NORTHERN NEIGHBOURS

NORTHERN NEIGHBOURS

SCOTLAND AND NORWAY SINCE 1800

Edited by John Bryden, Ottar Brox and Lesley Riddoch

EDINBURGH
University Press

Edinburgh University Press is one of the leading university presses in the UK. We publish academic books and journals in our selected subject areas across the humanities and social sciences, combining cutting-edge scholarship with high editorial and production values to produce academic works of lasting importance. For more information visit our website: www.edinburghuniversitypress.com

Edinburgh University Press Ltd
The Tun – Holyrood Road
12 (2f) Jackson's Entry
Edinburgh EH8 8PJ
www.euppublishing.com

First published in hardback by Edinburgh University Press 2015

Typeset in 10.5/12.5 Ehrhardt by
Servis Filmsetting Ltd, Stockport, Cheshire,
and printed and bound in Great Britain by
CPI Group (UK) Ltd, Croydon CR0 4YY

A CIP record for this book is available from the British Library

ISBN 978 0 7486 9620 8 (hardback)
ISBN 978 1 4744 1912 3 (paperback)
ISBN 978 0 7486 9621 5 (webready PDF)
ISBN 978 1 4744 0343 6 (epub)

The authors John Bryden, Agnar Hegrenes and Karen Refsgaard have received support from The Norwegian Non-fiction Literature Fund.

Contents

Acknowledgements

The editors would like to thank the authors, reviewers and editorial and publication team at Edinburgh University Press for their efforts in bringing this volume to print. This volume has been several years in the making, and during the process we received critical, but very helpful, comments from four anonymous reviewers, as well as from our authors and others who were approached for advice during the process.

Our editor at the Press, John Watson, and his team have been a constant source of support and encouragement during difficult moments when finding authors to write on new topics seemed almost impossible, as well as during the review and production process as a whole.

Professor Tom Devine kindly assisted with suggestions for several authors, and agreed to write the Foreword for the book.

In addition, we thank Tanera Astley, who advised on the title and front cover and wrote the new copy for the back page of the cover for the paperback edition, Pat Bryden, who copyedited the final draft chapters, and Anne Bente Ellevold and Karen Refsgaard then at NILF (Norwegian Agricultural Economics Research Institute), Oslo, who checked the formatting and consolidated the bibliography prior to submission. Thanks are also due to Professor Nadarajah Shanmugaratnam, Development Economist at Noragric in the Norwegian University of Life Sciences (NMBU) for his impartial comments on an earlier draft of Chapter 2. Professor Erik Opsahl of NTNU, Trondheim, also reviewed Chapter 1 and Chapter 5 and made a number of corrections regarding early local governance in Norway for which we are very grateful.

In the course of planning the book, and responding to reviewers' comments, we unfortunately 'lost' a few potential authors who nevertheless gave us some good comments and advice. Particular mention must be made in this regard of Professor Barbara Crawford of St Andrews University, Dr Liv Helene Willumsen of University of Tromso, Professor Rune Blix Hagen of the University of Tromso, Professor Steve Murdoch of St Andrews University, Professor David Arter of Helsinki, Professor Tom Devine, Professor David McCrone of Edinburgh, Dr Stig Gezilius (NILF), Dr Linda Riddell of Edinburgh University and Dr Vanessa Halhead.

Some of the Norwegian authors received crucial support for their writing work from the Norsk faglitterær forfatter- og oversetterforening (NFFO) or Norwegian Non-Fiction Authors and Translators Organisations, for which we are very grateful. NFFO is a trade union for non-fiction writers and translators in Norway, and has over 5,000 members. Its support programmes are funded by copying and library royalties.

We dedicate this volume to the neighbouring peoples of Scotland and Norway in the hope that their growing mutual understanding of an earlier shared – as well as a later and divergent – history will help them to greater future cooperation and friendship. If we have been able to play a small part in this process through this volume, then that is our just reward. We hope that the final result justifies the faith of all those who gave freely of their advice and encouragement.

Foreword

Tom M. Devine

The comparative approach is one of the most useful in the intellectual toolkit of the historian. It enables the scholar to determine what is distinctive and what is commonplace about the country he or she is primarily interested in studying. It encourages an analytical rather than a descriptive discourse as questions, paradoxes, problems and puzzles arise which would otherwise remain hidden or dormant without such a broader context of investigation. The pitfalls of exceptionalism, introspection, parochialism and navel-gazing in national histories can be avoided to some extent at least. Invaluable also is the fact that some features which domestic historians take for granted can often immediately seem striking and intriguing to the outsider.

The historiography of modern Scotland has already benefited significantly from the approach. In the final three decades of the last century a series of conferences, followed by publication of their proceedings, was organised to explore the comparative historical development of Ireland and Scotland. At the heart of the discussions was a central issue. Around 1700 the social, economic, resource and demographic contours of both countries seemed probably similar. Indeed, there was some evidence that Ireland showed more promise of material progress than Scotland. Instead, however, Scotland experienced rapid industrialisation from the middle decades of the eighteenth century and eventually a position of global economic hegemony while Ireland's tragic fate culminated in the horrors of the Great Famine, the most terrible human catastrophe in nineteenth-century Europe. Scholars on both sides of the Irish Sea learned much about the causes and nature of the development paths of the two societies until the project finally came to an end more than a decade or so ago.

Now in this important book we can read another exciting attempt to examine through the comparative lens the modern histories of Norway and Scotland. A team of interdisciplinary experts drawn from both countries and elsewhere in the

UK have been assembled to consider the radically different historical paths of two small nations and the social, political and economic consequences from c. 1800 to the present day.

As in the Irish case, before 1700 the similarities between the two were much more obvious than the contrasts. Both were relatively poor by the standards of contemporary England, France and Holland and practised a mainly subsistence form of agriculture in peasant communities with broadly similar endowments and challenges of land and climate. Each had experienced the full ideological and political impact of the Protestant Reformations of the sixteenth century, in the Scottish case rooted in Calvinism, in the Norwegian, Lutheranism.

By the mid-nineteenth century, however, the social and economic structures of both countries were diverging rapidly. Scotland's economic revolution in both manufacturing and agriculture was the fastest in Europe until forced Soviet industrialisation in the 1930s. It led to massive urbanisation, displacement of population and communities in the rural worlds of both Highlands and Lowlands, huge levels of internal migration and emigration, and eventually to a capitalist system of extraordinary material power feeding markets across the globe for ships, locomotives, steel, iron, engineering products and numerous other commodities. Norway's economic development was by contrast much less disruptive, more protracted and more benign, not least for the people of the countryside. Industry was less concentrated than in Scotland, a process aided by hydro-electricity as the power source rather than coal, which tended to localise population in areas of the best resources. The contributors to the book skilfully draw out the reasons for these different development paths while at the same time demonstrating convincingly that they have moulded the politics, social structures and popular cultures of Norway and Scotland down to the present.

This is, then, a fascinating study of comparative history. But it is much more than that. The historical background leads into pertinent assessments of how far in this year of the Scottish Referendum the much-vaunted 'Nordic Model' of higher taxation and a more potent welfare state is actually fit for purpose in Scotland given the radically different historical formations of the two countries. Here the volume contributes effectively not only to an understanding of the past but also to an important aspect of the constitutional and public policy debates of today and into the future.

CHAPTER 1

Introduction

John Bryden, Erik Opsahl, Ottar Brox and Lesley Riddoch

Hear me, Despot, I will be your bane, as long as I last. For Norway's law, in the peasant's hand shall smash your slaves' bonds.

Henrik Wergeland – *The Norwegian's Catechism*, 1832[1]

INTRODUCTION

This book is a comparative study of the economic, social and political development of Norway and Scotland since about 1800. Our main question is about how the development of these two small countries at the north of Europe, whose histories were intertwined from about the year AD 795 when Norse raiders sacked Iona Monastery, and whose economic, social, cultural and political structures had certain similarities in the early and late medieval periods, nevertheless diverged sharply in economic, social, political and other ways from the eighteenth century on. In seeking to answer that question, we inevitably move closer towards an understanding of the political, social and economic conditions that make an 'alternative' development possible. In this way we hope to inform debates about the future of Scotland after the referendum in Autumn 2014, as well as contribute to debates about present and future policy choices in Norway.

In this referendum, the Scottish electorate faced a choice of whether or not to vote for independence from the rest of the UK. In the political developments of the recent past that have led to this situation, there has been growing Scottish interest in Norway and the wider Nordic region, exemplified by Lesley Riddoch's lively 'Nordic Horizons' group. This interest has focused on issues such as education, land ownership, urban transport, green cities, elderly care, NATO, the management of North Sea oil and gas, local government, the welfare state and Nordic cooperation. The general tenor of the Nordic Horizon debates, as well as the White Paper on Scottish Independence produced by the Scottish Government in the Autumn of 2013, is that Norwegian – and wider Nordic – policies might offer some interesting ideas for Scotland should it become a nation-state again. Beyond that, some form of future alliance with the structures of Nordic and wider Scandinavian cooperation, in particular the Nordic Council of Ministers, is also under discussion. These issues, and in particular the perceptions around them, are further discussed by Hilson and Newby in Chapter 10.

This interest seems to have three main roots. The first is the historical relationships between the two countries, which included periods of conflict, occupation of the north and west of what we now know as Scotland, migration and settlement by both sides, trade, military and political alliances, connections during the World Wars, and the shared interest and cooperation around the development and exploitation of North Sea oil. The second is the fact that Norway gained independence from Denmark in 1814 and a Norwegian nation-state was re-established with a new, and for that time very liberal, constitution, an event that led to a long struggle for Norwegian identity. Norway was forced into a monarchical union with Sweden later the same year, a union which lasted until 1905, but after 1814 its control over domestic policies increased dramatically, as Brandal and Bratberg discuss in Chapter 3. There were two main political goals or strategies for Norway in the union: to resist interference in Norway's affairs by the Swedish Union Monarchy[2] which could reduce Norwegian sovereignty; and to attain as equal status as possible with Sweden in the union and reduce Swedish hegemony (first and foremost in foreign affairs). The first strategy was very successful, the second had growing success but led in the end to the dissolution of the union in 1905. Thirdly, as not a few observers have pointed out, there are many apparent similarities in the 'political sentiments' in the two countries, for example about the nature of democracy itself, peace versus war, nuclear weapons, equality and inequality, moral duties to the poor and excluded at home and abroad, education, and the management and rights and access issues around public goods (see also Chapter 11).

There is at least some plausible evidence to suggest that during most of the early, high and late Middle Ages, Scotland and Norway were more similar to each other than they later became after about 1700. Neither existed convincingly as cohesive kingdoms until after the eleventh century, being divided among clans and their chiefs in Scotland or earldoms and kingdoms in Norway and Norwegian-dominated territories. Neither were Christianised until between the eighth and eleventh centuries, at which point the Catholic Church started to accrue land and other property progressively until the Calvinist and Lutheran reformations of the sixteenth century. The western and northern isles, together with other parts of western and northern mainland Scotland, were effectively occupied and ruled by the Vikings and then the Norwegian kingdom[3] for various periods between the eighth and fifteenth centuries. According to Donaldson,[4] but based on the Norske Saga tradition, the Earldom of Orkney was 'founded as a Norwegian dependency by Harald the Fairhaired and for a long time included Shetland, Caithness, Sutherland . . . as well as occasionally other territories, and had a continuous existence for almost four centuries' until it was annexed to the Scottish Crown in 1472. The same source tells us, 'Another Norwegian dependency was established in the Hebrides . . . and took shape as a principality with its headquarters in [the isle of] Man.' The parliament in Man today claims direct descent from the 'Ting' established there in the Viking age. Some British[5] and Norwegian historians[6] are, however, sceptical of this tradition. The Sagas are written long after the actual events should have taken place, and probably with the aim of legitimising Norse power in the area. We do not know when the isles became Norwegian dependencies ('skattland'), but probably not until late in the eleventh century. The Orkney Earl and the King of Man were probably originally independent Vikings like the King of Dublin. After the death of King Haakon IV following the Battle of Largs in 1263, the Norwegians ceded the western isles to Scotland in the Treaty of Perth of 1266, thereby settling the territorial differences between the two countries at that time.[7] The Orkney Isles were pawned in 1468 and 1469 by the Union Monarch Christian I as Norwegian king, but this did not include transfer of the ultimate sovereignty, since the islands might be redeemed. James III of Scotland nevertheless acted on the assumption that he had acquired full royal rights. The islands have never been redeemed and it is generally held that in the course of time Orkney and Shetland have become Scottish by use and wont, and that Norwegian sovereignty has lapsed.[8]

AN AULD ALLIANCE

The alliance between Scotland and Norway was subsequently strengthened by the marriage of Alexander III's daughter Margaret to Erik of Norway, grandson of Haakon and son of Magnus VI of Norway.[9] Erik and Margaret had a daughter, also Margaret and called 'Maid of Norway', who had the right to succeed to the Scottish throne after the death of Alexander's remaining son in 1284. The plan was for her to marry the future Edward II of England, and so secure an alliance between Norway–Scotland and England. At this point there was a real prospect of a Scottish–Norwegian Union but it was frustrated by Margaret's untimely death about 26 September 1290 off the Orkney Isles while sailing to Scotland, at which point the throne was taken by Balliol as a vassal of England, leading to the subordination of Scotland under Edward I. Balliol's subsequent defeat and deposition led to the succession of King Robert Bruce to the Scottish throne. Bruce's sister had been the second wife of Erik of Norway after the death of Margaret, and in 1312 he concluded the Treaty of Inverness with his brother-in-law Haakon V of Norway, Erik's brother.[10] The Treaty of Perth was reaffirmed in the Treaty of Bergen in 1426 between the Union Monarch Erik as King of Norway and James I of Scotland, which was intended to extend friendship and reciprocal trade.[11] The Treaty of Bergen added a new clause to settle all remaining claims with the exception of an annual pension paid by Scotland to the Norwegian king to compensate for the transfer of the Western Isles to Norway under the Treaty of Perth.[12] This important clause increased mutual friendship between Scotland and the united kingdoms of Denmark and Norway[13] and led to an expansion of trade between the two parties that was seen as a welcome counterbalance to the dominant Hansa traders. Close political relations between Scotland and Norway continued until the Kalmar Union in the late fourteenth century[14] and thereafter between Scotland, Norway, Denmark and Sweden until the early eighteenth century. After 1426, Scottish traders were increasingly active in the Baltic, Danish and Norwegian ports, and many settled in them, further strengthening economic and cultural links between the countries.[15] Following the Kalmar Union of Denmark, Sweden and Norway the alliance with Scotland continued, but now in a new framework, within which power shifted away from Norway. Although the political focus of the Union shifted east and south in the first part of the fifteenth century, contacts with Scotland again intensified after 1452 and the *entente* between France and the Union under Christian I. Charles VII of France played a key role in arranging the marriage of Christian's daughter Margaret to James III of Scotland. Thereafter, marriage was arranged between Margaret's brother, and Christian's eldest son, John to Jeanne, daughter of Louis XI of France, thereby creating the French–Scottish–Scandinavian Triple Alliance ratified in 1494.[16] However, the triple alliance faltered under John, and was replaced after 1525 by an alliance between Scotland and the united kingdoms of Denmark and Norway,[17] and a separate alliance between Scotland and France. The latter lasted until the Treaty of Edinburgh of 1560, which secured English support for the Protestant reformers under Knox, and ended the Scottish–French alliance.[18]

Norway and Scotland had both been rather fragile monarchical unities in the early medieval period, power being retained in large parts of the respective territories by the local chieftains, or *Jarls* (Earls). In Scotland this situation lasted at least until the eighteenth century, at least with respect to the north and west of the country. In Norway, the role of the indigenous aristocracy was weakened with the Kalmar Union of 1397 between Norway, Sweden and Denmark. Norway's landscape and resources made the indigenous aristocracy, compared to its Danish and Swedish counterparts, more dependent on cooperation with the crown to secure its position as the country's political and military elite. The Kalmar Union ended the long and close cooperation between monarch and aristocracy in Norway. In the long run the Norwegian aristocracy did not manage to defend either Norway's political independence or its own position as ruling elite in the country, and the country was subdued to Denmark in 1536/7 as a 'dependent kingdom' ('*lydrike*').[19] Three hundred years of alliances formed between Scotland, Norway and Denmark–Norway in the period between the Treaty of Perth of 1266 and the Scottish–English Union of Crowns under James VI and I in the seventeenth century were essentially about mutual strengthening against a larger and more powerful England and mutual access to markets. For much of the last century of these formal alliances, and for a further hundred or so years afterwards, Scotland and Scandinavia had in effect created a region for 'free trade and movement of people' – in fact, a common market and one with a largely harmonised currency system linked to a silver standard.

There were close cultural and linguistic connections too: Norway's most famous composer, Edvard Grieg, came from a Scottish family in Aberdeenshire who settled in Bergen;[20] her most famous poet, Petter Dass, came from a Scottish family who settled in northern Norway; and the Christie family from Montrose settled in Bergen around 1650 – their descendants included the secretary to the 1814 Constitutional Commission, one prime minister and several other notable politicians. The Mowats, one of Norway's most prominent noble families in the sixteenth and seventeenth centuries, had Scottish ancestry. Not all were to be welcomed: John Cunningham of West Barns, Fife, was sent to serve King Christian IV and was appointed district governor of Vardøhus, Finnmark in 1619, where he infamously introduced witchhunts and trials.[21] The list is long. Equally, many Scottish families can claim Nordic ancestry, including the MacLeods, Kerrs, Gunns, and the Manx chief Somerled and his clan progeny (including the MacDonalds, MacRorys, MacDougals and MacAlisters), to name but a few. Norn, or old Norske language, was apparently spoken rather widely in Scotland, especially in the northern isles where there are people alive today who can remember their grandparents speaking at least some Norn. It is not surprising that there are also similarities in folk music – indeed, shared folk songs[22] – and in other arts and crafts.

The two countries also share some geographical similarities – for one thing, Norway is a continuation of the Caledonian mountain range and also experiences the moderating impact of the Gulf Stream on climatic conditions – and they each have roughly the same population.

Reckoned by some to be one of the six poorest countries in the world at the end of the eighteenth century,[23] Norway struggled to recreate and strengthen its identity and economy based on a Norwegian national state but eventually thrived after its independence from Denmark in the early nineteenth century,[24] creating a new social democracy, a strong municipal government system, and a universal education system that apparently served the country well.[25] By the end of the century it was industrialising rapidly on the basis of cheap hydro-power. It also established its own currency. Scotland also prospered in the period after 1750, playing a large part in British industrialisation, trade and the building of the Empire.

The social democratic order was built on what Heidar calls the 'culture of egalitarianism surviving from the old Lutheran peasant society'[26] and reinforced by the Church and religious movements. Heidar argues that the nineteenth-century mobilisation of the freeholding peasants and of the working class in the twentieth century both stressed egalitarian values and goals, and their eventual alliance was evidently founded not only on these shared values but also on the fact that many peasants were also workers, and aligned against the central bureaucracy and technocracy – officials of centralised executive power – which had remained after separation from Denmark in 1814. The foundation of the social democratic order, then, while rooted in the liberal constitution drawn up in April–May 1814 and, after some amendments, accepted by the Swedish monarchy has its roots in the weakening of the Norwegian aristocracy after the Black Death, during the Kalmar Union, and the loss of independence and the reformation which led to the collapse of the Norwegian nobility in the second half of the seventeenth century, all of which led to the dominance of the freeholding peasantry before 1814. On every meaningful indicator, Norway became the most 'democratic' state in the world after 1814, with 45 per cent of males over 25 having the vote – about 10 per cent of the then population of about 900,000. This was followed in 1898 when all men above 25 were qualified to vote, and in 1913 when universal suffrage was granted. A modified proportional representation system was introduced in 1896 for local elections, and in the period to 1921 a generalised PR system was introduced. The 1921 reforms allowed representation to come even closer to votes cast, and also opened the parliamentary door for the smaller parties.

Such a culture of egalitarianism and the development of social democracy in Norway contrasts sharply with the development of the British and hence Scottish political system, which remained firmly in the hands of the old regime. Although the skilled working class, artisans and sections of the professional middle classes in Scotland fought hard for greater political representation in the nineteenth century, the outcome, in the form of the Scottish version of the 'Great' Reform Act of 1832,[27] was a complete disappointment, especially to the working classes. The outcome was that although the electorate increased to about 65,000 adult male property-holders, this was only 2.5 per cent of the then Scottish population of some 2.6 million.[28] Scotland was also stuck with the British 'first past the post' system of elections and its consequences, at least in terms of Westminster government. The Scottish parliamentarians after 1999 have been elected by proportional representation, but voters in England and Wales later rejected such a reform. For Scottish voters, this, together with the weight of votes from the rest of the UK, has meant many decades of effective political disenfranchisement in which the party in power in Westminster has not had a majority of votes from the Scottish people. Indeed, the only time when this was *not* the case since the Union was in four elections during the period of liberal hegemony in the late nineteenth and early twentieth centuries, and very marginally in the 1955 election when 50.1 per cent of Scottish voters voted for the winning Conservative party.

Considering the similarities and connections between the two countries before 1800, as well as the present debates about Scotland's independence, and the related interest in Norway, it is surely both reasonable and helpful to ask why these two countries developed in such different ways, and with such crucial outcomes for such things as landownership and rights, the distribution of wealth and income, the economic benefits derived from North Sea oil, the nature of politics and forms of democracy, as well as related issues such as education, access rights and behaviour in relation to land and nature, taxation and the welfare state. By seeking to extend our understanding of the different development paths followed by Scotland and Norway in the period since 1800, and ultimately move towards an explanation of them, this book aims to inform debates about Scottish devolution and potential independence as well as debates in Norway and indeed Scandinavia and elsewhere on the significance of the Nordic Model and its future in the increasingly hegemonic world of development ideas.

Norway's independence from Denmark in 1814 triggered a period of reform and the reassertion of Norwegian national identity, and the book aims to show how and in what respects this has helped to make Norway the country that it is today.

The geographical scope of the book is mainly Scotland and Norway, but this is extended from time to time to the rest of the UK and Ireland, and the other Scandinavian countries. The temporal scope is mainly from Norwegian independence from Danish rule in 1814 to the present day, although we consider the earlier historical period when we think it helps us to understand the key differences at the beginning of our period, for example in landownership and religion. The subject matter and disciplinary scope includes history, politics, geography, education, economics, sociology and anthropology.

The book centres on an analysis of six core, and several attendant or related, reasons for the divergences between Scotland and Norway since the seventeenth century. These are, first, land and natural resource ownership, distribution, access and use rights, which we take up in some detail below as it is crucial for almost all other themes; second, that of union with a richer and more powerful neighbour in the case of Scotland, especially the Union of Parliaments in 1707, and independence from a richer and more powerful neighbour in the case of Norway in 1814; third, the development of political systems and politics, especially since the early nineteenth century, which were closely linked to religion and landownership; fourth, the evolution of local government since the mid-nineteenth century but reflecting the precursors of parish government and the role of religious governance; fifth, the development of the welfare state, especially in the twentieth century; and sixth, early and late industrialisation and, more recently, the development of North Sea oil.

LANDOWNERSHIP AND LANDED POWER

The character and distribution of land and natural resource ownership and rights in Norway was particular, even within the Nordic countries. The very different evolution of land ownership and occupation, and related power and influence of the 'old regime' in Norway and Scotland, is a crucial theme in our comparative analysis and arises in several chapters. It is vital in understanding the varying agrarian structures, distribution of wealth and power, treatment of natural resources, evolution of the franchise and political structures, rural and urban settlement patterns, and both agrarian change and industrialisation.

King David I introduced feudalism to Scotland in the twelfth century, along with a Norman aristocracy to whom he granted land charters in the south and east, areas of more productive land. He used the charters to try to force the pre-Reformation clan chieftains of the north and west into line, but largely failed in this effort,[29] which was taken up more ruthlessly in 1597 by James VI.[30] A similar process took place in Norway between 1000 and 1300, where the king forced the former chiefs to sign up to unification if they wanted to keep their land.

King David also gave large tracts of crown land to the monasteries, which held them – and indeed increased their holdings – until the late sixteenth century. As Cosmo Innes puts it, 'vast property were in the hands of churchmen, whether secular or regular' before the Reformation.[31] For example, the two great Benedictine monasteries of Kelso and Arbroath had extensive lands in the rich agricultural areas of the borders and Angus.[32] In 1500, the Church owned a quarter of the land of Scotland, and accounted for half of the national land tax revenue.[33] Indeed, it is frequently stated that in this period the Church was rich and the Crown was poor. However, the Crown (in particular, but not only, James IV and V) found that it could exercise patronage by securing a rich benefice for officers of state, other supporters and illegitimate sons[34] from the Pope.[35] Indeed, during the first half of the sixteenth century the Church was contributing one-half of total national tax revenues, while Church revenues at £300,000 a year comprised half of the national wealth, and over six times total royal revenues.[36]

The Reformation led by John Knox came to fruition only after the deposition of Mary Queen of Scots. Knox's plans for Scotland post-Reformation were published in the 'Book of Discipline', which planned to use the accumulated wealth of the Catholic Church for education, relief of the poor and remuneration of the ministers. However, in the event the wealth of the pre-Reformation church had mostly 'fallen into' the hands of the nobility and was largely irrecoverable.[37] There is no clear agreement among historians about the exact way in which this happened, but Robin Callander gives some details of the nefarious activities of Bishop William Gordon involving theft of church property and lands in the Parish of Birse and other church lands in Aberdeenshire.[38] James VI, faced with fractious landed aristocracy in the east, centre and south of Scotland – riven by religious differences – and by still- feuding highland chiefs in the north and west, adopted two strategies. First, through his Act of Annexation of 1587, he transferred the remaining property of the Catholic Church to the Crown and, being short of funds, redistributed this land to supportive landowners.[39] Second, in 1597, he brought the highland chiefs into line by threatening to seize – and in several cases seizing – the lands of any chief who could not produce titles.[40]

The Scottish Parliament
Pàrlamaid na h-Alba

17 ... 2019

MSP

Contact Visitor Services: 0131 348 5200
Email: visit@parliament.scot
www.parliament.scot

Code of Behaviour for the Public –
by order of the Presiding Officer
For all visits

Remember that this is a working parliamentary building

Obey all instructions from parliamentary officials

Keep all bags with you or place in the baggage store
(especially larger items)

Do not smoke in the building

Do not eat or drink, except in the restaurants

Collect any items retained by Security as you go out

For visits **to see parliamentary business**, please:

Switch off mobile devices, pagers and laptops

Enter the galleries quietly, take your seat and leave quietly

Obtain prior permission to paint, sketch or draw

Please note that the following are forbidden in the galleries:

Applause, shouting out or disrupting proceedings

The display of any banner or slogans, including on clothing

Use of cameras or recording equipment

The seventeenth and eighteenth centuries were a period of concentration and further extension of landownership[41] in Scotland, especially before 'improvement' became widespread in the mid-eighteenth century. The number of landowners in Scotland fell from around 9,500 in 1700 to about 8,000 by 1800.[42] For the entire nineteenth century, 90 per cent of Scotland was owned by fewer than 1,500 landowners.

In Norway too, the Church was the largest landowner. The percentage distribution is very uncertain, but according to one writer the Church might have owned an estimated 40 per cent of the land in terms of taxable value in the first half of the fourteenth century, a proportion that increased to 48 per cent by 1500.[43] The secular aristocracy in the king's service owned about 12 per cent, the Crown 4 per cent, and 36 per cent was in the hands of peasant proprietors. Some of it was owned by clergymen as private persons, and some also by the petty bourgeoisie of the small towns. This means that about one-third of the land might have been owned by freeholders, a very high proportion compared with Scotland. Another estimate for the same period shows the king owning 7–10 per cent, the Church 20–40 per cent and lay landowners (aristocrats in the king's service, townsmen and farmers/peasants) 50–70 per cent.[44]

The Reformation during the sixteenth century was a defining moment in both countries. In Scotland, most of the land formerly owned by the Church was appropriated by the large feudal landowners.[45] In Norway, the king annexed the former Church land but in such a way as to allow the income of 40 per cent of it to continue to support parish clergy, hospitals and almshouses.[46]

The remaining landed power in Norway was diminished successively by the appropriation of opposing chiefs' land to the Crown and its partial transfer to the Church and freeholders; by the Black Death and subsequent plagues which diminished the labour force; by climatic change; but mostly by the reduced power of the local aristocracy after the Kalmar Union.[47] Crown land, accounting for 52 per cent of all Norwegian land in 1661, was for the most part sold between then and 1821 in order to meet debts, and most of this land was ultimately bought by the farmer holders. As a result, the percentage of land owned by individual farm families increased from 19 per cent in 1661 to over 32 per cent in 1721, 57 per cent in 1801 and to an astonishing 70 per cent in 1835.[48] There was a steady decline in rented farms until 1917, but a small increase from 1917 to 1929. This is said to be a 'crisis phenomenon' as some mortgagees had taken possession of the collateral and leased it out. However, the result was that nearly 90 per cent of farmers owned their farm in 1929, and more than 90 per cent at the censuses of 1939 and 1949.[49]

Norway's land occupancy rights were mainly defined by ancient Udal (*Ódal*) tenure dating back to the late Viking age, and also influential in the Orkney and Shetland islands of Scotland, which were dependencies of the Norwegian Crown until the fifteenth century. Udal tenure comprised a set of inheritance rules assuring the hereditary right of descendants.[50] However, despite these rules the Church and other non-farmers became owners of land.

In Scotland, the feudal charters ultimately gave absolute power to the landed proprietors where before, especially in the Highlands and Islands, ancient Celtic law was a paternalistic system, under which the chiefs held the land in steward-ship, on behalf of the clanspeople. The 'first' agrarian reform[51] in Scotland involved the removal of peasants (who did not have formal property rights) from the land, a process known as the 'Clearances', and the creation of a new class of tenant farmers and crofters who were not freeholders but dependent on the landlord and owing service to him (or her).

AGRARIAN REVOLUTION 1750–1850

In Scotland, the 'Clearances' started in the Lowlands, and these have been little discussed by historians.[52] The legal insecurity of tenants and farming clanspeople in the Highlands and Islands was not significantly felt by them until after the failure of the 1745 rebellion. Before that, this remote region still had significant Catholic families and communities that had not experienced the Reformation, and they held to ancient Celtic laws and customs described by Sumner Maine.[53] The landowners at this point were almost entirely the descendants of the old highland chieftains, bound by the patriarchal obligations and moral economy of the clan, viewed as kinsfolk.

The harsh treatment of the Highlanders – who were at the forefront of the 1715 and 1745 Jacobite uprisings – after 1745 included expropriation of land, exile as indentured labour (for example, to the sugar plantations of the West Indies[54]), and proscription of Gaelic language and culture in general. The remaining and new landowners after the mid-1700s exercised the rights granted to them both by the feudal land charters and by the 1696 Act which authorised division of the commons by legal process, although neither of these 'rights' had previously been exercised outside southern Scotland. The 'new' landowners set about removing people from the land, sometimes forcibly, sometimes by organising emigration to the New World, sometimes by encouragement and resettlement on 'crofts'[55] in remote and unproductive areas of their land. The highland 'Clearances' mainly occurred between 1780 and 1855, but they continued as late as the 1880s in some cases.[56]

PROTESTS AGAINST THE CLEARANCES IN SCOTLAND

The lowland Clearances started in the 1720s, stimulated by favourable cattle prices following the Union of 1707. They provoked an armed rebellion – called the 'levellers' revolt' – in 1724, when several hundred armed men killed and mutilated cattle and broke down the dykes which marked new boundaries of enclosures.[57] This was the most serious eighteenth-century rural disturbance, followed later in the nineteenth century by the crofters' protests and uprisings in the western and northern Highlands and Islands,[58] and later still by the protests and land occupation following the First World War, when promises of land to Highlanders who joined the forces were not honoured.[59] The protests in the Highlands and Islands came mainly in the 1880s, triggered by the Clearances, the Irish Land Acts and failures of the potato crop, as well as incidents such as that at Pairc Estate on the island of Lewis, where the landlord wished to rent the land for deer-stalking rather than settle crofters on it. The crofters received support from the middle classes, including John Murdoch, proprietor of *The Highlander* newspaper, the Irish Land League, various land reform associations, and from the Liberal-voting working classes of the growing industrial belt around Glasgow. The cause of land reform – and the radicalisation of the working class – was also boosted by Edward McHugh's campaign for Georgist land reform in Skye in 1882 and Henry George's own lecture tours in Scotland in 1881 and 1884.[60] Many of the protests were met by military and police force. The protests after the First World War led to a limited amount of land settlement, through the creation of crofts and smallholdings on land acquired by the State for that purpose.[61]

The crofters' protests of the nineteenth century eventually led Gladstone's Liberal government to set up a Royal Commission on the Condition of Crofters and Cottars, known after its chairman as the 'Napier Commission'. When returned in 1886, Gladstone's government established the first Crofters' Commission to ensure security of tenure, regulated transfers, controlled rents and other means of protection.[62] The relatively strong regulation of crofters as a distinct tenant class was limited to the Crofting Counties which later became known as the Highlands and Islands following t he establishment of the Highlands and Islands Development Board by Harold Wilson's Labour government in 1965, and it has remained a feature of Scottish land law ever since. Among the most important features of this regulation were the control of rents, the right of succession by heritors, and control of decrofting of land and croft transfers outside the family.[63]

In 1976, crofters were given the right to buy their house and in-bye land, and in 2003 they were given the right to acquire their common grazings land in association with others. But most remain tenants today.

The situation in north-east Scotland differed from that of both southern Scotland and the Highlands and Islands, for here the landlords' aim was to create a full-blown capitalist farming system. However, as late as 1885, while nearly 58 per cent of farms in fertile East Lothian were over 100 tilled acres in total, in the counties of the north-east, only 17 per cent had over 100 tilled acres.[64] By way of contrast, farms between one and 49 acres in tilled land accounted for two-thirds of farms in the north-east counties, and just over one-third in East Lothian. As Carter argues, 'the social formations of East Lothian and of the northeast were radically different' and, further, that the capitalist mode of production was not in fact dominant in the north-east.[65] Carter's choice of date – 1885 – is important because this was just before the Napier Commission reported on the situation of crofters and cottars in the Highlands and Islands, and a time when the Liberal political hegemony was strongly supported by both small and many large (especially tenant) farmers in the north-east.[66] A Committee set up by the Aberdeen Liberal Association in December 1881 campaigned against high rents and tenant insecurity, and evolved into the SFA – Scottish Farmers Alliance, again with close links to the Liberal party. Although the SFA fought to have the north-east included in the Crofting Counties, the Lord Advocate ruled that only the counties in which the Napier Commission took evidence could be included. Carter suggests, however, that because the north-east peasants threw their lot in with the larger Liberal capitalist (tenant and also owner) farmers in this critical period, they failed to articulate their class interest at the critical moment when much stronger rights were given to crofters.[67]

NORWAY'S CROFTERS

Crofters (Husmenn) emerged in Norway in the later decades of the seventeenth century, not as a result of 'clearances' but rather following tax and inheritance laws from 1670.[68] The 'åsetesretten' law gave the eldest son the right to take over a farm without splitting it between his siblings,[69] while Kristian V's law of 1687 prohibited division of farms below a certain size limit.[70] Åsetesretten applied to properties owned by farmers and, as mentioned elsewhere, the share of farmer ownership increased steadily from 1660. Husmenn were tenants of owner-farmers or tenant farmers, often paying rent with labour time, although some were free pluriactive farmers paying a cash rent. The number of Husmenn peaked between 1855 and 1865, when the labour-intensive system of summer mountain dairy-farming (on what are known as shielings in Scotland) was also at its peak.[71] Thereafter, the number of Husmenn fell due to emigration,[72] urbanisation and the fact that some purchased their land and became independent smallholders. Other crofting units were absorbed into the farm from which they had been rented. Under the Jordloven of 1928, Husmenn gained the legal right to buy their plots. By 1917, the number of Husmenn had fallen to a quarter of that in 1857. At the time of the agricultural census in 1949, there were 1,476 Husmenn, a reduction from 3,741 in 1939.[73]

LANDED POWER AND PROTEST IN NORWAY

In Norway, 'serious peasant riots occurred . . . mostly in 1536–1660, and from the 1760s'.[74] Initially the riots were about increased burdens on farmers following the Reformation, which meant that farmers had to pay poor relief as well as the tithe. There were also protests in 1760–2 (*Strilekrigen*) when an extraordinary war tax was levied.

A different kind of protest broke out in the counties of Agder and Telemark in the late 1780s, led by the farmer and shipowner Kristian Lofthus (1750–1824).

This was a protest against the mercantilist privileges of towns, sawmills, mines and ironworks, which meant farmers had to buy expensive and poor-quality commodities and receive low prices for their timber, as well as getting low wages for their labour.[75] Another farmer leader with radical ideas on the same topic was the lay preacher Hans Nielsen Hauge (1771–1824) who also started many rural enterprises in opposition to the privileged towns. Underlying all this was a view that the Danophile ruling elite that took decisions affecting the mainly rural Norwegian people was culturally far distant, and also lacking knowledge of them and the conditions they worked and lived under, while taking too much away in terms of taxes and other burdens. The 'unquiet heads of Scandinavia', as the Norwegian peasants have been called, thus filled the role of 'heroes' in the years leading up to dissolution with Denmark in 1814.[76] Many followers of Hauge were in the national assembly at Eidsvoll, which made the enlightened constitution for the separate Norwegian state in 1814. 'Haugianism' was 'rooted in traditional orthodoxy and pietism as well as in enlightenment philosophy' and Gerdåker argues that it 'strengthened farmers' self esteem and inspired a growing number of them to active participation in local and national decision-making'.[77] The period after the 1790s was one of transition from protest and subversion to constructive and responsible participation in the evolving democratic state.

CONSEQUENCES OF LANDOWNERSHIP PATTERNS FOR THE POLITICAL FRANCHISE IN NORWAY AND SCOTLAND IN THE NINETEENTH CENTURY

Norway's 1814 Constitution gave male property owners and larger tenant farmers over the age of 25 the vote,[78] and this enfranchised 45 per cent of males over 25, including at least 70,000 property-owning farmers, in all comprising about 10 per cent of Norway's population.[79] This may be compared with a mere 4,500 property owners of all kinds who got the vote in Scotland after the 'great' Reform Bill of 1832, including landowning farmers, a mere 2.5 per cent of the population. The population of Norway at that time was about 885,000, compared with Scotland's population of some 2.1 million. By contrast with Scotland, Norway's small owner-farmers had thus achieved considerable political power by 1814. By 1833, farmers had a majority in the Norwegian Parliament (*Storting*), when forty-five farmers and thirty-five civil servants and military officers held office.[80] More importantly, the distribution of landownership at that time was much more equal than it was in Scotland, and it is today. And most important of all, this relatively egalitarian enfranchised population was increasingly in the 'driving seat' of politics after 1814.

In 1834, Fougstad wrote,

> there is no place on Earth where the common man has gained a comparable freedom, a comparable influence and independence ... This phenomenon has

awakened much attention. Some have called it the true development of freedom and the bringing to life of the constitution in common minds. Others have called it the triumph of ignorance and the forerunner of barbarism.

At this time, 90 per cent of the Norwegian population were peasant farmers/foresters/fishermen and their families.[81]

A third important theme concerns the processes of Union and separation that occurred in Scotland and Norway in the early modern period. Norway was freed from Denmark in 1814,[82] and even though it very shortly after was joined in monarchical Union with Sweden until 1905, it gained control of domestic policies at that time, and created its own constitution in the brief interregnum between Danish rule and Swedish political dominance/precedence (first and foremost in foreign affairs) in a union.[83] By contrast, Scotland had been going through the opposite process with the unpopular Union of Crowns[84] and the later and more significant (and possibly also more unpopular) Union of Parliaments (1707), which brought Scotland increasingly (and especially after the 1745 Jacobite rebellion) under the control of a hegemonic and centralised Westminster government in London, whose energies were devoted to the expansion of Empire. To this task, the Scots were evidently well suited due to their earlier and better education system, and their leading role in British industrialisation, banking, insurance and shipping. Until partial devolution and the restoration of a Scottish Parliament in 1999, Scotland's policies largely depended on English-dominated parliaments and governments, as well as being further constrained by the second chamber, the House of Lords, which time and again defended the interests of the landowning classes, for example in terms of land law. While the class formations evolving from feudalism and industrialisation in Britain led to confrontational politics, and favoured strong single-party governments, the closer social and economic position of peasants in Norway as well as their pluriactive character meant that they were able to share values and politics with the working class that emerged with industrialisation after the mid-1800s. The peasant–labour alliances that emerged in Norway in the nineteenth and twentieth centuries are much referred to, and were very important in the evolution of social democracy as well as consensual politics.[85]

In contrast to the development of a highly centralised government system in Britain and Scotland, with weak local government (see Chapter 5), Norway's liberation from Denmark led to efforts by the small farmers and farmer-fishermen to wrest power from the central Danophile elite of Oslo officials,[86] demanding strong municipal-level government.[87] Norway's freeholding peasants were strong Lutherans, and the pre-modern institution of the parish council is said to have been formative in the development of consensual politics of the nineteenth and twentieth centuries,[88] as well as in the development of education in the eighteenth century (see also Chapters 9 and 12).

The contrasting political developments in Norway and in Britain-Scotland led to different evolutions of the regimes for the welfare of citizens. In late medieval and even early modern times, responsibility for those who for different reasons were unable to look after themselves shifted between the church and parish council, with a significant burden falling on landowners, for example under the British Speenhamland system of income security. It was the poor laws of 1831 that led to the treatment of labour as a commodity, and forced reliance on paid employment for means of existence.[89] Although in Scotland the foundations of local provision for the poor can be traced back to the twelfth century,[90] it was industrialisation and dispossession that reinforced arguments that the able bodied might also need support, although the demands on local parishes increased with the number of landless labourers. At this point a kind of 'means testing' system emerged, where the level of support depended on income.[91] Within Esping-Andersen's typology of welfare regimes, this system stigmatised recipients and consolidated the social structure based on the liberal market regime.[92]

Like Scotland, Norway also had a Poor Law, but the foundations of a welfare state were put in place in the 1890s with the 'accident insurance law' funded by employers. In 1909, a similar scheme for health insurance was introduced. State pension and unemployment schemes were introduced in the late 1930s. The Beveridge Report, so influential in the development of the British welfare state after the Second World War, also influenced Norway's post-war welfare state, the difference being that Norway had persistently social democratic governments after the war, while Britain oscillated between two opposing class-based parties. The Norwegian system was, like the British system after Bevan's reforms, universalistic – in other words, it covered all citizens irrespective of their economic position and there was no means testing. However, the Norwegian system became much more generous as a result of the left and centre domination of post-war politics. In addition, the Norwegian system developed a much greater focus on children and young people, and on women – on the grounds that this was the foundation of a more equal society.[93] The political consensus around the welfare state, together with the willingness to pay for it, contrasted with Britain after 1980 when neo-liberal ideology became firmly entrenched in the politics of the main political parties, and there has been a gradual reduction in welfare benefits, and a shift from the universalistic basis back to means testing and stigmatisation. The contrasting development of the welfare state in Britain and Scotland and in Norway therefore forms an important element in understanding why indicators of social and economic inequality, including the distribution of income and wealth, gender equality, child poverty, human health and life expectancy, show such significant divergence in the two countries today (see also Table 1.1).

The landownership structures in Scotland, strengthened by feudalism, made it easy for the 'enclosures' or 'clearances' of the late medieval and early modern period to occur there, creating the large landless class that was crucial for the development of industrialisation in Britain-Scotland after 1750. Moreover, it was the accumulated wealth of the aristocracy and a wealthy trading class[94] that stood behind the evolution of banking to support industrial development.[95] This led to a kind of industrial feudalism, with the kind of exploitation of labour that moved Robert Owen to reforms in his New Lanark textile mill,[96] and later to Marx's analysis of the development of capitalism, and later still to Polanyi's 'Great Transformation' in which he notes the necessity of state action to prevent the consequences of free markets when applied to land, labour and money.

In contrast with Scotland, industrialisation came late in Norway, even though, as in Scotland, 'proto-industrialisation' was evident beforehand. However, as we see in Chapter 6, Norway's industrialisation did not rely on large-scale dispossession and displacement of peasants.[97]

One of the key economic benefits of the Union with England in 1707 was that Scotland gained access to the British Empire during its principal ascendency, as well as to the wider markets for its rapidly growing manufacturing industry. Initially this was mainly textiles but, increasingly from the mid-nineteenth century, it was also heavy industries, particularly marine engines, railway loco- motives, shipping and steel. By 1850, the Clyde was producing two-thirds of the tonnage of iron vessels in Britain. Coal production 'soared from 3m tons in 1830 to around 7.4m tons in 1851'.[98] Within a very short space of time, Scotland had become more industrialised than the rest of Britain.[99] By 1903, Glasgow was the 'biggest locomotive-manufacturing centre in Europe, with engines being produced in large numbers for the Empire, South America and continental countries'.[100]

Norway also experienced the development of large-scale textile factories from the 1840s, and heavier construction and shipbuilding industries later in the century. But it was the development of cheap hydro-electric power from the late nineteenth century that gave Norway a global comparative advantage that was to last up to the present day. Cheap electricity was used to develop the electro-metallurgical and electro-chemical industries based on Norway's natural mineral resources. Hydro- electric plants were established all over Norway, and especially in the western periphery with ready access to deep water as a means of shipping out the products. Norsk Hydro was founded by Sam Eyde and Kristian Birkeland in 1905 and used the Birkeland method[101] to produce artificial fertilizers by fixing atmospheric nitrogen from air. Later Norsk Hydro diversified into aluminium production and oil and gas production. In 2004, the agricultural divisions of Norsk Hydro became an independent company called Yara International ASA. The oil and gas activities were merged with Statoil in 2007. Norsk Hydro is now the world's fourth biggest aluminium producer and is also a major producer of hydro-electricity.[102]

A central political issue in Norway by 1906 was the regulation of the country's main natural resources, the outcome being the Concession Laws of 1906–9. These were intended to restrict the influence of large foreign capitalists on Norway's industrial and social development and retain control of natural resources and issues of industrial location.[103] As a result of the Concession Laws, Norway's central and local governments were ultimately able to retain stakes in all of its key natural resources, and to use these in productive ways including the retention of viable local settlements across the country. Related to this, while Scotland had access to the natural resources of Empire and was fully involved in their exploitation after Union with England in the eighteenth century, Norway had no empire to draw on during its early industrialisation and looked to its own natural resources to build globally competitive industry. Despite setbacks in the post-war global economic crisis, Norway weathered the storm better than Scotland, and emerged strongly after the war when its GNP tripled in real terms between 1946 and 1973. This post-war boom was of course common throughout Europe, including Britain, but in most countries it had faded by the 1970s and, as we see in Chapter 6, in Scotland the heavy industries, steel, shipbuilding and others were in a weak position by the 1960s, leading to significant unemployment.

The different industrial experiences of Norway and Scotland also informed the development of North Sea oil in both countries during and after the 1970s, Norway positioning itself with high levels of public ownership in the resource and its extraction, and creating an oil fund to avoid overheating the economy and provide for future generations. In the UK, however, policy led to the loss of national control and failed to generate an oil fund for future generations.[104] Perhaps it is not accidental that only the Shetland Islands, and to a lesser extent the Orkney Islands – despite opposition from the Westminster government of the day – were able to extract a semblance of rent from North Sea oil passing through them and thereby develop an independent oil fund.

These six themes help us to form a more coherent understanding of the differences between Scotland and Norway in the modern period. There are other related matters that are important, including the respective reformations under the influence of Luther and Calvin and extending between the sixteenth and seventeenth centuries, the development of money and banking, the evolution of education systems including nurseries and culture schools, the territorial equivalence and regional development policies, and attitudes and access to nature, all of which will be covered in other chapters of this book. The issue of religion is in part about the preconditions for developments in the nineteenth and twentieth centuries and is discussed in various chapters, but it is also about the emerging political differences in the main period covered by this book, and particularly the influence of the Irish Catholic community that migrated to Scotland after 1850 to find employment in the rapidly growing industrial and mining sectors, and the related divisions within the working-class movement.[105] These and related issues are covered in some depth in Chapters 6 and 9.

In addition, the different experiences of Norway and Scotland in the two World Wars, and the impacts of those experiences, also provide an important supplementary element. Ahlund argues that conditions arising from the First World War led to the radicalisation of the Norwegian labour movement, with important post-war implications.[106] During the Second World War, despite the evidence of positive efforts of Norwegian pockets of resistance and Scottish linkages (for example, the 'Shetland Bus'), some argue that a relatively small proportion of the

Norwegian population took an active part against Germany in the Second World War, thus challenging the national self-image promoted by films such as *Max Manus*. The question of defence alliances with other Nordic countries and the conditional membership of NATO after the Second World War also had important political impacts, mainly discussed in Chapters 3, 10 and 13. Moreover, the Second World War had important differential impacts on the development of the post-war economy in Norway[107] and in Scotland,[108] further analysed in Chapters 6 and 13.

We believe that the selected themes and linked chapters not only provide a coherent and balanced analysis of the key elements of differential political, social and economic development in Norway and Scotland, but also speak to contemporary debates in Scotland around the independence issue and forthcoming referendum. These debates are likely to become more focused and more intense in a post-referendum Scotland, whether or not the outcome is full independence, but especially in the cases of independence or 'devo-max' (maximum devolution within the UK). They include issues around national defence and Scotland's membership of NATO, including the issue of nuclear submarine bases; currency and banking; the welfare state; regional policy; land reform; the role and structure of local government; social democracy and the development of the political system; and national identity and Scotland's position within the EU, and potentially within the Nordic alliances. In a more general sense, in the event of Scottish independence, its people and government will face the same kinds of nation-building tasks that Norway faced after independence from Denmark in 1814 and Sweden nearly 100 years later, including the articulation of distinctive political values, governance and administrative structures; cultural markers; and where to position itself on a range of trans-national and global issues. The authors believe that the book speaks to these issues, and the related questions arising in people's minds, using the Norwegian case in a helpful but not uncritical way. Equally, we hope that it will help the Norwegian people – faced as they are with the pressures to reform the 'welfare model', to privatise some public services and to amalgamate municipalities, among others – to understand why it may be important to keep some of the key features of their own political and institutional system in place and, indeed, why they are there in the first place.

Anne Lie of the University of Oslo has reminded us recently of the hazards of seeking to draw lessons from history, pointing out that events are created by specific circumstances of time and place. Indeed, we must be very careful in moving from a comparison of various dimensions of the Scottish and Norwegian history since 1800 or thereby towards policy prescriptions for today in either country. Nevertheless, as Lie argues, studying history and, we would add, comparing the experience of broadly similar countries, can help us to make better decisions. In particular, the comparative approach allows us to see our own countries from a different perspective:

the examples I have referred to demonstrate perhaps the most important lesson of all. When we use history, we must try to keep the paradox I mentioned initially in mind – that history is both a process comprising unique events that cannot be repeated AND a treasury of examples to be followed or avoided. Even though history provides innumerable examples that can help us to make better decisions, we must remember that our time is unique, and that previous experiences cannot be directly transferred to the present. That is why historical examples must be used with care.[109]

We cannot, of course, cover the whole of Scottish and Norwegian history since the eighteenth century in one volume, but we believe that by selecting key themes and junctures we have been able to use the combination of social science and history to illuminate important and yet very different processes of long-term economic, social and political development in the two neighbouring countries. The thematic choices were also guided by the wise advice of anonymous reviewers of our original proposal to the Press, which we duly acknowledge.

Before concluding this chapter, we offer a few comparable facts about the contemporary economic and social situation in both Scotland and Norway that do not appear in other chapters.

As Riddoch points out, Scotland has prized natural and cultural resources, and yet at the same time has 'some of the worst health, employment and social outcomes in Europe, and one of the biggest income gaps'.[110] This situation is clearly revealed by a comparison of the key indicators between Norway and Scotland in Table 1.1. As the various contributions to this volume show, Norway's more egalitarian, healthy and participatory society has been created over a long period

Table 1.1 Some Facts on Norway and Scotland Today

	Norway	Scotland	Notes
Population	4,920,305	5,295,403	Total, de facto, 2011 official data
Fertility rate	1.88	1.73	2011 official data
Average age	39.4	38	Average, c. 2011
Density of population	16.5	65	Persons per sq. km
Labour force participation rate	78.4	72.8 (UK 77.10)	OECD data for Norway and UK
– males	80.7	80.5 (UK 83.2)	Scottish
– females	75.9	71.9 (UK 71.0)	Government data for Scotland
Unemployment rate	3.34%	7.13%	Average, 2009–11
Life expectancy, males	79.4	76.9	Official statistics
Life expectancy, females	83.4	80.9	Official statistics

Table 1.1 (continued)

	Norway	Scotland	Notes
Suicides per year	515	527	Intentional Suicide
GDP per capita, $US, 2011	99,143	38,806	World Bank data for Norway
Disposable income per head, NOK (average)	228,317	140,637	Gross disposable household income
Oil and gas production	1.9m (2013–14)	1.35m (90% of UK North Sea production of 1.5m in 2011)	Barrels of oil and oil equivalent (gas and condensate) per day
Renewables in electicity production	99%	40.3%	Gross renewable electicity production as a % of total electicity production
GINI coefficient for income distribution (a higher number indicated greater inequality)	23.9 (2012)	32 (2011–12)	SSB for Norway, Statistics Scotland for Scotland
Voter turnout – national elections	78.2% (2013)	50% (2011) 63.8% (2010)	Scottish Parliament UK elections
Voter turnout – local elections	64.5% (2011)	39.8% (2012)	Local government elections

of time, and is neither a myth nor simply attributable to 'oil', as some argue. Even if Scotland has a different history, and the world has indeed changed greatly since 1814, what we know from the Norwegian experience is that politics matter, and politics can change if people will it to do so.

Notes

1. Cited in Simon, 1985.
2. We refer in this book to 'Union Monarchy', by which we variously mean the double or triple monarchies of the various unions between Denmark and Norway (prior to 1397 and between 1522 and 1814), Sweden and Norway (1814–1905), and of Norway, Denmark and Sweden during the Kalmar Union of 1397–1522.
3. For the British, the Viking Age is held to have ended in 1066 after Edward expelled the Vikings in England and unified the country. In Norway, unification was a slow process from the ninth century, and is generally held to have produced a unified Norway during the first part of the eleventh century under

the reign of Olav Haraldsson (St Olav, 1015–28), Magnus the Good (1035–47) and Harald Hardrada (1046–66). Certainly, as Robert Bartlett (1993) argues, King Hardrada was much more than a Norwegian King – he was a European conqueror.

4. Donaldson, 1990: 46.
5. See Thomson, 2008: 24–39; and Alex Woolf, 2007.
6. Such as Steinar Imsen and Randi Wærdahl.
7. Riis, 1988: 15.
8. Thomson, 2008: 202.
9. Donaldson, 1990: 80–97.
10. This treaty reconfirmed the Treaty of Perth, but added no clauses.
11. Riis, 1988: 15.
12. Ibid.: 15.
13. Haakon VI of Norway, who came of age in 1355, married Margaret of Denmark who succeeded in securing the Danish Crown for their son Olav in 1375. Olav inherited the Norwegian Crown from his father in 1380, and this marks the beginning of the Danish–Norwegian union which lasted until 1814. Olav also had claims to the Swedish throne through the dispossessed Folkung dynasty which had ruled Sweden from 1250 to 1363 but his untimely death in 1387 at the age of seventeen prevented the ousting of the German King Albrecht from Sweden. However, the astute Margaret secured the support of the Swedish nobles and ousted Albrecht, and formed the Kalmar Union in 1397 at the coronation of her grand-nephew Erik of Pomerania. Interestingly, the Bishop of Orkney was the only representative of the Norwegian episcopate at the coronation in Kalmar (Derry, 1979: 72).
14. Haakon VI of Norway married Princess Margaret of Denmark in 1363, later founder of the Kalmar Union.
15. See especially Riis, 1988; Donaldson, 1990: 115–16; Murdoch, 2006.
16. Riis, 1988: 19.
17. This alliance lost its importance in Denmark and Norway under Fredrik I because of the issue of the redemption of the Orkney and Shetland Isles which remained unresolved, although it was 'on the agenda' on several occasions in 1524, 1533, 1549–50, 1563 and 1589, and related difficulties over 'reciprocal economic activities', especially trade and duties, that were not resolved until 1589 (Riis, 1988: 32–5).
18. Dickinson, 1961: 330.
19. Christian III promised the Danish Counsel of the Realm in his Danish *håndfestning* from October 1536 that if the king obtained control of Norway or parts of it, it was to become a Danish province. This promise was however never stated publicly and in reality Norway continued to be a kingdom but under Danish rule.
20. It is reputed that Grieg was related to Scotland's national poet, Robert Burns, through his grandmother, and also to Gavin Greig who was – with the Reverend James Duncan – one of Scotland's most famous and prodigious collectors of north-east Scottish folk songs, now published as a collection by the University of Aberdeen: Shuldham-Shaw & Lyle, 1983.
21. See Willumsen, 2008.

22. *The Young Laird of Logie* is a folk song about Margaret, a Danish attendant of Queen Anne, wife of King James VI, and her lover the Laird of Logie, then in prison in Edinburgh Castle. Margaret, with the help of Queen Anne, aids and abets the escape of Logie, who subsequently marries Margaret. That and other information about shared folk songs such as *The Young Allan* and *Young Aiken* is found in Shuldham-Shaw and Lyle, 1983.

23. How poor Norway was in the nineteenth century is nevertheless a matter of dispute (cf. Francis Sejersted, *Sosialdemokratiets tidsalder. Norge og Sverige i det 20. Århundre*, 2005: 520).

24. Caused mainly by the Danish State's large debts following defeat in the Napoleonic Wars, which it fought on the French side.

25. Although Norway gained control over domestic policies in 1814, it was in a union of crowns with Sweden until 1905. However, for our purposes 1814 is a more significant date than 1905, hence our focus on it and the period following. See, for example, Knut Heidar's *Elites on Trial* (2001).

26. Heidar, 2001: 4.

27. Representation of the People Act 1832 England and Wales. The Scottish Reform Act was based on it but was a separate Act in the same year.

28. Which compared with 5.8 per cent of the population of England and Wales having the vote after 1832.

29. Burton (1897, vol. 1, 426–44) tells us that King David had little or no control over the Highlands and Islands including Ross, as well as Galloway, and the Vikings controlled the Hebrides, Orkney, Shetland and Caithness. He also states that the Norman presence in Scotland at that time was tenuous, citing in evidence that there are no remnants of Norman castles in Scotland (434). Indeed, the 'motley tribes' of Scotland seem to have shared a 'spirit of alarm mixed with animosity' concerning the Norman 'threat' (435). King David led the 'motley tribes' against the Normans in the Battle of the Standard in 1138 and was criticised for this by the forebears of those later Scottish 'heroes' Robert de Bruce and Bernard de Baliol who had lands in both England and Scotland (Burton, 1897: 437; Innes, 1860: 95).

30. Dickinson, 1961: 375.

31. Innes, 1872: 188.

32. Innes, 1987: 165–6.

33. Indicating that Church lands included much of the better land: Johnston, 1909.

34. James V secured the rich abbeys of Kelso and Melrose as well as the priories of St Andrews and Pittenweem and the Abbey of Holyrood for three of his illegitimate sons while still in infancy. James IV likewise arranged for his illegitimate son Alexander to be made Archbishop of St Andrews at the age of eleven (Dickinson, 1961: 270).

35. Dickinson, 1961: 270.

36. Dickinson, 1961: 298.

37. Dickinson, 1961: 351.

38. Callander, 1987: 29–30. William Gordon was the fourth son of the powerful Earl of Huntly who was guardian of the bishops of Aberdeen, and used this position to appoint his son as bishop in 1546. Callander tells us that this was 'a

conspicuous example of the type of prelate that brought the Roman Catholic Church into disrepute before the Reformation of 1560'.

39. Dickinson, 1961: 357.
40. Dickinson, 1961: 375.
41. By processes of enclosure of former common lands, absorption of common rights into private rights, clearances of insecure peasants, extension of rights over the foreshore and over fresh fish and game. For an excellent account of the way in which landowners came to acquire foreshore rights in Scotland, see MacAskill, 2006.
42. Callander, 1987: 59.
43. Lunden, 2004.
44. The reason for having only one category of 'lay landowners' is the grey areas between the social groups. See Ugulen, 2005: 45–6.
45. See Dickinson, 1961: 353; Hume Brown, 1907: 329; Callander, 1987.
46. Lunden, 2004: 195.
47. Moseng et al., 2007.
48. Lunden, 2004: 197.
49. Norges offisielle statistikk (NOS) XI, 103: 48.
50. Øye, 2004.
51. Although not in fact the 'first' agricultural revolution, we will use this term here both because it is what is commonly understood, and also because the evidence is that patterns of landholding and rights before this time belonged to an age when by far the majority of people in both countries (and elsewhere in the world) lived in rural areas and worked the land mainly for subsistence, and which remained broadly static for several centuries. The first agrarian revolution can be thought of as the evolution of settled farming in the Middle East around 10,000 BC; the second might be regarded as the introduction of feudalism which was derived from the Carolingian Empire and codified in late Roman Law, but became established as a political, social and economic system in Britain after 1066 (Bloch, 1962: vol. 1, 187), although this is sometimes considered as a proto-revolution.
52. Devine, 1994; 1999.
53. Sumner Maine, 1890; 1901.
54. Their descendants include some of the so-called 'red legs', poor whites in Barbados, and the potato farmers of St Vincent, among whom one could find the name of 'Grant', for example, in the 1960s.
55. During the Clearances, clanspeople were displaced to make way for large sheep farmers and settled on smallholdings on poor land to the west and north. They had a small area of individual 'arable' or in-bye land, and a share in common grazings.
56. Including the notable case of Leckmelm estate in Sutherland, where a new owner cleared the land in 1880, leading to protests that Dunbabin (1974: 181) argues started the land reform movement.
57. See Devine, 1999: 129–30; Campbell, 1971: 27.
58. See Dunbabin, 1974: 181–210.
59. See Mather, 1978; Leneman, 1989.
60. Andrew Newby (2003: 74–91) argues that McHugh, an Irish Catholic who

migrated with his parents to Greenock in the early 1870s, played a crucial role in the spread of Georgist ideas in Scotland and hence to George's subsequent tour. McHugh's visit to Skye was sponsored by the National Land League of Great Britain.

61. See, in particular, Mather, 1978; Leneman, 1989.
62. See Hunter, 1976; Dunbabin, 1974; Smout, 1986; Richards, 1982.
63. For a formal definition of a croft, see Bryden and Houston, 1976: 33. A croft is a smallholding situated in the seven 'Crofting Counties' as defined in the 1886 Act and typically comprising an individually tenanted house and small area of arable or 'in-bye' land and a share in common grazings.
64. Carter, 1979: 29.
65. Carter, 1979: 29.
66. Carter (1979: 165–71) gives the examples of the famous Aberdeenshire capitalist farmer and cattle breeder William McCombie, who was president of the Scottish Chamber of Agriculture and, later, Liberal MP, and his 'lieutenant in all these endeavours' J. W. Barclay, who, in 1879, became vice-president of the new Farmers' Alliance founded to represent the interests of tenant farmers in England and Scotland. In 1881, following considerable agitation over rents during the agricultural depression, Aberdeenshire farmers spearheaded the creation of a Scottish Farmers' Alliance which became the Scottish Land Reform Alliance in 1886.
67. Carter, 1979: 170–4.
68. Sogner, 1996: 189.
69. Sogner, 1996: 192.
70. Lunden, 2004: 164.
71. Reinton, 1961: 404.
72. Emigration from Norway is said to have started in 1825. Before 1836, however, the emigration was moderate, and the large wave of emigration started in the 1860s. Emigration was mainly to the USA (Norges offisielle statistikk, 1921).
73. Norges offisielle statistikk XI 103: 48.
74. Lunden, 2004: 205.
75. Lunden, 2004: 206.   Several protests and riots are discussed in Dørum and Sandvik (2012), who classify the protests in two groups: tax riots and hunger riots. Both Strilekrigen and the Lofthus riot are classified as tax revolt. In addition, the Thrane-movement (1848) is discussed and one conclusion is that this was a product of a general political mobilisation and radicalisation.
76. Lunden, 2004: 207.
77. Gjerdåker, 2004: 237.
78. The franchise was given to males over the age of 25 who were or had been a senior official, an owner-occupier farmer or had owned or leased a farm in the land register (*matrikulert jord*) for over five years, were a township citizen or owned property in a township valued at more than 300 Riksbankdaler (see Chapter 8 in this volume). Stemmerettens historie i Norge at http://snl.no/Stemmerettens_historie_i_Norge (author's translation).
79. Heidar, 2001: 18.
80. This was called the 'Bondestortinget' or 'Farmer's Parliament'. Political parties

did not exist until 1884 when first Venstre (Liberal Party) and then Høyre (Conservative Party) were established.

81. Simon, 1985.
82. The settlement of the Napoleonic Wars (the Congress of Vienna was in 1815, which confirmed the new personal/monarchical union between Sweden and Norway) forced the King of Denmark, who had been an ally with Napoleon, to surrender Norway to the King of Sweden. For a few weeks the country enjoyed independence, before the personal/monarchical union with Sweden was enforced. In this very short time, Norway wrote a constitution inspired by French Revolutionary ideas, which was justly considered to be the most liberal in Europe.
83. Senghaas, 1985; Heidar, 2001.
84. See, for example, Devine, 1999: 9.
85. Bratberg and Brandal in Chapter 4 of this volume; Hilson, 2008: 39; Arter, 2008; Kane and Mann, 1992.
86. Initially the educated elite of officials in Christiania (Oslo) looked down on the newly enfranchised peasants as 'the estate of the most foolish' (Arter, 2008: 34) but this prejudice had been overcome by the mid-1800s when the liberal intelligentsia increasingly joined forces with the peasants to make government more responsive to parliament, thus weakening the old elite of officials (Heidar, 2001: 19).
87. The peasant opposition in parliament in the 1830s championed local government, and new elected representative municipal institutions were established in 1837, which restricted the local power of state officials. This was critical for the subsequent development of democracy (Heidar, 2001: 19).
88. Hilson, 2008: 74.
89. Polanyi, 1944; Esping-Andersen, 1990: 36.
90. Devine, 1999: 100.
91. Ibid.: 101.
92. Esping-Andersen, 1990: 26–9; Hilson, 2008: 89.
93. Kvist et al., 2012.
94. Reinforced by the 'Equivalence' payments following the Act of Union in 1707, which redistributed wealth to the landowners who lost money in the 'Darien Venture', and also the bribes that were paid to certain landowners by England to persuade them to vote for the Union.
95. Bryden and Hart, this volume; Saville, 1996.
96. Smout and Wood, 1990.
97. Indeed, Brox (2012) shows that the number of registered agricultural units in Norway increased during and after industrialisation, between 1875 and 1920 from 173,000 to 393,000 units.
98. Knox, 1999: 36.
99. Whatley, 1989.
100. Devine, 1999: 250.
101. Birkeland was also a Norwegian.
102. Norway's Centre Party PM, Per Borten, grandfather of the Oil Minister in the Centre-Left Coalition government up to 2013, secretly arranged with Hambros

bank, London, to acquire a 51 per cent majority stake in Norsk Hydro for the State in 1969, a feat which was accomplished by buying shares in various European markets in small lots in order to avoid increasing the share price. Borten subsequently won government approval for his actions, even though the Government was a Centre-Right coalition. Hogne Honset, 'Kronikk', *Klassekampen*, 26 April 2013.

103. Lange, 1977.
104. Harvey, 1994; Smith, 2011.
105. Knox, 1999: 37,41; Devine, 1999.
106. Ahlund, 2012: 34.
107. Grimnes, 2013: 162–4.
108. Knox, 1999: 254–71.
109. *On learning from history – Truths and eternal truths: A commentary*, Anne Kveim Lie, Associate Professor, University of Oslo. Norges Banks Skriftserie/Occasional Papers No. 46.
110. Riddoch, 2013: 17.

CHAPTER 2

Towards a Theory of Divergent Development

John Bryden

INTRODUCTION

The question I address in this chapter is how our findings on the long-term development of Norway and Scotland relate to some key themes in the Theory of Development. I approach this question in the first instance from a Classical economic standpoint. That is to say, I examine the key resources and the means by which these are transformed into improved economic welfare for people. In using a comparative approach, I look for explanations of the different development paths 'chosen' in Norway and Scotland first in ways in which land and natural resources are owned and managed through time, next in issues of human labour, ingenuity and reward for effort, then in capital and accumulation, and last but not least institutions. Within the rubric of institutions, I believe that our findings show that the State and State policies have played a key role in the processes of allocation, distribution and transformation of both resources and of rewards. Secondly, we find the notion of 'path dependency', as used by Bratburg and Brandal in Chapter 4, very helpful in thinking about the linkages between politics, resources, institutions and outcomes over relatively long periods of time.

LAND AND NATURAL RESOURCES

The first proposition is that the distribution of land was a founding factor in the emerging political, social and economic development of Scotland and Norway after the seventeenth century. While the roots of the market and fundamental differences in land ownership and rights between Scotland and Norway go far back into the mists of history, for practical purposes it is the period after the Reformation that is particularly important because, as Chapter 1 argues, the destiny of the land owned by the pre-Reformation Church was quite different in the two countries, and set a pattern for the following 400 years.

Adam Smith wrote that 'a man born to great fortune . . . is very seldom capable' of improving land with profit. The great landowners were more interested in land as a source of power and high office, in luxury expenditure to aggrandise (part of) their estates, and in dependent bondmen who both worked the land and formed the lord's military capacity.[1] Neither could improvement be looked for from the bondmen because 'A person who can acquire no property, can have no other interest but to eat as much, and to labour as little as possible'.[2] Any labour beyond that needed for subsistence was only extracted by violence. This was a state of underdevelopment, compounded by the numerous restraints on inland and external trade, 'privileges of fairs and markets'.[3] It was the normal state of most of Europe in the mid-eighteenth century, England being Smith's principal exception.

To Smith, the way out of this trap was to develop manufacturing, based on wage labour. This would free people from slavery or other bonds, allow specialisation and division of labour, create opportunities for capital accumulation, and ultimately lead to improvements in agriculture and reduction in restraints on trade in order to feed the manufacturing and urban population. The constraint on this process was diminishing returns to land, which Smith considered would raise the price of food and hence reduce the surplus, at least in the absence of expansion into virgin lands of the New World. To Smith, while the capacity of the human stomach has ultimately limited demand for food, people have limitless demands for manufactured products. The manufacturers are Smith's development heroes, because they fight against restraints on trade and monarchical privileges while seeking improvement in the incomes of ordinary people in order to widen the market for their products.[4] Their interests become the interests of the people, through the working of the 'invisible hand'.[5] They, along with labourers, artisans and the working farmers, constitute 'productive' as opposed to 'unproductive' labour on which economic progress depends.[6] They also recirculate a high proportion of their (working) capital in the local economy.[7] Moreover, it is important to Smith that the manufacturing units remain small and if possible individually or family owned, and that monopolies are avoided: he considered joint stock companies to be inflexible and subject to poor management.

For Smith, it was the reduction in monopoly power and privilege and the extension of the market, small manufacturing and wage labour that would lead to economic development. There is no mention in *The Wealth of Nations* of dispossession of 'peasants' in order to make way for large commercial farmers and certainly a strong inference that farmer-owners, rather than 'bondmen', were most likely to secure agrarian improvement.

Yet as we see in Chapter 4, the hegemonic idea of agrarian 'improvers' in Scotland from the mid-eighteenth century hinged around the idea of dispossession of individual and collective use rights – enclosures and clearances[8] – that would make way for the large capitalistic farmers. This was an idea that 'informed' agrarian improvers globally. But it was not the form of 'improvement' adopted in Norway, where no dispossession of peasants took place.[9] Indeed, later research has generally supported the Smithian view that oligarchic landownership retards structural change and economic development.[10]

Norway adopted another approach, where farms were mainly owned by the farmer, the farms remained small and the farm families were overwhelmingly pluri-active, earning their livelihoods from several occupations but certainly in large part from the manufacturing industry which, particularly after 1900, was decentralised. The decentralised nature of the new hydro-electric energy source that underpinned the form of Norwegian industrialisation that followed its development after 1900, plus the regulation of the location of industry that used it, worked in harmony with the nature of agriculture and the labour supply that it could provide without ceasing the production of food (see also Chapters 4 and 6). This contrasted with nineteenth-century industrialisation in Scotland, which used centralised and privately owned coal as the main power source, and which went along with rapid urban growth and migration. Urbanisation was thus both less likely and slower to occur in Norway than in Scotland, so that the demand for food by urban landless people did not expand rapidly in the nineteenth century as it did in Scotland. Ironically, in the context of what happened in Scotland after 1776, this was more as Adam Smith envisaged the development process.[11] As Giovanni Arrighi points out when discussing Smithian development in China, the focus was on development of the domestic market and allowing rural labour to gain more ready access to both education and off-farm work in factories and nearby towns.[12]

Chapter 4 discusses the issue of policy-making around agriculture, the land and rural development. Suffice to say here that Norway did not open its land market to non-nationals or corporations, and the market in land was heavily regulated in the interests of maintaining the resident working owner-farmer structure.

PEOPLE AND LABOUR

A second key theme concerns people and the supply of labour, and it is one deeply linked to the first theme, the occupation and ownership of land. The twentieth-century development economist and Nobel Prize winner Arthur Lewis considered himself to be a Classical economist in the tradition of Adam Smith. One of his most famous papers was 'Economic Development with Unlimited Supplies of Labour',[13] a thesis which rested on the commonly observed rural labour surplus, creating a labour force with a marginal productivity of close to zero which could provide low-cost labour for the development of manufacturing. Scotland had two apparently 'unlimited' sources of labour for the development of manufacturing industry in the period 1750 to 1850, one being Irish and the other being rural Scottish (see Chapters 6 and 7). These two migration streams kept wages relatively low in Scotland during the nineteenth and twentieth centuries, a situation aggravated by the weakness of the labour movement in this period. This weakness – partly itself caused by the streams of migrants struggling to survive in a context of anti-migrant poor laws – was compounded by religious and social divisions within the Scottish working class (see Chapters 6 and 9). In Norway, by contrast, industrial labour was to a large extent supplied *in situ* by the farm-based families and there was no large influx of industrial labour from elsewhere in the comparable period of industrial growth. The two main consequences were first a shortage of labour, and second a rural–industrial labour solidarity, which evolved into strong trade unions, all of which led to relatively high wages in Norway and a more or less endemic shortage of labour. The point is that in Norway cheap labour was not a main condition of industrial growth or its later sustainability in economic and social terms, whereas in Scotland it was seen, and is still seen, as a major cause of both the initial industrial expansion and of later industrial collapse. As we will see in Chapter 3, the rural–urban solidarity was in many ways also the foundation of the social democracy that emerged in Norway, a key element in its political development during the nineteenth and twentieth centuries.

CAPITAL AND ACCUMULATION

We know that most capital for the development of small manufacturing and other enterprise initially comes from the savings of entrepreneurs, their families and partners. As Adam Smith said, 'Capitals are increased by parsimony, and diminished by prodigality and misconduct'.[14] That is true even today. However, the Joint Stock Company that Smith did not care for became the principal vehicle for industrial and service sector development in Scotland in the nineteenth and twentieth centuries. This demanded shareholders and bank loans, for which there was a massive and rapidly expanding demand in the later eighteenth, nineteenth and twentieth centuries, a demand that was met mainly by Scotland's major banks (see Chapter 8). Accumulation came from three main sources in Scotland: first, the expansion of Empire, from whence surpluses returned to the UK to finance agrarian and manufacturing ventures; second, the accretion of property prices as a result of massive public and private infrastructure investments (principally road, rail and harbour) especially in the nineteenth century, and as a result of planning regulation in the twentieth; and third, as a result of the increase in the value of stocks in joint stock as well as private companies in the nineteenth and twentieth centuries. Since property was very unevenly distributed in Scotland, and since it was mainly the landed classes that accrued wealth from the Empire, including activities such as slave-trading, the landed aristocracy did well out of these capital gains. The landed elite was also heavily involved in the rapidly expanding – and relatively successful – banks. Scottish landowners were also involved in mining (especially coal) and in manufacturing, especially where the latter started as a rural industry based on hydraulic (water) power. However, there was also a growing merchant and trading class that benefited from urban expansion and the development of trade opportunities after the middle of the eighteenth century, and who also invested in the banks and manufacturing. Moreover, Young found that the main source of start-up capital for micro-enterprise in rural Scotland between 1840 and 1914 was savings from previous wage employment.[15] Indeed, referring to the UK, Crouzet argues that about 50 per cent of the founders of large industrial undertakings between 1750 and 1850 came from the working class or lower middle class, and less than 10 per cent of entrepreneurs were descended from a landed family.[16] Even if a significant contribution was eventually made by the Scottish banks, parsimony, it seems, was indeed at least as important as great wealth for the financing of rapid industrial growth in the nineteenth century.

In nineteenth-century Scotland, the links between coal-mining, iron and steel, heavy engineering and shipbuilding meant a rather dense inter-industry connectivity, even if the whole was driven by a somewhat fickle export demand. Chapter 6 makes it clear that by the early twentieth century there was a rather widespread view that Scotland's manufacturing sector was too much oriented towards iron, steel, shipbuilding and other heavy engineering industries, all of which were highly dependent on export demand, and too little oriented towards a rapidly growing domestic consumer demand for automobiles, etc. The two world wars were said to have saved these industries temporarily, but after the Second World War another hegemonic view emerged along the same lines, when shipbuilding, railway engines and other heavy industries faced increasing international competition from the USA, Germany and Japan. After a brief period of focus on 'indigenous industry' by the new Scottish Development Agency in the 1960s, support for the traditional industries faltered in the 1970s and was effectively ended by the Thatcher government in the 1980s. The focus switched to what Arthur Lewis called 'industrialisation by invitation', especially on inward investment by US multinationals in office machinery and light manufacturing. These multinationals preferred a non-unionised labour force, and reinforced Thatcher's anti-union policies and legislation in the 1980s. While other comparable countries managed to expand shipbuilding and heavy engineering, particularly Germany and Japan, and adopt new techniques, Scotland failed to do so, and the efforts to turn things around look, in retrospect, rather half-hearted.

The discovery of North Sea oil in the late 1960s and its exploitation in the 1970s provided little or no succour to Scotland's indigenous industries, as it came at a time when the relevant industrial base was weak and failing. Downstream and upstream activities mainly benefited US multinationals, while tax revenues accrued to the Westminster government and were used by it to bolster the Thatcher neo-liberal project, prosecute international aggression and bolster re-election prospects. For these reasons, Norman Smith calls his book on the subject *The Sea of Lost Opportunity*,[17] while Christopher Harvie titled his earlier book *Fool's Gold*.[18]

In short, the UK was following neo-liberal, free-trade approaches to everything, especially so from the 1970s, and failing to take the necessary action to retain and adapt its traditional and formerly highly successful skills and industries. It also became highly dependent on inward flows of investment, especially from the USA, both for oil development and for manufacturing generally, with the result that much of the value-added leaked out from Scotland, something that Adam Smith would surely not have supported.

Norway's approach to industrialisation, natural resource ownership, and oil specifically, was quite different from that of the UK, and by extension Scotland. First of all, Norway's industrialisation was based largely on hydro-electric power which was a dispersed resource seen to belong to communities rather than individuals, unlike coal which was a privately owned geographically concentrated resource in Scotland, mostly in the hands of the large landowners. Foreign investment in hydro power and related manufacturing was controlled by the Concession Laws which not only secured reversion of the hydro-power dams and related infrastructure to the municipalities and counties after a period of years, but also insisted that manufacturing should go hand-in-hand with the development of the hydro power. This manufacturing included the smelting of metal ores and the manufacturing of fertilisers and other chemicals, which required cheap energy. After twenty-five or thirty years, then, we see many years when the surpluses from hydro-electric generation largely accrued either to the State electricity companies or to the local authorities who were able to use them for local development purposes. This is still the case in many Norwegian counties and municipalities today, more than a century after the first Concession Laws were passed and despite the 'neo-liberal turn' in the 1980s and 1990s when local authorities were encouraged to sell off such assets, and some did.

The approach to hydro power was also followed with the development of North Sea oil, where ownership has remained in national, and to a very large extent government, hands. It is a largely state-owned company – Statoil – that owns the oil and exploits it. The revenues for the most part go into a Sovereign Oil Fund today worth more than £6 billion, or roughly £100,000 per citizen.[19] This helps to avoid 'Dutch disease' – or the super-inflation of the exchange rate – common in natural resource-rich economies. Just as important, it represents a fund to draw on when the oil is no longer there or exploitation ceases for other reasons. In addition, it is largely Norwegian companies that supply the oil industry, meaning that the revenues from oil have a much larger local economic impact than they do in Scotland.

Although Norway has also made mistakes, especially in the period since 1980,[20] the headline is that it has taken much greater care to ensure that it and its people benefit from its hydro-electric and oil resources than Scotland has been able to do, or the UK has been willing or inclined to do. This has not been because Norway led Scotland in traditional skills or enterprise relating to hydro or oil – indeed, the reverse is certainly the case with oil – but is because independence from Denmark in 1814 allowed it to develop better economic policies, rooted in a more democratic and participatory polity.

POLITICS AND POLICY-MAKING

In his critique of the prevailing hegemonic idea that free trade and movement of capital is inevitably 'good' for development, Dieter Senghaas points out that 'it has hardly ever been questioned whether, during its initial development stages in the nineteenth and early twentieth centuries, Europe itself had developed in such a way. And rarely have the repercussions of free trade in different societies been properly examined.'[21] Senghaas points out that Norway did not follow a conventional development path. It remained poor in the nineteenth century, when it was still exporting timber and fish, and its main export earner was in fact the Norwegian- owned merchant fleet, Norway having the third-largest tonnage after Britain and the US in 1860. To Senghaas, it was the coming of hydro-electric power and attendant industries, together with the State regulation of that process, which made the difference. Norway was able to 'disassociate itself' from the international economy, to use Senghaas' terms. Meanwhile, Britain was in a liberal period, having abolished the corn laws in the mid-nineteenth century, and of course having preferential trade arrangements with the British Empire, then at its apex.

Norway protected its land and natural resources from foreign exploitation and speculation, whereas Britain had a consistently 'open door' policy for most of the period in question. True, the coal industry was nationalised between 1947 and 1994 and Scottish hydro-electricity between 1943 and 1991, but in the case of coal this did not happen at a formative stage of industrial development,[22] while in the case of hydro power in Scotland the process of nationalisation was extremely centralised in its approach, leaving no surpluses for the local communities that they could deploy on their own account, but certainly leading to a large extension of electric power to rural households. What it did do was allow the electrification of most of the 50 per cent of homes in the Highlands and Islands that lacked electricity in 1950 during the following twenty years.

The choices made by Norway were made by it autonomously and against the hegemonic thinking of the time. They were made because of specific histori-cal, political and social conditions in Norway. Britain, on the other hand, was a major part of the hegemony, and it faced a different set of conditions. This is why Senghaas rejects both 'world systems' and 'core–periphery' theories that imply that the development of a core must necessarily be at the expense of a periphery, in a kind of zero-sum game.[23] Of course, core–periphery processes may occur, but only where the core exercises some kind of control over the periphery. As Chapter 3 makes clear, Denmark was a weak 'core' for Norway, and a non-existent one after 1814, while England was a much stronger core for Scotland, especially after the middle of the eighteenth century. The defining moment for Norway was indeed 1814, as within the Norway–Sweden Union of Crowns, Sweden started as more of an equal partner that became progressively weaker until the dissolution of the Union in 1905. While Scotland became more of a dependent periphery within Britain and the UK, Norway became increasingly independent within a framework of loose Nordic cooperation (see also Chapter 10).

Norway's choices were made in a political system that had been relatively democratic – certainly in comparison to Scotland – since 1814, due to the widespread and relatively even ownership of land on the one hand, and the related urban–rural alliance. Not only was the proportion of the enfranchised population significantly higher in Norway after 1814 than in Scotland even after the 1833 Reform Bill but, as we can see in Chapter 3, the grip of the old regime on Scotland's polity was very much stronger at the beginning of the nineteenth century and remained much stronger thereafter. Moreover, the rural–urban alliance, formed mainly in the nineteenth century, was strengthened in the crises of the twentieth century and underpinned the development of social democracy, a strong welfare state and a model of development that became known as a distinctive model.

Norway is one of the 'mixed economy' countries that, deliberately or otherwise, followed Karl Polanyi's (1944/2001) analysis of the failure of market liberalism, the hegemonic idea emerging from Britain's leading role in the world economy during the nineteenth century. In particular, the idea that the market is embedded in society and its institutions is one that is perhaps best exemplified by the Norwegian approach. This idea is precisely the opposite of that of neo-liberals who believe that society, if it exists at all, is or should be embedded in the market. While 'dislocation', as Polanyi calls it,[24] was common in Scotland in the nineteenth and twentieth centuries, it was far less so in Norway, at least until after the Second World War.

In his conclusions, Senghaas stresses three imperatives of development policy, mainly aimed at the 'third world' but founded on his analysis of the European development experience, and therefore relevant to our analysis. The first is the imperative of dissociation from the global regime, as only in this way can the necessary self-centredness that leads to an inward-orientated accumulation process be stimulated. The second imperative is socio-economic restructuring in a way that leads to what he calls 'building up of coherent accumulation structures' which, although he refers particularly to Freidrich List, is also – despite List–Smith disagreements – derived from Adam Smith. The third is both about the international division of labour and, perhaps more importantly, about the building up of sub-regional, regional and continental infrastructures and institutions that can counter the hegemony, wherever that is located. With regard to the first imperative, Norway dissociated itself in the early twentieth century by means of the Concession Acts. With regard to the second, the policy of location, ownership and linking of hydro-power plants and related industrial activities, as well as the structure of landownership and protection of that structure from external forces, was critical. With regard to the third, the development of Nordic cooperation, starting indeed in the medieval period but reinforced in the nineteenth and twentieth centuries, and the notion of the Nordic Model as a distinctive approach to development, political life and human welfare in the twentieth century are a clear example (see also Chapters 3 and 10).

By contrast, Scotland was politically unable to follow such a prescription after the Union of 1707, and its dependence on the central and increasingly central-ised government in Westminster increased, especially after the middle of the nineteenth century, with the only concession to Scottish governance up until devolution in 1999 being the establishment of an administrative presence in the form of a Scottish Secretary in 1885 and later a Scottish Office, both as part of the Westminster government (see Chapter 3).

CONSENSUS POLITICS

The political conditions facing Scotland since the Union have meant, for the most part, subordination to an increasingly centralised Westminster government, which was elected on a very limited and quite unrepresentative franchise in the nineteenth century, and which remained unrepresentative of Scottish voters even after the extension of the franchise for most of the twentieth and early twenty-first centuries. This lack of democratic representativeness was compounded by the bi-cameral system in the UK, with an unelected second chamber in the form of the House of Lords that, for most of the period under study, was peopled with the representatives of Britain's 'ancien régime', notably the upper echelons of the landed classes and members of the religious and legal elite.[25] Even in those rare periods when over half of the Scottish voters voted for the same party or coali-tion that won the UK elections under the first-past-the-post system, they had to contend with a House of Lords that was for the most part on the opposite side of the political spectrum.

As Tom Devine[26] has argued, the British Reform Bill of 1832 was hardly radical, and even less radical from a Scottish point of view where the franchise covered an even smaller proportion of the male population. Democracy was seen by the British elite as a threat, and the Reform Bill was aimed at preserving as much of the traditional landed power as possible. The legislation also allowed the corrupt practices amounting to 'vote-stuffing' to continue.[27] The failure of the Bill led to the rise of Chartism as a response to the failure to extend the franchise to the working class. Chartism failed as a political force in the later nineteenth century, but it did deepen and enlarge the Scottish radical tradition, already established in the 1790s.[28] It is also worth noting, in the context of our earlier discussion of land-ownership, that the Chartist Land Plan outlined a 'vision of smallholding colonies and agricultural self-sufficiency as an alternative to industrial capitalism'.[29] Nineteenth-century Scottish political ideas were anti-landowner rather than anti-capitalist, and contained strong elements of Scottish nationalism.[30]

Prime Minister Gladstone, a Liberal who was also popular in Scotland, won the UK elections in 1868 and in the same year the franchise was extended to the skilled working classes. There followed a period of Liberal dominance in both Scottish and UK politics which essentially lasted until 1914, albeit in an increasingly fragile political environment, and with some coalitions in the latter period. Although it could not be argued that Scotland as a whole was disenfranchised in this period, the period of Liberal dominance in Scottish politics is seen by Nairn as one of profound crisis for Scottish nationhood.[31] However, as Devine points out, this was also a period when Scots were prominent if not dominant in the Empire project, in industry and industrial inventions, in banking and in literature and academia.[32] Gladstone's government, with the help of the Crofters' Party, initiated the Napier Commission's enquiry into the condition of crofters and cottars that led to an important 'land reform' in terms of the granting of security of tenure to crofters, rent controls and other rights and protections in response to the abuses of the Highland Clearances, as discussed in Chapter 1. Those voters in general supporting land reform, home rule for Scotland and extension of the franchise voted Liberal in this period, and to a large extent this led to an alliance that cut across class boundaries.[33]

The Liberal hegemony collapsed after the First World War when, helped by the extension of the franchise in 1918, Labour gained a third of the votes in the elections of that year. However, the 'first-past-the post' system meant that only eight Labour MPs were sent to Westminster. The Irish Catholic vote moved from Liberal to Labour after the Irish Partition in 1920. Liberals lost votes because they provided neither promised land nor promised housing 'fit for heroes' to soldiers and sailors returning from the war. In the 1922 election, Labour became the largest party in Scotland for the first time with 32 per cent of the votes and 29 MPs in the UK parliament. However, Labour's fortunes were also to be affected by the Russian Revolution and the economic crises of the inter-war period, both of which polarised politics nationally and caused the middle classes to move to the right, a shift that Conservative Prime Minister Baldwin took advantage of, and which simultaneously deepened the marginalisation of the Liberals. Nevertheless, Baldwin's popular Conservative government of 1935 only polled 42 per cent of the Scottish vote. From then on, and up to the present day, Scottish voters have only once cast more than 50 per cent of their votes for the government in power in Westminster.

One can only conclude that because of the nature of the franchise – the first-past-the-post electoral system, different voting patterns between Scotland and the rest of the UK, and the existence of a second chamber dominated for most of the period in question by the landed elite – Scottish people have been in a very real sense disenfranchised by the British political system for most of the period between the Union of 1707 and the present day. The main exception seems to have been the period of Liberal hegemony between 1868 and 1914. It was perhaps in that period above all that we can see the glimmers of a kind of alliance between small farmers, working class and middle class that led to social democracy and consensus politics in the Nordic countries, but which ended in polarised and conflictual politics in the UK and Scotland in the twentieth century (see also Chapter 3).

In Norway, as Knut Heidar argues, people's political power was transformed by the new Constitution of 1814 when the vote was given to all owners of land and some tenants as well.[34] Because of the wide distribution of landownership, this meant that 45 per cent of males over the age of 25 were eligible to vote. However, the power of the parliament was for the time being restricted due to the Union Monarchy with Sweden: 'From about 1850 onward the liberal intelligentsia in the cities increasingly joined forces with the peasant groups in parliament in order to make government more responsive to parliament – at the expense of the old class of state officials.' In 1884, this coalition of forces came to power and secured a parliamentary form of relationship with the executive. All men were given the vote in 1898, and in 1913 this was extended to all women. Meanwhile, local government had been championed by the peasants in the 1830s and elected representative municipalities were established in 1837. Heidar argues that the local political autonomy created in 1837 was extremely important for later democratisation.[35] As Chapters 3 and 5 make clear, Norway created a local democracy that had and has very substantial powers and financing, as well as much greater representation and higher voter participation, than was or is the case in Scotland. This was the means by which the peasants successfully resisted centralised planning, centralisation, transfer of fishing rights to capitalist interests, and promoted concession laws and other progressive measures in the field of natural resources and land.[36]

Up to 1928, government oscillated between Liberals and Conservatives, although the Liberals were the 'natural party of government' in this period.[37] Labour benefited from universal male suffrage in 1898 and more so from the introduction of proportional representation in 1921, winning an eighteen-day control of government in 1928, and a more solid – if minority government – control in 1935 with support from the rural centre party, which gave it a thirty-year control of power broken only by the war period. This Labour government was a social democratic government, despite its history as a member of the Komintern[38] between 1919 and 1923, and it became the hegemonic party in Norwegian politics until the mid-1960s. During the entire period from 1950 to 1980, the Labour party was out of office for less than eight years. Heider states that

Social progress was founded on more or less continuous economic growth during this period. The state gave priority to industrial development, and a strong belief in progress, as such, permeated society. Planning was a central instrument in state economic policies, and sectors like agriculture, fishing, and transportation were all strongly state regulated. The social democratic order was also marked by a belief in a strong state. Primary public goals were full employment, social equality, and a high level of welfare. Accordingly, redistribution of resources was a major objective, and it was considered the responsibility of the state to provide free education and free health care and to look after important cultural institutions. In short, markets were to be guided, private solutions were eschewed, and the chances for 'opting out' were restricted.[39]

CONCLUSION

This chapter is titled *towards* a theory of divergent development, and so does not purport to be *the* theory of divergent development between Norway and Scotland. It is of course a matter of judgement whether any person likes the outcome better in Norway or, *vice versa*, in Scotland. I have used a Classical approach to the issue, married with Polanyi's approach which involves an economy embedded in society rather than the opposite. And I believe that this approach is the best one for explaining long-run divergence between two countries following, of their own volition or in a dependent manner, essentially different paths. I understand differences in the initial condition of land ownership and distribution to be central to these divergences, not just for their own sake but because they had an impact on political values and beliefs, as well as alliances and, ultimately, coalitions. These values and beliefs and political conditions in turn underpinned the dissociation from the global hegemony of free markets and capital movements at a critical juncture of history, notably the start of modern industrialisation on the strength of hydro-power resources at the end of the nineteenth century. They also underpinned the development of a more generous and universal welfare state in the twentieth century and the later development of North Sea oil. Taken together, I find much more of a 'Smithian' model of development in Norway than in Scotland.[40] However, perhaps it should be called a 'Smith-Polanyi' model because of the incorporation – whether by design or otherwise – of Polanyi's specific considerations relating to false commodities, land, people and money.

The dominant political cleavages in a rapidly industrialising Scotland in the nineteenth century were between workers and sections of the middle class, and the landed interests that were so much against the extension of democracy; and between the Protestant and (migrant Irish) Catholic working-class factions. The most powerful and enduring alliance was between the skilled workers and the urban middle classes that created the Liberal hegemony against large landowners and in favour of home rule, but ultimately fracturing into polarised Labour and Conservative regimes dominated by the Westminster government. In Norway, the dominant cleavages of the nineteenth century were first, between the towns formerly privileged by monarchs and the rural areas; second, between farm workers and their employers; and third, between workers and capitalists. The most powerful and enduring alliance was that between small family peasant farmers, many of whom were also small fishermen, and the growing working class, which led to the social democratic and consensual political system still enduring today. This was reinforced by early extension of the effective franchise and adoption of proportional representation. The two very different political systems that emerged help us to understand the different political choices made in Norway and in (but mostly for) Scotland in the modern period.

Does this comparative development 'story' have any more general theoretical pointers? We think it does. For one thing, the cases of Norway and Scotland do not support generalised 'stages' theories[41] that imply, for example, that an 'agrarian revolution' involving in particular the dispossession of peasants need precede an industrial revolution. For another, the cases demonstrate that peripheries are not doomed to remain dependent and poor, trapped in a vicious cycle. Yet again, there is no support from the Norwegian case for the notion that the development of market capitalism needs to precede 'social development' (the 'Sen-Bhagwati argument'), since 'trickle-down' from the development of capitalism will finance the development of education, health and other social supports. No doubt one could find many more examples but suffice to say here that it is important to examine the particulars of each case – Norway has its own very particular history, even distinct from the other Scandinavian and Nordic countries.

The story nevertheless has some pointers for both Scotland and Norway. Should Scottish people vote for independence, its new policy-makers can certainly find considerable support for the creation of a new political system, with multiple parties and proportional representation, and a much stronger local democracy to give those living in the very different parts of Scotland a real voice and powers to tailor policies to their needs and aspirations, and resist hegemonic ideas from the centre. New political leaders, parties and democratic elements can also drop the current obsession with the neo-liberal development path reflected by the policies of the main UK parties over the past thirty-five years, and emanating from the USA. They can, and hopefully will, open their eyes to other alternative development paths towards a more 'human' economy and society.[42] In this they will desirably be informed by the experience of the Nordic countries which have a robust alternative 'model', albeit one that has been formed in specific national political, social and economic conditions. To follow an alternative path, more like the Nordic social democratic path, Scotland will need solid alliances to counter the England–US axis, and these are also most likely to come from the Nordic countries, which already have a history of alliances between themselves in the Nordic Council of Ministers and the Nordic Council, to name but two. But opportunities will also arise in the EU, where Scotland would be in a position to play a more positive role than the remainder of the UK.

The issue of landownership and more generally the distribution of wealth and income also needs to be tackled in an independent Scotland, as do the related issues of control over land transactions and land value taxation. The very distorted distribution of wealth and income today in the UK has distorted democracy and disenfranchised the poorer section of society.

The role of the State will be critical in these and other matters, but to exercise that role properly the State must be legitimate and seen to be so. Politicians and the executive must be scrupulously just and fair, open and honest. Anything less should not be tolerated. People must trust the State and its institutions. The strengthening of social democracy must include the thoroughgoing reform of local government, including devolution of power, responsibility and taxation, and democratisation of the Non-Departmental Public Bodies (NDPBs) that dominate so many areas formerly under local government responsibility, including housing, water and sewage, recreation and the environment, flood protection, tourism, culture and economic development.

Notes

1. Smith [1776] 1910, Book III: 344.
2. Ibid.: 345.
3. Smith [1776] 1910, Book III: 351.
4. By and large this was also the view of the Scottish working class and liberal bourgeoisie in the nineteenth century, who supported a liberal trade regime, the notion of the 'good employer', with whom they were allied against the old regime of the landed aristocracy. See also Chapter 6.
5. Smith [1776] 1910, Book V: 400.
6. Smith [1776] 1910, Book II: 301.
7. Ibid.: 312.
8. We understand 'enclosures' to imply the individualisation of formerly common or collective property and other use rights such as the hunting of game, fishing, collecting of firewood and mushrooms, access and rights of way and the winning of peat for heating and cooking. We understand clearances to imply the removal of farmers, crofters or cottars from the land on which they had customary use for farming, etc.
9. Nor did it happen in Japan or, much later, in Italy.
10. See, for example, Binswanger et al. (1995) and Falkinger and Grossman (2012).
11. It is true that Norwegian industrialisation after 1847 adopted 'infant-industry' protection of the kind recommended by List (1789–1846), who opposed Smith on this point, at least for a period.   However, later in the nineteenth century Norway adopted free trade, although infant-industry protection was reintroduced for the development of the oil industry in the 1970s (see Chapter 6).
12. Arrighi, 2007: 359–64.
13. W. A. Lewis (1954), *Economic Development with Unlimited Supplies of Labour*, The Manchester School, May.
14. Smith [1776] 1910, Book II: 301.
15. Young, 1995.
16. Crouzet, 1985: 77.
17. Smith, 2011.
18. Harvie, 1994.
19. The Fund is now called the 'Government Pension Fund Global'.
20. This is not the place to list Norway's mistakes, but they include losing control of hydro power and Norske Hydro, and they currently include various privatisation projects in the public sphere, as well as proposals for local government reorganisation. Other mistakes are mentioned in Chapters 7 and 10 in particular.
21. Senghaas, 1985: 6.
22. At which time the British political system was firmly in the hands of the old regime (see also Chapters 1, 3 and 6).

23. Senghaas, 1985: 154–5. Senghaas here refers to a debate between T. C. Smout, the Scottish historian, and Immanuel Wallerstein, leader of the World Systems approach. One of the present authors (Bryden) also debated a core–periphery approach to Scottish development with Smout in an ESRC seminar in Edinburgh University on 21 March 1980. See also Seers et al. (1979) and Bryden's contribution in that volume. An unpublished postscript to that contribution was presented by Bryden at the Edinburgh seminar.

24. Some call this 'disembedding', a term not in fact used by Polanyi himself. By 'dislocation' Polanyi was referring to the commercialisation of those things such as land and people or even food that were formerly part of social institutions and 'places'. Polanyi [1944] 2001, Chapter 15.

25. In his John McEwen lecture, Bryden analysed Andy Wightman's data to show that over half of the top 100 landowners were also hereditary peers with the right to sit in the House of Lords (Bryden, 1996: 6, n4). Because of this, the popular cause of land reform in Scotland did not become politically feasible until after devolution in 1999, when Scotland took back control over its own land law. Also present were the bishops of the Church of England and the Law Lords. See also Wightman, 1996:142.

26. Devine, 1999: 274.

27. Ibid.: 274.

28. Devine, 1999: 280.

29. Ibid.: 280.

30. Knox, 1999: 169.

31. Nairn, 1977.

32. Devine, 1999: 289–98.

33. Knox, 1999: 163–74.

34. Heidar, 2001: 18. See also Chapter 3.

35. Ibid.: 19.

36. Brox, 2006: 33–42.

37. Heidar, 2001: 24.

38. The Moscow-based communist international organisation calling for armed uprising by the working classes. See also Heidar (2001) and Chapter 3 in this volume.

39. Heidar, 2001: 25.

40. See also Arrighi (2007). Arrighi explores Adam Smith's model as applied to China.

41. For example, those of either Marx, whose system in *Das Kapital* vol. 1, Chapter 24 depends so heavily on the enclosure movement in England, or Rostow's *Stages of Economic Growth* (1960). However, Gerschenkron (1962), who had a stage theory of his own, allows that it is neither necessary nor sufficient to have 'preconditions' for takeoff as well as the fact that each country need not go through the same set of stages.

42. For a discussion of 'Human Economy', see for example Hart et al. (2010).

CHAPTER 3

Cousins Divided? Development in and of Political Institutions in Scotland and Norway since 1814

Nik. Brandal and Øivind Bratberg

ABSTRACT

Scotland and Norway started the nineteenth century as political cousins with seemingly similar structural features with regard to the political unions in which they took part. Yet from that point onwards their national development diverged. Norway turned out to become a rapidly developing, consensus-oriented and egalitarian nation-state, where democratisation ran parallel with the pursuit of national autonomy. Its Scottish cousin, meanwhile, remained embedded in the Union of Great Britain. It was characterised by adversarial politics and sharp social inequalities and saw its national aspirations run awry. How and why two countries with a shared point of departure evolved into entities that differ so profoundly today provides the puzzle for this chapter. We assess the perceived similarity between Scotland and Norway at the start of the period, analyse the differences in the social and political models today and trace the factors that may account for how the gap appeared. Finally, we consider the implications for an independent Scotland with this historical backdrop.

INTRODUCTION

The *longue durée* of Scottish and Norwegian history gives ample reason to place the two under the same light of scrutiny. Both nations were unified as seaward empire-nations in the Middle Ages, only to move towards peripheral status under a stronger neighbouring centre during the phase of accelerated nation-building from the sixteenth century onwards. They both turned Protestant in the Reformation and concentrated heavy responsibility for cultural development and education in their State Churches. Both Norwegians and Scots, furthermore, maintained – even during the peak periods of political integration under the dominant external centre – distinctive legal traditions and institutions as well as urban corporations with some independence in their external trade relations. Finally, in cultural terms, both countries harboured progressive rural movements with the potential to forge links with an emerging industrial working class.

In the run-up to the referendum on Scottish independence in 2014 an argument has been made – especially by proponents for independence – that Scotland should regenerate its relations across the North Sea. However, as we will argue in this chapter, in social and political terms Scotland and Norway have diverged widely from a seemingly similar structural position, thus complicating any claim to familiarity today. From the starting point of 1814, Norway turned out to become a rapidly developing, consensus-oriented and egalitarian nation-state, with a social model that emerged from the parallel pursuit of democratisation and national autonomy. Its Scottish cousin, meanwhile, remained embedded in the Union of Great Britain. This was characterised by adversarial politics and sharp social inequalities and saw its national aspirations run awry.

How and why two countries with a shared point of departure developed along such different trajectories is one of the main questions that we will try to answer in this chapter. However, while the historical similarities are certainly glaring, it is also essential not to overstate these commonalities, and as the Norwegian political scientist Stein Rokkan has pointed out, significant differences in historical backdrop between Scotland and Norway extend from external geopolitics to internal territorial structure.[1] Even so, we will argue that the shared historical outlook of Scotland and Norway offers a useful point of departure for analysing the subsequent evolution in both countries.

In this chapter the analysis will focus on the political development in the two countries in order to assess the perceived similarity between Scotland and Norway at the start of the period, analyse the differences in the political and social model today and trace the factors that may account for how the gap appeared. In proffering not only the political but also the *social* model our argument is that patterns of political mobilisation in key phases of the two nations' histories have had a lasting impact on features such as welfare state development, labour market relations, social mobility and redistribution. While these aspects are only superficially treated in this chapter, they are part and parcel of any analysis of why and to what extent Scotland and Norway diverge politically – beyond the obvious difference in political institutions. We will return to this point in a brief concluding section to consider the potential implications for an independent Scotland on the historical backdrop that we sketch.

The analysis is informed by historical institutionalism, according to which the legacy of earlier institutional decisions impinges on current processes, reducing the scope for entrepreneurship and magnifying the significance of discrete choices in the past. Essential to this approach to politics is the concept of path dependence. What it suggests is that historical development follows a branching structure; decisions at critical junctures earn a momentous significance over time, thus making it increasingly difficult to diverge from a selected path to which vested interests and formal and informal rules are attached.[2] Analytically, the concept is particularly apt where the goal is to explain an outcome or structure where a casual reading suggests that history matters but with an insufficient grasp of how or why.

Path dependence thus appears as a particularly fruitful approach to make sense of a development characterised by 'contingency at the front end and some degree of determinism at the back end'.[3] This is precisely the striking feature for an informed observer of the social model attached to both the Norwegian and the Scottish polities. Significantly, path dependence need not translate into a vision of standstill and stasis between rare transformative events. Clearly, moments where the form and shape of political institutions are subject to full reordering are extremely rare. However, even in times of apparent stability there is scope for incremental adaptation to changes in the environment as well as for actors to fight their own turf. As argued by Wolfgang Streeck and Kathleen Thelen, 'political institutions are the object of ongoing skirmishes as actors try to achieve advantage by interpreting or redirecting institutions in pursuit of their goals'.[4] In the current chapter we will apply this broader view of path dependence to analyse the development in and of political institutions in Scotland and Norway since 1814.

CRITICAL JUNCTURE 1: A CONSTITUTIONAL MOMENT?

Path-breaker by Constitutional Design – Norway

The outcome of the Napoleonic Wars for Norway was radical in form and consequence. Externally, the consequences were mitigated by the fact that union with a foreign power was sustained, as Sweden was handed what Denmark was forced to relinquish at the Treaty of Kiel. Beyond the façade of great-power rivalry, however, Norway moved at one stroke from subservience to the enlightened rule of a monarch to a constitutional monarchy with an elected parliament at its heart.

Thus, if there was ever such a thing as a defining moment in the political history of a nation, for Norway it was the year 1814. Within just over seven months, Norway seceded from Denmark and was given to Sweden on 14 January, declared its independence in defiance of the major European powers and adopted a radical new constitution based on popular sovereignty on 17 May, and fought a short war with Sweden over the summer, ending in an armistice on 14 August. In its wake, the Norwegian Parliament voted in support of a Personal Union with Sweden on 20 October and elected the Swedish King Charles XIII as the King of Norway on 4 November. We will examine some of the key events and their consequences for later political developments in Norway.

Merely four weeks after the Treaty of Kiel,[5] a Meeting of Notables convened on 16 February to deal with its consequences for Norway.[6] The meeting had been called as a last-gasp attempt of retaining Danish sovereignty over Norway by the Danish Lord Lieutenant, the heir presumptive to the Danish throne, Prince Christian Frederick. However, it soon became clear that while the delegates were unanimous in their resistance to subjugation by Sweden, the principle of popular sovereignty was equally present among them. From this followed that if Christian Frederick should ascend the throne, it would have to be in a manner seen as democratic. At the conclusion the twenty-one Notables agreed to arrange for the election of a Norwegian Constituent Assembly that was to convene two months later, on 10 April, to draw up a separate constitution for Norway and elect a new Norwegian king.[7]

As such, the events in Norway in the spring of 1814 were a textbook example of negotiated elite-based pacted transition from authoritarian rule in the Linz-Schmitter tradition.[8] This was then followed by a mobilisation from below, in which all church parishes were firstly to swear an oath of loyalty to Norwegian independence, and then designate a number of electors to participate in electing representatives for the Constituent Assembly. Furthermore, military units were to elect two representatives directly, of whom one was an officer and one a representative for enlisted men. There were no clear restrictions on who had the right to participate in the vote, but the representatives selected for the electoral college and the Constituent Assembly were to be over the age of twenty-five and either public servants, burghers, freeholding farmers or leaseholding farmers on large properties, restrictions which were later to be found in the voting rules of the Norwegian Constitution. The assembly that gathered at Eidsvoll on 10 April 1814 could thus be seen as electives of the Norwegian people and represented a broad stratum of Norwegian society.[9] A committee charged with submitting a draft set out fundamental precepts which would underpin all subsequent work on the Constitution: that Norway was to be a free, independent and indivisible realm; the King was to have executive power, an elected national assembly was to have the power to pass laws and grant funds, and independent courts were to pass judgement; freedom of the press and freedom of religion were guaranteed.[10] After six weeks of deliberations, the assembly voted to approve a new Constitution and elected Christian Frederick as the Norwegian King on 17 May.

Norwegian independence was however short-lived, as a few military skirmishes between Norwegian and Swedish troops ended with an armistice at the Convention of Moss on 14 August.[11] Here, Christian Frederick agreed to relinquish claims to the Norwegian Crown if Sweden would accept the democratic Norwegian Constitution and a loose personal union. As such, the Treaty of Kiel was thus tacitly subdued and both the principle and substance of the Norwegian Constitution were accepted. Furthermore, Norway retained its own parliament and separate institutions, except for a common king and Foreign Service.[12] This was confirmed by the Norwegian Parliament, and the conclusion of the year 1814 was thus that Norway was not to be treated as a Swedish conquest but rather as an equal party in a union of two independent states.[13]

The short-term consequences were that culturally Norway remained a part of Denmark, while politically it became a part of Sweden. Meanwhile, with regard to trade and commercial interests it remained in all but name a part of the British Empire, due to the extensive merchant fleet and heavy emphasis on overseas trade with territories under British control. To the budding elites in Norway, the multifaceted relationship with its neighbours meant that the pursuit of national autonomy was never an all-or-nothing exercise against a dominant neighbour. Moreover, it left a significant space for triangulation, which was cleverly used in the first half of the nineteenth century.[14] In the longer term, by far the most important result of 1814 was the establishment of institutions which, according to the Norwegian historian Øystein Sørensen, would serve as hegemonic nation-building projects: the Norwegian Parliament (the *Storting*) and the Constitution.[15] Furthermore, as we will see in the following, the successful outcome of the mobilisation from below became a lesson learned for the political system.[16]

Significantly, while establishing the framework for a liberal democracy, the franchise established by the Constitution was exceptionally broad from a European perspective, as the right to vote was extended to about 40 per cent of all men over the age of twenty-five. This number decreased in the following decades since the number of cottars, proletarians, clerks and functionaries increased and the number of landowners dropped as a part of the population. By 1880 the number of eligible voters had thus dropped to 30 per cent of all men over the age of twenty-five, and in 1884 this led to the franchise being extended on the basis of taxable income. In 1898 it was extended to all adult males, and over the following years women were gradually included until the franchise encompassed all adults in 1913.[17]

While the breadth of the franchise constituted a promising point of departure for political mobilisation, it was aided by the local government reform of 1837 which introduced elected local councils with considerable political clout. Furthermore, the reform provided a democratic education for the electorate, especially in the peripheries, as thousands of farmers, burghers and others who would otherwise not have been involved in politics were given access to a political education, which in turn led many of them to seek higher office.[18] A latent centre/periphery cleavage was thereby given time and space to mature. The mobilisation from below – grounded in the assumedly 'national' culture of independent farmers – would be crucial for the parallel development towards a broadening of democracy (particularly by making the government accountable to the *Storting* in 1884) and national independence, finally obtained in 1905. Here, the budding alliance between the politics and culture of the periphery on the one hand and urban radicals on the other was crucial in transforming the political system towards a broadening of democracy on egalitarian grounds.

Constitutional Stagnation – Scotland

How does the nineteenth-century trajectory of Scotland compare with that of Norway? Scotland has been a constituent entity of what Rokkan and Urwin conceptualised as the union state. Here, '[i]ncorporation of at least parts of its territory has been achieved through personal dynastic union', permitting patchy survival of 'pre-union rights and institutional infrastructures which preserve some degree of regional autonomy and serve as agencies of indigenous elite recruitment'.[19] Scotland's path was one of incremental democratisation without national political institutions to operate within. While 1814 turned out to be a critical juncture for Norway in creating both an electorate and a parliament, the Scottish trajectory had involved no similar events since 1707. Through the Treaties of Union of that year, Scotland relinquished its Parliament in favour of representation in the House of Commons and adjacent institutions in London. While Norway in 1814 moved from colonial status under Denmark to a personal union with Sweden, Scotland went in the opposite direction: from a personal union with England and Wales (dating from 1603) to incorporation in the union of Great Britain.

In the absence of a Scottish Parliament, the Church operated as a surrogate institution of Scottish statehood after 1707, as a token of representation as well as a national rallying point. However, the General Assembly of the Church of Scotland was not democratically elected, nor did it exhibit any legislative powers. What was presented by some as a landmark event of Scottish national consciousness – the disruption of the Church in 1843 – could just as well be seen as a theological dispute. Likewise, evangelicals who rebelled against English-oriented landowners during those decades were arguably promoters of religious puritanism more than of Scottish autonomy.[20] The difference from Irish nationalism was notable; Scottish Presbyterianism never served as an anti-English rallying point from which political institutions could emerge. Interestingly, the role of the Church was just as much indirect, in serving as the anchoring for the Scottish educational system. When the role of the Church diminished in the latter half of the nineteenth century, the establishment of the Scottish Education Department in 1872 served to increase the role of the State while sustaining the perception of Scottish distinctiveness.[21]

If political mobilisation through parliament held few promises for Scotland, then the form and expansion of voting rights added to the differences from Norway. In Scotland, electoral reform for the UK Parliament included the Reform Acts of 1832, 1868 and 1885. All reforms built firmly on individual property as a criterion for political citizenship. In contrast with Norway, however, this excluded a large proportion of farmers – that is, the tenants and crofters that constituted a dominant segment of the farming population. Where Norwegian farmers were to a very large extent independent smallholders, the majority of Scottish farmers were tenants, dependent on the benevolence of landlords and disenfranchised even after the Reform Acts. In Scotland, the right to vote was extended to all male householders in 1868; however, landed property was maintained as a criterion in the county council elections.[22] Even following the 1885 reform, the franchise covered merely around 57 per cent of the adult male population.

The power of landed property thus meant fundamentally different things in the two countries, and the subsequent political mobilisation started from contrasting starting points. In the Norwegian case, a considerable proportion of farmers and fishermen were enfranchised prior to the industrialisation of the late nineteenth century that saw their offspring set out for industrial employment in and around the bigger cities. Liberal enfranchisement and an egalitarian social structure set the scene for the political mobilisation from the 1880s onwards – oriented, first, towards parliamentary government, then towards dissolution of the union with Sweden.

The critical juncture of 1814 set Norway on a path of increasing returns with regard to democratisation. According to Paul Pierson, path-dependent processes are characterised by (1) unpredictability before the process, (2) inflexibility once solutions have been found, (3) nonergodicity (small events at the start of the process have a disproportional impact), (4) potential inefficiency (outcome or arrangement may be suboptimal in functional terms), and (5) importance of timing (where the sequence in which events occur is critical).[23] Viewed against Pierson's indicators, the principles laid down by the Constitution were indeed unpredictable in advance; a compromise between rival strategies for an orderly transition from Danish rule, the Constitution was infused with a stronger democratic flavour than any of the dominant parties had voiced. On this basis, the events set in train at Eidsvoll in 1814 would also have a disproportionate impact on the succeeding development. Finally, the timing of the event was crucial; by laying the foundations for a liberal democracy at the exact time of a regime change, the Constitution would have a disproportionate significance as a rallying point for further democratisation as well as for the nationalisation of democracy over time.[24]

In Scotland, no space was provided for a similar mobilisation from below. Tenant farmers were considerably discriminated against, which placed a substantial barrier in the way of a rural/urban alliance akin to that of Norway. Moreover, prior to the establishment of county councils in 1889, there were scarce structures of local government in rural Scotland. Indeed, while urban centres had been given a solid platform for town councils by the Burgh Reform Act as early as 1833, local councils in the countryside were minimalist in form and policy content, serving the landed interests and counterproductive to channelling political mobilisation from below.[25] In Scotland, the alliance between small farmers and the industrial working class had had a propitious start in the early nineteenth century, united around anti-landlordism and favouring land redistribution. Later, its legacy can be detected in the decades between 1880 and 1920, when the quest for crofting reform, home rule and curbs on landed power were constituent parts of the Liberal hegemony. However, as we shall see below, this tentative alliance saw its opportunity pass as land reform came to little in substance, divisions between classes (and within the working class) remained stubbornly static and the home rule scheme turned into administrative devolution.

In the Norwegian political context this alliance was to prove crucial for the popular campaigns in favour of parliamentary government and national independence.

CRITICAL JUNCTURE 2: FROM DEVOLUTION TO INDEPENDENCE?

Democratic Mobilisation – Norway

Throughout the 1890s, the support for Norwegian independence grew steadfast among the national elites as well as the general public. The discord grew from a concurrence of cultural, economic and political currencies which at least for a few short years led to a bipartisan joining of forces. While the end result of this process – a peaceful dissolution of the personal union between Norway and Sweden in 1905 – was to a large extent a sequel to the events of 1814, there were also significant differences.

Firstly, while the independence movement in 1814 had by and large been driven by political opportunism among the national elites, the movement towards independence in 1905 was the result of political trends largely driven by elected officials with massive popular support, growing from the gradual building up of the Norwegian political system throughout the nineteenth century.[26] The introduction of yearly assemblies of Parliament in 1869 then moved power from the unelected ministers appointed by the Swedish king to elected representatives in the Norwegian Parliament, thus paving the way for the parliamentary system introduced in 1884, which by and large ended Swedish influence in internal Norwegian politics.[27]

Secondly, due mainly to a more favourable geopolitical situation in Europe, the major powers were more inclined to favour Norwegian independence from Sweden than they had been ninety years earlier. On the one hand, the poor display of Imperial Russia in the Russo–Japanese War of 1905 meant that the Russian threat was diminished for the Western powers, and accordingly the need for a strong Sweden to act as a buffer was off the table. On the other hand, dissolution of the union put Norway, and by extension the Norwegian ports, within the British sphere of influence, rather than the more pro-German-oriented policies pursued by the Swedes.

And thirdly, the claim for independent Norwegian statehood was underpinned by the presence of most, if not all, of the institutions and infrastructure of a sovereign independent state. Alongside the establishment of political institutions in 1814 and 1837, a Norwegian University in 1811 was followed by a national bank

(Norges Bank) in 1816 and the further establishment of a national system of credit especially from the 1850s onwards, the abolishment of the Swedish Vice Roy position in 1863, as well as the building of national infrastructure such as a railway system and national media in the latter half of the nineteenth century.[28]

As we have seen, the 1814 Constitution had by and large created an independent Norwegian state with its own parliament, judiciary and executive powers. The only exception was foreign relations, which had remained the prerogative of the Swedish king through the Swedish ministry of foreign affairs. This, however, was to prove a crucial issue in the dissolution of the union, as Norwegians more and more felt that their foreign policy interests were inadequately served by Sweden. There were several reasons for this. Firstly, the Norwegian economy was much more dependent on foreign trade and therefore sensitive to the increasingly protectionist measures adopted by Sweden. Secondly, whereas Sweden was traditionally affiliated with Germany, the import- and export-driven Norwegian economy both literally and figuratively sailed on the keel of the British Empire. To this came the geopolitical and economic fact that while Sweden faced east- and southwards, Norway was a westbound country with a long coastline and had greater interests outside of Europe than did Sweden. This was further intensified when the Interstate Laws (*Mellomrikslovene*) were abolished in 1895, thus putting severe restrictions on free trade between the two countries.[29]

These disputes were heightened by the sharp differences emerging within the political systems of the two states. While Swedish politics of the time tended towards conservatism and the king exercising greater discretionary power, in Norway the political system was increasingly dominated by liberal tendencies characterised by the establishment of a parliamentary system of government in 1884, very much against the will of Sweden.

The conflict came to a head over what has been known since as the 'Consular Affair', where successive Norwegian governments insisted that Norway establish its own consular offices abroad rather than rely on the common consuls appointed by the Swedish foreign minister. As the long-standing practice for the conduct of joint foreign policy had been that a Swede would always hold the office of foreign minister, the Swedish government and king rejected this insistence as an abdication of the throne's right to set foreign policy. The Norwegian reply was to adopt a unilateral course of action, and on 7 June 1905 the Norwegian Parliament deposed the king and declared the union dissolved. While much has been made of the supremacy of diplomacy in averting war between Sweden and Norway in 1905, in truth this was mostly the result of both parties recognising that the facts on the ground meant that any long-term hostility between the two countries would be untenable due to their geographical proximity. Added to this came the level of Swedish fatigue with the union, coupled with an acknowledgement that in case of war, the Norwegians would probably have more incentive to fight than did the Swedes. The union was thus dissolved in an orderly fashion at the Karlstad Conference in the autumn of 1905, whereby Sweden granted Norway the right to dissolve while Norway agreed to demolish its defence along the Swedish–Norwegian border.[30]

Another Swedish demand at Karlstad was that the Norwegian people should confirm their support of the government and parliament's aggressive politics by means of a ballot. This led to the first of two referenda towards the end of 1905, a simple 'yes' or 'no' vote on the union with Sweden spurring a massive government-led nationalist campaign to get the Norwegian populace out to vote for independence. The ballot results bear witness to a national awakening and unanimity seldom seen in democratic countries. An 85 per cent turnout among eligible voters resulted in a 99.9 per cent majority against the union.

The second referendum was on the nature of the political system, namely whether Norway should remain a monarchy after the Parliament had declared the Norwegian throne vacant on 7 June. As the government had already made it clear that its preferred choice was the Danish Prince Charles – and perhaps even more importantly his English wife Princess Maud – it was in reality an up or down vote on Charles as king rather than a vote on the monarchy itself. As in the first referendum, the government instigated an intensive campaign to get voters out, as the government and supporters of the monarchy claimed that the stability and peace of the country depended on a majority voting for the king. While both the turnout and the majority were smaller than in the referendum on the union, just short of 80 per cent voted in favour of a monarchy.[31]

Top-down Containment – Scotland

Scotland's path into the twentieth century was characterised by a widening of democracy echoing that of Norway but deprived of the dominant aspect of national mobilisation. In the Norwegian case, 1905 proved to be a logical end point of the popular mobilisation that was grounded in the wide franchise and national parliament of the constitutional settlement. Thus, democratisation and expanding national autonomy were concurring processes from 1880 onwards, reflecting the dynamic of increasing returns referred to by Pierson. The thirty-three years that followed saw the formalisation of political parties, the introduction of a parliamentary system of government, the attainment of national independence and the extension of the franchise to all adult men and women.

In Scotland, the dynamic was different. The meek Scottish parallel when it comes to institutional settlement was the creation in 1885 of a Scottish Secretary within the British Government. The territorial brief was sliced off from a portfolio otherwise served by the Home Office. It testified to the special attention now devoted to Scottish affairs within the union state. However, although the post was served by a small ministry from its creation, it was only four decades later that its head was raised to Cabinet status and the position of the ministry was secured. Administrative devolution is an appropriate concept for the model selected by the British Government; a model that was designed from above to enhance government coordination rather than develop from below. Perhaps the most significant contrast with the Norwegian trajectory is the frailty of the urban–rural alliance of the underprivileged. What essentially lacked in Scotland were channels and arenas for democratic mobilisation around a common cause. As we have seen from the Norwegian example, this progressive rural–urban alliance was the chief promoter of the twin ambitions of democratic empowerment and national sovereignty. A similar movement never obtained a sufficient foothold in Scotland, a stagnation which as we have seen can be attributed to institutional features such as electoral disenfranchisement and weak local government as well as cultural features such as the internal religious and class conflicts within the working class.

Evidently, developments in Scotland in the late-Victorian era must be considered within the wider framework of the British Isles. The search for a revised territorial settlement with Ireland was a dominant feature on the political agenda, as was the workload congestion of the UK Parliament in London. And the creation of an Irish legislature would be expected to have knock-on effects for Scotland. Thus, even within the constraints of top-down reform, space could have been found for a devolutionist settlement by default. This would have been the case had the Gladstonian vision of 'Home Rule All Round' been implemented.

For our argument in this chapter it is notable that the idea stalled not only due to the practical difficulties of incorporating England (or English regions) in this plan but also due to the scarce popular demand in Scotland for a devolved Scottish Parliament. The idea ebbed and flowed over the decades following 1880, where it was first suggested to Scottish voters during Gladstone's Midlothian campaign. In 1886, it was omitted from the (defeated) Home Rule Bill for Ireland. Ewen A. Cameron notes how Scotland was seen as 'the most comfortable of the three "Celtic" nations in its relationship with the United Kingdom', in which '[t]here was no substantial body of opinion in Scotland which seriously advocated fundamental change in the political relationship which had been established in 1707'.[32] The frustrated efforts of a small elite of Scottish nationalists were reflected in the thirteen resolutions on Scottish Home Rule being proposed in the House of Commons between 1890 and 1914, of which eleven were supported by a majority of Scottish MPs but without obtaining much further support or enthusiasm.[33]

As a consequence, the putative thirst for autonomy in Scotland did not translate into any scheme for government able to attract popular support north of the border. The late nineteenth century thus presents itself as a lost opportunity for territorial reform. Had initiatives been presented more forcefully, could a renewed territorial settlement have been consolidated prior to the momentous events of 1911–24, where House of Lords reform, Irish independence and the virtual elimination of Liberal hegemony followed in due order? If this institutional reordering could be seen as a lost opportunity for Scotland, we may add to it the unifying effects of the First World War: the picture that emerges at the beginning of the

1920s is one of British unionism, the fading of the home rule idea and the confirmation of London as the one and only political centre of what had now become the United Kingdom.

The failure of the home rule scheme thus reflected a general unwillingness to countenance alternatives to parliamentary sovereignty with Westminster at its heart. According to John Kendle, '[t]he only logical way the issue could have been resolved was by adopting a truly federal solution which [. . .] would have established not only separate legislatures for Ulster, the rest of Ireland, Scotland and Wales but would also have come to grips with the need to divide an oversized and all-too-powerful England.'[34] Support for a fully federal scheme was, however, minuscule. Indeed, the absence of any coherent idea of federalism is the core of Kendle's argument.

What unfolded instead was a territorial-administrative revision in Scotland in the form of the Scottish Secretary. The budding progressive political movement from earlier in the nineteenth century was never wedded to a campaign for national autonomy, a relationship which was so predominant in the Norwegian case. Moreover, the absence of political-institutional reform retarded bottom-up mobilisation, which rather than accelerating and uniting turned towards a more static and tribal form of politics, spearheaded by unionist parties centred in London. An institutional set-up that was conducive to bottom-up mobilisation in Norway had no equivalent in Scotland. Gradual democratisation on a national footing in the Norwegian case was matched by territorial management through top-down containment in Scotland.

CRITICAL JUNCTURE 3: EMERGENCE OF SOCIAL PACTS?

Negotiated Framework encourages Further Reform – Norway

The three decades from the end of the First World War to the aftermath of the Second World War constituted a transitional period for a range of Western democracies. It was an era of systemic changes as well as social unrest. In the Norwegian case, universal suffrage was introduced in 1913, fifteen years before the equivalent reform in Britain. Five years later, the Norwegian electoral system was reformed from a two-round majoritarian model to proportional representation through party lists. The reform emerged as a compromise between the Conservative and Liberal parties eager to avoid a socialist majority and a Labour party aspiring to see its electoral weight translated into a similar proportion of seats.

Contrary to the British Labour Party, social democrats in Scandinavia opted for proportional representation as the preferred option for the longer term, a position that is somewhat paradoxical given the electoral strength of these parties in the succeeding decades. The side-effect of setting a low threshold for representation was the gradual development of a multi-party system. In the Norwegian case, this included the Agrarian Party (1920) and the Christian Democratic Party (1933), both founded as splinter groups from the Liberals.

Another significant side-effect of the turn towards proportionality was found in the strengthening of cross-party coalitions, a broadening of civil society and the rise of the negotiated economy. During the 1920s, the extent of conflict in the labour market was dramatic. The parallels with conditions in Britain are striking, featuring a General Strike in 1921 and a premature and short-lived Labour government in 1927 before the Depression set in. Norway harboured no 'Red Clydeside' as in the Scottish case, but syndicalist tendencies were present in and around Oslo and Trondheim. What provided a critical juncture to the social and political conflict were two pivotal agreements of the mid-1930s: the Main Agreement between the social partners, and a political pact — the Crisis Settlement — between Labour and the Agrarian Party, both dating from 1935.

The consequences running from these two agreements were extensive. First, they punctuated the era of deep-seated and destructive conflict in the labour market by establishing a robust framework for negotiations over wages and work conditions. Secondly, this framework would then spill over to other areas of economic governance and contribute to the negotiated economy, which became a key aspect of the Scandinavian model. These would have clear corporatist features, based upon extensive participation by trade unions and employers alike in government committees imbued with the task of preparing or implementing legislation. It also spilled over into enhanced industrial democracy by ensuring a stronger participation by employees within the governance of corporations. And it set the train running for the all-encompassing, universalist approach to social policy. Where nearly everyone would be under the umbrella of one of the social partners, they would also be stakeholders in welfare state reform.[35]

Thirdly and finally, the broad agreements of the 1930s consolidated the cross-class electoral appeal of the Norwegian Labour Party, which thereafter emerged as the single party of government from 1935 to 1965, governing with a majority from 1945 to 1961. Its cross-class identity referred to the alliance between workers and the middle class; it was also grounded in the unity of urban and rural interests, captured in the 1933 electoral slogan of 'city and countryside hand in hand'.[36] The progressive alliance which in David Marquand's view failed to manifest itself in Britain during the 1920s was to a large extent fulfilled in Norway, in sociological if not in party political terms. Its consequences were momentous; aside from the negotiated economy of corporatism, a compressed wage structure and high participation in the labour market, the newly established alliance in Norway was also pivotal to the welfare state expansion in the post-war years. Here, Norway's trajectory was that of a path designed but not completed in Britain in the years following the war. In the Norwegian case, inspiration from the Beveridge Report and — though indirectly through influences from Sweden — from the Minority Report to the Poor Laws Commission of 1905–9, led to an expanding welfare state supported by increasing returns, not least because its welfare measures proved effective in ensuring high productivity and a safety net serving to regenerate rather than to pacify, decades before 'flexicurity' became a catchword depicting the Danish model.[37]

Thus, the negotiated framework emerging from the 1930s served to consolidate the social democratic welfare state in Norway, building upon the budding corporatism and activist industrial policy of that decade; indeed, it can be argued that it is only now that a distinct Scandinavian model emerges.

Stagnant Conflict in the Labour Market – Scotland

Developments in Norway through this period thus point towards the consensus around a social model and a negotiated economy whose consequences are detectable also today. Compared with this trajectory, Scotland's decades following the First World War are characterised by stagnant social reforms as a logical consequence of centralised command from London. Labour, which took over the mantle as the leading party of Scotland following the Liberal debacle of the early 1920s, was centralist to its bones in its ambitions for welfare state development and redistributive taxation. Despite the independent ideas evolving with Labour in Scotland, there was little political clout to bring them to bear, with Labour remaining too weak to obtain a governing majority at Westminster, unable to forge an alliance with the Liberals and unable to fathom how a renewed territorial settlement for the Union could look.

The place where a real reordering of the priorities for Scotland took place was in the Scottish Office, which was characterised by 'an increasing responsibility for Scottish administration, a greater physical presence in Scotland and the professionalisation of the business of the Office'.[38] Prior to the First World War, the Scottish Secretary had not had a Cabinet position, and the Scottish Office had resided in London. Its work was supplemented by a broad range of public boards catering for regulatory work in Scotland on the government's behalf. It was under a Conservative government in 1926 that the Scottish Secretary entered Cabinet. Two years later, the boards were reformed into departments of state, and in 1937 the real breakthrough appeared when these departments were made accountable to the Scottish Secretary and underpinned by civil service standards. At the same time the civil service of the Scottish Office was moved to Edinburgh.

In 1939, the recommendations of the Report of the Committee on Scottish Administration, better known as the Gilmour Report, were implemented in law, which provided the Scottish Office with four functional departments: Agriculture and Fisheries, Education, Health and Home.[39] Following the Second World War, the expansion of the State machinery in London was more than matched by Edinburgh. Overall, between 1937 and 1970, the number of civil servants in the Scottish Office almost tripled, from 2,400 to 8,300.[40] Scottish recruitment became the general rule, and an evident north-of-the-border identity was consolidated. Aiding the development of a stronger Scottish dimension was the fact that policy areas imbued with great esteem and significance in Scotland – such as agriculture and education – were conspicuously lower in priority and prestige among ministries in London.

Interestingly, the relationship between Scottish Office and local government was hampered by acrimony through the post-war decades. According to Cameron, the resistance by local councils could be seen as 'a badly needed contribution to the balance of democratic forces within the Scottish political context'.[41] The anxiety was about excessive concentration of power in the Scottish Office which, despite its acquired Scottish identity, was not accountable in any meaningful way to the Scottish public, let alone a representative assembly elected by the Scots. The need for stronger democratic scrutiny of the executive was acknowledged through the existence since 1907 of the Scottish Grand Committee in the House of Commons, which was later accompanied by two Scottish Standing Committees, set up in 1955 and 1963, and a Scottish Select Committee dating from 1969. Yet the sentiment remained that scrutiny in Westminster gave scarce attention to Scottish concerns as a political entity, reflected in the perception that Scottish MPs represented primarily a local constituency perspective rather than a Scottish dimension as such.[42]

The real barrier to a similar pattern of change as in Norway was thus of an institutional nature. Firstly, the electoral system permitted no similar blossoming of civil society and sectoral groups as in Norway. Secondly, the exclusion and majoritarianism of the political system fed into the economic sphere, where there was no capacity to forge a negotiated economy with corporatist features similar to that which evolved in Norway in response to the international crisis. Thirdly, in the search for a consensus arising from the centre-left, it was nowhere to be found in the Scottish case. Working-class solidarity was falling short, reflecting a structural and cultural conflict between the indigenous, Protestant working class and Catholic-Irish labour, which was generally lower paid, lower skilled and estranged. Together, these institutional characteristics meant that no window opened in Scotland during the inter-war period for political and social change of the sort appearing in Norway. Consequently, the two countries were accelerated on separate trajectories.

CRITICAL JUNCTURES OR INCREMENTALISM?

An important modification of historical institutionalism is the fact that change is dynamic and occurs between path-breaking events as well. In its simplest form, path dependence denotes essentially two modes of institutional development: long periods of stability punctuated by brief and dramatic moments of reform. Kathleen Thelen has been a leading proponent in conceptualising change under the surface of stability. This may, for example, take the form of new institutional arrangements that are layered on top of old ones which are allowed to remain; or old structures that are filled with new content and tasks. The core of her argument is that the process could be gradual without any observable juncture, thus amounting to 'incremental change with transformative results'.[43]

How does the divergent historical development of Norway and Scotland measure up against this elaboration of path dependence? In pursuit of critical junctures, 1814 stands out as holding quintessential importance for the Norwegian course of democratic collectivism within the bounds of an emerging nation-state. The constitution and the creation of a parliament (alongside the replacement of a somewhat quasi-colonial status under Denmark with a personal union with Sweden) represented a leap away from institutional stasis towards the blossoming not only of national fervour but of democratic renewal as well. Scotland finds itself on the opposite side here: if 1707 with the Act of Union is the critical juncture, the long nineteenth century seems to represent precisely the increasing returns that Pierson refers to in his elaboration of path dependence. Political stability, imperial opportunities and economic dynamism were underscored by the existence of the Union, or they were seen to be. At the same time, the alternative of pursuing independence was one that would yield negative returns; the more embedded Scotland was in the English economy, the weaker the case for independence, and the longer down the path to modernity without a separate legislature, the more natural the Anglo-Scottish partnership seemed to be. The Church, as we have seen, did little to strengthen Scottish national aspiration. Arguably, through the crucial Victorian era, its dogmatic disputes with the Anglican Church served to *divert* attention from nation-building rather than *assist* in it. Scotland's path was one of consolidation of the union state.

If 1814 and 1707 were the first critical junctures, their value was in creating favourable conditions for the rise of democratic collectivism cum patriotism in Norway and much weaker conditions for a similar development in Scotland. Where egalitarianism through corporatism, public welfare and the strong state are added to the picture, a second critical juncture presents itself. In the 1930s, key alliances were forged in the labour market and between social democratic and agrarian parties in Norway. The absence of the same in Scotland held great importance for the different paths when it came to welfare state development and the mixed economy pursued from the post-war era onwards. The significance of that critical juncture was consolidated immediately after the war, when Norway chose what was arguably the path not taken by British welfare reformers. Instead, the intellectual gist of the Beveridge plan was taken forward as key inspiration for the Norwegian welfare state.[44] Thereafter, increasing returns has been the key mechanism in further welfare state development in both countries; while in Norway universalist features have been consolidated by middle-class support and high participation in the labour market, means-testing and a widening gap between insiders and outsiders have driven the opposite dynamic on the Scottish side.

Nevertheless, the path-dependence model does not account for Norwegian–Scottish divergence in full. The gap between the countries has been underscored by the differences in the labour market regime, where small wage differentials have helped sustain the legitimacy of the welfare state in Norway, in as much as it has been subject to a much smaller redistributive burden to rectify social inequality. But there is no law-like relationship between centralised settlements in the labour market and the particular distributive form characterising the Scandinavian model. Developments under the surface of institutional stability have altered the relationship between employers and trade unions in very different ways in Norway and Scotland respectively, as witnessed by the last three decades of increasing sectarianism and emasculation within the British legislative framework against the expanding role of trade unions in negotiating industrial renewal and wage compression in Norway. Agency matters within existing institutional settlements, and significant actors with coherent strategies can generate the incremental changes with the transformative results that Streeck and Thelen refer to.

Finally, it is worth asking whether Scotland and Norway really did look as similar in the early 1800s as is contended above. First, Denmark was a much weaker outside centre than England, as it did not command the resources of a vast overseas empire and could not offer as many tempting opportunities to the talents of the periphery. Secondly, there was much less intermingling of elites between Norway and Denmark than between Scotland and England. While the bourgeoisie of the Norwegian cities was markedly international, this was a reflection of the overall dynamics of North Sea trade since the days of the Hanseatic League rather than a result of a Danish political dominance. Thirdly, Norway was clearly not a colony for Danish settlement. It was the weaker partner politically and culturally but it commanded a variety of independent economic resources. And this did not change fundamentally with the establishment of the union with Sweden in 1814, as Norway established a broad range of distinctive institutions and was only deprived of full sovereignty in external and military affairs. And fourthly, in contrast with Scotland, landed property was never an obstacle to popular mobilisation around a national cause in Norway. A nation of largely independent farmers, there was no necessity for land reform as a prerequisite for internal solidarity. And to the extent that landownership was a source of political power at all, it was primarily through the Agrarian Party that emerged as late as the 1920s, only to lend its support to the social democrats in the following decade.

Scotland became more thoroughly integrated with England at the economic level, yet maintained its institutional identity much more clearly than Norway did in its union with Denmark. While Norway maintained its distinctive legal institutions, the officials of the Absolutist State were trained and certified in Copenhagen. The Scots, by contrast, not only maintained their separate legal system and their own judiciary, but also established their own universities before the Union and have been able to sustain these separate channels of elite recruitment ever since. This created a combination of economic interdependence and professional autonomy that served to pacify the elites. According to Rokkan, it was precisely the pull of the Empire and the maintenance of distinctive agencies of elite recruitment that were the main explanation behind the weakness of the

Scottish drive for separate sovereignty.[45] On the one hand there were the patent pay-offs of union with England, and on the other hand there was no great rush to erect new institutions in order to sustain a Scottish identity. Finally, landed power worked against any attempt to forge a Scottish political entity along a similar path to that of Norway. Landownership evidently encompasses much more than property itself. In the Scottish case, the political institutions served to reflect and consolidate the skewed distribution of land and power; the electoral system for the House of Commons as well as the sustained presence of nobility in the House of Lords. Together, these features represented a fundamental barrier to any form of democratic mobilisation with egalitarian nationalism as its cause.

If we consider the political outlook of the Norwegian elites, they had no empire to tempt them and, moreover, they had no university of their own until 1811 nor a national system of credit until 1816. Thus the outward ties to the metropolitan centre were weaker and the need for distinctive institutions greater. The result was a much earlier wave of national mobilisation, and as such this goes a long way in explaining the explosive Norwegian development of national ideology at all levels during the nineteenth century. In Scotland the economic ties to the larger system kept nationalism at bay during the heyday of the Empire, and it is instructive that the successes of the SNP followed only after the decline and loss of imperial ties.

CONCLUSION: JUNCTURES IN THE PAST, PATHS TO THE FUTURE

2014 marks a prominent anniversary of national significance on either side of the North Sea, commemorating the Battle of Bannockburn and the 1814 Constitution respectively. It is also the year of the Scottish independence referendum. On the threshold of independence, Scotland finds in the Scandinavian countries its alternative to the England-dominated path of development which has characterised the three centuries since 1707. There is, obviously, a particular case to be made for a parallel to Norway, given the latter's century-old liberation from junior status in a union in favour of national construction of a welfare state supported by small inequalities, high labour market participation and gender equality. If we allow ourselves to pursue that analogy further, there is room for a comparison between the Norway of 1905, with its preceding decades of national mobilisation through its national parliament, and the Scottish trajectory of 1999–2014; indeed, the fifteen years of the Scottish Parliament could be seen as a fast-forward version of nation-building and democratic collectivism as witnessed in Norway during the second half of the nineteenth century.

The analogy is, however, flawed with regard to some of the choices that would need to be made for the two countries to chart a similar developmental path. This is not primarily due to lack of capacity or political will but rather timing and sequencing.

Some features seem on the face of it to be equally incorporated in both countries today. The pursuit of a more inclusive politics – grounded in proportional representation and characterised by cross-party collaboration and coalition governments – certainly counts among them. Since the creation of its Parliament in 1999, Scotland has seen coalition government (1999–2007), then single-party minority government (2007–11) and, finally, a single-party majority government by the SNP (2011–). Thus, in the space of fifteen years, Scottish politics has acquired wide experience of the shifting modes of a parliamentary system. The accompanying political culture is more difficult to assess. A stated ambition of a devolved Scotland has been to foster an alternative to the majoritarian Westminster model, characterised by the ritual conflict between two rival political camps with disproportionate parliamentary representation. The Scottish mode would be one of mature debate across party lines. It is doubtful that this has been fully accomplished; moreover, it has certainly not been facilitated by the independence debate.

When there is reason to be cautious with regard to transferability between the two paths, it is first and foremost related to timing and sequencing. On the Norwegian side, proportional representation was introduced in 1918, which meant that the systemic features for multi-party politics were installed precisely at the time that the main pillars of the party system were falling into place. Just as significantly, the negotiated settlements that emerged from the new electoral system also helped establish the social pacts of the 1930s, which turned the page on extensive labour market conflict and enabled a negotiated economy to emerge.

Cooperation and flexibility are thus appropriate catchwords for the economic model on which post-war Norway was constructed. It is equally apt to describe the Nordic community in which it has been embedded. A region consisting of five small and politically close countries prepared not only for parallel trajectories but also for mutual learning. The argument is particularly relevant for the Scandinavian core of Sweden, Denmark and Norway, which share key features of inter-war conciliation between the social partners succeeded by accelerated post-war welfare state development. A dominant social democratic party also played a similar (and ideologically deeply related) role in all three countries through the second half of the twentieth century. Finally, although the three countries have been characterised by different foreign policy affiliations, it has not hindered a strong community of ideas. Denmark and Norway were both founding members of NATO but parted company vis à vis European integration when Denmark acceded in 1973. Sweden has remained outside NATO and only became an EU member in 1994. Nevertheless, they have shared a sufficient set of characteristics for their foreign policy to be broadly similar in content. Small, outward-looking economies based on egalitarianism at home and competition abroad; oriented towards international trade but also institution-building and global development; in terms of foreign policy, small-country status has permitted the Nordics to cultivate a role that Scotland has been barred from as part of the Union of Great Britain.

If the path dependence perspective is conducive to the analysis of institutional change, this is perhaps the most evident example in comparing the economic model on the two sides of the North Sea. In Norway, as in the other Scandinavian states, the pacts of the 1930s succeeded by immediate post-war welfare reforms set in train a social market economy characterised by small wage differences coupled with an extensive welfare state. Just as reversing the trajectory would prove difficult in the light of the trust and interests that are invested in the model, so would transferring the path to a different context at a different time be difficult.

Notes

1. Rokkan, 1975.
2. Krasner, 1984; see also Mahoney, 2000.
3. Thelen, 2003: 219.
4. Streeck and Thelen, 2005: 19; see also Peters et al., 2005: 1277–8.
5. Cf. Stortinget, 2014b.
6. Frydenlund and Storsveen, 2013; see also Dyrvik, 2005 and Steen, 1989.
7. Frydenlund, 2013: 23–42.
8. Cf. O'Donnell et al., 1986.
9. Hommerstad and Ottosen, 2013; see also Michalsen, 2013 and Langeland and Michalsen, 2014.
10. Cf. Stortinget, 2014c. Jews, Jesuits and other religious orders of Catholic persuasion, however, were to remain barred from entering the realm. Cf. Mendelsohn, 1969.
11. Glenthøj and Ottosen, 2014.
12. Cf. Stortinget, 2014d; see also Frydenlund, 2014 and Ottosen, 2013.
13. Cf. Stortinget, 2014a.
14. Sørensen, 2004.
15. Sørensen, 1988 and Sørensen, 1998.
16. Hommerstad, 2012.
17. Myhre, 2012.
18. Pryser, 1999, especially Chapter 14.
19. Mitchell, 1996: 86. Cf. Rokkan and Urwin, 1982.
20. Macwhirter, 2013: 99–101.
21. Mitchell, 1996: 87.
22. Cameron, 2010: 56, 70.
23. Pierson, 2000: 253.
24. Sørensen and Stråth, 1997; see also Sørensen, 1996.
25. Ibid.: 62–3.
26. Sørensen, 1998; see also Sørensen, 1994 and Nerbøvik, 2000.
27. Nerbøvik, 1999; see also Grepstad and Nerbøvik, 1984.
28. Nerbøvik, 1999.
29. Sørensen and Nilsson, 2005.

30. Ibid.
31. Bjørklund, 2005: 68–73.
32. Cameron, 2010: 66.
33. Morton, 2008: 241–2.
34. Kendle, 1997: 61.
35. Brandal et al., 2013.
36. Ibid.
37. Ibid.
38. Hutchison, 1996: 49.
39. Cameron, 2010: 174.
40. Hutchison, 1996: 50.
41. Cameron, 2010: 61.
42. Ibid.
43. Streeck and Thelen, 2005: 9.
44. Brandal et al.: 2013.
45. Ibid.

CHAPTER 4

Agrarian Change in Scotland and Norway: Agricultural Production, Structures, Politics and Policies since 1800

John Bryden and Agnar Hegrenes

INTRODUCTION

The contrasting evolution of landownership in Scotland and Norway is discussed in Chapter 1, as it affects so many social, economic, political and other processes between the Reformation and the present day. One of these concerns agriculture, especially changing agricultural structures, agrarian politics and policies, and rural settlement.

This chapter focuses on four main processes that we consider to have underpinned the important differences in the structure and nature of agriculture and rural settlement and indeed in policies between the two countries today. These four processes are firstly, the timing and nature of the 'first' agrarian revolution which to a large extent followed the reorganisation of land ownership and rights and was a much earlier and more powerful movement, and, significantly, driven by different hegemonic ideas about 'improvement', in Scotland than in Norway. Secondly, the free trade period and wartime food shortages in the second half of the nineteenth and early twentieth centuries. Thirdly, the development of agricultural policies and extensive State intervention in the inter-war period and immediately after the Second World War. Finally, the 'second' agrarian revolution, mainly after the Second World War, involving large-scale mechanisation and the application of artificial fertilisers and chemicals, and new plant- and animal-breeding methods and objectives, and its subsequent consequences and policy responses after the implications of this form of agriculture became clear.

Before moving on to discuss these themes in greater depth, we present some comparative data that illustrates some of the differences between agricultural structure, production, incomes and their evolution over the past two centuries or so.

Table 4.1 Land Use in Scotland and Norway, c. 2004

	Scotland	Norway
Land Area, ha	7,710,000	30,786,000
Agricultural land, ha	5,604,104	992,000
Grass & rough grazings	67 per cent	65 per cent of ag. land
Forest & woodland	17 per cent	38 per cent of land area
Urban	8 per cent	1.1 per cent
Crops and fallow	7 per cent	3.3 per cent
Other ag. land	2 per cent	

In terms of land area and its utilisation, Norway is roughly four times larger than Scotland, but has a lower proportion of land used for agriculture and more than twice the proportion of land in forests and woodland. Farming in Norway extends well north of the Arctic Circle, especially near the coast which benefits from the Gulf Stream. However, average temperatures are lower.

Although commodities grown are similar in Norway and Scotland, Norway has a higher proportion of oats in cereals grown, and a lower proportion of barley. The proportion of wheat is almost the same. Much fewer oilseed crops are grown in Norway. In general, crop yields are higher in Scotland. There are more dairy cows in Norway, and fewer beef cows and sheep. Norway has relatively more fruit trees and fruits, especially plums, apples and cherries in the sheltered fjords of west Norway where there is a special summer microclimate.

As our later discussion of farm structures shows, Scotland has a 'dual' structure, with a higher proportion of very large and very small farms than Norway. Both the average and the median size of Norway's farms are smaller than those in Scotland. In total, there are 52,625 agricultural holdings in Scotland,[1] somewhat more than Norway's 43,525 holdings in 2013.

In Norway, part of the land that is not classified as agricultural land (*utmark*) is used for grazing during the summer. Estimates indicate that the feed uptake from such pastures accounts for 10 per cent of total feed from Norwegian resources.[2]

In both countries, but more so in Norway, multiple job-holding or pluriactivity is very important for the livelihoods of farm families in almost all size categories. The relatively small farm size in Norway means that as many as two-thirds of the farmers get less than half of their income from farming.[3] Indeed, there is a long tradition in Norway of combining farming and other activities, such as farming and fishing along the coast, farming and forestry, farming and mining, farming with manufacturing near to the hydro-power sources and related industries, farming and tourism, farming with 'green care', and farming and various forms of trade and professional activities. Such a tradition also exists in Scotland, especially among crofters whose holdings, for the most part, could not provide a family income.[4] This was not really 'noticed' by policy-makers until the 1980s, set as they were on the imaginary model of a full-time commercial farmer imbued with the logic of the market and

Table 4.2 Agricultural Land Use and Production in Scotland and Norway, 2012

	Scotland			Norway		
	Area, ha, or number	Production, tonnes, or other	Yield, tonnes/ha, or other	Area, ha, or numbers	Production, tonnes, or other	Yield, tonnes/ha, or other
Wheat	100,637	673,300	6.69	66,900	247	3.32
Barley	332,039	1,723,500	5.19	155,900	577	3.70
Oats	23,672	108,200	4.57	69,200	236	3.38
Oilseeds	36,611	101,000	3.42	5,500	10	1.91
Potatoes	29,536	983,000	33.28	13,000	243	18.7
Fruit and veg.	16,308			10,600		
Grass	1,325,187			648,770		
Rough grazings[a]	3,080,483					
Other land	609,572					
Common grazings	583,685					
Dairy cows	182,184	1.3 mill. lit.	7,136	238,702	1.54 mill. lit.	6.452
Beef cows	452,438			73,319		
Total sheep and lambs	6,735,974	56,400		2,222,400	22,292	
Pigs	363,439	54,300		839,433	131,215	
Poultry	14,693,988			18,270,215		
– chickens		84,300			79,593	
– eggs		1,082 m			c. 1,000 m	

Sources: Agricultural Statistics Scotland, 2012. Statistics Norway, 2012.

Note:
[a] Not included in rough grazings

technology.[5] In Europe as a whole in the 1980s, as in previous centuries and later decades, it was possible to argue that it was multiple job-holding or pluriactivity of farm families that was the norm for winning livelihoods, rather than the exception.

The real, as opposed to the imaginary 'virtual', farming family today, as in earlier times, wins a livelihood from as many sources as it can because family income from farming is always relatively small, risky and uncertain, being subject to the caprices of nature, the vagaries of markets that he or she cannot control, and the whims of politicians often in far away places.

Table 4.3 Income of Farm Households in Norway's FADN Sample, Average for 870 Holdings, 2012

	Thousand NOK	Per cent of gross income	Per cent of net income
Agriculture	380.0	42.5	47.8
Forestry	14.4	1.6	1.8
Other	50.7	5.7	6.4
Other businesses	34.4	3.8	4.3
Wages	339.2	37.9	42.7
Pensions	39.8	4.4	5.0
Interests and dividends	30.2	3.4	3.8
Family labour on farm investments	6.2	0.7	0.8
'Gross income' (GM)	894.9	100.0	112.6
Interests on liabilities etc.	100.0	−11.2	−12.6
Net income	795.0		100.0

Source: Norwegian FBS 2012, main Table 18.

Figures in NOK. At the time of writing approx. NOK 10 = £1.

In the Norwegian sample, 42.5 per cent of gross income comes from agriculture and 57.5 per cent from other sources, of which 37.9 per cent is from wages and 3.8 per cent from other businesses. It is important to point out that the Farm Business Survey (FBS) data is biased towards larger and more 'commercial' farms, such that pluriactive farm households are underrepresented in the sample. Moreover, only the incomes of spouses or other resident family members who are actually working on the farm are included. The FBS data therefore understates the significance of non-agricultural incomes for farm households.

By comparison with Scotland, Norwegian farmers have a much higher proportion of income from non-agricultural sources, including non-farm work and farm-based businesses including forestry. This broader mix of income is facilitated by the higher proportion of owner-farmers in Norway.

As in Norway, the FBS data on non-farming income in Scotland understates its importance for farm household incomes, both because of the nature of the FBS sample and because of the methods of data collection. Other studies on farm household pluriactivity in Scotland indicate much higher levels of non-agricultural income.[6] Nevertheless, it is unlikely to be as high as in Norway.

Table 4.4 Income of FBS Farms in Scotland, 2011–12

Number of farms	502	
Av. farm size, ha	272	
Av. agricultural business income	£42,033	78 per cent
Av. diversification margin	£ 3,333	6 per cent
Av. off-farm income, farmer and spouse	£ 8,736	16.1 per cent
Total income per farm	£54,102	

Source: FBS. Scottish Agricultural Statistics.

THE INFLUENCE OF THE EVOLUTION OF LAND OWNERSHIP AND RIGHTS ON FARMING STRUCTURES IN THE TWENTIETH CENTURY

The influence of the very different evolution of land ownership and rights in Scotland and Norway (see Chapter 1) is reflected in the different structures today, especially in the more pronounced 'dual' structure of Scottish farms. However, the pace of structural change has increased in Norway in the last twenty years, with the proportion of farms of 20 hectares or greater increasing from 12.2 per cent in 1989 to 40.8 per cent by 2012.

About 31 per cent of farmholdings in Norway are less than 10 hectares, and only 7.9 per cent are over 50 hectares. This compares with Scotland, where 51.7 per cent of holdings are less than 10 hectares, but 26.7 per cent are over 50 hectares. However, in both countries about 60 per cent of farms are less than 20 hectares.

The very small Scottish holdings include some 8,000 crofts in the Highlands and Islands, most of which also have a share in common grazings not included in the data above.

In Scotland the distribution of the agricultural area is therefore highly skewed.

Table 4.5 Farm Structures in Norway

Year	Number of holdings	0.5–4.9 ha %	5–9.9 ha %	10–19.9 ha %	20–29.9 ha %	30–49.9 ha %	Over 50 ha %
1929	208,550	72.2	17.7	7.6	2.3		0.2
1949	213,441	70.3	19.9	7.3	2.3		0.2
1969	154,977	57.1	27.3	11.6	2.5	1.2	0.3
1979	125,302	49.5	26.1	17.3	4.5	2.1	0.6
1989	99,382	37.3	25.1	25.5	8.0	3.3	0.9
1999	70,740	20.5	23.6	31.5	14.7	7.5	2.2
2012	44,673	13.3	17.5	28.4	18.1	14.8	7.9

Sources: Calculated for 1969 to 1999 from Almås (2004; 331) and, for 1929, 1949 and 2012 from Statistics Norway.

Table 4.6 Farm Structures in Scotland[a]

	Number of holdings	0 – <5 ha per cent	5 – <10 ha per cent	10 – <20 ha per cent	20 – <50 ha per cent	Over 50 ha per cent
1972	37,930					
2000	49,783	35.9	11.3	9.6	12.6	30.5
2012	50,625	39.6	12.1	9.8	11.7	26.7

Source: 2000 and 2012 Computed from Economic Reports on Scottish Agriculture, 2001 and 2013.

Note:
[a] Data refer to 'significant holdings' under the Eurostat definition. The highest proportion of insignificant holdings is in the Highlands and Islands, and include both crofts and very large holdings which are now sporting estates.

There were 4,464 holdings (8 per cent of the total) with more than 200 hectares, accounting for 76 per cent of the total agricultural area. At the other end of the spectrum, there were more than 27,000 holdings with less than 10 hectares of agricultural land, accounting for only 1.6 per cent of the total land.[7] Measured by European Size Units (ESU),[8] as many as 73 per cent had less than 4 ESU. Approximately 23 per cent had more than 8 ESU, and almost one-half of these had more than 40 ESU.[9]

The number of farmholdings in Norway was at its highest just after the Second World War. Since then the number of farmholdings has been decreasing while the number of farm properties has been rather stable. An increasing share of the arable farmland is rented, and in 2010 as much as 42 per cent of total agricultural land was rented. Tenants of agricultural land are often farmers who also own land.

Some 75 per cent of the total Norwegian land area is owned by agricultural landowners. In addition to agricultural land, farmers own and work forest and other land. These areas are used for a variety of purposes, including rough grazing. At present, sheep are the most important animals utilising rough grazings and account for two-thirds of the feed uptake from *utmark*[10] and cattle most of the remainder. Earlier, cattle were more important than sheep, but the cattle:sheep ratio has swung steadily against cattle.

FARMERS AND POLITICS

Norwegian farmers played a more central role in political developments after 1800 than did their counterparts in Scotland, a further important consequence of the much wider and more evenly distributed ownership of land in Norway. Kane and Mann explore the case of Norway as one of the few cases where 'a numerous peasantry was pushed leftward into allying first with liberal bourgeois elements, then with the working class'[11] with whom they faced a weak and impoverished monarchy and aristocracy (see also Chapters 1, 2 and 3).

Norwegian farmers are today organised in two unions: the Norwegian Farmers' Union (*Norges Bondelag*) and the Norwegian Farmers' and Smallholders' Union (*Norsk Bonde- og Småbrukarlag*). The Norwegian Farmers' Union was established in 1896 as the *Norsk Landmandsforbund*. From the beginning it was both a union of farmers and a political party. In 1920, the organisation split into a farmers' union (*Norges Bondelag*) and a political party (*Bondepartiet* – the Farmers' Party). The Farmers' Party changed name to *Senterpartiet* (the Centre Party) in 1959. The Norwegian Farmers' and Smallholders' Union was established in 1913. Traditionally there used to be close links between the Farmers' Union and the Centre Party and between the Smallholders' Union and the Labour Party, but these links have become less close over the years. The Farmers' Union is by far the largest of the two unions with approximately 60,000 members, while the Smallholders' Union has about 7,000 members. The two unions have equal rights in the annual negotiations with the government on agricultural prices and support. There are similar negotiations and agreement regarding reindeer-farming. As far as we know, Norway is the only country where the farmers' unions and the government still negotiate on prices and support, although a similar system applied in the UK between the Second World War and the UK's entry to the EEC in 1972.[12]

In Scotland, the dominant farmer organisation since the Second World War has been the National Farmers' Union of Scotland, although various attempts have been made to create a representative voice for crofters, currently in the shape of the Scottish Crofters' Union, re-formed in the 1980s. Farmers were seen as being closely allied to the Liberal Party during the period of Liberal hegemony between 1880 and 1920. The small tenant farmers and smallholders of Scotland have been consistently underrepresented and lack a clear and consistent political voice.

THE 'AGRARIAN REVOLUTION' IN SCOTLAND

As a result of the very different patterns of landownership discussed in Chapter 1, the nature of agrarian change in Scotland and Norway was completely different. By 1800, Scottish agriculture was in the middle of a revolution that started seriously around the middle of the eighteenth century. The slow recovery from the financial losses of the Darien venture, together with the bad weather at the end of the seventeenth century and the demands of the Union with England after 1707, as well as the quasi-revolutionary state of much of Scotland at the time, especially north of the highland line, set back the progress that had been made. However, as a result of higher cattle prices following the Union of 1707, landowners in southern Scotland undertook significant enclosures after 1720. As Devine points out,[13] this indicates that the 'improvers' were at work before the middle of the eighteenth century, and that a key part of their ideas was the consolidation of farms under a single tenant, with more human and financial resources, and the goal of increasing production and rents for the – mostly large – landowners.

The middle of the eighteenth century appears as a watershed in Scottish agrarian history. Then the majority of Scots lived and worked in the countryside, and even urban dwellers went back to their family lands at harvest time. While some were tenant farmers/crofters, the majority were cottars with a house and a small area of ground for self-provisioning, and often working in a rural trade such as blacksmith, carpenter, weaver, miller or shoe-maker, as well as constituting a 'reserve army' of seasonal labour for agriculture.[14] Unlike in England, there were few entirely landless people in Scotland at the beginning of the eighteenth century, and even they often had access to land – or married into tenant or cottar families.

In the course of the following century, Scotland experienced an unprecedented parallel agrarian and industrial revolution. However, the agrarian revolution was primarily aimed at rapidly increasing both the production of food and the proportion that was marketed. It was not aimed at the replacement of labour as such, since farming operations remained relatively labour intensive. Between 1750 and 1850, the urban population increased by a factor of over four, while the rural population increased by 80 per cent. The urban population increased from 13.4 per cent to 31.9 per cent of the Scottish population, leading to a rapid increase in the domestic demand for food from the towns and cities. Yet the rural population was also increasing in this period, if at a much slower rate.

Although there is a view that Scottish agriculture had been entirely static and focused on subsistence prior to this period, evidence indicates significant changes in the Lowlands of southern Scotland during the sixteenth and seventeenth centuries, and significant trade in agricultural commodities on the 'eve' of Union in 1707.[15] Scottish agriculture was also on the whole successful in meeting the needs of the population for food, and providing a small surplus for export. Moreover, a set of complex social institutions had clearly evolved that were to be swept away by the ideas of the eighteenth- and nineteenth-century 'improvers'. These institutions were focused on the food security of farming communities, and ensuring fair distribution of the produce of scarce arable land, and included the runrig system and joint farming. Devine's research in the Lowlands suggests that more than half of the farms were in 'multiple tenancies' at the time of the Union, but by the 1740s the majority were in single tenancies.[16] These institutions, evolved over a long period of time, were designed to secure more equal access to scarce good land but also to share the access to poorer land. Such ideas were not at the forefront of the minds of the 'improvers'. Indeed, the Reverend Adam Dickson, who was the first Minister to join the Honourable Society of Improvers, and whose *Treatise on Agriculture* (1762) was 'widely read and highly regarded', believed that the number of small tenants was 'an obstruction to agrarian change' and provided 'powerful ideological and moral backing' for the expropriation of the peasantry.[17]

In retrospect, the hegemonic ideas of the improvers have provided one 'story' of Scotland's agrarian revolution from the mid-eighteenth to the mid-nineteenth centuries, with few dissenters. Many historians have accepted that there was no doubt about the 'improvement' brought on by the 'improvers', including eminent economic historians such as Roy Campbell,[18] although Ian Carter and Tom Devine are notable exceptions. Ian Carter went so far as to call it a 'Whig theory of agrarian change',[19] even if it also later became a Marxist theory of agrarian change. This 'story' of agrarian improvement is about placing the overwhelmingly tenanted farms in the hands of capitalist farmers who would hire regular landless labour, occupy full-time farms of 100 acres or more, install drains and efficient farm buildings, adopt regular rotations, introduce new crops – especially barley and turnips, abolish the infield-outfield system, and the rig-and-furrow method of cultivation.[20]

While up to the 1760s the structure of the Scottish countryside looked much as it had done for centuries 'with its open fields, long sinuous rigs and huddled townships', the rapid growth of the number of landless urban workers created market pressures. By 1830 'a recognizably modern landscape of trim fields and compact farms, separated by hedges and ditches, had emerged . . .'[21] The transition from subsistence to market was also greatly assisted by the expansion in the road network after the 1715 and 1745 'rebellions', and the roads' later improvement in the first quarter of the nineteenth century.[22]

According to Devine, the agrarian revolution of this period resulted in a doubling or tripling of crop yields.[23] Livestock yields also improved through new breeding methods using the Shorthorn, or developing new indigenous breeds, in particular the Aberdeen-Angus, as well as through the development of the division of cattle- and sheep-breeding from the function of fattening and finishing, the former being an increasing specialism of hill and upland farms, the latter being linked with low-ground arable farms increasingly using the high-yielding turnip or swede as a fodder crop. The potato, introduced in the mid-eighteenth century, became very important as a subsistence crop, especially in the western Highlands and Islands, by 1800. James Small's swing plough[24] was another important eighteenth-century innovation, later improved by the addition of iron mouldboards. Andrew Meikle's winnowing and threshing machines, improving earlier versions from Holland[25] and England, were further important eighteenth-century inventions introduced, as was Patrick Bell's horse-driven reaper, in the early nineteenth century.[26] However, these reapers were hampered by the lack of tile drainage, which meant that the old ridge- and-furrow technique was still in use during the early nineteenth century. Long-term loans were offered to landowners for draining in 1846 and 1849, and from the middle of the century drainage and levelling took off, preparing the way for the machine age.[27] Writing in the mid-nineteenth century, Louis de Lavergne, Professor of Rural Economy at the National Agricultural Institute in Paris,[28] said, 'Scotch agriculture is at this day superior even to English, in some districts at least'. He ventured the estimate that 'total production during the last hundred years has increased tenfold'.

The introduction of horse-drawn reapers and threshing machines saved much hard labour and increased the number of horses. Between 1856 and 1869 the number of horses employed on Scottish farms increased by nearly one-third.[29] The introduction of horse-drawn machines released farm labour at this time.[30]

Although Britain was in the vanguard of the eighteenth- and nineteenth-century reforms in Europe, they were also occurring elsewhere on the Continent.[31] However, they were not occurring evenly, and regions that were at one moment in the lead ceased to be in that position at other moments. Nor, as we have seen in the comparison between Scotland and Norway, did they necessarily take the same pathways. In particular, in the Norwegian case there was no mass dispossession of farmers in the late eighteenth and nineteenth centuries, no rapid urbanisation that created a nationally increasing demand for a marketed surplus of food from farmers, and no clearances that separated people from their means of subsistence, but instead the development of a close alliance between industrial, agricultural, fisheries and forest work and workers that served the emerging social democratic political system well.

The potato was introduced in Norway around 1750. Its role was vital for many people during the Napoleonic Wars. By 1835 'the potato had become a major condition for the lower rate of mortality and the rise in population of the period'.[32] Potato blight was a problem from 1846 onwards but the effects were not as catastrophic as in Ireland and Scotland.

As we see in Chapter 6, the industrial revolution came relatively late in Norway. The first steam-driven textile factory was established in the 1840s. Sawmills driven by steam engines came in the 1860s. Pulp and paper industries came in the 1860s and 1870s. From the early twentieth century hydro-electricity became an important element in the industrialisation of Norway.[33] One innovation of special interest for agriculture was the Birkeland-Eyde method for producing nitrogen fertiliser. That was the basis for the industrial complex Norsk Hydro established in 1905.

POLICY DEVELOPMENT: NINETEENTH-CENTURY FREE TRADE TO INTERVENTION IN THE INTER-WAR PERIOD

In the nineteenth century the protection of grain-farming by means of the corn laws and their equivalents in other European countries gave way to a period of free trade after their abolition in Britain in 1846, and the signing of the Anglo–French Treaty of Commerce in 1860.[34] The opening up of the American and Canadian prairies and the Russian plains, and the extension of the railways across the US and Canada and Europe in the second half of the nineteenth century, as well as the development of steam ships, transformed the locus and supply of grains. Between 1870 and the end of the century, wheat exports from the USA, Canada and Russia increased from 116 million to 307 million bushels. This resulted in a collapse of grain prices and an agricultural depression initially in grain-farming areas, but which ultimately spread to livestock-production areas as well. The depression led to the reimposition of protection for agriculture until, on the eve of the First World War, it was between 20 and 30 per cent in most countries of Western Europe, the main exceptions being Britain, Denmark and the Netherlands.[35] During the First World War, tariffs were generally suspended and prices were high, but depression returned in 1921 and, after a brief respite, again in 1926. In 1927, Norway introduced a tariff, as well as a 'milling ratio' for wheat which set a minimum for national grain content. Norway also established a state company with an obligation to buy all Norwegian grain and with a monopoly on importing feed grains. Britain converted to protectionism in 1931–2 but not for Empire trade. In 1932, the Wheat Act also reintroduced guaranteed prices for wheat subject to a cap on the total output that would be supported. The support was paid as a 'deficiency payment'[36] and financed by a levy on all wheat flour, most of which was imported. Similar support was given for sugar beet and sometimes also for other farm products such as butter and bacon.

Both Norway and Britain took measures to manage the markets for agricultural produce in the 1930s. In Britain this took the form of the statutory Marketing Boards for milk, potatoes, eggs and hops. These were essentially farmer-controlled monopolies intended to manage markets and counter the monopsonistic power of large wholesalers and retailers. They mainly survived until the 1980s in the UK, when the neo-liberal politics of the day decided to throw the farmers back into the hands of the increasingly oligopolistic food manufacturers and retailers.

In Norway, cooperative marketing of milk was made compulsory for all milk producers in 1931, and the system created a model much examined by other nations at the time.[37] 'Milk centrals' were in effect cooperatives of the milk producers, and they were organised in the different regions, with support varying from 75 to 97 per cent. By 1937 there were eight such cooperatives covering the whole country. Like the Milk Marketing Boards in Scotland and the rest of the UK, they managed the market for liquid milk alongside that for milk destined for manufacturing, maintaining a higher price for liquid milk and a lower price for milk destined for manufacture in the creameries, which in the Norwegian case were also farmer cooperatives but in Scotland belonged to the regional Milk Marketing Boards. The system could only work with national or regional monopolies controlled largely by producer interests, because it involved internal cross-subsidisation, such that the dairy farmers received the same price for their milk within each region. Indeed, Grimley hints that the British Milk Marketing Board system may well have been at least partly based on the Norwegian model.[38]

These inter-war policies strengthened farming in both Norway and Scotland, and placed the sector in a stronger position to face the problems of food supply during the Second World War. Churchill sought a 'large but not excessive' increase in the production of food during the war, and guaranteed prices for milk, cattle and sheep were introduced in 1944 to help to achieve this.[39] In the same year, the Annual Review and Determination of Guarantees was introduced, involving annual negotiations on prices and other matters of agricultural policy between the government and the farmers' unions, and based on evidence about movement of production, prices, costs and incomes.[40] Norway also developed an Annual Review system after the war that involved the two unions representing larger farmers on the one hand and the smallholders on the other, as well as the government.[41]

POLICY DEVELOPMENTS AFTER THE SECOND WORLD WAR

Food shortages persisted after the end of the war, and most European governments took steps to raise the self-sufficiency of food supplies while at the same time relieving the balance of payments deficits. In Britain, the 1947 Agriculture Act set the framework for the next twenty-five years, institutionalising the system of guarantee payments implemented through the deficiency payment system and intervention purchases, along with Marketing Boards.[42] The stability provided by agricultural policies at this time, as well as the institutional arrangements for their review, provided a more predictable environment for farms to invest in new techniques and expansion. Production and productivity both expanded rapidly, and mechanisation, especially the switch from horses to tractors and related new machines, expanded by leaps and bounds. By 1960–1, UK agricultural output was some 55 per cent above its pre-war levels in real terms, while labour productivity was 46 per cent higher in 1959 than it was in 1949.[43] Shortages were turning to surpluses, and the costs of agricultural guarantees were expanding as world market prices for many commodities fell. By 1961, the Chancellor of the Exchequer was stating, 'We shall have to look critically at the level of agricultural subsidies during the 1962 Review'.[44] Standard quantities for the main commodities were introduced in the 1960s to limit support to a ceiling. Despite this, production of most commodities continued to expand rapidly during the 1960s and 1970s. Thus, total output of Scottish agriculture in current prices increased by a factor of about nine between 1950–1 and 1980–1, while the physical output of cereals increased by 224.8 per cent, milk and milk products by 167.6 per cent and fatstock by 174.1 per cent in the same period.[45] However, the net output of Scottish agriculture fell in the period between 1970 and 1980 due to rapidly increasing input prices caused largely by the oil shocks of 1973 and 1979.

The 1946 Hill Farming Act and Marginal Agricultural Production scheme (MAP) introduced differential and regionally specified support for breeding cattle and sheep in much of southern and northern Scotland. This support was explicitly covered in the UK's accession negotiations in 1971–2 and, after a visit to the Highlands and Islands by the EC Agricultural Commissioner Sicco Mansholt, it was agreed that there would be a 'common' policy for the so-called 'less-favoured' agricultural areas in the member states, to be part-funded by the common budget of the CAP.

Agricultural policy changed quite radically when Britain joined the EU in 1973. In particular, EU policy derived mainly from the policies of the founding member states[46] and was based on a regime of external tariffs and quotas, export subsidies and intervention buying, to reach target prices. In this system, the costs of agricultural policy support shifted from taxpayers to consumers. In preparing for EU entry, however, Britain had an interest in increasing production as much as possible, and in the 1971 Annual Review the value of agricultural guarantees was increased by £138m, which represented 'full recoupment of increased costs of all the main commodities except eggs'.[47]

The shift in the burden of support brought consumers into more direct conflict with farmers, and the former political consensus on farming broke down. Nevertheless, for at least some years during and after EC entry, Scottish agriculture enjoyed a certain prosperity, helped in the middle of the decade by good years for potato prices and yields at a time when English farmers were facing much less favourable growing conditions.

Apart from growing consumer resentment of high and increasing food prices, the environmental interests were becoming more powerful at a time when the form of agriculture which emerged from the 'second' agrarian revolution of our period led to the removal of hedgerows and copses, adverse pesticide impacts on insect and bird life, herbicide impacts on plant biodiversity, pollution of the water table by fertilisers and animal manure, and other negative 'externalities'. Moreover, the CAP was absorbing the majority of the EU budget at a time when other demands, such as southern and later eastern enlargement, were increasing and fiscal constraints were rising. At the same time, the export of production surpluses arising from EU agricultural policy caused problems for traditional food exporters of temperate products, especially the USA, Canada, Australia, New Zealand and Argentina, as well as for some tropical and semi-tropical products (sugar, tobacco, cotton). In this respect, the UK had significant concerns about the reaction of Commonwealth countries.

In addition to market policy, the EC had developed an agricultural structures policy during the 1960s and early 1970s which, from the 1972 Directives, encouraged farm enlargement and modernisation, the development of extension services, and retirement of older farmers in favour of younger farmers. In 1975 the Less Favoured Areas Directive was introduced, which covered differential support for hill and mountain livestock farmers. The policy was based on the 'Mansholt Plan', which presented an image of a 'modern' farmer and farm, the farm being large enough to support at least the farmer and family, and the farmer being both educated in modern techniques and a full-time professional. These 'modern' full-time professional farmers were those who had been driving, and would continue to drive, the second agrarian revolution. As with the images of commercial farmers in the first agrarian revolution, so influential for related ideology and policy, here again we had an image that did not reflect the reality of most of Europe's farmers, and certainly not the reality of farming in Scotland, with its distinctive dual structure, or in Norway, which is not an EU member state. Much of this original structures policy still exists as part of what is now called Rural Development Policy, although other elements have been added, in particular agri-environmental policies added during the 'greening' of the CAP that followed the GATT Uruguay Round Agreement in 1994 and the 1992 CAP reform that was linked with it.

Subsequent CAP reforms have further decoupled subsidies from production, such that over 60 per cent of market support now comes from 'direct payments' first introduced as temporary compensation for decoupling in the 1992 CAP reforms but which have become a permanent feature. In addition, the environmental component of policy has increased in two main directions: firstly, the compliance with environment directives as a condition of direct payments has been strengthened; and secondly, the elements of environmental measures, such as water protection, biodiversity, forestry and landscape cosmetics, have also been widened and better financed within the 'rural development' pillar of the CAP that now replaces agricultural structures policies. The grounds are based on 'payment for public goods' and related 'multifunctionality' arguments.[48]

THE EVOLUTION OF AGRICULTURAL POLICY IN NORWAY

Norway's agricultural policy development shows some parallels, even if the goals and nature of policy measures remain significantly different from the EU policy that now dominates in Scotland. However, a particular dimension of agricultural policy in Norway was regional agricultural pricing introduced with the regulation of key markets in the 1930s, and strengthened after the Second World War. Prices were set to ensure that farming continued throughout Norway rather than becoming concentrating in the favoured agricultural areas and around the large towns and cities.

During the nineteenth century, Norway, like many other European states, moved towards economic liberalism. However, during this period the Norwegian Government introduced a number of policy measures to promote agriculture, some of which are mentioned elsewhere in this chapter.

Free trade contributed to an inflow of cereals from North America and some European countries, and reduced prices. As a response, farmers put less weight on cereal-farming and more on dairy-farming.[49] Farmers asked for protection from imports, as did manufacturers of industrial products. A major revision of the import tariffs in 1897 introduced or increased import tariffs on several products but agriculture had less protection than manufacturing industries.[50] The Farmers' Union demanded import tariff parity with manufacturing industries in 1912.

During the First World War supply was scarce but grew relatively rapidly afterwards. Around 1930, import tariffs were not sufficient to secure satisfactory farmers' prices and incomes. Market regulation became a main part of agriculture support.

After the Second World War, the government took a greater responsibility for social and economic conditions. Income parity between farmers and other groups in society became a policy goal. The operational definition was decided only in 1964, by the select committee for agriculture in Parliament, and in 1975 Parliament decided that the income goal should be fulfilled within six years. In 1982, the farmers' unions and the government agreed that this goal was fulfilled. In 1993, Parliament again discussed goals and measures for the agricultural policy. Income was now regarded as a means for reaching other goals, and the income goal became less binding.[51] However, the negotiations on agricultural prices and support continued.

While Scotland has been part of a larger market, first within the UK and the Empire and then the EU, Norway has been on its own. It is mainly the GATT/WTO agreements that limit the Norwegian use of import tariffs, export subsidies and internal support.

After the Second World War, the government maintained price control. From 1947, prices were settled in negotiations with the farmers.

From 1944, all producers in northern Norway and in the so-called '*Fjord- og fjellbygder*' in southern Norway received a special price support of four *øre* per kg of barley. This continued until the mid-1970s, when a system of regional cereal prices was introduced and maintained until 1992, when it was replaced by regionally differentiated acreage support.

Price support for milk produced in some specific areas such as northern Norway had been implemented during the Second World War. In 1945, the government decided to give a subsidy of three *øre* per litre of milk to producers in north Norway and mountainous municipalities and municipalities along the west coast.[52] The system was subsequently extended to more zones in milk production, and also to meat, especially beef, mutton and lamb.

The regional support for milk and barley can be regarded as the early stages of regional support to Norwegian agriculture. Cost compensation is a main criterion for the regional support. Coordination of the zoning of regional differentiation of agricultural support with the zoning of general regional support has been discussed on several occasions, but has not yet been implemented.[53] Nevertheless, in principle, regional elements in agricultural policy are seen as a part of the important Districts Policy, which emphasises that people should have free choice to settle wherever they want. Four key areas of policy effort have been prioritised in recent years, notably:

• real freedom of choice about where to live;
• regional strategy to sustain the current pattern of settlements;
• facilitating economic developments in all parts of the country;
• facilitating fair distribution of growth between cities and rural areas.

These regional policy goals have been facilitated by the important devolution and decentralisation of government (see Chapter 5), and by an active regional policy targeting the most difficult areas such as northern Norway, as well as by regional agricultural policies.

Within agriculture, payments per hectare and per animal and welfare payments have a long tradition in Norway but became more important around 1990. This was partly to make agricultural production less intensive to curb surplus production but also to make agriculture more environmentally friendly and to increase competitiveness.

CHANGING REGIONAL AND COMMODITY CONTRIBUTION TO AGRICULTURE

The nature of agrarian change in the different regions of Scotland has been studied by several writers, even if it remains a somewhat neglected topic in both Scotland and Norway.[54] Bryden also examined differential regional trends in agricultural production within the main Scottish regions, mainly for the period after the Second World War II,[55] while Shucksmith et al. studied the regional impact of the CAP at EU level.[56]

According to Bryden,

> [t]here is a good deal of evidence to suggest that the effects of technology, price support, and structure support have been additive, tending to favour arable and dairy farms as against beef and sheep farms, tending to favour larger as against smaller farms, and tending to favour the geographically more favoured agricultural areas.[57]

Although this was written in 1985, there is little subsequent evidence to support another conclusion, either for the period to 1985 or after it, despite fairly radical policy changes.[58] Indeed, in the preparatory documents for the 1992 reforms of the CAP, which started the process of decoupling of agricultural support from production, the then Commissioner for Agriculture and Rural Development in the EC, Ray MacSharry, pointed out that 80 per cent of CAP support went to about 20 per cent of the largest farmers.[59] The following figures give some indicative, long run, data.

We can observe that the north-west, which is the most remote and agriculturally challenged region of Scotland, including most of the Highlands and Islands, has consistently lost its share of arable crops and cattle since 1800, while also gaining a greater share of sheep in the period overall, but with some glitches in periods when sheep-farming was economically challenged or hunting activities were especially lucrative or popular. Here, too, the dramatic increases in the sheep:cattle ratio since 1800, and associated with the Clearances, are now generally recognised to have been damaging for the natural environment.[60]

We can also observe that cereals have gravitated to the north and south-east of

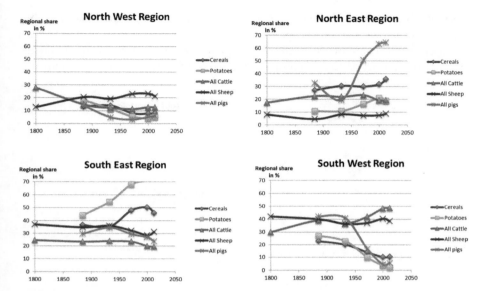

Figure 4.1 Regional Agricultural Trends since 1800, Scotland (regional shares in crop areas and livestock numbers)

Sources: Derived from data in Sinclair's *General Account of the First Statistical Account of Scotland* . . . (1804), 1885–2012 Agricultural Statistics, Scotland reported for the early years in Trs. RH&AS, 1885–1933, and from Table 2 in Bryden (1995), and for 1972 and 2012 derived from data in Agricultural Statistics, Scotland.

Scotland, and cattle (especially dairy cattle, although we cannot see that in this figure) to the south-west.

In terms of the value of gross output, the work on regional agricultural output in Scotland in 1951/2 and 1961/2, and 1971/2,[61] strongly suggests that the relative position of the Highlands and Islands deteriorated in each of the two decades from 1951–61 and 1961–71, while it is probable that the south-east improved its relative position in both decades.[62] Such changes were not just caused by market forces: the differential support for cattle, sheep and arable production[63] in the Highlands and Islands was steadily eroded following EC entry in 1972, even though such support became part of the CAP in 1975.

The regional distribution of agricultural production has also changed in Norway. From 1850 to 1900 the population of Oslo (Kristiania) increased from less than 50,000 to more than 250,000. The market for milk and other dairy products developed accordingly. The agricultural 'crisis' after 1875, and new technology, also helped to encourage a switch from cereals to dairy in many areas.

As late as 1949, more than 90 per cent of all holdings over 0.5 hectare grew potatoes and had dairy cows. Two-thirds of the holdings had sheep, the highest share in western and northern Norway. About half grew cereals, although fewer in northern Norway and in some parts in the west. About 56 per cent had pigs, but less than 15 per cent in northern Norway.

Since 1949 the number of holdings has fallen by 80 per cent and production has become specialised on the remaining holdings. Cereal production is concentrated

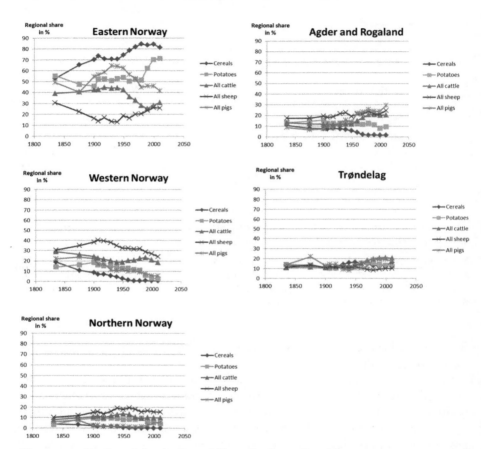

Figure 4.2: Regional Agricultural Trends since 1835, Norway

Sources: Data for 1835, 1875 and 1900 are from Norwegian population censuses, while the other data are from agricultural censuses with approximately 10-year intervals.

Notes:

[a] Regional classification: Eastern Norway is the counties of Østfold, Akershus, Oslo, Hedmark, Oppland, Buskerud, Vestfold and Telemark; Agder and Rogaland are Aust-Agder, Vest-Agder and Rogaland; Western Norway is Hordaland, Sogn og Fjordane og Møre og Romsdal; Trøndelag is Sør-Trøndelag og Nord-Trøndelag; Northern Norway is Nordland, Troms og Finnmark. Note that many counties have changed name during the period. Some borders have changed, but at regional level this will have only minor effects.

[b] Units: Cereals are in hectares, except for 1835 when the measure is seed. Animals are in numbers.

in eastern Norway and Trøndelag. Two-thirds of commercial potato production is now in eastern Norway and Trøndelag. Potato production has almost disappeared from western and northern Norway. Dairy production has increased relatively in Rogaland and Trøndelag. Western Norway has about the same share as in 1949, while the shares for other regions have fallen, mainly in eastern Norway. The development in cereal- and dairy-farming since 1949 is partly a result of a policy to increase cereal-growing in eastern Norway and stimulate dairy-farming in areas well suited for grass production. In sheep-farming, western Norway has reduced its share while eastern Norway has increased its share. The other regions have been more stable. Pig production has increased substantially but at variable rates. The increase has been especially large in Rogaland, while the rest of southern and western Norway has had a similar decrease of their share. The production and consumption of chicken was rather insignificant until about 1970 but the production is now larger than the production of beef and is concentrated in some regions within eastern Norway – Rogaland and Trøndelag.

MECHANISATION AND THE SECOND AGRARIAN REVOLUTION AFTER THE SECOND WORLD WAR

The steam engine, although often mentioned, had very little practical impact on agriculture in Scotland, and working horses continued to be used in relatively large numbers until after the Second World War. Although tractors started to be used in significant numbers in the later 1930s,[64] it was Harry Ferguson's hydraulic three-point linkage system in 1938 and its use in mass-produced tractors after 1952 that finally ended the dominance of horse power in Scottish agriculture.

The tractor also released arable land, because horses were normally fed on a diet of hay and oats, both typically produced on the farm, and requiring about 3–4 acres per horse.[65] Between 1950 and 1970, at least 169,800 acres of arable land, or roughly 5 per cent of the Scottish total, were released by the switch from working horses to tractors on Scottish farms.

A similar process occurred in Norway but about a decade later.

Table 4.7 Horse and Tractor Power in Scottish Agriculture

	1886	1933	1950(a)	1960	1970(b)
Working horses (c)	141,522	113,886	58,000	8,400	1,402
Tractors (d)	nil	n/a	21,835	60,000	58,200

Sources: Working Horses: Agricultural Statistics, Scotland.
Tractors: Rettie, W. J., *Mechanisation of Scottish Agriculture*, SJAE.

Table 4.8 Horse and Tractor Power in Norwegian Agriculture

	1939	1949	1959	1969	1989
All horses	204,000	198,000	117,000	41,000	17,000
Tractors	3,000	9,500	47,250	88,470	158,000

Source: Statistics Norway.

The mechanisation of agriculture in Norway started with the introduction of the threshing machine. The second phase was the introduction of the mowing machine in the 1850s.[66] Thereafter, a number of improved machines were introduced. The introduction of horse-drawn mowing and threshing machines released labour. Further advances were made with the rapid electrification of farms in both Scotland and Norway after the Second World War. In 1949, about 65 per cent of Norwegian farms used electricity for lighting, and 44 per cent for cooking.[67] A representative census in 1957 found that 91 per cent of the holdings had installed electricity in the farmhouse, while 78 per cent had installed electricity in the outbuildings.[68]

ANIMAL-BREEDING

Animal-breeding and changes in feeding methods have been important in both countries since the 'first' agrarian revolution. Building on the work of English cattle- breeders such as Bakewell[69] and Cully towards the end of the eighteenth century, breed improvements first occurred in southwest Scotland based on the Ayrshire cow, and in southeast Scotland based on the Shorthorn. The English approach used larger breeds for crossing but this was less appropriate in Scotland, which quickly introduced its own approaches using indigenous breeds including the Highland, the Galloway, Aberdeen-Angus and the Ayrshire dairy cow.[70]

Analysis of the famous Perth Bull Sale data between 1969 and 1983 revealed a considerable decline of bulls of British breeds, including Aberdeen-Angus, and a corresponding increase in the heavier and larger continental bull breeds over this period.[71] In the case of sheep, new breeds were introduced to Scotland by the improvers of the late eighteenth and nineteenth centuries, especially the Cheviot and the Leicester, while the indigenous Blackface from southern Scotland remained on poorer land. The original dun-faced or white sheep formerly spread throughout Scotland were displaced.

The dominant Norwegian cattle breed, the Norwegian Red, was created in the 1930s by crossing local Norwegian breeds with Swedish Red and White cattle and Finnish Ayrshire cattle. The Swedish Red and White Cattle breed is also strongly influenced by Scottish Ayrshire cattle. The change to the Norwegian Red was influenced by the use of deep-frozen semen and artificial insemination.

Aberdeen-Angus is one of the most common beef cattle breeds in Norway, where there are breed organisations for Aberdeen-Angus, Highland and Galloway cattle.

The Cheviot sheep came to Norway around 1860 and played an important role in Norwegian sheep-breeding, although only 2 per cent of the Norwegian sheep population was classified as Cheviot in 2013. The Cheviot has been crossed with other breeds which became the Norwegian white sheep. Blackface and North Country Cheviot sheep have also been imported to Norway. The Border Collie is also a well-known sheep dog in Norway.

AGRICULTURAL MARKETING AND COOPERATIVES IN NORWAY

The former dairy marketing organisation is now called TINE SA and organised as a national cooperative owned by more than 15,000 Norwegian dairy farmers.[72] The members deliver 1.4 billion litres of cow's milk and about 19 million litres of goat's milk every year, giving a market share of over 90 per cent. The TINE Group also consists of several wholly owned and partially owned subsidiaries. Besides dairy products the group manufactures products ranging from ice cream and juice to marine products. The dairy cooperative is one of Norway's largest food manufacturers, with a total of 5,485 employees and an annual turnover of NOK 19.7 billion (roughly £2 billion) in 2012.

Nortura SA is an equally large marketing and processing cooperative for meat and eggs. The current Nortura SA group has 5,500 employees, approximately 18,800 owners and operations in thirty municipalities all over the country. It is the result of a long journey since the establishment of the first cooperative breeding association for laying hens and the first farmer-owned slaughterhouse around 1900.[73]

The main agricultural supply cooperative is Felleskjøpet, which buys cereals from farmers, produces and sells concentrates, and sells farm inputs (fertiliser, machinery, seeds, plant protection, etc.). It also sells feed for pets and equipment for consumers.

Norway has many other cooperatives, including one for example for the processing, grading and marketing of honey. In addition, there are various arrangements for joint operations in dairying and machinery sharing.

AGRICULTURAL RESEARCH, EDUCATION, TRAINING AND EXTENSION

This section will be brief, not because the subject is not interesting, rather because the evolution of the agricultural research, training and extension systems in Norway and Scotland were rather similar, at least up until the 1970s. Formal agricultural training in Norway started with a private agricultural school in the 1820s. From 1825, the government supported the training of farm boys,[74] and this is recognised as the start of the agricultural schools in Norway. After ups and downs in the nineteenth century, every county had at least one agricultural school in 1910.[75] From its establishment in 1900 and until 1990 the Ministry of Agriculture had responsibility for agricultural schools. In 1990, the schools became part of the upper secondary school system under the Ministry of Education.[76]

Higher education in agriculture began in 1859 when the Higher Agricultural School at Ås enrolled its first students. In 1897, the school got the status of a university college. The Norwegian School of Veterinary Science was established in the 1930s. The responsibility for the Norwegian Agricultural College (the Norwegian University of Life Sciences since 2005) and the School of Veterinary Science, which were merged in 2014, was transferred to the Ministry of Education in 1995. The Norwegian Ministry of Agriculture and Food, working mainly through the Norwegian Research Council, is a major research department. Additional research funding is provided through an R&D tax on agricultural and forestry products, and the annual agricultural agreement. Overall, about £60 million (NOK 600 million) is allocated for food and agricultural research.[77]

During the nineteenth century and up until 1950, Norway established a large number of experimental stations and research institutes. After a series of reorganisation processes, the Ministry of Agriculture and Food currently owns four research institutes and has a responsibility for the basic funding of two institutes organised as foundations (*stiftelser*). Together, the University of Life Sciences, some regional university colleges and the research institutes cover the main fields of agriculture, forestry and food sciences.

Scotland also had a number of agricultural schools at upper secondary level, including Oatridge (Lothians), Lawers (Perth), Elmwood (Fife), Barony (Dumfries) and Balmacara House (Wester Ross). However, these were either closed or later merged with the Scottish Agricultural College to form the Scottish Rural University College in 2012. At higher level, the North of Scotland, West of Scotland and East of Scotland Colleges of Agriculture were established in the late nineteenth and early twentieth centuries and became closely associated with their nearby universities (Aberdeen, Glasgow and Edinburgh respectively) after the universities established chairs of agriculture and degree courses in the early twentieth century. This system meant a close and fruitful relationship during most of the twentieth century between the colleges delivering practical education at diploma and later first degree level, the research activities related to agriculture, and the extension service, which was also operated by the three colleges. In addition, there are a number of agriculture and food-related research institutes in Scotland, including the Hutton Institute,[78] the Moredun Institute and the Rowett Institute. Together, the agriculture, food and environment research institutes have annual funding from the Scottish Government of around £50 million a year. In addition, there is research funding from the EU Framework Programmes for RDT&I, the UK Research Councils, foundations and private sources, so that the total is probably not very different from that in Norway today.

AGRICULTURAL DILEMMAS TODAY

Many writers and organisations today believe that the world stands on the threshold of a climate crisis, a food and nutrition crisis, an energy and an environmental crisis, all of which are inter-linked, and all of which have some roots in the second agrarian revolution that we have discussed in this chapter.[79] For both Norway and Scotland, livestock represents a major part of agricultural output and value-added, and the livestock industry represents a major part of the problems referred to above. However, the problems referred to are also deeply linked to crop-farming.

The twenty-first century promises a higher global population, and climate change and considerable global political changes. In this context, providing everyone with a sustainable and sufficiently nutritious diet represents one of the great challenges of the century. The challenge coincides with the emergence of global rules – Trade Related International Property Rights (TRIPS) – that will affect our ability to meet this challenge. Among other things, the proposed Transatlantic Trade and Investment Partnership (TTIP) agreement between the EU and the USA is an effort to strengthen the future clout of two key players and their large food corporations in TRIPS in terms of WTO rules, and Norway and Scotland will both be subject to this agreement. TTIP is also the forum within which the USA seeks greater market access and laxer European rules for their food products, including GMO-based products.

Two main paradigms are being proposed to meet the food and nutrition challenges.[80] The first, and the one being promoted by the key commercial and political interests behind TRIPS and the application of patents to genetic materials, as well as some 'hard' scientists,

> involves a highly technological, highly controlled, broad application, wide adaptation approach . . . with large production units and professionalized supply systems from inputs and seeds to final consumers. This future is more monocultural, industrial, corporate-dominated and dependent on IP [intellectual property].[81]

The second involves an 'ecologically integrated paradigm' that 'recognises mutual dependencies, symbiotic relationships, and more subtle forms of manipulation, and . . . aims to preserve ecological diversity'. It promotes diversity, producer–consumer links, and 'favours the micro, small and medium-sized enterprises rather than the transnational'. Local takes priority over global: 'It promotes organic, integrated pest management, low external inputs, more skilled, open systems of exchange, family-based biodiverse farming, healthy diets, and keeping cooking and farming skills alive from farm to flat.' It favours an open-source regime over an IP regime in relation to food.[82] Among supporters of this paradigm are those who favour a diet with a higher proportion of vegetables and a lower proportion of meat, especially meat based on feedingstuffs that compete with human food, such as cereals and vegetables, for land.

The current IP regime provides incentives for innovation by large commercial interests[83] and favours the first paradigm over the second. However, such a solution causes problems for both Norway and Scotland because of the relative importance of small farmers and crofters on the one hand and higher dependence on livestock sectors on the other, especially in more vulnerable rural areas.

The tendency among policy-makers and hard scientific organisations and interests is to follow the 'productivist' option. However, this will not necessarily be a politically, socially, economically or environmentally feasible option in either country in the medium and long term. Both countries are therefore potentially interested in alternative paradigms, such as the second paradigm mentioned above or variants of it. These alternative paradigms are generally seen more positively by environmental and social interests as well, and so are likely to be more politically legitimate.

Both Scotland and Norway are also quite dependent on food- and drink-manufacturing industries for internal and external markets. In Scotland, food- and drink-manufacturing accounts for 29 per cent of Scottish manufacturing exports and gross value-added, and 25 per cent of all manufacturing employment. The Norwegian food and drink industry accounts for 18 per cent of value-added and 21 per cent of all manufacturing employment.[84] The processing of fish constitutes about 20 per cent of employment and value-added in the food and drink industry. The Norwegian agri-food-processing industry concentrates on the domestic market, while the fish-based industry is largely export-oriented.

Cross-border trade with neighbouring Sweden presents something of a challenge because of the higher price levels in Norway, and something similar may be faced in an independent Scotland, although if both Scotland and England remain in the EU such problems would be avoided by the common policy and tariff regime. During the past decade there has been an increase in cross-border shopping, that is, Norwegians travelling to Sweden to buy food products such as meat and cheese. One of the major issues of the Report to the *Storting* No. 19 (1999–2000) was that the target prices should be kept low enough so that the price difference between Norway and the EU (including the neighbouring countries of Denmark and Sweden) did not increase. Important goals were to keep Norwegian food prices under control, enable market balance and maintain the competitiveness of the Norwegian food industry.

As of 1 July 2001, the value-added tax on foods was reduced from the general rate of 24 per cent to 12 per cent, that is, to the same level as in Sweden. This measure was mainly introduced to reduce consumer food prices and thus limit Norwegian border trade in Sweden and Denmark. Even though consumer prices did fall as expected, cross-border shopping continued to increase. After several changes the VAT rate on food is now 15 per cent, while the general rate is 25 per cent. The cross-border trade is influenced by differences in taxation of alcohol and tobacco, not only differences in agricultural policy and prices and exchange rates.

The subsidy regimes in Scotland and Norway have become more similar in recent years, with a much higher proportion of support coming in the form of direct payments and payments for environmental activities and services of one kind or another. In the end that means increasing taxpayer-funding, since high tariffs are forbidden under the WTO regime. In order to sustain such high tax-payer support, policies must be seen to be legitimate. The science-IPR regime is less likely to be seen in this way.

In addition, though, Norway, unlike Scotland, has used tax relief as an element in agricultural policy. For the fiscal year 2013, the income allowance consisted of a flat-rate base allowance of NOK 63,500 per holding and an additional allowance of 38 per cent of agricultural income higher than NOK 63,500. The maximum allowance is NOK 166,400, which is obtained if the income is NOK 332,100. Income from production of bio-energy from wood can be included when estimating the allowance.

CONCLUSIONS

The historical, social, economic and political processes reviewed in this chapter and in Chapter 1 seem to provide a useful framework for understanding the considerable differences between Scotland and Norway in terms of the evolution of landownership, agricultural structures, income and settlement patterns, and agricultural production and its regional distribution. Running throughout are the differences, perhaps in degree rather than anything else, in geography, size and latitude. At the root of the differences are the differences in land ownership and tenure that impacted also on the nature of agrarian change, settlement patterns and farmers' role in politics, as well as the ultimate outcomes in terms of policies and the political system as a whole. In turn, these differences go back at least to the medieval period, the power of the landed aristocracy, and the fate of pre-Reformation church land, all influenced by incorporation in larger political entities – Sweden and Denmark between the fifteenth and nineteenth centuries in the case of Norway, and England and the United Kingdom in the case of Scotland.

These long-term and emergent processes and the differences they have created are likely to have ongoing implications for the different ways that Scotland and

Norway handle present and future dilemmas in relation to the CAP and global trade issues, which now dominate agricultural policy.

Notes

1. This compares with 49,783 holdings in the 2000 census, 31,413 significant holdings in the 1980 census and 61,911 holdings in the 1959 census (Bryden, 1985).
2. Hegrenes et al., 2012: 49.
3. Rognstad and Steinset, 2012: 100.
4. Collier (1953) gives some data for 1938 for non-croft family income in three areas of the Highlands and Islands.
5. See, for example, Jan Dowe Van der Ploeg's fine study of the 'Virtual Farmer', a product of the 'expert system' that creates the kind of hegemonic view of what policy should aim at, and leads to a kind of hegemonic view of future agrarian development paths (Van der Ploeg, 2003).
6. For example, Shucksmith et al. (1991) and Dalton et al. (1995).
7. This average does, however, exclude crofting common grazings in the Highlands and Islands, which amount to about half a million hectares.
8. A measure of farm business size based on standardised gross margins.
9. Economic Report on Scottish Agriculture, 2013 edition.
10. More than one-third of the feed uptake for sheep is probably from *utmark*.
11. Kane and Mann, 1992.
12. The Annual Review and Determination of Guarantees. The National Farmers' Union of Scotland (but none of the then crofting unions) was party to these negotiations, along with the Farmers' Union for England and Wales.
13. Devine, 1999: 130.
14. Ibid.: 130.
15. Smout, 1963.
16. Devine, 1999: 128.
17. Smout, 2012: 135.
18. See, for example, Roy Campbell (1971: 24). Campbell is an enthusiastic supporter of the 'improver movement'.
19. Carter, 1979: 179.
20. Fiona MacKenzie cites a nice phrase from Anne Frater's poem, *Aig an Fhaing/At the Fank*: 'The nails of improvement have left me stiff in the wind.' Pers.Comm.
21. Devine, 1999: 134.
22. Youngson, 1973: 153–60.
23. Devine, 1999: 134, 137.
24. James Small was a native of Berwickshire who started as an apprentice carpenter and plough-maker, and later wrote a *Treatise on Ploughs and Wheel Carriages* (1784). He was familiar with the early Rotherham Plough introduced in 1730. The latter is illustrated in Higgs (1965), Plate 101. See also Handley, 1953: 217.
25. See Handley, 1953: 218–19. Hadley tells us that it was Andrew's father, James, who went to Holland in 1710 on the advice of Andrew Fletcher of Saltoun in East Lothian, who wanted to transfer the Dutch inventions. Fletcher was an exception to what Smout (2012: 127) calls the 'culture of disinterest' in agrarian

improvement in 1700, his private library – the second-largest private library in the British Isles at the time – having ten volumes on husbandry.

26. The Highland and Agricultural Society of Scotland offered a prize for the invention of a reaping machine in 1803, and two Scots, Gladstone from Castle Douglas in Kirkcudbrightshire and Smith from Deanstone in Stirlingshire, produced reaping machines based on rotary cutters. However, it was Patrick Bell from Angus who invented the 'mechanised scissor' type of cutting blade still used today. By 1832, at least ten of his machines were in use in east-central Scotland (Fenton, 1987: 114–15).

27. Fenton, 1987: 116.

28. Lavergne visited England, Scotland and Ireland four times between 1848 and 1854. His original book was in French and first published in 1854. See Lavergne, 1855: 285.

29. Orwin and Wetham, 1964: 114.

30. The Dutch agrarian historian Slicher Van Bath (1962: 302) cites Lavoisier's estimates that an eighteenth-century day-labourer who worked 200 days a year would spend 28 days on the cereal harvest, 24 days on hay-making and carting, and 130 days on threshing. Lavoisier's estimates are in turn found in Labrousse, 1932: 503, n.1.

31. Van Bath, 1963; Tracy, 1982.

32. Lunden, 2004: 178.

33. Taugbøl, 2013; Bull and Tvedt, 2013; see also Chapter 7.

34. Tracy, 1982: 19.

35. Tracy, 1982: 25–6.

36. A 'deficiency payment' bridges the gap between import prices and guaranteed prices, and it became the basis for market support to most of British agriculture after the Second World War and up until EEC entry in 1972.

37. Grimley, 1937: 79–80.

38. Grimley, 1937: 79.

39. Tracy, 1982: 232.

40. The evidence was drawn from farm accounts supplied by cooperating farmers to the Colleges of Agriculture in Scotland, which then provided data for each farm type to government and the unions. This eventually became known – and still exists in the EU as – the Farm Accountancy Data Network or FADN. Norway is not part of this system but has a similar system and the data is gathered by NILF.

41. Norway has an annual review process and data is prepared by the Agricultural Budgeting Committee.

42. Bryden (1985: 141–4) discusses three periods in post-war agricultural policy; what follows draws on that and updates it.

43. Tracy, 1982: 233–4.

44. Rt Hon. Selwyn Lloyd, MP reported in *Farming Leader*, NFUS, Edinburgh, 1 September 1961. Cited in Bryden, 1985: 141.

45. Bryden, 1985: 145.

46. France, Germany, Italy and the Benelux countries. See also Tracy (1982) for the evolution of EC Agricultural Policy after the Treaty of Rome, which laid down its aims, and the Stresa Conference which agreed its principles and key elements.

47. Annual Review and Determination of Guarantees, 1971. Cmd.4623. London, HMSO.
48. For a detailed account, see Bryden et al.: 2012.
49. Aresvik, 1954; Gjerdåker, 2004: 270–1.
50. Hovland, 1990: 120.
51. St. prp. Nr 8 (1992–3).
52. Lidtveit, 1979: 456.
53. For example, Landbruks- og matdepartementet, 2011: 116.
54. Ian Carter (1979) studied farm life in north-east Scotland between 1840 and 1914, while Jim Hunter (1976) studied the making of the crofting community in the Highlands and Islands, Tom Devine (1996) studied farm servants and labour in lowland Scotland between 1770 and 1914, while John Bryden and George Houston (1976) studied agrarian change in the Scottish Highlands, to name but a few.
55. See Bryden, 1985; 1995.
56. Shucksmith et al., 2005.
57. Bryden, 1985: 142.
58. The work on the CAP and the regions edited by Mark Shucksmith, Ken Thomson and Deb Roberts supports the regional concentration thesis at EU level, for example (Shucksmith et al.,2005).
59. MacSharry, R. (1991), Foreword to *The Development and Future of the Common Agricultural Policy: proposals from the Commission*, Brussels: Commission of the European Communities, 2/91. The issue was also discussed in the earlier Reflections Paper, published in February 1991.
60. See Frank Fraser Darling's *West Highland Survey* (1955).
61. See Mackenzie (1965), whose work was partially updated for 1971/2 by Bryden and Houston (1976).
62. Bryden, 1985: 157.
63. A Cropping Grant was also given to crofters up until about 1972.
64. Binswanger, 1986: 38.
65. Although discussing the different context of the USA, Olmstead and Rhode (2001: 2) estimate that a working farmhorse required 3 acres of cropland for feed each year.
66. Tveite: 1990.
67. NOS X 103: 238–41.
68. NOS XI 308: 58.
69. Handley (1953: 225, n.1) cites Sir John Sinclair that Bakewell 'often declared that he wished he had laid the foundations of his improved breed with the Kyloe, or West Highland cattle, for they wanted nothing but size to be perfect'.
70. Handley, 1953: 221–4.
71. Bryden, 1985: 152.
72. See also http://www.jarlsberg.com/about-tine (last accessed 31 March 2014).
73. Nortura's short presentation of its history can be retrieved from http://www.nortura.no/historie_2/ (last accessed 31 March 2014).
74. See Kile, 1997: Chapter II.
75. Landbruksskole (22 February 2013). I Store norske leksikon. Last Accessed 25 February 2014 from http://snl.np/landbruksskole.

76. The upper secondary schools aim at the 16–18 age group. The name of the responsible ministry has changed several times. We refer to function more than the name of the department.
77. Landbruks- og matdepartementet, 2011b: 59.
78. The Macaulay Land Use Research Institute and Scottish Crop Research Institute joined forces on 1 April 2011 to create the James Hutton Institute.
79. McCalla, 1994; FAO, 13 June 2011. The Save and Grow Programme. See http://www.fao.org/news/story/en/item/80096/icode/ (last accessed 2 April 2014); UNEP, 2011.
80. Tansey and Rajotte, 2008; Lang and Heasman, 2004. These issues are also much discussed by NGOs, including OXFAM, World Development Movement and Action Aid.
81. Tansey and Rajotte, 2008: 215; Lang and Heasman, 2004.
82. Lang and Heasman, 2004; Tansey and Rajotte, 2008: 215.
83. See, for example, Winson (1993), who stresses the increasing dominance of the 'agribusiness complex'.
84. Rålm, 2013.

CHAPTER 5

The Evolution of Local Government and Governance in Scotland and Norway

John Bryden, Eberhard Bort and Karen Refsgaard

INTRODUCTION

Local governance is one of the key areas flagged up whenever the 'Nordic model' is being compared to the UK or Scotland. In this chapter we discuss the main political, social and economic factors and processes that explain the very different structures of local governance and powers and autonomy of local government in Norway and Scotland today.

Our story starts in the medieval period, when functions of local governance in both Scotland and Norway were essentially divided between the monarch's secular local supporters and appointees, and the organs of Church government, centred around the parish. Local governance was very important in this period because communications by land and sea were slow, difficult and dangerous, and centralised governance was impossible. The kingdoms were also fragile, and support from local powerholders had to be won, and kept.

The Reformation did not greatly change the nature of local governance, especially those functions accorded to the Church, which included providing subsistence to the poor and maimed, and in the later period schools as well as certain quasi-judicial matters, especially before the Enlightenment when moral offences were punished by the congregational 'courts',[1] the most severe punishment being banishment or exile.

However, the nature of local government changed in the late eighteenth and nineteenth centuries, in Scotland following Union with England in 1707 and nineteenth-century extensions of the franchise, and in Norway after independence from Denmark in 1814. Our focus in this chapter is mainly on this period and subsequent major reforms, partly associated with the extension of the franchise in the later nineteenth and early twentieth centuries. However, we also examine and describe the structure, functions, powers and financing of local government in Scotland and Norway today, highlighting some of the key differences, and the political, economic and social consequences of these differences in the context of devolution and the independence referendum.

MEDIEVAL LOCAL GOVERNANCE IN SCOTLAND AND NORWAY

Although accounts of early local government and governance in Scotland and Norway are rare, the available historical evidence suggests that they had similar origins. Both countries were founded when central monarchical governments were weak and contested, both had large and difficult terrain and geography, and sparsely settled and small populations, implying difficulties of communication and central control, and both were experiencing emerging nationhood and national identity. In medieval times, social organisation was around kinship, clans being the Scottish term. Clans sometimes fought for kings or would-be kings, and often on opposite sides. National identity was weak or non-existent in the early Middle Ages. At that time in Norway, the king recruited *lendmen and årmenn*[2] from his army to be responsible for tasks related to justice, taxes and fines, and order in areas that were later designated counties (*fylker or sysler*).[3] However, Norway already had district 'parliaments' (*Ting*), such as the *Gulating* for the western coast and *Frostating* for central Norway, in the ninth century.[4] They were participatory parliaments where new laws were read to the people in the open air on a hill.[5]

As national identity became stronger and clans or families united against common enemies, monarchs appointed trusted members of the aristocracy or officials as their local administrators – in Norway known as *lensherrer* and mainly lords of Danish origin, and in Scotland as mormaers, thanes and, later, sheriffs.[6] The *lensherrer* were mainly located in the larger towns where the king's residences were, and they eventually acquired *sysselmen* to assist them in their work.[7] The Scottish equivalent was sheriffs, also until recently organised at county level, equivalent to Norway's *syssel*.

Christianity spread in Scotland under St Ninian and after St Columba had arrived from Ireland and established his monastic settlement in Iona in the mid-sixth century. Norway was converted later, mainly under Olav II, in the eleventh century. As explained in Chapter 1, the Church, including the parishes and the monasteries, became powerful in the subsequent period, at least up to the Reformation, owning much land and other property in both Scotland and Norway.

However, while Norway's landed aristocracy was weakened between the high and late Middle Ages by the processes explained in Chapter 1, this did not happen in Scotland. As a consequence, the clan chiefs and the king's appointees retained local power in Scotland,[8] and the landed aristocracy and their later replacements in the form of wealthy industrialists continued to play an important role in local as well as national government up to, and in some cases beyond, the Wheatley reforms of the 1960s.

The second party in the development of local government in both countries was the Church, especially as it evolved after 1066 in its parish governance system. The parishes survived in Scotland until the local government reforms of 1929, but were combined into the municipalities in Norway in the nineteenth century.

In Scotland, local government can be considered as having its origins in the 'sheriffdoms' created probably first by King Malcolm II in the eleventh century, and certainly by Alexander I and David I in the twelfth century,[9] although it must be remembered that at this time the inner and outer Hebrides and the Orkney and Shetland islands, as well as Caithness and Sutherland and parts of Argyll, were still ruled by Norwegian earls, and to a large extent under the control of the Archbishop of Nidaros (Trondheim) for Church matters, while other parts of the Highlands were run by clan chiefs. However, in mainland Scotland, at least south and east of the 'Highlands', the early thanages and sheriffdoms formed the basis for 'shires',[10] which became known only much later as counties. King David I created the first royal burghs in the twelfth century.[11]

In 1305, twenty-five sheriffdoms were ordained in the public ordinances.[12] The sheriffdoms were commonly sub-divided into 'districts', 'bailliaries', 'Quarters' or 'Wards'.[13] Much change apparently took place in Scotland between the tenth and the thirteenth centuries; while Innes lists only thirty-seven 'places' identified on a map showing Scotland in the tenth century, no fewer than 435 'places' were listed on a thirteenth-century map. This period followed the partial unification of the Picts and the Scots in the ninth century under Kenneth Macalpine, and the introduction of both Christianity and feudalism. Christianity brought churches, monasteries and the 'parish', in Scotland the latter coming to mean the baptismal church territory.[14] The number of shires, burghs and parishes gradually expanded, thirty-three shires being named in the Local Government (Scotland) Act of 1889, which also tidied up boundaries and definitions.[15] However, the structure of local government – parishes, shires, burghs – remained basically the same until the twentieth century.

In Norway, we have to go back to around 1500 to understand the development of the need for local governance there, and how the situation differed between rural and urban areas.

Norway's Urban Areas after 1500

From the mid-1500s, the burghers had gained a central role in the daily governance of the towns, with specified rights for business life and trade in the towns and surroundings.[16] Normally, four to six councillors (*rådmenn*) and one mayor were elected from the burghers, often the larger merchants. The mayor and the council had the responsibility for the budget, the accounts and the town tax, and also served as the higher court of law.

Throughout the seventeenth century, the King of Denmark-Norway attempted to increase his power over the town governments by delegating more authority to the *lensherrer*.[17] In 1660/1, the king introduced absolutism, at which point the burghers ceased to elect the councillors and mayor, who became the king's officials. The leader became the town clerk, which marginalised burgher power. However, the king needed the burghers' support, and Næss[18] refers to a case in Bergen where representatives for the burghers from different towns met in 1661 to plead on behalf of the towns concerning privileges and governance. Although their pleas went unheeded, in 1671 the king decided that the towns could elect a fixed number of burghers (*elegerte*) to confirm that the budget was in balance. Initially, large merchants dominated the *elegerte* but after 1800 craftsmen and others gained more influence, giving a broader representation, even if large merchants remained a dominant group.[19]

Rural Areas

In 1600 and thereafter up until about 1945, the majority of Norway's population lived in rural areas (see Figure 6.2 in Chapter 6).[20]

Until 1837, local governance in rural areas was very different from that of the towns. Rural communities had been split into secular and clerical administrative areas since the 1600s. In the lowest secular tier (*Skipreide*), the governing assembly (*Ting*) decided local disputes and enforced documents.[21] In addition, the *Ting* negotiated taxes, fees and defence with the bureaucracy. Both freehold and tenant farmers were obliged to meet at the *Ting*, but decisions were made by a committee of six or twelve jury men (*lagrettsmenn*), mostly coming from resourceful and powerful families.[22] The *Skipreide* was administered by an official (*Fogd*) from 1660, but the laws were given by the king in Denmark and often not adjusted to Norwegian conditions. Eventually, the king employed local sworn scribes (*sorenskriver*) who later became the administrators and judges[23] to help farmers with complicated cases, while the jury men lost influence. In the 1790s, the farmers gained more power and responsibility – partly to save the authorities costs caused by an increase in the number of petty cases. Private disputes were then dealt with by a lay magistrate (a farmer) and a civil servant in a so-called conciliation commission (*forlikskommisjon*),[24] which in some cases would be the *lensman* and the minister – in other cases not.

Alongside the secular *Skipreide*, the clerical parish dealt with support for the poor and the school system. In the mid-1700s, absolutism took initiatives to remedy the problem of the poor but, in practice, the work had to be done by the local bureaucracy. Further, the introduction of confirmation in 1736 implied a need for (Christian) education. The ministers were given the main responsibility to organise the poor and the school system in rural areas, and also chaired these commissions, the costs of which were met by the farmers. The farmers therefore became members of the poor and school commissions in rural areas in addition to the sheriff or the bailiff.

THE EVOLUTION OF LOCAL GOVERNMENT IN NORWAY AND SCOTLAND IN THE MODERN PERIOD

It is after 1800 that we see the greatest divergence in local government and governance systems in Scotland and Norway. In Norway, the mainly rural population of small farmers and farmer-fishermen and their families dominated. For them, strong local government, founded first on the small local municipalities and then on the counties, was seen as a way of distancing the elite from local decisions and diminishing central power after independence in 1814.[25]

Scotland, by contrast, ceased to be an independent nation after the Union of Parliaments in 1707. The Union of Parliaments was not popular, and riots broke out in Edinburgh, Glasgow and elsewhere, while the Jacobites, still powerful in the north and west, remained wholly opposed to the Union, supported by England's main enemy of the time, France.[26] England very much needed and wanted the Union in order to advance its military and colonial ambitions,[27] while the unrepresentative members of the then Scottish Parliament were more susceptible to English bribes[28] and blandishments – 'bought and sold by English gold', as Robert Burns would have it[29] – than to popular opinion.[30] Especially after the 1715 and 1745 'Jacobite' rebellions, the English extended their military control of Scotland, which suffered from a political vacuum. Post-Union local government was dominated by the Kirk (also guaranteed in the Union) and landed interests favourable to the regime in London. However, London was preoccupied with managing the British Empire rather than micro-managing Scotland and, as Smellie observed about nineteenth-century England, it had 'no Ministry of the Interior able to manipulate the political and administrative life of local areas in the interest of the government of the day'.[31] This situation only changed with the advance of transport and communication technology and the concomitant centralisation brought about by the two world wars and the introduction of the (centralised) welfare state in the twentieth century. While the UK (and Scotland) was, until the late nineteenth century, one of the most decentralised countries in Europe,[32] less than a hundred years later it had become one of the most centralised.

Norway's Freedom Letter (Frihetsbrevet)

The defining moment for modern local government in Norway was its separation from Denmark in 1814. Several attempts followed thereafter to get a Local Government Act. Shortly after 1814, an effort was made to introduce a more coherent system in the Legislative Committee of the Parliament, and in 1821 a proposal for rural local government similar to that in the towns was introduced in Parliament. However, many officials criticised these initiatives, arguing that farmers lacked the ability and knowledge to deal with public issues. In 1830–1, the liberal-minded minister Jonas Collett proposed a law with government at county as well as local level and open meetings, but it was not approved by the king and the ministry in Stockholm. The larger[33] farmers then made an alternative proposal which would give most power to the local authorities and no supervision by local bureaucrats, county governors or central government, but also without open meetings.[34] Steen perceives Collett's proposal as aiming for the ultimate goal of 'the self-sufficiency society',[35] by which he meant 'the need to govern the contributions to the public purse within the local units in order to reduce these contributions to the least necessary'. The final law, sanctioned by the king on 14 January 1837, was a compromise, with representative government rather than direct democracy. As Næss concludes, the fact that farmers had had experience as jury men, sheriffs and lay judges gave them influence in the local community and prepared them for work in local government.[36]

Norway's Local Government Act – 1837 and Beyond

The Local Government Act consisted of two parts, one for the towns and one for the rural areas: *Lov om Formandskaber paa Landet samt om Bestyrelsen av Districternes almindelige Commune-Anliggender* and *Lov om Formandskaber i Kiøbstæderne*. The law for the rural areas also included the regulations for the county. The Local Government Act must be seen first and foremost as a constitution for the municipalities.[37] It clarified the territories, institutionalised the governance bodies, laid down rules for the municipal governance procedures, drew up the limits for the municipalities' independent competence and regulated the relationship between municipality and state.

As in the 1814 Norwegian Constitution, representation was the major principle. The 1837 Act called for direct elections to a local governing body, and an indirect election by the council for the mayor and executive body, with elections every fourth year. The executive had considerable power[38] but the full council had to approve all cases where municipal operations were discussed and where economic decisions were made.

The common definition of a municipality today, according to Hovland, is a locally delimited public community, subject to the state. It is a delimited geographical area where the inhabitants are organised in a community with rights and duties.[39] This community or municipality is an individual legal entity, which can contract debts and accumulate wealth. For the towns, the creation of the municipalities in 1837 was more or less based on the existing management units. The challenges of distinct boundaries were greater in the rural areas: initially, the legislators were inclined to build on the old secular districts (*Tinglagene*) but this approach was soon dropped and the clerical parish normally became the municipal unit. As Hovland argues, this was a natural unit, as the management of both schools and the poor was closely integrated with the church parish governance.[40]

The county executive was formed by the rural municipal mayors. The county governor had a veto and certain other powers, although only at the first reading in a local government. In cases with large economic impact it was left to the king to approve the decision, that is, when the municipality was obliged to make payments for more than five years, as in new long-term jobs or loans.

Three levels of rural governance were established in 1837: the parish municipality (*prestegjeld*), the sub-parish municipality (*sogn*) and the county, which were all called 'general municipalities', being responsible for legislation and governance.[41] This was to distinguish them from the 'special municipalities' which were responsible for roads, the church, schools and the poor. The latter had a combined local government where the former professional members (the minister, the constable and the clergy) sat together with the councillors. These special municipalities were subject to economic control by the general municipality, which also appointed their treasurer and auditors. The county level of local government was a kind of superstructure for the rural municipalities with responsibility for tasks that were too large for them. The primary tasks here included responsibility for the judicial system, the health system and the roads. The town municipalities were not part of this authority.

The 1837 Act led to 392 new local government units, of which 355 were classified as rural and thirty-seven as urban.[42] The rural population remained dominant at this time, and rural interests were also relatively strong in the Parliament. As such, decentralisation was very much a part of the Norwegian independence process. Transfer of power to the local authorities was one way to break the dominance of the former elite and related foreign influence.

Participation in the Elections

The national franchise also applied at local levels. Article 50 of the Constitution limited the right to vote at national and municipal levels to men over the age of twenty-five, being township citizens, senior officials or farmers with ownership or leasehold of land. In 1814, 40 to 45 per cent of males over twenty-five had the right to vote in parliamentary elections.[43] Although this proportion decreased during the nineteenth century due to an increase in the number of landless labourers and property-less people, the Norwegian Constitution has remained one of the most radical and democratic in Europe.[44]

In rural areas, it was mainly the larger farmers, constables and teachers who voted, while ordinary farmers were less interested. Even fewer voted in local government elections than in national elections. In rural areas, between 10 and 30 per cent voted in the 1840s and 1850s. Steen argues that this might have been due to lack of knowledge of the impacts, which might also have been the case in the towns, where even fewer voted – often only between a third and a fifth of the electors.[45]

According to Steen,[46] the socially and economically better off, such as larger farmers, dominated both the executive and the council, while ordinary farmers and other 'small people' were less represented. In about one-third of the rural municipalities, the minister was elected as mayor, reflecting old paternalistic customs, where the minister was the leader on municipal issues. However, from the 1860s onwards, the balance changed. Many of those who had been part of the earlier councils or commissions were also the first ones to be elected to local governments. By 1862, the number of farmers who were mayors had increased to 73 per cent, and the number of teachers who became mayors also increased as they were the most literate rural men. Furthermore, the representatives, functioning as a parliament, gradually gained more power, while the executive increasingly functioned as the government.

Different reasons are given for the introduction of local government in Norway through the *Formannskapslovene* of 1837.[47] Some argue that it was inspired by the liberal ideas of the French Revolution, where local governance was seen as a way of liberating people from central government's control. In Cappelen Dam[48] it is argued that, as nearly half of the MPs of *Stortinget* were farmers in 1833, the lack of democratic determination at local level, where the bureaucracy dominated, became ever more obvious, leading the farmers to demand change. For others, local governance was regarded as a locally initiated administrative apparatus to be used as an instrument of central government to implement its policies. Over time, the idea that local governance was a necessary element of a democratic political system became more or less taken for granted.[49] The establishment of local authorities and related institutional structures offered a training ground for local governance and democratic practice,[50] even if suffrage and participation were initially restricted. The basic principles underpinning local government in 1837 have persisted until today, such as direct elections to a council, local political government basically ruled by laymen, representative government in councils as well as executive boards and standing committees, a basic organising principle with collegiate decision-making, and a system with three levels, the national, county and municipal.[51]

After 1837, a more homogenous institutional and economic foundation emerged for the increasing exercise of local governance that reconciled the bureaucratic and democratic elements.[52] This process included subordination of the special municipalities within the municipal council, more uniform taxation procedures, and settlement of property and income as the main tax base. The municipal taxation laws were completed in 1882.[53] The strong municipal tax powers meant that by 1910 municipal taxes accounted for around 85 per cent of total direct taxation.[54] In 1911, an upper level was set for the municipal taxation and the proportion decreased following the First World War.

This strengthening of the municipalities was first motivated by needs for improvement in the sanitary sectors. Later, the development of hospitals, infrastructure for power and communication by municipal monopolies and emerging social policies became important drivers. Consequently, in 1896 the municipal franchise was freed from the constitutional rules for national elections and extended to a much larger proportion of the male population, qualified only by a rather low income level.[55]

Women also started to act more politically at this time, and in 1884 Norwegian women founded the Nordic countries' first society for women's suffrage.[56] In 1901, men got general – and women limited – suffrage to local authorities and then, finally, in 1910 women achieved full civic suffrage in local elections[57] followed by universal suffrage in 1913.[58]

The 392 authorities established in 1837 increased to 722 during the period up to 1950. However, during the 1960s many amalgamations took place, reducing the number to 443 by 1975. These were a result of government decisions, and caused by changes in communications and demography. Nevertheless, the most important development was the recognition that some of the existing units were too small to be able to take effective responsibility for the new welfare state reforms, such as the introduction of nine-year elementary schools and nursing homes for elderly people.[59]

The Emergence of Local Government in Scotland

In Scotland, by then fully absorbed into the United Kingdom, the 1889 Local Government Act laid the foundations for the 'modern' local government systems.[60] At this time, the following local government authorities appear to have been active in Scotland:

      4 Counties of Cities
     21 Large Burghs
    176 Small Burghs
     33 Counties
    878 or thereby Parishes[61]

The parishes were abolished as local government entities in 1929, and 196 county or landward districts were introduced in the same year. The functions of the parishes were transferred to the remaining 430 local government entities, while the smaller burghs lost some power to the counties. The reform of 1929 'swept away many small units of local government and transferred their responsibilities to county and burgh councils'.[62] A pattern of logic was evolving which increasingly accepted the primacy of (alleged, but never proven) improvements in efficiency over a strong local democracy: 'While many, mostly Liberals and Labour, deplored the elimination of small local democratic institutions, the government stressed the gains in efficiency and professionalism that would ensue.'[63]

This was essentially the situation up to the time of the Wheatley Commission[64] on Local Government in Scotland (1966–9), which led to the 1974 reform of local government in Scotland:

> Wheatley recommended the creation of seven new regional authorities, with responsibility for strategic services, the major local government functions of police, fire, water and sewerage, roads and transport, education, social work, housing and planning; and 37 district councils responsible for environmental and amenity services of a local nature. Recommendations were also made for a system of community councils with consultative powers to act as a voice for local communities.[65]

Following the 1974 reforms, Scottish local government had two tiers consisting of nine regional councils, fifty-three district councils, and three all-purpose island councils serving Orkney, Shetland and the Western Isles, having the functions of both regions and districts elsewhere. Regional councils were responsible for major functions such as education, transport and strategic planning, while more localised functions such as urban recreation, housing, libraries, development control and local planning were the responsibility of district councils. Meanwhile, especially from the 1970s onwards, local government lost powers in the domains of the environment, water and sewerage, economic development, public housing, health and policing, all of which were transferred to quasi-autonomous public bodies (Quangos), or NDPBs[66] as they are known today. These included Scottish Natural Heritage, the Scottish Development Agency, the Highlands and Islands Development Board, Scottish Water and Scottish Homes.[67] Industrial and regional development powers were also exercised by central government.

LOCAL GOVERNMENT IN SCOTLAND TODAY

The structure of Scottish local government today resulted from the Local Government (Scotland) Act 1994. The subsequent 1996 reorganisation abolished the nine regions and fifty-three districts and replaced them with twenty-nine single-tier bodies, the three unitary island councils remaining unchanged. The argument was that single-tier authorities would result in a more economic, cohesive, accountable and effective system. These thirty-two councils are responsible for all the local government services formerly administered by their predecessors, with two main exceptions: water and sewerage passed to Scottish Water, a centralised and unelected NDPB; and the reporters to Children's Panels were also recentralised. Harvie[68] summed up the effect: 'Since councillors were fewer, and as many formerly regional functions were now carried out by joint boards or the new water authorities, government was even more remote.' Riddoch[69] gives an example:

The Highland Council covers an area the size of Belgium with a population the size of Belfast. Councillors drive hundreds of thousands of miles a year to create a sense of connection through meetings, surgeries and local events. Despite such superhuman efforts, many remote communities still feel excluded – reduced to questioning, suspecting and vetoing whatever emanates from the centre.

Meanwhile, the Labour government elected to Westminster in 1997 saw through the Scottish Devolution Bill in 1998, giving Scotland its first parliament in nearly three hundred years – but this time with universal suffrage and a proportional representation system more like the Nordic system. This limited devolution of powers to Scotland represented an important contextual shift.

While it was understandable that the new Scottish Parliament in its early years refrained from fundamentally reorganising local government (the system was still reeling from the Tory reform of 1994/6), it established the McIntosh Commission,[70] followed by the Kerley Commission, and in the second session passed the Local Government Bill, introducing proportional representation through STV, the single transferable vote. This had 'large repercussions on the balance of influence within the Scottish body politic', as it destroyed 'the one-party municipalities which are the power base of the Labour machine'.[71] Indeed, Labour was returned in overall control of just two councils, rather than thirteen, as in 2003,[72] and a majority of voters gave preferences to candidates from more than one party.[73] It was an important step with regard to the electoral system but otherwise hardly a bold change in the power relations concerning local government. Apart from introducing STV for local government elections from 2007, the Local Government (Scotland) Act 2003 made the following provisions:

- Lowering the age at which people can stand as a councillor from twenty-one to eighteen;
- Removing unnecessary political restrictions on council employees standing for local authority elections;
- Establishing an independent remuneration committee for councillors;
- Reducing to three months the period during which most former councillors are able to take up employment with the council after their period of service as a councillor comes to an end;
- A one-off severance payment to councillors who decide not to stand at the next local government election;
- Powers to introduce a pension scheme for councillors that allows future service to count for pension purposes.

There are at least four other important contextual points to note about local government in Scotland when comparing it with Norway or indeed other countries. First, local governments are 'creatures of Statute' and the doctrine of *ultra vires* is of crucial constitutional importance. This means that a local authority must be able to point to specific statutory authorisation for everything it does, a situation that contrasts with that in continental Europe and elsewhere.[74] It also means that local governments occupy an ambivalent position in the democratic arena, since they are creatures of central government, and answerable to it, as well as being locally elected. Devolution did not change that relationship:

> local councils have the same constitutional, statutory and legal limitations on the extent of their independent activities as before devolution. They are constitutionally just as subordinate to Scotland's devolved institutions as they were to the Scottish Office and the UK parliament.[75]

Secondly, Scotland is, as a consequence of the Act of Union of 1707, part of the United Kingdom and, although it has a different structure of local government, it is subject to essentially the same legal and constitutional framework.

Scotland, as part of the United Kingdom, is also a member of the European Union. The devolved parliament is constrained by the single market and the common security area throughout the whole of the United Kingdom, as well as the welfare state settlement and membership of the European Union.[76] Such factors 'encourage policy convergence with the rest of the United Kingdom'.[77] Scotland's capacity to fund such policies as free personal care for the elderly and the abolition of university tuition fees 'relies heavily on favourable financial decisions made at Westminster, due to the workings of the Barnett formula'.[78]

Thirdly, and most importantly, the process of transferring power from local government to statutory agencies, noted in the Wheatley report, has continued largely unabated into recent times. This concerns the steady loss of powers, functions and budgets relating to public health, hospitals, water and sewerage, environment, countryside, countryside recreation, tourism, public transport, airports, economic development, police, children's panels and housing. However, although there has been a process of centralisation, 'quangoisation' and privatisation, hollowing out local democracy, this has been accompanied by a rhetoric of 'decentralisation'. This has meant some transfer of responsibilities as a consequence of 'downsizing' of the State during and after the Thatcher period, for example for 'care in the community' of people formerly in public institutions. In some cases this 'downsizing' has involved non-governmental institutions (voluntary organisations becoming quasi providers of public services), in others it has been partial or complete privatisation. In Scotland, as elsewhere, there is a debate about the impact of 'new public management' enshrined in ideas of partnerships, modernisation and the 'new way' but ideologically rooted in the unilineal 'Washington Consensus' discourses of welfare state reform, competition and enterprise, and globalisation. On the one hand there is a rhetoric of 'decentralisation'; on the other a reality of great centralised control and management through targets, performance indicators or, under the SNP government, 'concordats' and 'outcome agreements.'

Fourthly, it is important to recall that although some women were able to vote in Scottish local government elections from 1881, universal and equal voting rights to all adults were not granted in the UK until 1928. However, although the UK parliament in 2010 had only 21 per cent women, the Scottish Parliament had 34 per cent in the 2011 elections.[79] The figures in Scottish local government are less impressive, with only 23.4 per cent women candidates, and 24.3 per cent elected in 2012.[80] Women lost out under the old 'first past the post' electoral system but the introduction of STV in the 2007 elections has not yet led to any substantial improvement. We return to discuss some of these issues in greater detail later.

THE DIVISION OF POWER IN SCOTLAND

As explained earlier, the formal powers are granted to local governments by central government, and their activities are constrained by these powers, as well as by finance. Before 1999, all legislation affecting local government in Scotland emanated from the UK Parliament. The Scottish Office played some role in shaping that legislation but had no legislative power in its own right. Following the Scotland Act 1998 and the subsequent establishment of the Scottish Parliament on 1 July 1999, the Scottish Parliament has the power to enact legislation relevant to local government in Scotland but local authorities may only act within the powers bestowed upon them by the Scottish Parliament. In practice, however, most of the legislation relating to structures and functions of local authorities was previously established by Westminster.

Midwinter[81] sums up the 'essential characteristics' of local government in Scotland:

- councils are directly elected by popular franchise;
- they are multi-purpose;
- they have responsibility for service provision within a defined geographic area;
- they may only act within the specific powers set by Parliament;
- they have power to raise local taxation (council tax is roughly 20 per cent of local government expenditure);
- they are corporate bodies whose powers are vested in the whole council.

Local authorities in Scotland have a range of mandatory and permissive powers. Mandatory powers include 'the provision of schooling for all 5- to 16-year olds; provision of fire cover; promotion of certain social work services; provision of housing for the homeless; making arrangements to secure Best Value; and, initiating and facilitating Community Planning'.[82] In addition, local authorities 'have a range of permissive powers, which they are legally allowed to exercise, but are not required to do. These include: giving permission for civil marriages to take place in venues other than local registrars' offices; promoting economic development; promoting arts and tourism; producing local bye-laws in areas specified by ministers; and to cut service provision, as long as it does not interfere with statutory obligations.'[83]

Scottish local governments are both service providers and regulatory authorities, for example issuing licences for taxis and public houses (bars), regulating trading standards and environmental health, and also granting planning permission for new housing, offices and industrial buildings. Local authorities also perform an advocacy role, promoting the interests of their local communities, as well as fulfilling their statutory requirement to initiate and facilitate community planning.

Lynch[84] makes the point that local government reorganisation in the mid-1990s made local government in Scotland 'structurally more complex'. Some of the thirty-two unitary councils are based on former regions (for example, Dumfries and Galloway, Fife, Highland, Scottish Borders), some on former district councils (for example, Argyll and Bute, Dundee, Glasgow, Stirling); some result from amalgamations of former councils (for example, Aberdeenshire, East Ayrshire, North Lanarkshire, South Lanarkshire); and then there are the three island councils (Western Isles, Orkney, Shetland). The small size of some of the councils (for example, Clackmannanshire, with a population of less than 50,000) necessitated 'joint arrangements' to provide strategic public services, manifested in the establishment of 'joint boards between authorities'. They may safeguard efficient services but they also 'blur democratic accountability'. In the larger councils, 'internal decentralisation' saw the creation of 'area committees' and 'area management offices'.

The reorganisation of local government, and the loss of key powers to centralised bodies, has unquestionably affected the development prospects of the peripheral mainland areas such as Caithness and Sutherland in the Highlands, and Wigtownshire in the south-west. People in these areas feel particularly disempowered by the shift in decision-making and loss of effective representation.[85]

THE FINANCING OF LOCAL GOVERNMENT IN SCOTLAND

Local government is largely financed by the Scottish Government, which currently, following seven years of a government-imposed Council Tax freeze, supplies about 86 per cent of its revenue expenditure.[86] This compares with the situation in the late 1960s which the Wheatley Report said was causing 'grave disquiet', notably that '57 per cent of the net revenue expenditure of all local authorities in Scotland was met by Government grant'.[87] Although this high dependence on government grant was exacerbated by the switch to a Poll Tax in the 1980s, and the only partial return to rates on property in 1993[88] it has been the growing importance of key areas of public expenditure processed through the local authorities but decided by central government that has been the most important cause.

Local councils are therefore in a very dependent position today: decisions made by the Scottish Government and the Scottish Parliament about the overall level of revenue-funding have a very significant impact on the local choices of councils. The 'Gearing Effect', as it is known, means that if there are cuts in central government funding (as there have been since 2010), then local councils can only maintain their budgets by much higher increases in their Council Tax. But that route was closed by the Council Tax freeze put in place by the SNP government in 2007.

In addition, ring-fencing of spending and spending caps imposed by central government further limited the room for manoeuvre of local authorities. When the SNP minority government took office in 2007, it promised to liberate and empower local communities by removing ring-fencing. The 'concordat' between the councils and the SNP government

> was supposed to set councils free again after decades of servitude to the central government. They were to be allowed to spend more of their allotted funds as they saw fit, not have it ring-fenced around the government's priorities. But instead we have them tied into 'single outcome agreements' covering all sorts of central government targets, including a council tax freeze. The result is that councils are left paring away at their services, unable to make one bold cut – like closing under-utilised schools, or pulling out of nursery provision or care homes. Nor are they able to go the other way and increase taxes.[89]

The situation means that in effect most local governments have very few 'free resources' that they can decide to allocate in accordance with the wishes of their local electorate. The main exceptions to this are Orkney and Shetland, which both, as a result of their own initiatives, managed to extract royalties from the North Sea oil passing through their islands, and used these to create 'oil funds' which could be used for social and developmental purposes.[90]

Overall, we can say that Scottish local government has lost power steadily in modern times due to an accretion of power at national and supra-national levels over things formerly decided at local levels. In part, of course, this is due to the extension of the welfare state after the Second World War, and efforts to provide 'equivalent' public services and other conditions to people irrespective of their place of residence or other personal characteristics. But in part it has also been due to the recentralisation of many functions due to reorganisation and the establishment of non-elected NDPBs or 'Quangos'. Neither has Scotland been free of the neo-liberal 'modernisation' and 'new public management' tendencies of all recent governments, but notably the Blair government after 1997.[91] According to Clarke and Glendinning,[92] under New Labour 'the practice of "modernisation" and the "new way" have been cloaks obscuring yet greater central direction and resource control', processes which have affected the whole of UK (including Scottish) public life and governance. Central government regarded local government 'as little more than a subordinate piece of administrative machinery rather than a key partner in the system of government'.[93]

The lack of local decision-making power is also reflected in the lack of fiscal autonomy at the local level due to the singular dependence on the Council Tax,

Table 5.1 Tax Revenue over which Local Authorities have Some Discretion as a Percentage of Total Revenue exceeding Borrowing

Country	First tier	Second tier of local government	Third tier
Denmark	46	63	–
Finland	43	–	–
France	46	61	48
Spain	35	–	16
Netherlands	8	19	–
Sweden	56	66	–
Scotland	20*	–	–

Source: Loughlin et al., 2005, pp. 4–5.

Note:
* Until the Council Tax freeze by central government in 2007.

and massive dependence on central government grants. There is no land taxation – a policy the Greens have unsuccessfully pursued in the Scottish Parliament. Furthermore, the SNP and Liberal Democrat models of a local income tax – a system used in Norway, for example – could not be synthesised, and the SNP government refrained from introducing its Local Income Tax Bill to Parliament. Even now that the SNP has an overall majority at Holyrood, there has been no attempt at introducing that Bill in Parliament.

Moreover, there is no transparent system of fiscal equalisation between authorities to compensate for higher costs of service delivery or lower own revenues, as there is in Scandinavia and Germany. Higher service delivery costs occur due to things like remoteness and scattered population, or larger proportions of ethnic minorities. Lower tax revenues result from lower property values and larger numbers of exemptions for persons or properties, as well as greater or lesser collection differences due to poverty.

The Scottish situation contrasts markedly with that in Norway, with its core revenue from local income tax and a well-developed and transparent fiscal equalisation scheme which compensates municipalities with higher costs of service delivery (for example, through remoteness and scattered settlements) and lower revenues (for example, because incomes are low). It also contrasts with most other Scandinavian countries.

ARRESTED DEVOLUTION

The greatest disappointment with devolution since 1999 has been that it stopped at Holyrood. This was not originally envisaged, and it has gone from bad to worse under a centralising SNP government: from the regressive Council Tax freeze (depriving local authorities of their only relevant means of influencing their own budget) to the introduction of a central police and fire service, the forced merger of colleges and the programme of court closures.

Local government in Scotland is, in large parts of the country, not 'local', and it is about administration – as an executive arm of central government – rather than about democratic decision-making. As has been pointed out by the Jimmy Reid Foundation's report *The Silent Crisis*, Scotland has a local democracy deficit.[94]

There are only thirty-two councils with a total of 1,223 councillors for the whole country; community councils are, by and large, toothless, powerless and even more poorly supported than local authorities; distances, particularly in rural council areas, can be prohibitive. Towns of over 50,000, like Kirkcaldy,[95] East Kilbride and Cumbernauld, are without their own governance structures. Nowhere else in Europe is such a state of play remotely imaginable.

Not only does Scotland have far fewer elected councils per population and area than the rest of Europe, it also has far fewer elected councillors and candidates standing in council elections. The numbers speak for themselves.[96]

Table 5.2 Contraction of Local Authorities

Country	1950	2001	Average population
Austria	4,065	2,359	3,437
Denmark	1,303	276	19,381
France	37,997	36,585	1,615
Germany	33,932	13,854	5,931
Italy	7,802	81	7,141
Switzerland	3,097	2,867	2,488
Norway	744	435	10,295
Scotland	236	32	163,200

Source: Bort et al. (2012).

Table 5.3 Proportion of the Population standing in Local Elections

Country	Population in mill. people	Candidates in all local elections	Proportion of population standing as candidate
Finland	5.4	38,509	1 in 140
Norway	4.8	59,505	1 in 81
Baden-Wurttemberg	10.7	75,726	1 in 141
Sweden	9.4	64,810	1 in 145
Scotland	5.2	2,607	1 in 2,071

Source: Bort et al. (2012).

Table 5.4 Number of Candidates contesting Each Seat

Country	Candidates in all local elections	Number of seats in all local elections	Number of candidates contesting each seat
Finland	38,509	14,412	3.7
Norway	59,505	10,785	5.5
Baden-Wurttemberg	75,726	21,279	3.6
Sweden	64,810	14,631	4.4
Scotland	2,607	1,223	2.1

Source: Bort et al. (2012).

Scottish local democracy has been compared to a ladder, with the lower rungs missing. It is excluding Scots from running their own local affairs, denying them access to – and participation in – democracy. Add to that the loss of power through centralisation and privatisation, emphasising the 'customer' rather than the 'citizen', and the catastrophically low turn-out at local elections[97] is hardly surprising: Scottish voters clearly experience local government as something they are being excluded from and ignored by, and which they see as remote and lacking power.

Devolution was widely seen as part of decentralising power, according to the principle of subsidiarity. As Trevor Davies[98] has argued,

all public service provision should be devolved to the local, except those reserved to the centre. The same reserved powers principle is embedded in the Scotland Act which set up our Scottish Parliament and itself reflects the principle of subsidiarity upon which governance in most of the rest of Europe is based.

That principle means local NHS services being governed, provided and audited locally. It means education being governed and provided according to local needs and direction. It means roads and transport and regeneration being funded and determined locally.

And it must mean a far greater proportion of taxation to do all that being set and raised locally, leading even to different taxes in different places. A shocking thought in Scotland yet commonplace throughout Europe where people seem to do very well by it.

In the run-up to the Scottish independence referendum, a debate about the structure and the powers of local democracy has begun – from the studies of the Jimmy Reid Foundation and Reform Scotland[99] at the time of the 2012 Local Election to political parties committing to 'localism'. Over the summer of 2013, local government itself intervened, in three stages, on behalf of its interests in what it perceived as a referendum discourse falsely limited to the power relations between Westminster and Holyrood. First, the three island councils of Shetland, Orkney and the Western Isles added their demands for greater autonomy to the debate; then the Cities Alliance chimed in; and, finally, CoSLA (The Convention of Scottish Local Authorities, the umbrella body of the thirty-two councils) installed a Commission on 'Strengthening Local Democracy' with the remit of looking into the purpose of local government.

The Scottish Government responded to the demands of the three island councils, set out in their *Our Islands – Our Future* document, with the 'Lerwick Declaration', installing a ministerial group under Local Government Minister Derek Mackay that is supposed to look into the possibility of devolving powers to the three councils – if the Scots vote Yes in the referendum.[100] The Scottish Labour Party's Devolution Commission, whose recommendations for more devolved powers for Holyrood were unanimously passed by the Labour Party conference in March 2014, makes explicit mention of a new power arrangement for Shetland, Orkney and the Western Isles, regardless of the referendum outcome. The islands' main demands are:

- Control of the seabed around the islands, allowing revenues currently paid to the Crown estate to be channelled into local needs.
- New grid connections to the Scottish mainland to allow world-class wave, tidal and wind energy resources to generate maximum benefits for the islands.
- New fiscal arrangements to allow the islands to benefit more directly from the harvesting of local resources, including renewable energy and fisheries.[101]

Glasgow City Council published a report by its chief executive George Black, which contrasted the UK Government's handing of greater powers to English city authorities 'in recognition of their pivotal role in supporting economic growth' with Scotland, 'where there has been increasing centralisation of powers to the Scottish Government'.[102]

In October 2013, CoSLA launched its Commission on Strengthening Local Democracy in Scotland, which was to look at reforming local government in Scotland before the independence referendum.[103] CoSLA president David O'Neill warned the 'centralising' Scottish Government against future power grabs and called for the role of councils to be enshrined in law.

CoSLA's 'vision for stronger local democracy in Scotland' speaks of 'local services that are built around local democratic choice.' It rejects the increasing 'centralisation' of services epitomised by the Council Tax freeze, the merger of the eight regional police forces into a single force, and the loss of powers on public health and economic development. 'Over the decades,' according to David O'Neill, 'we have moved away from the local aspect of almost everything. More and more services are being run by distant bureaucracies and often those services are being done to people rather then delivered with them'.[104]

The interim report by CoSLA's Strengthening Local Democracy Commission, published on 24 April 2014, could not have been clearer: local democracy 'has been gradually dismantled over the last 50 years', from over 400 elected local governments in 1946 to thirty-two today. The erosion of powers held by councils in Scotland is 'significantly greater than elsewhere internationally', and voters are 'losing trust and confidence' in democracy. Communities have 'very limited local tax capacity and a high dependency on grants from national government', and only 'a radical and fundamental overhaul' of local democracy in Scotland will resolve the issue, the report said. It called for more powers to be devolved from Holyrood and Westminster to councils.[105]

Local government's push for more powers is a welcome reminder, in the run-up to the referendum, that devolution of more (or all) power to Holyrood is not the only item on the agenda, that devolution was never meant to stop at the Edinburgh Parliament, and that the Parliament's founding principle of sharing power with the people has, so far, not extended to sharing power with local democracy. On the contrary, as Andy Wightman[106] has commented: 'At the same time as Scotland is on a journey to greater autonomy as a nation, the opposite is happening at the local level.'

While proposing that local government would be made statutory in a Scottish Constitution after a Yes vote, and underlining the principle of subsidiarity, the Scottish Government's White Paper, *Scotland's Future*,[107] states: 'On independence, the responsibilities and services of local government will continue as normal, as councils' statutory basis, funding, contracts and workforce will remain in place.' This emphasis on continuity is truly baffling: there is, after all, nothing 'normal' about the organisation of local democracy in Scotland.

Regardless of the outcome of the referendum in September 2014, making Scottish local government truly local and truly democratic should be on the agenda of any Scottish government, devolved or independent.

LOCAL GOVERNMENT IN NORWAY TODAY

The principal units of local government in Norway are municipalities, of which there were 428 in 2013. These vary enormously in size: the smallest municipality is Utsira, with a population of 211; the largest is Oslo, with 634,000.[108] However, 45 per cent of the municipalities have fewer than 20,000 inhabitants.[109] The main intermediate government unit in Norway today is the '*fylke*' or county, of which there are nineteen.

The popularly elected councils are the supreme governing bodies in Norwegian municipalities. The turnout in the municipal and county council elections in 2011 was 64.5 per cent. This is the highest voter turnout seen in the 2000s, but still lower than in previous local elections.[110]

The total number of local councillors is 10,785, of which, after the 2011 elections, 38 per cent are women. Moreover, 22 per cent of the mayors are women.[111] We may note that this is a much higher proportion than in Scotland, where in 2012 only just over 24 per cent of local councillors were women.

In Norway the council appoints an executive board from among the councillors. The executive board prepares proposals to be decided upon by the council, but may also decide on matters delegated to them by the council. The council also selects the mayor from the members of the executive board. In addition, the council selects members of a number of other committees dealing with specific tasks. Since the 1980s, municipalities have had four standing committees covering the main sectors of public policy: educational affairs, health and social affairs, cultural affairs and technical affairs.[112] The municipalities also establish committees with specific tasks. These local committees have a strong influence on local politics in the Norwegian context. The committees either have the authority to decide upon the distribution of the budget in their policy field, or they can submit proposals to the municipal council.

The Local Government Act has been revised several times but it remained basically the same between 1837 and the major revision in 1992. The idea behind the new Act was to give local authorities increased freedom and scope for problem-solving by giving them more autonomy in the choice of organisational solutions for their various activities. However, the Act combined the idea of autonomy with the idea of integration and partnership of local and central government. On the one hand, it gave a high degree of autonomy when it comes to how to structure the internal organisation of the municipalities; on the other hand, it offered integration regarding the content of the substantive policies of the municipalities. Hence, the basic model was for the municipalities to function as implementers of centrally formulated and decided policies.[113]

The role and activities of the councillors have changed during the last twenty years. Councillors elected by popular vote have two important functions: representation and management.[114] The first function means that the representative, on the basis of a party programme, is given a mandate from the electorate. Traditionally the councillor was willing to compromise with other councillors on behalf of the voters. During the 1990s, attention was drawn to political divisions, and it became important to put responsibility on the political majority. The second function, management, presupposes that the representatives have a real influence on policy. Traditionally, management was taken care of by politicians who were 'experts' in certain fields, such as schools or elderly care. However, one consequence of New Public Management ideology is that the representatives should concentrate on strategic thinking, overall objectives and principles, and not interfere in details. This means that the representatives have to create new roles.

During the revision of the Local Government Act in 1992, Norwegian authorities at the national level decided to establish legal quotas to change the biased gender balance in politics at local level.[115] The quotas refer to local public committees. The Norwegian Local Government Act states that local public committees should consist of a minimum of 40 per cent of each gender. The intention of the legislation was to increase the numbers of women in the local public committees.[116] The gender quotas target appointment procedures to the municipal public committees[117] and the executive board, the appointed bodies elected by the members of the popularly elected local assemblies.

The members of the committees are mainly appointed from among the members of the local council but other candidates can be elected as well. For example, if the proportion of women in the local council is low, female committee members can be appointed from outside the council.[118] However, members of the executive board can only be elected from among council members.

The Local Government Act also contains a paragraph on 'supervision and control'.[119] The Ministry of Local Government and Regional Development, through the county governors, has the duty to provide information to the municipalities on the rules concerning the implementation of gender quotas. In accordance with certain criteria, the Ministry is required to check the legality of decisions made by municipal councils. The Ministry also has a duty to annul a decision in the event of errors which render the decision invalid.

The Powers of Norway's Local Authorities

An examination of responsibilities, functioning and financing helps us to understand how much power municipalities have. The responsibilities of the

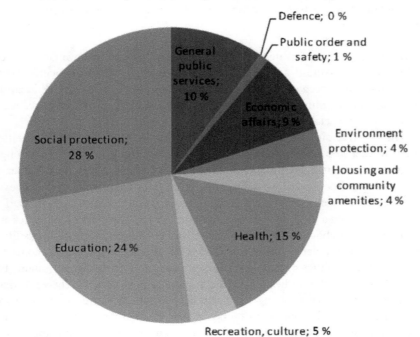

Figure 5.1 Norway: Local Government Expenditure, percentage by sector, 2013

Source: Statistics Norway 2013: General government revenue and expenditure, 2013, available at https://www.ssb.no/statistikkbanken/selectvarval/saveselections.asp (last accessed 16 April 2014).

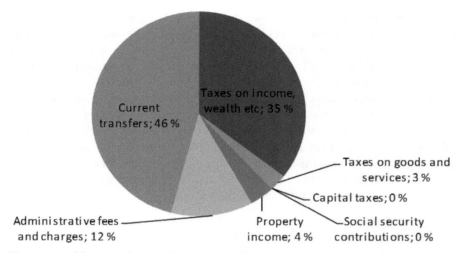

Figure 5. 2 Norway: Local Government Revenues, percentage by sector, 2013

Source: Statistics Norway 2013: General government revenue and expenditure, 2013, available at https://www.ssb.no/statistikkbanken/selectvarval/saveselections.asp (last accessed 16 April 2014).

municipalities are concentrated around production of national welfare services (see Figure 5.2). Around a quarter of municipal expenditures concerns social care. Another large responsibility is in primary and lower secondary education. In addition to that, municipalities also have responsibilities for childcare, waste management and social services.[120]

On the revenue side, in addition to having significant tax-raising capacities, municipalities also profit from hydro-power schemes and benefit from a strongly developed fiscal equalisation scheme which transfers resources from richer to poorer municipalities and so enables the delivery of 'equivalent' if not even 'better' public services in remoter and more sparsely populated communities. Tax revenues (including a local income tax) and block grants, earmarked subsidies and user fees comprise about 70 per cent of the income revenues in the municipalities, although the income varies a great deal between the municipalities. Income tax revenues are split between municipalities, counties and central government, but municipalities have the highest share. Each level of government receives a fixed percentage of revenues accruing from the 28 per cent flat-rate tax on personal income. In 2006, the division was 13.6 per cent as a maximum tax rate for municipalities, 3 per cent for the counties and 11.4 per cent for central government. The progressive rate for higher income brackets is reserved to central government.[121] Norwegian local governments have only a modest share of property tax compared to most OECD countries, at around 2 per cent of municipal revenues.[122]

The Meaning of Local Governance in Norway

The classical tripartite value base for local governance is defined in NOU (Norwegian Official Report)[123] as democracy, autonomy and effectiveness.

The value of democracy is related to local political participation as an instrument to strengthen democracy through activation of the citizens,[124] but it is also a question about 'localness' between citizens and politicians. Or, as Aodh Quinlivan put it: 'The very strength of local government is the fact that it is local and accessible.'[125] Local democracy contributes both to social and physical 'closeness' between citizens and politicians, as well as to politicians' knowledge of the needs and priorities of the inhabitants. And, of course, local democracy allows space for democratic variation.

The value of autonomy emphasises that local institutions need a certain amount of independence from the State for local governance to be real. 'Subsidiarity' implies that tasks should be fulfilled by the lowest possible level, although the State often decides which tasks are to be fulfilled at municipal level.

The value of efficiency is the last of the central–local governance principles. It has traditionally two main forms: a) that the municipalities are cost-effective; and b) that the municipalities demonstrate adaptative or allocative effectiveness.[126] The request for cost-efficiency is legitimately to prevent unnecessary waste of public resources[127] and to control the growth in public expenditure. Adaptation efficiency is related to responsiveness to local needs and circumstances. The municipality is the institution best able to answer the needs of the inhabitants. It is closest to the inhabitants and knows the local challenges, constraints and resources, so enabling better services. In this respect it is important to note that local needs vary, which requires a political adaptation of services in the municipalities and therefore coordination between different levels of government. This vertical coordination between central and local governments is facilitated by the County Governor's office in each county, where there are representatives of all central government departments.

Does Norway's System make a Difference?

If one of the goals of our democracies is indeed to foster democracy in the form of people's participation in local decisions affecting their lives, then it is clear that this is much more possible in Norway than in Scotland. The difference is measured by comparison of the powers and financing of local government, their local presence and character, voter turnout at elections, and coordination between levels of government. The fact that there are much higher turnouts at local government elections in Norway than in Scotland shows that people recognise that local government matters, and is really a voice that can speak for them at all levels.[128] The stronger fiscal position of local government in Norway with respect to its own revenues is also very important. Moreover, the much greater number of elected representatives in Norway means that people have more and better access to local politicians than in Scotland.

The presence of democratic government and governance at local levels in Norway also provides the means to tailor national policies to local circumstances and needs which, as in Scotland, vary considerably across the national territory. In Scotland, policies are much more of the 'one size fits all' variety.

Powerful, well-funded local government with wide powers and duties also provides good employment opportunities for local people in Norway, a factor which is critical for the survival and development of remoter and more sparsely populated communities, including those on islands. It is particularly, but not only, important for women's employment, a *sine qua non* for the sustainability of local populations and societies.

Last, but by no means least, strong local government has provided a powerful voice for local people with respect to central government that has helped to avoid the worst excesses of centralised power in Norway.[129]

CONCLUSION

We may conclude that Scotland has much to learn from Norway about local government (institutional framework) and governance (decision-making processes). There are strong arguments, based on the Norwegian experience, for a much more decentralised system of government and governance in Scotland. We would in particular find support in Norway for the following five key reforms in Scotland:

- The reinstatement of a two-tier system of municipalities and counties, and the introduction of a county governor system which allows representation of all the relevant ministries of central government at county level.
- The abolition of most of the NDPBs and quangos which have taken over and centralised many powers that properly belong to local democratically elected authorities. These powers and duties – and the funds and employment that go with them – need to be returned to municipal and county levels.
- The collection of income taxes at municipal level, and retention of some proportion of those taxes as may be negotiated.
- The introduction of a general land value tax system at local level, with revenues accruing to municipalities.[130]
- The introduction of a transparent fiscal equalisation system for municipalities and counties which factors in the higher costs of delivering services in remote and isolated communities, or for large proportions of non-English-speaking immigrants or other disadvantaged groups as well as the lower local tax revenues in poorer municipalities and counties.

Local government is too often seen in Scotland as a rather tedious and uninteresting topic. We hope that the reader is now convinced that this is not the case.

As for Norway, local government is always threatened by neo-liberal tendencies, technocratic modernising forces including those promoting new public management, and by those who believe that you can treat democratic local government like a business where the only thing that matters is often ephemeral economies of scale, and the thing that matters least is the authentic voice of local people. Brox[131] has shown clearly how important local political institutions and political resistance to centralising and technocratic tendencies has been to modern Norway, and Norwegians need to remember this when they become too self-absorbed in their life of material plenty, or too attracted to technocratic solutions. There are contemporary threats to the Local Government Structure in Norway arising from those on both right and left of the political spectrum who favour large-scale local government on grounds of 'efficiency', and it is important for Norwegians to remember why they have the structure they do, and how important it is for settlement patterns and Norwegian identity today.

Notes

1. For example, it was both a sin and a crime in the eighteenth century to have a child born out of wedlock that was the result of *leiermaal* (fornication or adultery). Those who were caught had to stand up in church and publicly confess to the congregation. This confession (called *publice absolverede* and also referred to as *skrifte*) was abolished in 1767.
2. *Sysselmenn/syslemenn* were established in the twelfth century. Before that the king used *lendmenn* (high-ranked persons) and *årmenn* (low-ranked persons) in his administration. The *årmenn* disappeared in the High Middle Ages but the *lendmenn* existed until the first half of the fourteenth century. See also Moseng et al., 2007.
3. Counties, or *fylker*, are known in the Early Middle Ages from the western and the central part of Norway, not from the eastern part. A *syslemann*'s administrative area was called a *sysle*. Norway was divided into approximately fifty *sysler* around 1300 (see Moseng et al., 2007: 199, 201).
4. The only surviving example from the Viking period is the Tynwald, the parliament of the Isle of Man, which has two branches, the Legislative Council and the House of Keys, and claims to be the oldest continuous parliament in the world.
5. Grimley, 1937: 21.
6. On Mormaers, Thanes and the development of Sheriffdoms in Scotland, see Muir 1975: 27, 30.
7. *Syslemenn* existed until the beginning of the fifteenth century. In the Late Middle Ages *syslemenn* were replaced by *fogut/lensherrer* and the original administrative areas (*syslene*) were reorganised into *len*. The *lensherrer* had *fogder/futer* and *(bygde)lensmenn* to assist them in their work. Until 1537, most of the *lensherrer* in Norway were native-born or naturalised Norwegian noblemen, but the Union Monarch placed Danish noblemen in strategic castles to secure the control of Norway from the early sixteenth century. After 1537, Danish noblemen dominated as *lensherrer* in Norway. (Pers. comm. Erik Opsahl, 2014).

8. Of course, there were changes. Some clan chiefs had their clan's land (it was not their own) forfeited because they refused to accept land charters granting them and their heirs property rights; others lost it by being on the 'wrong' side of wars or rebellions (as in the Jacobite rebellions of 1715 and 1745); some, like Breadalbane, lost it by gambling; while some gave it to the monasteries and the Catholic Church. Others gained it by being on the 'right' side, by taking Church land at the Reformation, by purchase, or by other means, including enclosure of common lands and communities. See also Chapter 1.

9. See Muir, 1975: 30.

10. The word 'sheriff' has Anglo-Saxon origins, being derived from 'shire-reeve' or 'county official', taken as appointed by the king.

11. Duncan, 1975: 32.

12. Innes, 1860: xix.

13. Innes, 1860: xviii–xxi.

14. Innes, 1861: 1–2n.

15. Shennan, 1892.

16. Næss, 1987: 13.

17. Næss, 1987: 14.

18. Næss, 1987: 14.

19. Næss, 1987: 16.

20. Reference for Figure 6.1.

21. Næss, 1987: 23.

22. Næss, 1987: 24.

23. The Norwegian nobility asked the king in 1591 to establish '(ed)svorne skrivere' (sworn scribes), to be called 'sorenskrivere'. Over a couple of generations this secretary became a judge. Imsen and Winge, 1999: 408–10.

24. Næss, 1987: 25.

25. Heidar, 2001: 18.

26. Devine, 1999. The pre-Union alliance against England also included Denmark-Norway. See also Chapter 1.

27. Macinnes, n.d.

28. Fletcher of Saltoun, a member of the old pre-Union Scottish Parliament known for his honesty and integrity as well as his intellect, was the source of much information on 'English bribes'. The evidence about a sum of £20,000 'to be sent to Scotland between the conclusions of negotiations and the opening of the final session of the Scottish parliament' is discussed in Scott, 1992: 182–4. But the larger part of the bribe was the 'Equivalent' which compensated certain members of the aristocracy for their losses incurred in the Darien venture.

29. Robert Burns, 'A Parcel o' Rogues' (Burns, 2001: 394). 'Ye Irish Lords, ye Knights an' Squires, Wha' represent our brughs an' shires' were chosen without a pretence of popular election, and were mostly in the pay, by 'pension, post or place', of '. . . a chap that's d-mn'd auld farran, Dundas his name' (Mitchell, 1897: 113). Henry Dundas was the Government's 'manager' for Scotland, who had comfortably manipulated most of the meagre Scottish electoral system in his interest by the 1790s when he personally controlled thirty-four of the forty-one Scottish constituencies contested. Dundas, who later was made the first Viscount

Melville, was to many the personification of the serious corruption of Scottish governance of his time (Devine, 1999: Chapter 10 *passim*).

30. Even by 1831 a mere 4,500 men, out of a population of more than 2.6 million people, were entitled to vote in parliamentary elections. Universal suffrage did not arrive in the UK until 1918, and even then only women over thirty had the vote. In the nineteenth century, voting rights were mainly given to the landed classes and those property owners in the cities and royal burghs, even after three reforms.
31. Smellie, 1946: 53.
32. See Devine, 2006: 288; Paterson, 1994: 54.
33. Hovland, 1987: 32.
34. Pryser, 1987: 251.
35. Steen, 1962.
36. Hovland, 1987.
37. Hovland, 1987: 35.
38. Hovland, 1987: 39; Pryser, 1999.
39. Hovland, 1987: 35.
40. Hovland, 1987: 37.
41. Hovland, 1987: 39.
42. Offerdal, 2007.
43. Available at http://www.regjeringen.no/nb/dep/bld/kampanjer/allmenn-temmerett/tidslinje.html?id=661778 (last accessed 15 April 2014). See also Myhre, 2012: 16.
44. Available at http://www.nrk.no/nyheter/distrikt/nrk_ostlandssendingen/sendinger_nrk-ostlandssendingen/lang_lunsj/2765204.html (last accessed 15 April 2014).
45. Steen, 1962 (cited in Hovland, 1987: 50).
46. Steen, 1962 (cited in Hovland, 1987: 50).
47. Available at https://www.stortinget.no/no/Stortinget-og-demokratiet/Historikk/Historisk-dokumentasjon/Formannskapslovene-av-1837/ (last accessed 15 April 2014).
48. Cappelen Dam, 2014: Chapter 4.
49. Offerdal, 2007.
50. As John Stuart Mill argued in *Representative Government* (1861).
51. Larsen, 2007.
52. Danielsen, 1987: 309.
53. Danielsen, 1987: 310.
54. Ibid.: 310.
55. Hovland, 1987: 111.
56. Raaum, 1999: 33.
57. Hovland, 1987: 111.
58. Raaum, 1999: 32.
59. Larsen, 2007.
60. See Midwinter, 1995: 11; McConnell, 2004: 44.
61. This number is obtained from the Wheatley Report (1969), 143.
62. Hutchison, 1996: 60.

63. Hutchison, 2001: 52.
64. Lord (John) Wheatley, a well-known judge, led the Commission. John Wheatley was – some may consider ironically – the nephew of a well-known 'Red Clydesider', the trade unionist and radical ILP politician John Wheatley. He was also father of Kathleen, who married Tam Dalyell, the Labour politician famous for his framing of the 'West Lothian Question' about the voting on 'English' questions by Scottish MPs in Westminster after Scottish devolution in 1979, while he, as a West Lothian MP, could no longer vote on matters of his Scottish constituency. The report had two main dissenters, Betty Harvey Anderson and Russell Johnson, both being concerned about the sparsely populated regions, and especially the proposals for the Highlands and Islands. Their points were partly heeded by the government in implementing the reforms.
65. Midwinter, 1995: 16.
66. NDPB is a Non-Departmental Public Body, normally responsible to a specific government minister who also appoints the board members who run the body in question. According to Nick Clegg (2010), there are 'now 790 listed quangos, all taking decisions on behalf of government. Some estimates say in reality there are more than 1,160' in the UK.
67. McConnell, 2004: 8.
68. Harvie, 1998: 178.
69. Riddoch, 2013: 208.
70. Lynch, 2001: 221–5.
71. Keating, 2005a: 46.
72. Curtice et al., 2009: 11.
73. Curtice et al., 2009: 174.
74. It is a matter of some historical debate that in the Act of Union, 1707, the shires or counties and burghs were constitutionally protected, but this apparent protection mattered as nothing in the post-Wheatley reforms of the Heath Conservative government. In the negotiations over the deeply unpopular Act of Union, 1707, the Scots failed to get a federal arrangement but did secure the continuation of the Scottish legal system, education and Church, and maintenance of the privileges of the Scottish royal burghs. See Paterson, 1994.
75. McGarvey, 2009: 125.
76. Keating et al., 2003; Keating, 2005b.
77. Haydecker, 2010.
78. Haydecker, 2010.
79. The first Scottish Parliament elections in 1999 returned 37.5 per cent women; the number of women MSPs rose in 2003 to 39 per cent, and stood at the beginning of the fourth session in 2011 at 34.5 per cent.
80. Kenny and Mackay, 2013.
81. Midwinter, 1995: 13.
82. Anon., n.d.
83. Anon., n.d.
84. Lynch, 2001: 207–9.
85. Bryden et al., 2004: 79.
86. 'The council tax freeze has been in place since 2007 and that is going to go on

until the end of this parliament which will be 2017, ' according to CoSLA president David O'Neill. 'During that time, local government's ability to raise its own finances has been reduced from only 20 per cent down to 14-ish per cent' (quoted in MacNab, 2013).

87. Wheatley, para. 1031.
88. The Poll Tax – an infamous uniform tax on persons introduced by the Thatcher government – was replaced by the Council Tax in 1993. Council Tax is a local tax on domestic property with a property and a personal component – a 'hybrid' tax with elements of the old rating system on domestic property and of the Poll Tax. Some property is exempt from Council Tax, some people do not have to pay and some get a discount. All homes are given a Council Tax 'valuation band' by the Valuation Office Agency. The band is based on the assessed value of a home on 1 April 1991. The rate of Council Tax varies according to the band.
89. Knox, 2010.
90. Morgan, 2009.
91. McGarvey and Cairney, 2008: 145, 151.
92. Clarke and Glendinning, 2002: 46.
93. Sinclair, 1997: 14.
94. Bort et al., 2012.
95. Kirkcaldy in Fife has a history going back to the Bronze Age. It was also the birthplace of Adam Smith, and at one time a Royal Burgh. Its population of just under 50,000 can be compared with that of the Arctic town of Bodø in Norway, which has a population of 47,000, its own municipality, a university, and is also the administrative centre of the county of Nordland.
96. For these statistics, see *The Silent Crisis* (Bort et al., 2012).
97. Turnout at the 2012 local elections was under 40 per cent.
98. Trevor Davies, 2012.
99. Reform Scotland, 2012
100. *The Herald*, 2013.
101. Available at www.orkney.gov.uk/Council/C/our-islands-our-future---faq.htm (last accessed 15 April 2014).
102. Brown, 2013.
103. CoSLA, 2013.
104. CoSLA, 2013.
105. CoSLA, 2014
106. Andy Wightman, 2013.
107. Scottish Government, 2013.
108. Statistics Norway, 2014b.
109. Parliamentary Bill, 2008.
110. Statistics Norway, 2011b.
111. Statistics Norway, 2011a.
112. Offerdal, 2007.
113. Offerdal, 2007.
114. Vabo, 2002.
115. Norway Local Government Act 1992, §36–8.
116. NOU, 1990.

117. That is to say, the main political public committees at the local level, such as the committee for health and social care, the committee for school and daycare issues, culture and economic development.
118. Norway Local Government Act, 1992.
119. Ibid., §59.
120. OECD, 2007.
121. OECD, 2007.
122. OECD, 2007.
123. NOU, 2005. NOU means Norwegian Official Report (*Norges offentlige utredninger*).
124. Sharpe, 1970; Kjellberg, 1990.
125. Aodh Quinlivan, 'Strength of local government is the fact that it is accessible', *Irish Examiner*, 17 October 2012.
126. NOU, 1988, 1990; Hagen and Sørensen, 2001; Bukve, 2002.
127. NOU, 1988: 38.
128. While in Scotland not even 40 per cent of the electorate voted in the 2012 local council elections, in Norway the turnout for the 2011 municipal elections was 63.6 per cent and for the county elections 59.2 per cent.
129. As in the attempts to centralise communities in northern Norway after the Second World War. See Brox, 1993, 2006.
130. See also the arguments for Land Value Tax in Scotland in Bryden, 1995.
131. Brox, 2006.

CHAPTER 6

The Development of Industry and North Sea Oil in Scotland and Norway

John Bryden

INTRODUCTION

There are striking differences between the respective stories of industrial development in Scotland and Norway since the eighteenth century. These especially concern the timing of the shift from 'proto-industrialisation' to 'modern industrialisation' based on the factory system; the relationship between agrarian, rural, urban and industrial development, especially concerning the peasantry, migration streams and urbanisation; working-class divisions and alliances; attitudes and policies concerning foreign interest and capital in relation to basic resources; the source of energy for modern industry and its impacts on the location of industrial development; the importance of domestic and overseas markets and industrial protection; different ideas on the role of the State and protectionism; and the differential impact of neo-liberal policies after 1970. Mainly as a result of these rather deeply rooted differences, but also because of Scotland's constitutional position within the UK, the story of the development and exploitation of North Sea oil after about 1970 is also quite different, as are its social and economic consequences.

Between 1750 and 2010, Scotland gained and lost a world-class – and world-scale – manufacturing industry. Scottish textiles, iron and steel, coal, ships, railway engines, and the steam engines to drive them all, together with a host of interconnected industries, were the engines of industrial development. At the beginning of this period and for nearly a century, this industrial development was mostly rural, involving pluriactive farmers and their households, based on power from water, charcoal and wood, iron ore from the hills, and linen and wool from Scottish farms and crofts. Until the later stages of the twentieth century, it was also mainly Scottish-owned. At its peak it was largely based on export-orientated 'heavy' industry, and for this reason Scottish manufacturing and the people who worked in it suffered disproportionately in recessions. By the middle of the twentieth century, the experience of recessions filled the memories and future thoughts of many. The increasingly hegemonic idea among decision-makers was that Scotland was far too dependent on heavy industry, and that what was needed were more consumer industries. Government policies focused on this task periodically after the Second World War, and traditional industries were either propped up or left to die. When North Sea oil appeared in the early 1970s, neither Scottish nor UK heavy industry was in a position to participate to any real extent. The final blow was the neo-liberalism of the Thatcher government, later reinforced by one of Mrs Thatcher's favourite EU policies – the European Single Market and accompanying, if less well known, 'competition policy' – which led to the removal of remaining subsidies and denationalisation of the remnants of shipbuilding and steel.

The parliamentary Union with England in 1707 provided important access to the markets of a growing empire. It is tempting to argue that it was this same Union that finally destroyed Scottish manufacturing industry, through the election of a neo-liberal government that had little support in Scotland. Yet this would be a distortion, as the evidence is that many Scots, including industrialists, officials and academics, also supported the hegemonic and essentially defeatist idea that heavy industry just could not compete with Japanese, German, Norwegian and North American rivals. Moreover, this idea emerged long before Mrs Thatcher's election in 1979. Scottish industrial capital and skills moved out as a result. It is therefore at least questionable whether the outcome would have been very different under any alternative government.

Norway's industrialisation was equally impressive, but the development of 'modern' factory-based industry started in the middle of the nineteenth century, much later than in Scotland, and it had a different relationship to agrarian and urban developments, and took a different social and spatial form. This was because it was founded on decentralised energy and mineral sources, and a dispersed labour force from the small farms, rather than centralised fossil fuel deposits and landless labour. Like Scotland, however, Norway's industrialisation also started with a 'proto-industrial' development of rural raw materials and using power sources such as water, charcoal, and human labour. We will briefly discuss this proto-industrialisation before moving on to analyse the key differentiating themes.

PROTO-INDUSTRIALISATION IN SCOTLAND UP TO 1800 AND NORWAY UP TO 1850[1]

Proto-industrial manufacturing activities were present in both countries, and based on similar sources of energy, natural resources and labour. The commodities in question can be identified in late-medieval trade and shipping records for the various Scandinavian and Scottish ports.[2]

Before the later decades of the eighteenth century, manufacturing and mining in Scotland was a mainly rural phenomenon, often undertaken with water power and skilled human beings, typically transforming raw materials such as wool, flax, timber and iron ore into higher-value items for human use or mining raw materials and metal ores such as lead and iron ore, the latter using charcoal for smelting.[3]

Equally, the manufacturing labour force was a rural labour force. Indeed, Scotland's main cities and towns with a population of upwards of 3,900 in the mid-eighteenth century contained only 13.5 per cent of the Scottish population of just over 1.2 million. By the first decade of the nineteenth century, this proportion had risen significantly but was still small at 20.7 per cent.[4] By 1850, Scotland's urban population, defined as those living in cities of over 10,000, had grown to 32 per cent.[5] But this still left a sizeable population in the smaller towns and rural areas and, due to high fertility rates, this rural population had continued to grow, reaching a peak around 1860. As Devine points out, 'As late as the 1830s . . . around two-thirds of Scotland's handloom weavers of cotton, linen and woollen cloth lived in country villages or small towns.'[6]

Textiles comprised one of the most important elements in this proto-industrial structure. According to Smout, 'Spinning, weaving, or knitting, either of flax or wool, must have been carried out in most parishes in Scotland'[7] in the period leading up to the Union of 1707. He reinforces the rural nature of such activities with a quote from an unnamed source that textiles were 'maid and wrocht in the countrie, quhairby the peopill ar sett to labour'. Yet the Union of 1707, while providing greater market access and more secure trade conditions between Scotland and England, was not at first an unmitigated blessing for textiles, which were exposed to greater competition from technically superior products while lacking the necessary capital to adapt.[8] Nevertheless, the Board of Trustees for Manufactures, created in 1727, sought to transform the linen industry by bringing in expertise from Holland and France – among others – and providing some 'pump priming' finance.[9] The establishment of the British Linen Company in 1742[10] was also important not only for the provision of credit to linen spinners and weavers but also through engagement in market operations to improve production and bleaching methods. Partly as a result of such efforts and innovations, linen output 'rose three-fold in volume and four-fold in value' between 1736–7 and 1768–72.[11]

Iron ore was found in Scotland, for example in the hills at the Lecht near Tomintoul, where by the 1720s it was carried to Strathspey by pack horses and reduced to pig iron at the Abernethy Iron Works of the York Building Company using charcoal produced in the local forests.[12] However, it was only in the nineteenth century that it became a staple industry. The first modern blast furnace was founded at Invergarry near Fort William in 1727, again because of the importance of charcoal to the smelting process at that time.[13] It was followed by the Bonawe or Taynuilt furnace in Argyll in 1753. These and the later plant at Furnace on Loch Fyne continued to work well into the nineteenth century, and all were notably 'rural'. However, the foundation of the large and technologically advanced Carron

Iron works in 1759 marked a major change in the location of the industry because although it used native ores, the smelting process was based on coke rather than charcoal. This new technique led to a centralisation of the iron and steel industry close to the major coal-mining areas of the centre and west of Scotland.

Although textiles and iron were important in the seventeenth and eighteenth centuries, and, later, their place in the order of things, as well as their predominantly rural location, was increasingly threatened by new growing industries as steam power displaced water power for spinning and weaving, non-indigenous cotton increasingly displaced indigenous linen and wool as the main spinning activity after 1780, and coal and coke replaced charcoal from the forests as the means of smelting iron ore. The sources of energy for manufacturing shifted (to coal) in the nineteenth century, and again (increasingly to liquid fossil fuels, and to a lesser extent hydro power) throughout the twentieth. In addition, Scotland's growing merchant class took full advantage of the post-Union access to North American and West Indian raw material supplies, especially tobacco, cotton and sugar, for which the Clyde estuary was favourably located. Scotland became a major player in the European tobacco trade in the eighteenth century, and merchants later diversified into cotton for the growing spinning industry, and sugar from the West Indies to meet rapidly growing consumer demand. Scottish textiles – wool and linen – were very much part of the 'triangular trade' with the West Indies and southern States, which returned tobacco and sugar for refining in Scotland. As we shall see, the merchants involved in such colonial trade later became a direct and indirect source of capital for Scottish industrialisation.

Norway's proto-industrialisation looked somewhat similar to that of Scotland and included textiles based on hand and water power, wood and metal crafts, shipbuilding,[14] tar, and whale and cod oil.[15] There were also a few silver and copper mines, and some charcoal-based iron works mainly for local and regional markets for iron stoves, agricultural tools and suchlike. It was also rural in character, and involved small-scale pluriactive subsistence households[16] who formed the majority of the population until the end of the nineteenth century.[17] Agriculture, forestry and fishing, and related processing and manufacturing, together with shipping, underpinned the Norwegian economy until hydro-electric power came at the end of the nineteenth century. The expansion of shipping was a major stimulus to economic growth in the second half of the nineteenth century, and the American historian Thomas Derry points out that '[i]n 1880 Norway possessed the third largest of the world merchant navies'. However, although Norway was clearly producing ships competitively at this time, Derry's claim that its crews were also cheap because they were 'drawn from a countryside where the agricultural crisis reduced employment'[18] is a misunderstanding based on a standard Anglo-Saxon view of the processes of agrarian change involving dispossession of the peasantry, something that did not happen in Norway, as we have seen in Chapters 1 and 4. At this time, Norway's agriculture was mainly for subsistence, and its peasants were interested in seasonal wage labour on ships or anywhere else they could find it.

As late as 1875, a mere quarter of Norway's population lived in cities and urbanised areas, and it took until just after the Second World War before half of the population lived in these areas, about a hundred years after the similar crossover point in Scotland.[19]

Norway's 'modern' industrialisation came after Scotland's, starting around the middle of the nineteenth century with the first textile mills, in the early days water-powered as in Scotland, and then pulp and paper mills around 1880. The real 'new dawn' came around the turn of the twentieth century, when the development of cheap hydro-electric power and available natural resources in the form of metal ores led the development of new electro-metallurgical and electro-chemical industries.

THE LABOUR SUPPLY FOR THE INDUSTRIAL REVOLUTION AFTER 1800

The stark contrast between Scotland's and Norway's industrial labour supply is also discussed in Chapters 1 and 7. In Scotland there was an abundant supply of labour, first from landless peasants 'cleared' in the eighteenth and nineteenth centuries, second from Irish migrants, and third from a rural labour surplus due to relatively high fertility rates and early mechanisation, especially the reaping and threshing machines (see Chapter 4).

In Norway, the labour came mainly from pluriactive peasants and their families, as well as surplus rural labour generated by relatively high population growth. The geographical distribution of industrialisation in Norway discussed below also meant that the rural population had access to wage employment in industry. In Norway, the 'reserve army' of industrial labour, as Brox argues in Chapter 7, came from the families of small subsistence farmers and fishermen.

During the period of Norway's modern industrial development from the late nineteenth century, the number of farms continued to increase, only peaking in 1949. Unlike the British (and Scottish) case, rural Norwegians could maintain and even improve their pre-modern, subsistence economy adaptation in the nineteenth and much of the twentieth centuries (see Chapter 7).

As we see elsewhere in this book and below, these crucial differences are also closely and directly linked to the nature of political alliances, religious conflicts, the power of the working class, and the development of politics and political systems in the two countries since 1800.

SCOTTISH INDUSTRIAL GROWTH

Industrial production and employment grew rapidly, and were also transformed, in nineteenth-century Scotland, as Table 6.1 indicates.

Table 6.1 Indicators of Scottish Nineteenth-century Manufacturing Growth

		1775–1800	1800–1825	1825–1850	1850–1875	1875–1900
Employment	Manufacturing employment	>200[1778]	300,000 early 1800s	525,000 early 1800s		
Textiles	Cotton imports, thousand lbs		about 7,000[1801]	about 41,234[1831]	about 62,400[1867]	37,400 to 49,900
Energy	Coal			3 mill. tons[1830]	7.5 mill. tons[1854]	
Iron	Furnaces			27[1830] to 100[1844]		
	Pig iron, share of British output			5%[1830] to 25%[1849]		
Shipbuilding	Clyde's share of employment			3%[1831]	21%[1871]	
	share of tonnage of British iron vessels				66%[1850]	
Steel	Production				1,119 tons[1873]	485,00 tons[1890]

Superscript numbers indicate year.

Sources: Employment: Figure for 1800 is based on Sinclair's estimate that 275,000 were employed in fabrics and textiles in the early 1800s, and that this represented 90 per cent of all manufacturing employment. See also Devine, 1999: 108. The figure for 1851 is from Lee (1979).
Cotton: Derived from Campbell, 1965: 104–5. Campbell gives data in 'bales' after 1801, which has been converted at 1 bale = 480 lb.
Coal: Knox, 1999: 35–6.
Iron: Campbell, 1965: 119–21.
Shipbuilding: Knox, 1999: 85–6.
Steel: Campbell, 1965: 231.

In Norway, manufacturing employment amounted to only about 17,000 in 1825, but increased to 95,000 by 1851 and 169,000 by 1911. In 1951, it reached 358,000 and although there was a subsequent decline, it remained at 236,000 in 2011, higher than the Scottish figure of 194,000 in the same year. These figures should be seen against the relative size of population: around 1800 Scotland's population of 1.6 million was about 70 per cent greater than that of Norway; in 1900, Scotland's population of 4.4 million was more than twice that of Norway's; today the two countries have almost the same population.

The main Scottish industry at the beginning of our period, textiles, developed rapidly between 1780 and 1840,[20] after which it slowed and subsequently declined after the American Civil War. In 1831 and until after 1840, the industry was dominated by handloom weavers, a situation that persisted due to the flow of cheap labour and the inadequacies of the Scottish Poor Law.[21]

However, while cotton was slowing down, coal production was increasing. Like linen weavers, coal miners were often agricultural smallholders.[22] Coal-mining was still mainly for local markets. However, between 1830 and 1849, Scotland's share of British pig iron output grew rapidly, followed by intensive railway-building in the 1840s. By 1850, the Clyde was producing most of the tonnage of iron vessels in Britain. Whatley argues that it was in this rather brief period of rapid growth that Scotland became more industrialised than the rest of Britain.[23]

The labour for the rapid industrial expansion in Scotland between the mid-eighteenth and mid-nineteenth centuries came mainly from the increasing 'clearance' of cottars, crofters and small farmers from the land in both the Scottish Lowlands and, later, in the Highlands and Islands as part of the agrarian revolution, and related migration to the increasingly urban industrial areas. By 1851, 54,000 Highlanders had settled in the west of Scotland. Moreover, by 1841 44,000 or 16 per cent of Glasgow's population was Irish-born.[24] This rapidly increased after the Irish potato famine of the mid-1840s, with a thousand Irish migrants arriving every week by 1848. Ireland provided mainly Catholic and anti-landlord labour, mainly from rural areas of the South, but also some Protestant migrant labour from the North. The seven crofting counties (later known as the Highlands and Islands), which were in this period the main site of clearances and dispossession, also provided a steady flow of labour that was largely but not wholly Protestant in faith, and anti-landlord in sentiment. This flow of migrants was fuelled by the potato famines and poverty, but also maintained by high fertility rates. Together, Ireland and the Highlands and Islands provided a large 'reserve army of labour', as Arthur Lewis later termed it,[25] and this kept wages in Scotland persistently lower than in England. These very different migration streams also created the basis for an important dimension of Scottish religious conflicts (see Chapter 9); for the pro-Irish independence movement; for the Scottish home-rule movement; and for the anti-landlord or land reform movement.

While the textile industries had been the motive force in Scotland's industrial development up to the 1830s, it was the development of heavy industries that

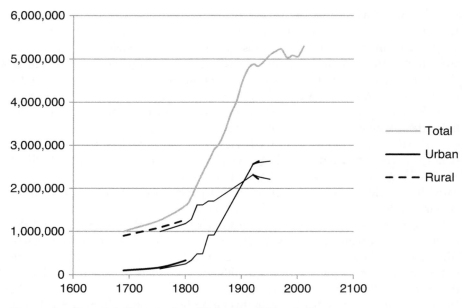

Figure 6.1 Scottish Population, Urban and Rural, from 1700

Sources: 1690: Smout, 1969: 119. Urban population for 1755, 1801 and 1821 is the population of the cities and largest towns: Smout, 1969: 261. Population census data for total population since 1801. Urban population from 1921 is the population of the large burghs, including the 4 large cities. 1841, based on Smout's (1986: 9) estimates for towns over 5,000 inhabitants.

Note:
Missing data on the size of the rural and urban population for several years are calculated as sliding number averages.

made it one of the greatest industrial centres in the world by the late nineteenth century, and Glasgow a great world city at its core. In this period, 'coal, iron, steel, shipbuilding and engineering took off and transformed Scotland into a manufacturer for the world'.[26]

Iron production became markedly more competitive as a result of Mushet's discovery of blackband ironstone in 1801, and the new hot-blast smelting technique invented by Neilson in 1828.[27] By 1854, Scotland provided 90 per cent of total UK exports of pig iron. Thereafter, growing competition came first from the north-east of England and later from overseas.

From the third quarter of the nineteenth century, it was shipbuilding and the related industries of steel-making and marine engineering that became the leading sectors in Scottish industrialisation. They were centred around the Clyde estuary between Glasgow and Greenock, which had a leading position as a result of the change from wooden to iron and steel hulls, and from sail to steam propulsion. Both of these changes built upon earlier Scottish expertise in steam engines, and in

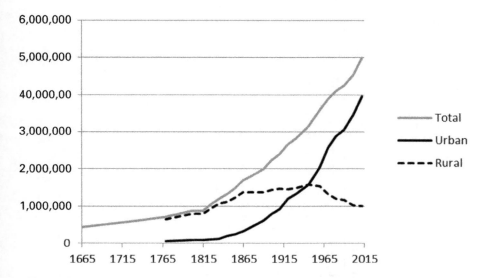

Figure 6.2 Norway's Population, Urban and Rural, from the Eighteenth Century

Sources: Population censuses after 1769. Earlier data from Dyrvik et al. (1992, 3rd edn), pp. 124–6.

iron and steel production. Between 1870 and the outbreak of the First World War, shipbuilding was the main growth industry in Scotland. In 1871, just under half of the total British tonnage launched was in the Clyde,[28] and by 1913 Scotland produced more tonnage than the combined German and US shipbuilding industries, at 756,976 launched tonnes that year.[29]

Scottish expertise in steam engines supported and linked with the shipbuilding industry as well as the rapidly growing railway engine industry in the second half of the nineteenth century. Springburn in Glasgow was the leading supplier of locomotives in the world by the last quarter of the century.

Steel-making was also a major growth industry in the second half of the nineteenth century when the Bessemer converter and the Siemens–Martin open hearth furnace technology were adopted, later improved upon by Gilchrist-Thomas.[30] The main market was the growing shipbuilding industry, with which its fortunes (and fluctuations) were tied. Two firms – Beardmores and Colvilles – came to dominate the steel industry by the end of the nineteenth century, and they and their successors continued to dominate it until its virtual demise in the late twentieth century.

The close inter-industry connections between iron, steel, coal, shipbuilding and railways were a strength of Scottish industrialisation in the nineteenth century. However, the export dependence of shipbuilding, locomotive and related industries made Scottish industry and its employees vulnerable to fluctuations in external demand, while the close inter-industry connections meant that slumps

Table 6.2 Indicators of Scottish Manufacturing Decline in the Twentieth Century

		1900–1925	1925–1950	1950–1975	1975–2000	After 2000
Employment	manufacturing	735,000 (1911)		748,000 (1951)	596,000 (1979)	176,000 (2010)
Energy	coal production, million tons	42.5 (1913)	20.3 (1938)	17.2 (1961)	7.1 (1981/2)	
Shipbuilding	tons launched	650,000 (1919)	74,000 (1933)	33,400 (1950)	27,000 (1978)	
Steel	% of British output	23% (1920)	15% (1937)	13.5% (1951)	11.3% (1980)	

Sources: Manufacturing employment: Shipbuilding and steel output in 1919 and 1933 from Knox, 1999: 190.
Coal production: Payne 1985: 80.

permeated throughout the economy and had an exaggerated impact. By the beginning of the twentieth century, growing competition from other UK centres including Tyneside and Belfast, as well as from new industrialising countries, reduced profitability in the shipyards, in turn threatening the dependent steel industry.

The situation was temporarily saved by the First World War, and the involvement of several major shipyards in building ships for the British Navy,[31] as well as the reorientation of heavy industry into munitions in general. The basic industries, including jute in Dundee, did well from the war, and capacity expanded in the postwar boom. However, Scotland's competitors in the US, Japan, the Netherlands and Scandinavia also expanded capacity in this period and boom turned to bust in the 1920s. Shipbuilding and engineering output fell between 1919 and 1933, as did steel. The demand for the other major nineteenth-century industries including coal and jute also fell or remained static in this period. As Devine and others point out, Scotland's problem in the early twentieth century was that it had too few industries – with too few employees – supplying the growing domestic consumption market.[32] Those that did exist – such as the manufacture of carpets and linoleum, hosiery and knitwear – did relatively well between the wars, but their impact could not counter the loss of exports and employment in the heavy industries. Although efforts to diversify into new consumer products were made, such as the vehicle- manufacturing activity of Beardmore and the Albion company, these failed due to distance from markets and a reluctance to adopt the new 'Fordist' methods.[33]

The mantra of diversification into light industries remained at the forefront of Scottish development debates and public efforts thereafter, some would argue diverting attention from the needs of the traditional heavy industries which remained important at least until the 1970s.[34] As we shall see later, others argue that the neglect of Scotland's traditional heavy engineering industries was one factor leading to the UK's failure to gain significant economic advantage from the development of North Sea oil after 1970.[35]

Norway's industry remained proto-industrial in character until much later. In 1829, 83 per cent of what was defined as 'manufacturing' was sawmilling, and a further 7 per cent was distilleries and mills, leaving about 10 per cent for all other branches. Nevertheless, like Scotland, Norway started 'modern' industrialisation based on the factory system with textile mills in the 1840s. After the middle of the nineteenth century, consumer industries started to develop such as shoe manufacture, canned foodstuffs and tobacco-processing, while the construction and shipbuilding industries developed to modernise the merchant and fishing vessels. Communications, especially the railways and then telecommunications, both created new demands and opened new and better markets.[36] For example, the Lofoten telegraph line was completed in 1861, connecting nine fishing villages during the season. Its long length of undersea cables and landlines comprised the country's first telegraph line that was independent of the main network.[37] By 1906, Sørvågen in the southern end of the Lofoten Islands had its first wireless telegraph – the first in Norway. Norwegian railways also expanded in the second half of the nineteenth century, especially with the completion of the Rørosbanen between central Norway and Oslo in 1877. In 1883, the entire main railway network was taken over by the national rail company, NSB, although private companies continued to operate a number of industrial railways. A second railway construction boom in the 1920s connected east and west Norway, and electrification of the railway system also started in this period.

Manufacturing was probably the most dynamic part of the economy by the turn of the century. However, in 1865 only about 6 per cent of Norwegians were involved in industry, compared with about 65 per cent in agriculture, forestry and fishing.[38] In the same year, industrial exports accounted for about 8 per cent of total exports. It was 1957 before manufacturing employment exceeded that in the primary industries, and – astonishingly – this was more than a century later than the comparable crossover point in Scotland.[39]

THE CONTRASTING SOURCES OF ENERGY FOR INDUSTRIAL DEVELOPMENT

Norway and Scotland have contrasting transitions in the main energy source used for modern industrial development, although both were indigenous. In Norway,

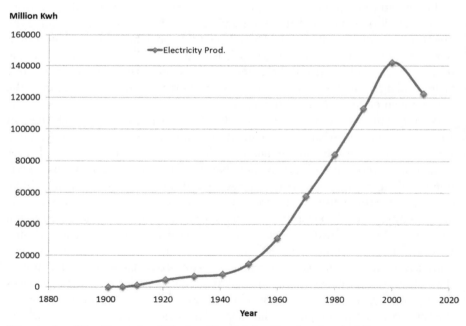

Figure 6.3 The Growth of Hydro-Electricity Production in Norway, 1900–2011 (million Kwh)

it was hydro-electric power from the late nineteenth century. In Scotland, it was coal. Hydro power gave a major boost to Norwegian industrial development. The first hydro-electric power plant was erected in Skien in south Norway in 1885 by a wood-processing plant on Skien river which also supplied the small town, and the first municipal hydro-power plant was opened in Hammerfest in north Norway in 1891. By 1920, all towns, and 64 per cent of Norway's population, had a hydro-electricity supply. It was the development and institutionalisation of cheap hydro-electric power that gave Norway a global comparative advantage that was to persist up to the present day. Cheap electricity was used to develop the electro-metallurgical and electro-chemical industries based partly on Norway's natural mineral resources. Norsk Hydro, currently the fourth-largest integrated aluminium company worldwide, was founded in 1905 by Sam Eyde, who used the Birkeland[40] method to produce artificial fertilisers by fixing atmospheric nitrogen from air. Hydro plants were established all over Norway, and especially in the western periphery with ready access to deep water as a means of shipping out the products. Norsk Hydro is now joined with Statoil, and remains over 40 per cent owned by the State.[41]

In Scotland, the energy for industry was initially provided by indigenous coal, which was also used to produce coke and gas. Coal production also grew rapidly in the nineteenth century as a result of rising domestic demand for steam-driven engines and iron production, as well as growing overseas demand. Of the total production of just under 7.5 million tons in 1854, about one-third was consumed by the iron works. By 1873, production had more than doubled to just over 16.8 million tons, of which only 2.7 million tonnes was consumed by iron works, while half was exported.[42]

INDUSTRIAL CENTRALISATION AND DECENTRALISATION

As we have seen, Scotland's industrial activity and labour force were overwhelmingly rural up until at least the first quarter of the nineteenth century. The majority of industrial workers were small farmers, crofters and cottars, and, after 1800, increasingly landless rural labour. However, the advent of coal and steam power and related development of heavy industries in the nineteenth century led to a centralisation of industry in and around the main cities, especially Glasgow and Dundee. This relocation of industry also led to significant urbanisation in the nineteenth century.

The shift in the energy source for manufacturing in Norway did not lead to the centralisation of industry in urban centres as it did in Scotland, but rather the reverse – a new form of essentially rural industrial development that provided more opportunities for the small farm families, as well as a by now growing working class – within the rural areas and small towns. This was an important emerging difference between Norway and Scotland, which, when taken alongside the dominance of small freeholding peasants and the absence of enclosures or clearances in

Norway, underpinned the very different migration and settlement patterns, class formations and alliances that emerged and persisted during and after the nineteenth century.

THE LABOUR MOVEMENT, SOCIAL CLEAVAGE AND LABOUR POLITICS

The two migrant streams to industrial Scotland underpinned the weakness of Scottish working-class politics and solidarity in the later nineteenth and twentieth centuries and kept wages relatively low. This helps to explain the Liberal hegemony between about 1880 and 1920. In Norway, however, Brox (see Chapter 7) argues that industrial labour came largely from the non-urbanised peasantry with access to subsistence. This led to the development of close worker–peasant relations, while the lack of a significant reserve army of labour in the form of in-migrant streams meant that wages were generally higher. In addition, as Rosie and Amundsen point out (see Chapter 9), sectarian divisions between Catholic and Protestant workers, and also within the numerous Protestant factions in Scotland, had no parallel in Norway. In Chapters 1, 3 and 4 we discussed the importance of the alliance between the peasants and the industrial workers. The Norwegian Labour Party (AP), founded in 1886, has been the largest party since 1927 and has dominated the country's politics from 1935, being a core member of social democratic coalitions. Until the 1970s, the party was completely dependent on the small farmer vote.[43]

As Knox[44] argues, cleavages emerged in the Scottish working class in the nineteenth century based on social differences between skilled and unskilled workers, initially between largely Protestant handloom weavers in the east and factory weavers in west of Scotland towns such as Paisley. They were exaggerated by (largely Catholic) Irish migrants, then generally viewed as poor, illiterate and drunken. Knox argues that between the late eighteenth and the mid-nineteenth centuries, the political culture of Scottish workers reflected the values of the skilled, Protestant workers whose position was increasingly threatened by mechanisation and specialisation, notably 'democracy and social justice, which in turn rested on a value system which derived its strength from independence, temperance and religion'.[45] They created alliances with the middle class to fight for the extension of the franchise before the 1832 Reform Act, but felt badly let down by the ultimate result, which gave the franchise only to propertied males, a tiny proportion of the Scottish population.[46]

Radicalism in the working class originated in the Irish Catholic and Highland migrants whose own life histories encouraged a focus on anti-landlord, anti-British State-ism, which was seen as supporting the old regime, and related 'home rule'. This radicalism was ruthlessly suppressed in the Radical Wars and the related march on the Carron Iron Works in the 1820s. Moreover, debates over 'the future of the Church of Scotland in the early 1840s distracted a great many artisans from radical politics'. Indigenous and Northern Irish Protestant hatred of Catholicism also 'ensured a large measure of hostility to Irish immigrants throughout Scotland, and confined Catholics for generations to come to unskilled, low paid work'.[47] These sectarian hostilities, related skill, status and wages issues, and consequential social divisions – coming on top of the divisions within the Protestant community in the nineteenth century – constrained working-class political solidarity in a period when it was perhaps most needed.

Although there was interest in Robert Owen's cooperative socialism reflected in his New Lanark Mill, Owenite secularism and ideas for gender equality deterred the working-class movement from its political programme.[48]

The working class took an interest in the UK Chartist movement for electoral reform, whose 1938 Charter sought, among other things, voting rights for all males over twenty-one who were not criminal or insane. Knox argues that Scottish Chartism was infused with moralism, temperance and radical religious movements, and favoured moral rather than physical force as a route to social and political change.[49] However, after the Commons rejected the Chartist petition in 1839, the influence of moderate Chartism declined as a more radical branch favouring physical violence and strike action became more influential for a time.

The Scottish skilled working class and middle class had shared Enlightenment ideas, including those of free trade and attachment to religion, but the turn to a more violent strand of Chartism and demands for universal suffrage in the late 1840s frightened the middle classes and led to their alignment with the interests of property.[50] This was a turning point for working-class politics in Scotland, which thereafter 'would be democratic, evolutionary, independent and morally infused by the interaction of temperance, religion and respectability. But they would be understood within a language and meaning system which recognised the validity of class as both an abstract ideological formulation and a lived experience.'[51]

Knox and Devine argue that there was no real clash between workers and capitalists, or indeed the middle classes, in nineteenth-century Scotland. The working classes were against landlordism, and control of the State by the landowning classes, at this time, blaming this system for the evils of low wages, the inadequacy of the poor laws, and poor housing conditions. The paternalism of many entrepreneurial families such as the Coates in cotton and Beardmores in steel also helped to avoid worker–capitalist conflicts. Moreover, the values of the 'respectable' skilled working classes were very close to those of the middle classes, supporting self-improvement, education, religious values and thrift.[52] As we have seen in Chapters 1, 2 and 3, this absence of radical labour politics, acceptance of liberal values and alliance between middle and working classes, together with the limited franchise, led to the Liberal political hegemony in the UK, including Scotland, between 1868 and 1914.

Because of the weakness of the Scottish working class movement in the nineteenth century, trade unionism remained weak and fragmented in Scotland until after 1900. In 1892, there were only 147,000 trade union members. However, militancy and trade union membership and coherence increased between 1900 and 1914, when affiliations to the General Trades Council grew. The Scottish Trades Union Council (STUC) was established in 1897, and after reforms in 1923 it led all trade union activity in Scotland. By 1924, trade union membership in Scotland had increased to 536,000, although by this time somewhat less than half of these belonged to 'purely Scottish' unions.[53]

Trade union activity was interrupted during the war and muted in the post-war boom, but continued in the recession of the 1920s and 1930s, which affected Scotland more seriously than other parts of the UK. The inter-war period was 'marked by a large-scale accretion in employer power as mass unemployment and a decline in trade union membership weakened worker resistance to the imperatives of capital and the impact of technological change on the distribution of skills in the workplace'.[54] Employers introduced new technocratic management regimes, intensifying industrial discipline and speeding up production, especially in coal. Deskilling occurred in coal- mining and engineering. In short, the 'proletarianisation' of the working class intensified.

WORKING-CLASS POVERTY AND THE DISTRIBUTION OF INCOME AND WEALTH

Despite rapid industrial and urban growth in Scotland during much of the nineteenth century, poverty remained endemic – especially among women and children – and health deteriorated at a time when changing capacities and ideologies made the response of the poor law less and less effective. Reliance on parish revenues to fund poor relief became problematic as destitute migrants from Ireland and rural Scotland flooded to the cities in numbers that could not be absorbed even by a rapidly growing industrial economy. In addition, there were persistently low wages in Scotland, and divisions between the skilled and the unskilled continued. The period between 1880 and the outbreak of the First World War was one of increased overseas competition for Scottish industry, forcing the introduction of new technology and new management practices that subordinated labour to capital.[55] The period between 1830 and 1914 was also one of very high out-migration from Scotland to the New World and to England: the rate of out-migration at this time was comparable with Norway and Ireland, topping the European league, indicating the poor wages and living conditions experienced by the working class and their families.[56] Evidently the quite extraordinary industrial growth during the nineteenth century had failed to deliver commensurate material and quality of life benefits to many workers and their families.

A very unequal distribution of income and wealth emerged in nineteenth-century Scotland. A few industrial families became very rich and a prosperous professional and business middle class of around a quarter of a million people also emerged in this period, while the majority survived on low wages and in uncertain employment.[57] Baxter estimated that almost a million people were in his unskilled or lower skilled categories in 1867, mainly male labourers who earned less than £50 per annum on average.[58] Scottish industrial wages were lower than those in England, while living costs were higher.[59] Such wide disparities in income and wealth, compounded by the skewed distribution of landownership, contrast with the Norwegian distribution discussed in Chapter 1, which was and has remained much more equal.

INDUSTRIAL CAPITAL

Despite the tendency to portray Scotland as an impoverished backwater before the Union in 1707, the evidence is of a thriving merchant class, active for example in the Baltic and Scandinavia, as well as significant cultural and educational achievements, including four universities.[60] Massive financing was needed for the development of Scottish Industry after the late eighteenth century, and this came partly from merchant capital, landlord capital and the relatively advanced banking system discussed in Chapter 8. In the eighteenth century, the rural location of mining and manufacturing, as well as their dependence on water power, charcoal and raw materials such as flax and wool, naturally involved a close association with the more innovative and resource-rich landowners, many of whom were also involved with the rapidly growing banking sector.[61] Successful Scottish merchants were involved, not least among which were the Glasgow 'tobacco lords', more than half of whom 'had shares in industrial ventures in the eighteenth century into linen, cotton, coal, sugar-boiling, glass-making and many other activities', and who also founded Glasgow's first three banks, the Ship Bank, the Arms Bank and the Thistle Bank, in the second half of the eighteenth century.[62] In the early stages of industrialisation, new technology was typically 'borrowed' from elsewhere. English and Welsh entrepreneurs, attracted by persistently low wages, were also investing in Scotland at this time, notable examples being Robert Owen's father-in-law David Dale, Hargreaves and Arkwright in textiles and textile machinery, and the Carron Company in iron-smelting. Thereafter, however, 'a whole stream of key inventions started to emanate from Scotland', including James Watt's steam engine, Archibald Buchanan's integrated cotton mill, Henry Bell's iron ship *Comet*, and J. B. Neilson's blast furnace.[63]

Scottish merchants and landowners were also involved in investments in land and sub-surface assets in the West Indies, USA, Australia, New Zealand and elsewhere. The Alliance Trust, founded and still based in Dundee, was established by the wealthy jute families of the nineteenth century to invest in land and subsurface minerals (including oil), as well as railway stocks, in the southern USA.[64] Devine shows that Scots were very active in sugar plantations in the West Indies in the eighteenth century.[65] Even at a time of rapid industrialisation, Scotland was exporting capital at a disproportionate rate. The trial of the City of Glasgow Bank

directors in 1878 revealed investment in 'doubtful or altogether hopeless speculative securities, such as Erie shares and other American railway stocks, buying
land in Australia and New Zealand', as well as in the East India Trade.[66] In the
last two decades of the nineteenth century, the Bank of Scotland shifted resources
to London as well as directly investing in US, colonial and railway stocks in
North and South America and India, among others. It also had significant, if less
profitable, interests in Trinidad sugar estates.[67] In the first decade of the twentieth
century, Thomas Aitken, the manager of the London branch of the bank, had
made large advances to Canadian and Brazilian enterprises which turned out to be
bad investments.[68]

Nevertheless, despite this and other evidence of capital outflow, sometimes into
bad or highly risky investments, the question of what happened to this undoubtedly great wealth, and the skilled workers, entrepreneurs and inventors who
created it, by the second half of the twentieth century, when Scotland was portrayed as a nation of 'spongers' dependent on State handouts and capital inflows,
remains to be answered.

THE COLLAPSE OF HEAVY INDUSTRY IN SCOTLAND

Scotland's economy faltered in the inter-war period when growth was much slower
than the UK as a whole and rates of migration and unemployment were much
higher.[69] Although several traditional heavy industries, such as shipbuilding and
mechanical engineering, had maintained their position in this period, consumer
goods remained underrepresented and several promising developments in the
vehicle and aircraft industries and related supply sectors failed. The 'main feature
of the Scottish economy between the wars were the heavier commitment to industries that were stagnating or in decline . . . [and] at the same time, an inability to
secure a share in the 'new' growth industries of the 1930s'.[70] By the later 1930s,
reports from the Scottish Development Council and related Scottish Economic
Committee were united in demanding greater efforts on industrial diversification,
as well as a uniquely Scottish approach. The acceptance of the role of the State
by an organisation in which industrialists were very well represented was unique
within the UK and influenced post-war structures and policies.[71] However, the
thinking of the civil servants and planners during this period was overwhelmingly
dominated by the idea that the poor prospects for traditional heavy industries
discouraged investment and new ideas.[72]

Heavy industry was saved again by the Second World War and its immediate post-war boom, which obscured latent competitive problems in coal, steel,
shipbuilding and locomotive-manufacturing until the late 1950s. By the 1960s,
unemployment had increased, heavy industry was stagnating, diversification was
minimal, and the majority of larger manufacturing plants were no longer owned
by Scottish interests. Not only had outward migration of people continued apace

in the 1950s but so too had the export of Scottish capital. By 1958, the Clyde shipyards launched only 4.5 per cent of world tonnage, compared with 18 per cent in 1947.[73] Industrial employment reached its peak around 1960, and declined relatively and absolutely thereafter. Within industry itself, the balance shifted to consumer-orientated industries including electronics, symbolised by the IBM plant in Greenock. Increasingly these new consumer industries were owned by foreign capital, and they had few of the inter-industry connections that typified Scottish industrial development between the eighteenth and twentieth centuries. Thus Campbell[74] points out that whereas before the war about two-thirds of the tenants occupying about half of the floor space were Scottish concerns, by 1960 only one-third, renting some 15 per cent of the floor area, were Scottish. He further states that these were largely American concerns. A later study by John Firn showed that in 1973 only 41 per cent of manufacturing employment was controlled in Scotland, American-owned firms accounting for 15 per cent of manufacturing employment. Moreover, the five fastest-growing sectors in the early 1970s had less than 14 per cent Scottish control.[75]

One bright star on the post-war Scottish economic horizon was hydro-electricity, the development of which was earlier opposed by landowners, preservationist bodies and coal-owners. The great wartime Secretary of State Tom Johnston persuaded Parliament to pass the Hydro-Electric (Scotland) Act, which vested responsibility for all developments north of the 'Highland Line' between Dumbarton and Montrose in the new Hydro Electric Board. The background is that before the Second World War there were only six hydro-electric works in the Highlands – three for aluminium-smelting in Fort William, Kinlochleven and Foyers, and three for general purposes at Rannoch, Tummel and Loch Wishart. Six further proposed developments had been turned down by Parliament, while others never reached Westminster.[76] Electricity was nationalised by the post-war Labour government, and the North of Scotland Hydro Electric Board (NOSHEB) was created to absorb the Grampian and other smaller electricity producers in the north of Scotland. By 1950, hydro-electricity generation capacity controlled by the Board was 644,600 kW. By 1965, fifty-four main power stations and seventy-eight dams had been built, providing a total generating capacity of over 1,000 megawatts. NOSHEB was privatised by the Thatcher government in 1990.

Despite the early development of aluminium-smelting based on hydro power by the British Aluminium Company at Foyers in 1886, and the later development of two other smelters, the view of the Board was that power should be transported to industry, rather than locating industry where the power was produced. This appears to have been an effort to keep the conservationist and landowning interests quiet. Yet it deprived the Highlands of a potential source of industrial regeneration. Nevertheless, the Hydro Electric Board did have development responsibilities, which it interpreted as encouraging the subsidisation of electricity connections to the farms and crofts, and indeed private homes, scattered across this sparsely populated region. The success of this policy is regarded by some historians as a great achievement.[77] However, it neither provided cheap power to the Highlands nor led to industrial development there. Today, in Inverness, electricity from the inheritor company of Scottish hydro-electric dams (now part of Scottish and Southern Energy) is more expensive than several other suppliers, and some 40 per cent dearer than in Norway.[78]

During the 1950s and 1960s, as in earlier crises of Scottish industry, reports on the economic situation argued that Scotland was far too dependent on traditional heavy industries, particularly in the west-central area around Glasgow and Lanarkshire. The government's strategy, through the Scottish Development Department established in 1962 and a central Scotland development plan, was to bolster heavy industry by massive investment, in particular in Colville's strip-mill at Ravenscraig, while forcing light manufacturers to move to Scotland under rigid industrial planning laws. This included the Rootes car plant at Linwood and the BMC truck plant at Bathgate. Ravenscraig, then part of British Steel, finally closed on 24 June 1992, effectively symbolising the end of significant heavy industry in Scotland. The Linwood car plant was bought by Chrysler UK and then Peugeot and closed in 1981, most of the factory being demolished soon afterwards. Tractor assembly at Bathgate ended in 1982, following sale to Marshall Tractors who transferred production to England. Truck assembly ceased in 1985, and the plant closed in 1986.[79] Although the Executive Committee of the Scottish Council (Development and Industry) described the three projects as 'the largest economic advance made by Scotland during the century', the advance turned out to be unsustainable in the face of adverse exchange rates facing exporters and Mrs Thatcher's neo-liberal policies. The old engineering and shipbuilding industries were being closed down at a critical juncture, notably the discovery of North Sea oil in 1969. The drive for inward investment, muted when the Scottish Development Agency was established in 1974, intensified in the 1980s with the establishment of Locate in Scotland. It seemed that nobody in authority any longer believed in indigenous Scottish enterprise.

Some writers[80] are enthusiastic about the impacts of the efforts at attracting light manufacturing and related inward investment to Scotland through the Scottish Development Agency (later named Scottish Enterprise) and Locate in Scotland, just as was the eminent economic historian Roy Campbell of earlier efforts. However, it is important to reflect that manufacturing employment in Scotland peaked at around 748,000 in 1954, and remained as high as 596,000 in 1979 before collapsing to its 2010 level of 176,000. The mainly US multinationals who came to Scotland in the 1950s wanted a pool of cheap, flexible labour, and opposed the support of traditional heavy industry which they considered would keep wages at too high a level.[81] As part of this, they viewed the run-down of traditional heavy industry as 'too slow', a view increasingly reflected in subsequent government policies. Yet other advanced countries such as Germany, Japan and Norway were developing heavy industry at the same time. It seems probable that future historians will wish to review the almost total acceptance by the Scottish elite in government, industry and finance that efforts to modernise Scotland's once-dominant shipbuilding and engineering sectors were doomed to failure. As we have seen, this view took root slowly during the twentieth century and finally triumphed in the Thatcher years when the proud legacy of Scotland's industrial achievements – which might otherwise have served Scotland's future oil economy well – was swept aside by neo-liberal ideology and politics.

NORWAY'S POST-WAR INDUSTRIALISATION

As Brox argues (see Chapter 7), post-Second World War economic vitality in Norway's rural areas had positive consequences for the working class, including the end of poverty, the expansion of rural opportunities, and investment in infrastructure and public transportation. This maintained the scarcity of labour in rural and urban labour markets, and kept wages high.

POLICY DIFFERENCES: PROTECTION AND LIBERALISATION

Scottish industrial growth in the nineteenth century could not have occurred at such a rate and in such a form without a rapid and sustained widening and deepening of the market which was largely a consequence of the Union, and the active participation of Scottish interests in British Empire-building. While in the eighteenth century and earlier, markets for manufactured products were to a large extent local, and demand consequently constrained by low population and purchasing power, by the middle of the nineteenth century the markets for the products of Scottish manufacturing had become both UK-wide and international.

Norway, like other countries, had to face the British lead in industrial development in the nineteenth century. Senghaas suggests six types of response to the challenge posed by this lead,[82] which basically 'peripheralised' industry in the rest of Europe and elsewhere: Dissociative development (Type I); Associative development (Type II); Associative-dissociative development (Type III); Dissociative State-capitalist development (Type IV); Dissociative State-socialist development (Type V); and delayed development in newly industrialising countries (Type VI). By 'association', Senghaas basically means free trade and global association, and by 'dissociation' he means selective delinking from world markets based on the 'infant industry' arguments of Friedrich List.[83] Senghaas places Norway in Type III, where industrialisation begins with an export-orientated associative phase linked to the primary sector – agriculture, forestry, minerals – and moves on to a dissociative phase based on import substitution. This in turn eventually leads to a new associative stage based on free trade for specialist manufactures, as occurred in Norway after the Second World War.[84] However, the Norwegian case is special because it achieved integration into world markets in the second half of the nineteenth century through its large merchant shipping fleet, the third-largest in the world after Britain and the USA. In 1880, 40 per cent of Norway's export earnings, and over 10 per cent of national income, came from shipping.[85]

Yet, despite the undoubted advances in Norwegian industrialisation before the Second World War, the share of manufacturing industry in GNP in 1950 at around 15 per cent was still lower than that in Denmark and Japan (17 per cent), Argentina (21 per cent) and France, Germany and the UK (between 27 and 29 per cent).[86] Moreover, the bulk of industrial activity in 1949 was accounted for by 'relatively simple transformation of foods and raw materials', which accounted for over three-quarters of exports in 1949. Finally, manufacturing activities were aimed at the home market – only 3 per cent of output of final manufactured goods was exported in 1949, and manufactures accounted for less than 10 per cent of merchandise exports.[87]

Nevertheless, between 1950 and 1966 output of final manufactured goods increased rapidly and by 1966 these accounted for nearly one-third of merchandise exports. Belassa attributes this growth to Norway's decision to opt for 'associative' policies that stimulated exports and increased foreign competition in domestic markets. Whereas the earlier development of consumer – final manufacturing – industry took place in a context of 'moderate protection', the new approach favoured lowering of tariffs and the maintenance of competitive exchange rates for the Krone.[88] In 1959, Norway – with the active support of industrialists - became one of the founding members of EFTA – the European Free Trade Area – after which the remaining tariffs for non-agricultural products were reduced and eventually dismantled within the EFTA area. This opened the export market for Norwegian manufactured products as EFTA then included the UK, Austria, Denmark, Finland (as an associate), Portugal, Sweden and Switzerland.

The post-war expansion of manufacturing industry in Norway led to the share of this sector in all commodity production value added increasing from 37.1 per cent in 1949 to 48.4 per cent by 1966, while that of intermediate products at lower stages of transformation also increased from 21.3 per cent to 27.2 per cent. The most rapid expansion was in electricity-intensive industries, especially carbide, ferro-alloys, aluminium and fertilisers, but food, drink and tobacco also experienced rapid growth. In addition, there was a shift to higher stages of processing requiring more skilled labour, as well as specialisation.[89] At the same time, industries relying on unskilled and semi-skilled labour such as textiles, clothing, leather and leather products, and footwear were static and subsequently declined. In the period before North Sea oil, as a result of these transformations, wage levels in Norway had grown to approximate those in other major European countries. The growth in production of specialised iron and steel products, mechanical-handling equipment, shipbuilding and other products between 1949 and 1966 also helped to place Norway in a stronger position when oil exploitation started.

Foreign ownership also increased in Norwegian industry in the 1990s, from about 13 to 20 per cent of manufacturing employment and from 18 to 28 per cent of production between 1995 and 1999.[90] However, this was a much lower proportion than in Scotland where, by 1973, 41 per cent of manufacturing employment was controlled by foreign companies.[91]

RIGHTS TO NATURAL RESOURCES

A central political issue in Norway by 1906 was the regulation of the country's main natural resources, the outcome being the Concession Laws of 1906–9. These were intended to restrict the influence of large foreign capitalists on Norway's industrial and social development, and regulate control of natural resources and issues of industrial location.[92] This has been a consistent dimension of natural resource policies, which extended to public access to land and foreshore (see Chapter 11), hunting rights and, later, North Sea oil and gas.

The Concession Laws applied to the exploitation of waterfalls, mines and forests, and required government permission in each case. Certain conditions were applied to concessions granted, the most important of which concerned the reversion of ownership after forty to sixty years. There was considerable argument that the Concession Laws would deter foreign and domestic investment, and hence slow down industrial developments, apparently accepted by many historians such as Wilhelm Keilhau.[93] However, Lange's own more quantitative analysis shows no evidence of decline in foreign or domestic investment, or production, in any of the affected industries after the Concession Laws were passed in 1909. Indeed, Lange points out that 'the period 1905–1916 was the longest continuous period of economic growth in modern Norwegian history before the Second World War' and, further, 'those branches that were most closely connected with the expansion of electric power and mining . . . were also those that enjoyed by far the greatest growth during this period.'[94] Industrial production increased by 5.7 per cent a year between 1905 and 1916, while the annual rate of growth for the chemical industry was 18.3 per cent, for extraction of ores and metals 15.9 per cent, and for timber-processing 7.3 per cent.[95] Electrical energy from hydro power increased by over 500 per cent between 1906 and 1914.[96] Lange also provides data that shows increasing investment between 1909 and 1912 compared either with previous periods or with comparable rates of investment in Sweden and Denmark. Finally, Lange and others argue that this period was 'the era of the breakthrough of large-scale industry in Norway'.[97]

As a result of the Concession Laws, Norway's central and local governments were able to hold increasing stakes in all of its key natural resources in the twentieth century, and to use these in productive ways, including the retention of viable local settlements across the country.

While coal, hydro-electricity dams and considerable forest land were in public ownership for varying periods in twentieth-century Scotland, there was no equivalent to the Concession Laws, and no linking of rights to exploit natural resources to industrial development. Nor was there a political consensus or consistent policy on such issues.

THE ROLE OF THE STATE AND THE CONTRASTING HISTORIES OF NORTH SEA OIL IN SCOTLAND AND NORWAY

As argued above, a consensus on the role of the State in industrial change emerged between capital, labour and government in Scotland in the 1930s, and this consensus was largely maintained in the post-war period up until the 1970s. However, the lack of faith in traditional heavy industry and its ability to adapt to competitive pressures, reinforced by a political regime that first lost the confidence of the working class, manifested in a series of 'damaging' strikes during the Heath and Callaghan governments in the 1970s and, after 1979, transformed under a more liberal market-orientated regime, surely forms an important element in any explanation of the failure of Scottish industrial entrepreneurs to respond to the new demands of the North Sea oil industry.[98] The Offshore Supplies Office (OSO) was set up in 1973 with the aim of increasing local content in the oil-exploration industry to 70 per cent after the government realised that local content and related employment was likely to be too low during the development of the northern oil basin.[99] However, unlike Norway, there was no local content requirement established in licences awarded. In the event, local content in 1974 only amounted to 'about 40 %'.[100] Tony Benn's efforts to secure benefits for British industry after he became Energy Minister in 1974, by creating the British National Oil Corporation (BNOC) and leaning on the two British-based oil multinationals, BP and Shell, also failed,[101] foundering under the ideological weight of Heath's 'Selsdon Man' in 1971, much reinforced after 1979 by Thatcher's 'liberalism', as well as related trade union strife and continued collapse of UK-owned heavy engineering, shipbuilding and other related manufacturing. As Kemp says in a classic understatement in the official history of North Sea oil, 'The incoming Conservative Government was unenthusiastic about the advantages of a state oil company',[102] and BNOC was privatised in 1982.

The Norwegian case is very different. Despite Norway's open economy policies after the war, the discovery of North Sea oil was seen as creating a strong need for government intervention, involving itself as both owner and entrepreneur.[103] As Austvik argues, 'the state managed to create a competitive national petroleum industry from nothing in only a couple of decades. It also managed to take most of the profits from the activities itself' and, one might add, invest much of those profits in a national oil fund for the future of Norway, the value of which was NOK 3,961 billion (roughly £400 billion) at the end of 2012.[104]

Unlike the UK, Norway had very little knowledge about the oil industry before the start of oil activities in the North Sea in the late 1960s and early 1970s. However, it put together a very clear and overtly protectionist policy for its development by 1971, which gave the State a central role as resource-owner, regulator and entrepreneur. Policy was agreed in the Industrial Committee and presented to the *Storting* (parliament) on 14 June 1971. The policy laid down the 'ten commandments' for the oil industry, which together aimed to secure benefits for the whole nation from its development.[105] These were:

1   Securing national management and control over all operations on the Norwegian continental shelf;
2   Exploiting discoveries in a way that minimises Norway's external dependence for crude oil supplies;
3   Developing new industrial activities based on oil;
4   Taking the necessary account of existing industries as well as the protection of the environment in the development of the industry;
5   Flaring of usable gas not to be permitted except for brief periods of testing;
6   North Sea oil to be landed in Norway, with exceptions only based on specific national policy issues;
7   The State to become involved at all appropriate levels in a coordinating role to ensure the creation of an integrated Norwegian oil community with both national and international ambitions;
8   A State oil company to be established to look after the State's commercial interests and to collaborate with domestic and international oil interests;
9   The pattern of oil activity north of the 62nd parallel to satisfy the special policy concerns in this area;
10 Large-scale Norwegian oil finds could add new dimensions to Norway's foreign policy.

In 1972, the fully State-owned company Statoil was established. Preference was given to Norwegian suppliers of equipment and services, and Statoil (and later on Norske Hydro) got the best licences, representing a form of 'infant-industry' protection. Although later partly liberalised, Norway did not liberalise the oil sector as part of the liberalising tendencies of the 1980s and 1990s. The State is still in control at all levels, and the mainly-State/part-private model is hardly controversial in Norway, even today with the Conservative-Populist coalition.

CONCLUSION

This comparison between the development of industry in Norway and Scotland since about 1800 has revealed six key, and often related, differences, which seem to us to have crucial importance for any understanding of the general economic, social and political development of the two countries in the modern period. We also believe that these differences still have important messages for countries still in the early stages of industrialisation.

The first important difference lies in the fact that while Scotland's industrialisation coincided with a form of agrarian change that required the removal of the peasantry from their means of subsistence in the form of smallholdings and their displacement to the urban centres, Norway's industrialisation coincided with a growth in both the number of smallholdings and in the peasant population itself, and took the form of a decentralised, even rural, industrialisation which provided an additional means of survival on small farms. Moreover, it was the 'surplus' peasantry from both Scotland and Ireland that provided a 'reserve army' of labour for the rapid Scottish industrial development of the nineteenth century, and kept wages low, while labour was persistently in short supply in Norway, keeping wages relatively high and forcing attention increasingly on higher value-added products that increasingly built on Norway's highly competitive energy resources in the form of hydro power and also skilled labour.

The second key difference concerns the development of working-class politics during and after the nineteenth century. Scotland's working classes and the mainly rural Scottish and Irish migrant streams that continually augmented it in the nineteenth century, were mainly focused on the injustices of landowner power and its impact on the highly unrepresentative political system, and yet also divided by religion. Norway's working classes, however, did not face the power of great landowners by the early nineteenth century and were essentially 'rural' and mainly small farmers in a period when representative liberal constitution drafted by Norwegians in 1814 allowed them a much higher degree of political engagement than was possible in Scotland.

The third important difference is that the Norwegian peasants and working class during the nineteenth century were more or less one and the same, since most of those working in industry were also peasants or their families. Their main concerns, which were shared, were earning a fair income for them and their families, securing their rights over resources, and avoiding exploitation by foreign capital. This contrasted with Scotland, where the largest part of the industrial working class by the second half of the nineteenth century was landless labour that had migrated to the rapidly growing cities.

The fourth key difference lies in the nature, location and governance of the energy supply used for industrial development, which was coal in the case of Scotland and hydro-electric power in the case of Norway. While coal deposits were largely concentrated in and around the central belt of Scotland, hydro-electric resources in Norway were scattered throughout the country. The exploitation of coal by modern Scottish industry in the nineteenth century, and parallel development of steam engines, led to a centralisation of industry in the central belt, and an early urbanisation of the population in that region. Such a movement of population, and urbanisation, was not, however, required in Norwegian industrialisation, and nor did it take place.

A fifth important difference was the impact of neo-liberal economic policies from the 1970s. In a very real sense these policies, encapsulated by some in the UK as 'Selsdon man'[106] or, later, 'Thatcherism'[107] but more generally as the 'Washington Consensus',[108] brought the not insignificant remnants of Scottish steel, shipbuilding and other engineering to their deaths and precluded significant State involvement in the emerging oil industry. While neo-liberal policies were not without impact on Norway in the longer run, Norway was much more resistant to them than Scotland because of its strong social democracy, the political consensus on welfare state policies and its strong economy during the 1970s and 1980s.

The sixth and final key factor concerns the rights of people to common property. Norwegians have a strongly held political idea that natural resources are common property, and their use should benefit all. This approach is certainly reflected in the Allemannsretten law granting public rights over land and sea as well as certain other rights, such as the right to pick mushrooms and berries. It was also reflected in the treatment of hydro-electric resources, which eventually reverted to the counties and municipalities and added to their revenue streams. And it was also reflected in the policies for the development of North Sea oil, particularly that 'the natural resources on the Norwegian Continental Shelf should benefit the entire nation',[109] that its exploitation should be under national management and control, that a State oil company should be established, and that new industrial activities should be developed on the basis of petroleum.[110] Contrast this with the strong position of private property in Scotland, rooted in the dispossession of the people from their land between the sixteenth and nineteenth centuries through clearances and the erosion of common rights, the political presence of large landowners in the House of Lords, and the ultimate treatment of Scotland's natural resources of coal, hydro power and oil.

Notes

1. By 'proto-industry', a pre-factory mode of production is usually implied. See also Mendels (1972: 241–61) and Hovland et al. (1982: 45–56). The concept is generally attributed to Mendels, who used it to 'describe the expansion of domestic industries producing goods for non-local markets . . . [and] which employed previously untapped labour resources . . . and occurred in symbiosis with agriculture' (Hutchison, 2012: 4).

2. See, for example, Riis (1988), Smout (1962), Murdoch (2006) and Hutchison (2012).

3. See Campbell, 1971: 54–67; Smout, 1969: 244–255; Devine, 1999: 54–5, 111–12, 142.

4. Smout, 1969: 261.

5. de Vreis, 1984: 38–48.
6. Devine, 1999: 157.
7. Smout, 1963: 232.
8. Campbell, 1971: 54.
9. Campbell, 1971: 60.
10. Tom Devine states that the British Linen Company, which later became the British Linen Bank, was the only eighteenth-century chartered bank in Britain explicitly devoted to industrial expansion (Devine, 1999: 105–6).
11. Smout, 1969: 244.
12. Iron works had been set up at Abernethy before 1730, with four furnaces using charcoal made from the Abernethy pine forest (Grant, 1994: 11; Murray, 1883).
13. Campbell, 1971: 64.
14. Smout (1963: 49) states, 'Norwegians learned to mass-produce ships at a very much cheaper rate than had ever been possible in Scotland' in the seventeenth and eighteenth centuries.
15. Hovland et al., 2011; Heidar, 2001.
16. Hutchison (2012: 62) discusses pluriactivity in relation to Norway's proto-industrialisation between 1750 and 1830.
17. See also Chapter 4 for an account of the enclosures and clearances as part of the agrarian revolution or 'improvement' in Scotland from the mid-eighteenth century.
18. Derry, 1979: 252.
19. Heidar, 2001: 14.
20. Knox, 1999: 34.
21. This argument is made by Rosalind Mitchison (2000).
22. Knox, 1999: 35–6.
23. Whatley, 1997.
24. Knox, 1999: 37.
25. W. Arthur Lewis' famous article, 'Economic Development with Unlimited Supplies of Labour', was published in *The Manchester School*, May 1954. In it Lewis was reflecting the assumptions of the classical economists from Smith to Marx that an unlimited supply of labour was available to be deployed on capital accumulation at subsistence wages.
26. Devine, 1999: 249–52.
27. Campbell, 1965: 119–21.
28. Knox, 1999: 85–6.
29. Ibid.: 132.
30. This last process allowed higher phosphorus iron to be used. See Campbell, 1965: 231.
31. Devine, 1999: 265.
32. Devine, 1999: 266–8; Knox, 1999: 190.
33. Campbell, 1965: 272–3.
34. See, for example, Campbell, 1965: 323–5.
35. Harvie, 1994; Smith, 2011.
36. Heidar, 2001: 20.

37. Norwegian Telegraph Museum, Sørvågen, Lofoten.
38. Grimley, 1937: 53.
39. Lee's (1979) historical data for Scotland gives 316,257 employed in agriculture, forestry and fishing compared with 525,343 in manufacturing in the 1851 census. See also Table 7.1. Since about 500,000 were occupied in agriculture, forestry and fishing in 1821, compared with about 300,000 in manufacturing, the crossover took place between 1821 and 1851.
40. Birkeland was also a Norwegian.
41. Norway's Centre Party PM, Per Borten, grandfather of the Oil Minister in the last Stoltenberg government, secretly arranged with Hambros Bank, London, to acquire a 51 per cent majority stake in Norsk Hydro for the State in 1969, a feat which was accomplished by buying shares in various European markets in small lots in order to avoid increasing the share price. Borten subsequently won government approval for his actions, even though the government was a centre-right coalition. Hogne Honset, 'Kronikk', *Klassekampen*, 26 April 2013. Hambros Bank was founded by a Danish family, and traditionally dealt with Scandinavian business in the London markets.
42. Campbell, 1965: 130–2.
43. Brox, 2006: 21.
44. Knox, 1999: 41, 43–6.
45. Ibid.: 56.
46. This compared with a tiny 2,665 voters, all male, of whom 1,318 were 'non-resident appointees of the greater landowners who owned the superiorities' in the 1788 elections (Saville, 1996: 172, 196). By 1830, Scotland's electorate was less than 4,500 out of a population of 2.3 million. After the 1832 Reform Act (Scotland), 2.2 per cent of adult males qualified for the franchise, while in the burghs it was 3.7 per cent (Pentland, 2013).
47. Knox, 1999: 46. See also Devine, 1999: 163.
48. Knox, 1999: 64.
49. Ibid.: 68–9.
50. Knox, 1999: 76–7.
51. Ibid.: 78.
52. Knox, 1999: 109.
53. Campbell, 1965: 315.
54. Knox, 1999: 203.
55. Knox, 1999: 145–53.
56. Devine, 1999: 263.
57. Ibid.: 261–3.
58. The Victorian economist R. D. Baxter (1867) cited by Devine, 1999: 263.
59. Devine, 1999: 263; Rodger, 1988.
60. See Smout, 1963; Grosjean and Murdoch, 2005; Murdoch, 2006; Riis, 1988; Campbell and Skinner, 1982: 42–7.
61. The fascinating example of the Malcolms of Poltalloch is explored in Macinnes (2007). The Malcolms became plantation owners in Jamaica after the Union of 1707, also becoming merchants trading in sugar, rum, cotton and livestock as well as slaves, and expanding their operations to central America, the rest of the

Caribbean, Australia, Scottish and London property and Scottish provincial banking, among others, all founded on wealth repatriated from Jamaica.

62. Devine, 1999: 115.
63. Ibid.: 115–16.
64. The Alliance Trust is the subject of a new history by Charles Munn, *Investing for Generations – A History of Alliance Trust*, published by Dundee University Press in 2013. The company was incorporated in 1888 by the merger of two Dundee-based investment and mortgage companies. The volume makes clear that the founders had made their fortunes in jute production and formed ventures to lend money to immigrant farmers in Washington State and Oregon as well as to sugar planters in the Hawaiian Islands. The book follows the company's move into US railway bonds, mineral rights and fixed-interest securities, ultimately to become one of the largest generalist UK investment trusts, managing assets of around £2.7 billion. The Trust continues to hold some oil and gas properties in Texas, Louisiana and Oklahoma, which remain from the original mortgage business of its founding companies, and continue to generate considerable income.
65. Devine, 1999: 120.
66. Wallace, 1905: 7.
67. Saville, 1996: 441–2.
68. Ibid.: 468–9.
69. Saville, 1985: 4.
70. Buxton (1980), cited in Saville, 1985: 11.
71. Saville, 1985: 15–17.
72. Ibid.: 26.
73. Devine, 1999: 571.
74. Campbell, 1965: 325.
75. Firn (1975), 'External Control and Regional Policy', in Brown, G. (ed.), 'The Red Paper on Scotland', EUSPB, Edinburgh. Cited in Bryden, 1985: 265–6.
76. Saville, 1985: 27.
77. See, for example, Devine, 1999: 558–9.
78. Personally checked online by the authors on 4 November 2013. Scottish Hydro quoted 14.459p/kwh, which compared with 13.104p/kwh quoted by E.ON, 14.102p/kwh quoted by British Gas and 88.1 øre per kwh (9.270p/kwh) average for the second quarter of 2013 quoted by SSB in Norway.
79. Peden, 2012: 659.
80. For example, McCrone and Randall in Saville, 1985.
81. Saville, 1996: 653.
82. Senghaas, 1985: 32.
83. Senghaas, 1977; 1985: 2.
84. Belassa, 1969.
85. Senghaas, 1985: 33.
86. Belassa, 1969: 346.
87. Ibid.: 349.
88. Belassa, 1969: 349.
89. Ibid.: 355.

90. Statistics Norway. Manufacturing statistics. Foreign ownership in manufacturing. Increased foreign ownership in manufacturing. Published 2 August 2001. Also available online at http://www.ssb.no/energi-og-industri/artikler-og-publikas-joner/increased-foreign-ownership-in-manufacturing (accessed 11 March 2014).
91. Firn, 1970.
92. Lange, 1977: 311.
93. See Kaelhau, 1938: 158 (cited by Lange, 1977: 313).
94. Lange, 1977: 319.
95. SSB, 1955.
96. Based on figures in Lange, 1977: 326.
97. Ibid.: 319.
98. Harvie, 1994.
99. Smith, 2011: 21.
100. Ibid.: 21.
101. Harvie, 1994: 5.
102. Kemp, 2012: 682.
103. Austvik, 2012.
104. Government Pension Fund Global: Annual Report to the Storting, 2012.
105. Based on Austvik, 2012: 326–7.
106. Harold Wilson, the Labour PM of the day, coined the phrase after a meeting in 1970 of the Conservative shadow cabinet in Selsdon to plan their campaign. It was at this meeting that the Conservative party adopted free-market policies, setting up the Selsdon Group to ensure their continuance.
107. Margaret Thatcher became PM after the 1979 election, and remained in post until 1990, winning two further elections. Her economic policies stressed deregulation, reducing the power and influence of trade unions, flexible labour markets, privatisation of State companies, and generally a reduction of the State in favour of the free market.
108. 'Fiscal austerity, privatisation, and market liberalisation were the three pillars of the Washington Consensus' (Stiglitz, 2002: 53), which term encapsulated the policies of the International Monetary Fund (IMF), World Bank, US Treasury and UK Government after 1979.
109. Industrial Committee Report to the Storting, 14 June 1971.
110. Austvik, 2012.

CHAPTER 7

Reflections on the Making of Norway

Ottar Brox

INTRODUCTION

This chapter is an attempt to tell Scottish readers how another small, peripheral country became a reasonably economically efficient but relatively
egalitarian nation – in marked contrast to the kingdom of which Scotland is a part.
My contribution is based on a lifelong study of the history of modern Norway,
fieldwork in many different local communities – mostly in the northern part of my
country, where I grew up – and serious participation in local and national politics.
But I have learned a lot about Norway through fieldwork and shorter trips to comparable situations abroad, in Newfoundland, Iceland and Scotland, where I have
had the good fortune of having friends and colleagues like the late Robert Storey,
his wife the Gaelic scholar Lisa Storey and our common friend, John Bryden.

In April 1964, I spent a week on Vatersay, at the southern tip of the Outer
Hebrides. At that time, I worked as a research assistant on the project 'Human
geography studies of North Norway' at Tromsø Museum. The anthropologists
at the University of Edinburgh invited me as a visiting 'Northern Scholar' for a
month, including a grant for travelling around the country.

I must admit that I, as an agricultural economist with some social anthropology and sociology in my tool chest, was rather unprepared for my North Norway
project, which I tried to develop in the direction of finding differences between
declining coastal villages and those that seemed to be able to survive – comparing their access to natural resources, ability to raise capital, access to markets,
and so on. But my observations and conversations with people on Vatersay and
Barra were a very important impulse to expand my set of interacting explana-
tory categories beyond ecology and local culture. The decisive importance of the
politically manipulable rules of the economic game became very easy to discover
– like in fields such as fish marketing and subsistence agriculture – and the natural

conditions in Vatersay were favourable as compared with many Arctic local communities, where people carrying on subsistence agriculture and seasonal fishing
fifty years ago enjoyed a living standard indeed comparable with urban wage
labour anywhere. In the around twenty fishing villages in the two municipalities
on the exposed western coast of Senja, where I grew up, the population increased
from 2,822 in 1930 to 3,590 in 1960, and the number of fishing boats less than 30
feet from 62 in 1934 to 307 in 1962.[1]

THE SUBSISTENCE ECONOMY IN RURAL NORTH NORWAY
AND THE HIGHLANDS AND ISLANDS OF SCOTLAND

The main conclusion from my research in coastal villages was that established
subsistence farm households, earning most of their cash income from seasonal
small boat (18–30 feet) fishing, or odd jobs in construction or services, seemed
to be uninterested in modern industrial employment in regional urban centres,
or stable, rather well-paid jobs in offshore fishing based in central harbours. It
was hard to find households willing to move to cities or towns even if they would
be secured jobs giving wages three times their previous cash earnings. Local tax
records of 1960 indicate that small farmer cash incomes of NOK 5,000 to 6,000
(£249–299 at October 1960 exchange rates) p.a. seemed to be standard, while the
unskilled urban worker could earn NOK 15,000 to 18,000 (£748–898) if permanently employed. I must stress that I am now referring to established households,
as young, unattached individuals are a different matter, being more mobile, as well
as propertyless.

Comparing Histories

The contrasts in demographic development between the two nations are indeed
striking: Norway had only about half the population of Scotland in 1801. But
today, the two countries are both home to five million people. Norway's population has been growing rather fast lately, also through immigration, whereas
Scotland has experienced zero growth for most of the period since 1951.

Natural conditions are similar in the two countries – except for the cold Arctic
climate and the somewhat richer fish resources of northern Norway, whereas
much more of the land is suitable for agriculture and pastures in Scotland. I hope
to show, however, that political factors, such as the division of power, property
relations and the development of the labour market, can explain more of the differences in economic and social development. Before the beginning of industrialisation in the United Kingdom – around 1750 – the life of ordinary Norwegians had
very much in common with rural life in Scotland. Both populations were still in
feudal harness, in the sense that most of the land was owned by larger or smaller
noblemen, merchants, clergy or others belonging to classes above those who

Table 7.1 Manufacturing Employment, 1825–2011, Scotland and Norway (thousands)

	1825	1851	1911	1951	2001	2011
Scotland	350[a]	525	735[b]	748[c]	299	194
Norway	17	95[d]	169[e]	358[f]	285	236

Sources: Norway: SSB (Statistics Norway) Historical Archives to 1951, then labour force survey.

Scottish 1825 data on manufacturing employment is based on Sinclair's estimate of 275,000 employed in fabrics and textiles in the early 1800s, and which represented nearly 90 per cent of all those working in manufacturing at the time. See also Devine, 1999: 108. The 1851 data for Scotland is from Lee, C. H. (1979) *British Regional Employment Statistics 1841–1971*, Cambridge.

Notes:
[a] estimate based on 1801 data.
[b] 1907 data.
[c] 1954 data.
[d] 1875 data.
[e] 1910 data.
[f] 1950 data.

worked the land, although even then, as Chapter 1 makes clear, an important difference in landownership structures and landed power had emerged between the two countries. The second important difference may be the fact that Scotland had four universities by the sixteenth century and some of the most well-known intellectuals and inventors of the world.[2] The level of literacy was – as in Scotland – relatively high in Norway, probably due to legal rules to the effect that one had to be confirmed, which implied being able to read the Bible, to be allowed to marry.

Norwegian peasants lived in a subsistence economy: most of the households generally produced food, clothes and housing for their own consumption – as in most of the rural world before as well as after the industrial revolution in Great Britain. They grew and collected food, as well as fodder for their animals, and tried to minimise their need for money, which was hard to get. Norwegian tenants usually paid their rents and taxes in kind (butter, dried fish and other naturalia), whereas cottage industries like spinning, weaving and knitting of wool and linen became a source of necessary cash in rural Scotland. But during the latter part of the eighteenth century the two countries started to develop along different paths. In Norway, the 'old-fashioned' subsistence economy continued largely as before, even if the export of fish, timber and planks – mainly produced by farmers between agricultural seasons – to Western Europe continued with varying success. A few silver and copper mines were operated, and some large landowners established charcoal iron works, mainly for their regional markets for iron stoves, agricultural tools and the like. A couple of very simple statistical tables which

Table 7.2 Number of Agricultural Units in Norway, 1819–1949, by Size
Category

	1819	1870		1907	1939	1949
Parcells	5,000	24,500	All sizes	247,000	328,000	345,000
Small farms	45,500	84,000				
Medium farms	40,500	35,500				
Large properties	2,400	2,000				

Note:
[a] Detailed and reliable statistics are available only from 1907, but a statistical publication from 1873, based on material like reports from province governors, census papers, etc., compares the number of farm units of four different sizes in 1819 and 1870. The categories compared are *'parceller'*, *'smaabrug'* (small farms), *'middelsbrug'* and *'store eiendomme'* (large properties). *'Parceller'* were assumed to feed a 'half dairy cow', and yield 1.5 barrels of grain and two barrels of potatoes, and even if the author calls this output insignificant, he assumes that even these small properties are important socially, as 'many of the working class own house and land'. *'Smaabrug'* were supposed to feed a 'half horse', three to four cows and seven sheep or goats, as well as yield 15 barrels of grains and 18 of potatoes. These units are supposed to give 'a very important contribution to subsistence', and, like *'parceller'*, they are mostly owned and worked by fishermen, workers, artisans or sailors. *'Middelsbrug'* are supposed to be large enough for a stock of animals equal to 26 or 27 dairy cows, and yield 60 barrels of grains and 70–80 of potatoes. 'Large properties' are owned by rich people who employ servants and labourers, and keep on average animals equal to 109 cows. Data for the period after 1870 are from *Statistiske Oversikter* of 1948.

augment the data given in Chapters 4 and 6 highlight two very important factors explaining the striking contrasts between the economic and social development of the two countries. First it should be noted that an increasing number of these units were very small, often≈less than one hectare of arable, fully cultivable land. But the number of Norwegian farms continued to grow during the first half of the twentieth century – after a hundred years of industrial expansion. Second we should note the much faster growth in industrial employment in Scotland, at the same time as hundreds of thousands of new – and most of them very small – agricultural units were established in Norway. As we have seen in Chapter 4, the number of small farms continued to grow in the twentieth century, until after the Second World War.

URBANISATION – AND ITS CAUSES?

As an implication of the rapid industrialisation, and the out-migration of rural families, British urbanisation proceeded very fast. The share of the population living in urban areas (towns and cities with more than 20,000 people) grew from 10 per cent in 1801 to 58 per cent in 1901 in England and Wales. In Scotland,

32 per cent of the population was living in cities of over 10,000 by 1850.[3] At this point the most important difference between the two countries should become visible: there was no clear-cut causal connection between economic development and urbanisation in Norway – even if towns and cities increased their share of the population.

As explained in Chapter 6, industrialisation started late in Norway. Industrial growth took off around 1840 or a few years later,[4] even if Norwegians had sawn timber into planks, smelted iron and built wooden ships for centuries, generally between agricultural seasons, and even if in the seventeenth century there were sawmills in places like Christiania. But around the middle of the eighteenth century, there were textile factories and tool-making industries, and year by year more modern branches, like wood pulp and paper mills, were established. In 1851, the country had 95,000 industrial workers.

If we assume that economic growth implies that labour moves from agriculture, fishing and other primary economic activities to manufacturing and services, it is indeed striking that the number of farm units increased so fast in Norway even after the start-up of industrialisation. We could ask: Did young people have no choice? Did lack of opportunities of the kind available in the rapidly growing industries of the British islands – available to their propertyless Scottish counterparts – force young Norwegians to go into the birch forests and swampy bogs with an axe and a spade to drain and cultivate enough land to feed a cow or two and grow a few barrels of potatoes?

Alternatively, subsistence farms can be considered a positive opportunity in Norway, an option that the Scottish working class did not have. If we accept Polanyi's analysis of the British industrial revolution – that the opportunities for maintaining the pre-industrial subsistence system were eliminated by those in power[5] – it may become more interesting to focus on the fact that the opportunities for rural Norwegians to continue their pre-modern, subsistence economy adaptation not only were maintained but even improved after the Napoleonic Wars.

It goes without saying that 'easy entry' to subsistence farming and a competitive self-employment economy must influence the level of attraction of industrial jobs or other urban adaptations – to make rural people willing to make the move. We simply have to ask: In spite of the high level of productivity in British industry, was the life of an industrial worker family preferable to life on a family-owned subsistence farm? It would obviously depend on the wage level. A report from the Norwegian Ministry of Finance in 1842 considers that Norwegian manufacturing could hardly be competitive – because of the 'generally high wages here in Norway.'[6] If such differences in industrial wages can be documented, we have to conclude that keeping the opportunities for subsistence-farming and pluriactivity open implies a certain degree of market power for the labour side.

The sociologist Eilert Sundt, who studied poverty in Oslo in the 1850s, concluded that the problem only could be solved in the rural area from which the poor came, which may mean publicly supporting the establishment of small farms – 'homesteading'.[7]

The keys to the very different development of our two countries should not be too difficult to find:

1 Contrary to most of Scotland, and at any rate the Lowlands, Norway has very little land of commercial agricultural value, apart from a few areas around the bigger cities. The feudal owners of the many marginal and small rented farms had no motivation to get rid of their tenants, as leaseholding to many landowners was the only way in which they could get any income from their properties. As argued in Chapters 1 and 4, 'clearances' were not a theme. It is indeed a paradox that having marginal natural conditions was an advantage to the rural, peasant population. But at the same time, marine resources were plentiful in many coastal areas, and they were common property. Besides, some of the biggest landowners were positively interested in having many subsistence farmers on their land, simply because they needed seasonal forest workers. At any rate, the 'frontier' regions in the north of the country – with no manufacturing worth mentioning but rich common fishing grounds – increased their populations faster than the south through most of the nineteenth century, in spite of the fact that many, if relatively fewer than from the southern provinces, emigrated in this period.

2 As we have seen in Chapter 4, before 1850 most of the tenants had bought the farms that their forefathers for some reason had transferred to the Church in medieval times, and nobody could stop farmers from dividing their properties between children, or give them cultivable land (bogs, woodland), which many did. Towards the end of the century, most of the *husmenn* (cottars) had either bought their *parcells* or otherwise quit for something better – their own small farms, manufacturing industry or any kind of service work, often pluriactivity, or emigrated to North America.

3 Compared with the Scots, Norwegian small farmers lived in a very different political world: even if the propertyless could not vote, over 40 per cent of adult men over 25 had full political rights, including the right to be elected as MPs early in the nineteenth century. Owning a very small area of undrained bog was said to be enough. From 1898, all men had the right to vote, and from 1913 all women. From the 1830s, the higher urban classes referred to the Norwegian Parliament as *Bonde-Stortinget* – that is, the Peasant Parliament. It is no exaggeration to say that providing young families with the opportunity to get hold of a farm, even if small, was supposed to be a national priority, up to as recently as after the Second World War.

But possibly yet more important was the fact that even if poor rural people did not leave their cottages to go to the cities in the hope of finding a manufacturing-industry job, preferring subsistence farming *in situ*, they were intensely interested in all kinds of paid employment that did not imply moving house permanently.

In modern terms, they were 'under-employed'. Work at a wage level too low to pay for moving, even for limited periods, may indeed be attractive on top of what a family could get out of a small subsistence farm – one or two cows, a few sheep and a potato plot – and often certain opportunities like fishing and hunting. And if one's employer went bankrupt, it was less of a catastrophe for a small farmer than for a family with urban housing and food costs.

In a certain sense, we may conclude that to coming entrepreneurs, the large and expanding smallholder population of Norway could be considered a labour reserve as important to economic growth as the urbanised masses were to British industry. Local and regional studies support the architect R. Kyllingstad's pointed generalisation: 'For Norway, manufacturing industry became an element of the rural economy.'

Contrary to that of Great Britain, the economic growth of Norway was not based on urbanised industrial labour but rather on natural resources – including hydro power – and easily mobilisable surplus and seasonal labour from the large subsistence farm population. The most important Norwegian export goods were not produced in cities: timber and planks, salted and dried fish, ore and, in the twentieth century, products from the chemical industry based on hydro power. It is important to note that at the same time as Norwegians individually had relatively easy access to land, most important national resources that only could be exploited by organisations larger than the household, like water power, minerals and oil, were considered to be common property, owned and controlled by the State or municipality.

In a certain sense, we could conclude that Norwegians maintained, developed and improved their pre-industrial economy, based on a subsistence economy combined with fishing for the market, and any opportunities for cash income that might turn up. The new industrial opportunities that came along from the middle of the nineteenth century came on top of a pre-industrial, maintained and improved production system, contrary to what happened to rural Britain, where one can say that the subsistence economy of the poor and powerless rural masses was more or less destroyed through 'enclosures', 'clearances' and measures of that kind.

Chapters 1 and 3 outline some of the important preconditions for the economic development that I have tried to describe. Most important is the close cooperation between trade unionist and small farmer interests, especially through the Labour Party. At the same time as the sociologist Eilert Sundt found that poverty in the towns could be solved by 'homesteading' in the regions where the poor came from, Marcus Thrane, who organised exploited workers of all kinds, from farm labourers and cottars to craftsmen and apprentices, argued strongly for distributing land to the poor, to improve their bargaining position with their employers.[8] From the start in the 1890s to the 1980s, the Labour Party was as much a small farmer party as it was a party of wage-earners. Culturally, there were few differences, as most trade unionists would have parents or siblings working small farms.

In a certain sense, one may talk about a *moving equilibrium* between rural self-employment and urban wage work: the relative attractiveness of subsistence farms had a strong effect on industrial and service wages. By supporting small-scale farming, the Labour Party improved the market power of wage-earners. As the rural living standard improved, employers would have to follow up in order to recruit and keep employees.

But we cannot assume that the Labour leaders had developed a conscious strategy based on these relationships. This conclusion can be drawn not only from the absence of this kind of thinking in Labour programme documents and many conversations and confrontations with party politicians, but also from events like the general national congress (*landsmøte*) in 1933, where rural party members proposed an agricultural programme against unemployment. They lost against an ambitious industrialisation plan proposed by the economist Ole Colbjørnsen, who had experience from the Soviet planning organisations as well as from the City of London. However, many of the practical measures against rural unemployment carried through by the Labour/Farmers' Party coalition government from 1935 created many opportunities for the subsistence farmers. For many years, Labour leaders were unable to avoid decisions against their 'technocratic' master plans, as long as they ran contrary to rural smallholder interests. Politically, this is easy to understand: in the province of Troms, with very little modern industry, where I grew up, Labour won four of the six seats in the first elections after the Second World War. The 'Fresh Fish Act' of 1938, giving fishermen's organisations better control of landing prices, making small boat fishing really competitive as employment, was without a doubt the main reason for the preference for Labour in the north.

The post-Second World War economic vitality in rural areas had important and positive consequences for the urban working class. According to reports from the labour market authorities, most urban centres, large and small, suffered a permanent shortage of labour during the first decades after the Second World War, which meant that urban poverty evaporated rapidly. Somehow, rural development transformed the urban rag-proletariat into petty bourgeoisie. The abilities of and opportunities for rural people to protect and improve their adaptations, and realise their projects, maintained the scarcity of labour on the urban market, and urban poverty disappeared as soon as a surplus of labour became a thing of the past.

For many years after the war, rural opportunities – such as landing prices for fish – improved so much that urban employers must have had problems getting and keeping employees. Many *gründers* (or entrepreneurs) had to establish their production units outside cities to be able to recruit workers. According to Skonhoft,[9] most of the industrial growth of the 1970s took place in small centres, often far from big cities. It may be worth noting that all shipbuilding and related industrial development and repair work has disappeared from Oslo, Bergen and Trondheim, but thrives profitably in small centres along the coast, with the benefit of stable and well-trained labour, probably often retrained small farmers and their well-educated children.

Coming now to the recent past, many of the opportunities for rural households to realise their projects have disappeared since the 1980s. Professional fishing seems about to be privatised, and salmon-farming monopolised by big business. Many fish-farming corporations as well as whitefish processors/packers hire cheaper labour migrants from Eastern Europe rather than train and pay local youth according to national norms, which stimulates rural–urban migration of natives. Traditional small-scale opportunities have been only partly compensated by growing employment in public or private services. Most fishing villages seem to be losing inhabitants.

CONCLUSIONS

I hope to have shown that the establishment, maintenance and development of small farms – households combining subsistence agriculture with fishing, forestry and all kinds of other opportunities available locally or within commuting distance – must have played a very important role in the economic and social development of modern Norway. And I must assume that the negligence and what must be called destruction of the rural part-society during the industrial revolution must be an important factor in the more unfortunate development of Scotland, a country with probably better natural conditions for general economic and social progress. The opportunity for people without property to establish subsistence farms – up to the middle of the twentieth century – made the modernisation of Norway's economy less traumatic for the majority of the population than was the case in countries where the rural poor had very limited access to land for subsistence.

To put my main conclusion in very simple words: Many Norwegian small-farmer-labourer-families were able to maintain and develop their subsistence base at the same time as they took advantage of 'modern' opportunities that turned up, while in Scotland – as in most of the United Kingdom – the pre-industrial subsistence system was largely destroyed. Since the welfare gains of subsistence agriculture, and other values produced in households for consumption in the households, as we all know has been badly recorded in national statistics, the level of general welfare in Norway – before the oil age – has probably been underestimated. But I also have to conclude that many historians and other social scientists by and large have neglected the contribution of the small farmer as an important actor in the making of modern Norway. Probably because national histories are seldom based on close comparison with other nations – close in the sense that the reader can see concrete differences in the opportunities and restrictions encountered by ordinary people in their economic struggle. A practical consequence of this neglect must be the fact that the general public, including Norwegian politicians, journalists, commentators and teachers at all levels, know so little about the most important material and political processes that have generated the national society. This must be the main reason why Norwegians seem unable to maintain certain qualities that we have attempted to describe in this chapter, like keeping rural areas habitable, as well as the equality-maintaining scarcity of manual labour.

I find it necessary to emphasise that the social qualities I have tried to describe cannot be explained with reference to anything like the ideology or ethical standards of Norwegian leadership, or the professional quality of our development planners. The point is rather that the peripheral and rural population has happened to be strong and efficiently enough organised politically to resist planning. One of our master planners in the 1960s blamed what he called 'the Norwegian immobility preference' for the slow modernisation of the country. In this chapter, as in my earlier 1993 paper, I have tried to argue for the opposite point of view.[10]

Notes

1. My research on the maintenance and depopulation of north Norwegian fishing villages in the 1960s is summed up in my doctoral lecture, given as partial fulfilment for the degree of PhD at the Norwegian College of Agriculture, spring 1970. Published in English as Brox, 2006, Chapter 4. A more detailed Norwegian version may be available as Brox, 1971.
2. Aberdeen, Glasgow, St Andrews and Edinburgh universities, the first three of which were established before 1500. At the time, England had but two universities – Oxford and Cambridge – serving a much larger population. See Cant, 1982.
3. de Vreis, 1984: 38–48.
4. Lange, 1983: 142ff.
5. Polanyi, 1944: Chapters 4 and 8 in the Norwegian version.
6. Report on the state of the economy in the Kingdom of Norway from 1836 to 1840.
7. Christophersen, 1979: 449.
8. Bjørklund 1951: 122.
9. Skonhoft, 1982.
10. Brox, 1993.

CHAPTER 8

Money and Banking in Scotland and Norway

John Bryden and Keith Hart

INTRODUCTION

In this chapter we look at the history of money and banking in Scotland and Norway, and make some comparisons between the monetary experience of the two countries in the period up to the recent financial crisis and its immediate aftermath, with the main focus being on Scotland. We then consider the options facing small open economies like these two countries at a moment of dramatic change in the global organisation of money. This in turn allows us to open up important questions about the future that as yet are hardly being considered in the debates over Scotland's possible independence.

The referendum debates have identified three main monetary alternatives in the event of Scottish independence:[1] to remain in the sterling area; to join the European Monetary Union (EMU); and to issue an independent currency, with or without a peg to sterling or the euro. There has been no discussion so far of a dual or multiple system where the national currency coexists with others as legal tender – as in Zimbabwe today or indeed Scotland before the late seventeenth century,[2] Scandinavia between 1873 and 1914,[3] and the Hanseatic city states between the thirteenth and fifteenth centuries.[4] Indeed, we will argue that national monopoly currencies were an invention of the mid-nineteenth century and are now in disarray, as are fixed-exchange rate currency unions. Throughout history the circulation of several independent currencies within a territory has been normal and this situation is being restored now. It would be a shame if the debate concerning Scotland's money system after possible independence were limited to models that are already anachronistic.

Both the reports cited above agree that the optimal solution is to stick with sterling in a monetary union after independence. The UK Government report, however, emphasises that effective 'supervision' will limit Scotland's fiscal policy independence. Many other observers have made the same point, while some have ruled out such a solution even before negotiations.[5] However, a recent paper by Angus Armstrong and Monique Ebell on 'Monetary Unions and Fiscal Constraints', argues that 'any negotiation to form a monetary union between two sovereign states substantially different in size, and each acting in their own self-interest, is likely to result in a currency arrangement that resembles "dollarization" in practice', and that fiscal control by the larger partner is neither necessary nor feasible.[6]

Norway faced a similar question when it separated from Denmark in 1814 and gained control over its domestic economic and social policies as part of the Union of Crowns with Sweden for the following century. In that period, it variously established its own currency and central bank, joined a Scandinavian currency union, and then reestablished its own currency. Remaining in a Union of Crowns with Sweden did not oblige – or even encourage – Norway to use Swedish currency.

More than three centuries of independent Scottish banking ended after the merger of the Bank of Scotland with the Halifax Building Society in 2001 and then its enforced takeover by Lloyds TSB, followed by the collapse of the Royal Bank of Scotland (RBS) in 2007. This followed its ill-advised acquisition of the derivatives-stuffed Dutch bank ABN Amro just when the derivatives market was collapsing. RBS briefly became the largest bank in the world with a balance sheet of £2 trillion, but its leverage ratio was then 31.2, compared with 22.1 in 2004 and a mere 1.7 in 1850.[7]

The two largest Scottish banks, rivals for 280 years, not only shredded the proud reputation of Scottish banking, they brought the UK economy to its knees by exploiting the vacuum created by Margaret Thatcher's 'big bang' deregulation of 1986, and later by the botched regulatory reforms of Blair and Brown after their electoral victory in 1997.[8] The Scottish banks were not alone, of course. Deregulation caused the broad liquidity ratio of UK banks to fall from 30 per cent in 1968 to below 5 per cent after 1983, a ratio which persisted up to 2011.[9] This compares with an average liquidity ratio of the London clearing banks in the first quarter of 1938 of 29 per cent.[10] Indeed, an informal rule emerged in the nineteenth and early twentieth centuries that 'banks tried to maintain at least 30 per cent of their total deposit liabilities in ... liquid assets' comprising cash, money at call or short notice, and bills.[11]

How then might the history of money and banking in Norway and Scotland inform discussion of the options facing Scotland should it decide for independence? First we look at Norway, which developed after independence from Denmark in 1814. Next we look at Scotland, which had its own banking system until the Union of Parliaments with England in 1707 and then was increasingly integrated with the UK banking system. Norway and Scotland are two small countries with open economies and we must place them comparatively within a changing global context. The gold standard ended when Nixon took the US dollar off gold in 1971;[12] the consequent liberalisation of financial markets was the ultimate cause of the global economic crisis of 2007–8.[13] As a result the twentieth-century norm, which we identify as 'national capitalism' with its central bank and single legal tender, has been giving way to a new world regime of multiple competing currencies. The debate over Scotland's future would do well to take these developments into account.

KEY FEATURES OF NORWEGIAN BANKING AND MONETARY POLICY

The Norges Bank (Norway's central bank) was established in 1816 as a limited liability company, in part with private shareholders.[14] The new bank organised the changeover from the old Norway-Denmark currencies – *riksbankdaler* and *courantdaler* – to the new *speciedaler*, backed by silver from 1842 and by gold after 1874. The bank's head office was in Trondheim and five branches were established by the 1830s, with two more by 1860.

The Norges Bank was the only one operating until the first savings bank was established in 1822 and the first commercial bank in 1848. Thereafter both types increased steadily, reaching a peak around 1925.[15] In addition, there were State-owned commercial banks, the first being Kongeriket Norges Hypotekbank (1852–1903) which was funded by issuing bonds – often floated in Denmark and Hamburg – and mainly making mortgage loans to farmers. Savings and commercial banks were not permitted to issue bonds until 1897 and were discouraged from doing so until deregulation in the 1980s. Deposits were therefore the main source of commercial and savings bank finance, although share capital was also increased from time to time, especially during the real-estate boom of the 1890s. The number of commercial banks increased from 48 in 1895 to 82 in 1900, when the boom collapsed and many went bankrupt or suffered high loan losses.[16] Both commercial and savings banks were local, normally single-office affairs, although the commercial banks were usually larger. Once established they, and to a lesser extent the savings banks, increased their share of the financial market, together accounting for around 75 per cent of total lending by 1875. The Norges Bank's share declined accordingly, as a matter of policy, and became negligible after 1925.

For a small 'emerging' country with a population of around one million in 1820, interest rates were remarkably low. In 1820, the Norwegian Government was paying a premium of 2.5 percentage points over what the British Government paid on its foreign bond transactions, and the difference subsequently narrowed. This was a low when compared with the five percentage point premium for 'emerging market' bonds in today's market.[17] Up to 1842, the real interest rate was 5.4 per cent, remaining around 5 per cent until the outbreak of the First World War.

If one of the arguments for Scotland staying linked to sterling is that it would face higher borrowing rates on government bonds if it had its own currency, we should note that this has not been Norway's experience. Indeed, ten-year government bonds in Norway currently yield 2.92 per cent, only marginally higher than the UK rate of 2.90 per cent.[18]

In 1875, Norway joined the Scandinavian Currency Union (SCU) (*Skandinaviske myntunion*), first formed by Denmark and Sweden in 1873. The members fixed their currencies to gold, at par with each other, and Norway fixed the kroner at 0.403 grams. The gold-based crown (krone/krona/kroner) of the SCU replaced the three former national currencies at the rate of 1 crown = ½ Danish rigsdaler = ¼ Norwegian speciedaler = 1 Swedish riksdaler, although the three countries continued to issue their own currencies.[19] The SCU provided monetary and exchange rate stability, until Sweden left the gold standard in 1914, leading to the break-up of the SCU in 1921. The general view of economists has been that, despite apparent similarities in economic structure, the SCU was not an optimal currency area.[20] Nevertheless, the years from 1906 to 1914 were stable for Norway. We return to the optimality of the SCU later.

The First World War ended Norway's stability as well as the SCU. It saw considerable expansion of the money supply (Mo and M3),[21] while the number of commercial banks grew from 125 to 200 by 1918. The banking structure became less concentrated, while lending expanded due to increasing deposits and share capital. By 1920, commercial banks' share of lending had increased to 60 per cent. However, the boom ended in 1920–2, when the non-financial sector increased its debt considerably, and the number of bankruptcies rose to historic peaks.[22] This liquidity and solvency crisis particularly affected the commercial banks. The global depression of the early 1930s only made things worse. Norges Bank suspended the gold standard in 1931. The number of State-owned banks and mortgage companies grew and they increased their share of total lending, while non-financial companies and local authorities turned to bonds as a financing mechanism. By 1933, the economy had returned to a period of growth that lasted until the Second World War. This brought the German occupation, which printed money to finance its needs, and inflation increased rapidly. Deposits increased but lending fell, the banks holding treasury bills and bonds which they converted back into commercial lending during the post-war boom. Regulation was tightened but commercial and State-owned banks enjoyed stable expansion until the 1980s, with interest rates low or even negative.

Encouraged by the USA,[23] the banking system was deregulated around 1980, leading to rapid expansion of the commercial banking sector, which was now open to foreign-owned finance houses. The level of indebtedness increased and by 1987 the banks again faced serious problems. Since 1993, however, despite the reintroduction of stricter bank regulation after 1990, there has been strong growth in both bank lending and total credit, although the number of banks has fallen due to mergers and acquisitions, as elsewhere.

According to Norges Bank governor Svein Gjedrem,[24] three lessons were learned from the 1990s banking crisis. First, that bank rescue does not need to be costly for taxpayers if the State injects equity capital and then sells it when the crisis is over. Second, it is not always essential to create a 'bad bank' to take the most problematic loans, as was done in Sweden and Finland. In Norway, the originating banks were thought to be best placed to deal with problem loans, which were in any case relatively small scale. Third, if prompt action is taken to recapitalise the banks and write down problem loans, a banking crisis need not be prolonged.

Gjedrem did point out that the 2007 crisis effectively ended the era of bank concentration; and that deregulation had led to a rapid rise in cross-border banking, which cannot be bolstered by national government guarantees in times of crisis. Like Basel III,[25] the governor believes that reserve ratios and liquidity buffers will need to be increased and that financial regulation should move away from having pro-cyclical effects back to counter-cyclical effects, as Keynes advocated. He also stressed the need for international cooperation to address financial globalisation, without much evidence for it so far. Without it, the position of small countries with their own currencies, including Norway, must remain fragile. This vulnerability is accentuated by foreign ownership of finance – four of the five largest banks in Norway are foreign-owned.

Midthjell[26] identifies several factors that allowed Norway to avoid the worst effects of the financial crisis: the generous Norwegian welfare system, low interest rates, lack of any dramatic decrease in domestic demand, and the higher capitalisation of Norwegian banks than elsewhere. This last was a result of the 1990s financial crisis, along with stricter regulation of what could be included in 'core capital'. In addition, the creation of the Norwegian Bank Guarantee Fund helped a lot. Norway was affected by the global crisis and did introduce a stimulus package in 2009; yet, at £20bn, this was only 0.84 per cent of GDP, compared with a UK stimulus package of 2.2 per cent of GDP. Beltratti & Stulz[27] showed that, unsurprisingly, those countries with stricter capital requirements, more independent bank supervision, and more restrictions on the activities of banks performed better. Norway was one of them.

Norway's experience shows that small countries can develop successful independent monetary and banking systems. Its finances could be described as 'conservative' or 'prudent', not unlike Scotland's before the 1980s, allowing for periodic booms and busts. In both cases a 'rule' was adopted to hold secondary liquidity ratios around 30 per cent; this was enshrined in Norway's Monetary and Credit Policy Act of 1965.[28] Both abandoned this rule under the neo-liberal drive for deregulation after 1980. But the Norwegian financial crisis of 1990 caused a degree of reregulation of the banking sector, which contributed to weathering the much more serious global crisis after 2007.

SCOTTISH CURRENCY AND BANKING BEFORE AND AFTER THE UNION

Banking developed earlier in Scotland. Even before the establishment of the Bank of Scotland in 1695, there were several sizeable merchant discount houses in the main ports. These financial intermediaries – as was common in Europe in the late Middle Ages – discounted bills of exchange used as means of payment, especially in foreign trade.[29] The currency was the Scots pound, shilling and pence, with the merk (worth 13 shillings and 4 pence) occasionally minted, but normally used only as a unit of account. The silver penny was the first truly Scottish coin, minted by King David I, while the noble was the earliest Scottish gold coin, minted by David II who also minted the silver groat, originally worth four pence. The country was on a silver standard and in theory 240 pennies weighed one pound of pure silver. As a source of funding to the Crown, the real silver content was about 5 per cent less and further debasement led to wider divergence from the English pound, until the exchange rate was fixed at 12:1 on the Union of Crowns in 1603. Because Scotland was frequently short of coinage, foreign coins were also in use, including Roman coins, silver pieces of eight (from Spain), and silver thaler or daler (from Austria and Norway, for example). Scotland before the Union was thus a multi-currency country, like most countries before the modern era, but with the common, if variable, element of silver.

The Bank of Scotland was established by an Act of the Scottish Parliament in 1695. It was a joint stock company with a nominal capital of £Scots 1.2 million, but with a maximum permitted holding of £20,000.[30][31] Its first potential competitor was the Company of Scotland, founded by William Paterson,[32] a London–Scot who was involved in the establishment of the Bank of England but then fled on a charge of treason. This company sought to break the monopoly of the English East Indies Company and, having failed, promoted the colonisation of Panama (Darien). Although the Bank of Scotland was not supportive, the colony's failure almost broke the bank.[33]

The Scottish adventurer John Law was also involved with the Company of Scotland. He escaped from London to France, to found the Banque Royale there. Both the Bank of England and the Banque Royale were financed through 'debt-equity swaps': in exchange for financing the large war debts, they were granted monopoly privileges. Law's efforts as a pioneer of financial capitalism generated the Mississippi and South Sea 'Bubbles', plus two financial collapses that temporarily removed confidence in paper currency.[34] Law was also heavily involved in the Darien disaster which brought on the Union, and was later castigated by Adam Smith for contributing to the banking profligacy of the period.[35]

The Bank of Scotland's effective monopoly was broken by the establishment of the Royal Bank of Scotland in 1727 and the British Linen Bank in 1746. Numerous smaller private and local banks were founded in the eighteenth century.[36] The Bank of Scotland introduced two banking innovations before Union in 1707: the issue of bank notes and the remittance trade with London and Amsterdam. Unlike similar currency initiatives around this time, Scottish paper succeeded, despite having little backing from precious metals, thanks to the Bank's strong political connections and strong support from the Scottish landed aristocracy, merchants, lawyers and other professionals.

Yet Scotland's economy was particularly weak just before the Union. Apart from poor harvests, Darien absorbed up to a quarter of Scotland's total liquidity at the time.[37] Scottish cloth manufacturers were also experiencing increased competition. The English Alien Act of 1705 increased pressure by imposing barriers to Scotland's exports of coal, linen and cattle there.[38]

The Union brought harmonisation of customs and excise duties. Moreover, part of Scottish fiscal revenue was used to service England's larger national debt accrued before 1707. Scotland received payment of 'the Equivalent' as well as an 'Arising Equivalent' calculated annually as compensation for revenue raised in Scotland. These funds were to be used for servicing Scotland's own national debt, compensating losers from currency harmonisation, including Darien investors, and assistance to the woollen industry, among others.[39] These provisions were inadequate, however, and even when losers were compensated with debentures, they were not redeemable or convertible and paid no interest.[40] Economic growth before the 1760s was too weak to generate additional imports, while 15–20 per cent of Scottish fiscal revenue was sent to Westminster. The Union's 'financial provisions did not provide a ready-made solution' to Scotland's economic problems.[41] The rebellions of 1715 and 1745 probably owed something to the financial provisions of the Union. The Hanoverian government nevertheless encouraged technical improvement of Scottish manufactures, especially linen, wool and the herring fisheries.

Against the wishes of the Bank of Scotland, the Royal Bank was founded in 1727 by former holders of Scottish national debt, who were paid in unsecured debentures and eventually sold most of these at a discount to English speculators.[42] The latter, who faced difficulty when collecting interest in Scotland, formed the Society of the Subscribed Equivalent Debt. When frustrated in its efforts to establish a bank in England,[43] this company was permitted to fund the Royal Bank of Scotland under the authority of the Great Seal of Scotland.[44]

The Royal developed the world's first overdraft facility, the 'cash accompt', in 1728.[45] It was also politically opposed to the Bank of Scotland's supposed pro-Jacobite sympathies. Each bank proceeded to try to destroy the other in an 'exhaustive bank war'.[46] This ended just before the 1745 rebellion. It engendered a cautious banking approach in the Bank of Scotland, while the truce paved the way for a more cohesive, even collusive, relationship between them.

With the addition of the Linen Bank in 1746,[47] Scotland had three joint stock banks by the middle of the eighteenth century, all with branches throughout Scotland. The Bank of England, by contrast, retained its monopoly and a single head office in the City of London, with a host of private banks underneath. Whereas it was formed by the merchants and goldsmiths of the City of London, the Scottish joint stock banks were formed by the landed aristocracy, merchants and others from across Scotland.

Scotland also developed housing insurance. The parent company of the 'Edinburgh Society for insuring houses against loss by fire' was the Society of the

Subscribed Equivalent Debt; and three of its founders were active in forming the Royal Bank. It seems to have been more interested in trying to generate a run on the Bank of Scotland than in insuring houses.[48]

Scotland's new banking system was more stable, if more conservative, than England's. This slowed down lending at a time of rapid industrial and commercial development, largely to the detriment of Glasgow and the west of Scotland. Below the large joint stock banks, local chartered banks developed. Finally, there were private banks, some of which pre-dated the Union.

The Scottish banks issued paper notes and, when credit was scarce, there was a tendency to over-issue them, leading to inflationary pressures and balance of payment deficits. Adam Smith observed that almost all the Scottish banks paid dearly for excessive circulation, but that 'the Bank of England paid very dearly, not only for its own imprudence, but for the much greater imprudence of almost all the Scotch banks'.[49] Smith also noted that the paper money issued by the Scottish banks tended to exceed what 'the circulation of the country could easily absorb and employ', yet the commercial sector still argued for more credit, which they satisfied by the relatively costly method of drawing and redrawing bills of exchange, a practice known as 'raising money by circulation'.[50]

The Ayr Bank's policies on printing notes were 'more liberal than any other had ever been'[51] and it duly collapsed in 1772, triggering the fall of several private banks in London and Edinburgh. This led to alterations in Scottish banking structure and to the triumph of conservative banking policies. But the Scottish economy picked up, sustaining stable growth until the next financial crisis in 1793.[52] This crisis deepened when the Bank of England suspended cash payments, leading the main Scottish banks to suspend convertibility of notes into gold. They moved towards cooperation in this period, perhaps forming an oligopolistic cartel. This return of the 'old regime' was led by Henry Dundas in resistance to the new wealth gained from industry and empire.[53] Dundas secured an increase in the capitals of both chartered banks against the wishes of the Bank of England and the East India Company, ensuring only a limited role in Scottish banking for the Bank of England thereafter.

By 1796, the capital of each main bank had reached £1 million. In 1804, this was raised to £1.5 million each, making them the largest banks in Britain after the Bank of England and among the largest in the world.[54] The British Linen Bank was very much their junior partner and the two chartered banks opposed its expansion up to 1810. The Commercial Bank was set up as a joint stock bank in 1810 by Whigs dissatisfied with Tory control of the older banks. Even so, its initial policies were also highly risk-averse and by 1815 the Edinburgh meetings of the Scottish banking 'cartel' included both the Linen and the Commercial banks.

The Scottish Enlightenment school of economists, including Sir James Steuart and Adam Smith, promoted the idea that the issue of paper currency could 'far exceed the monetary base of banks and contribute to the long-run accumulation of capital'.[55] John Law must also be credited with this idea. But how to avoid the over-issue of paper currency, especially by more speculative, even dishonest, operators? Steuart (1767) advocated State regulation and the 'transparency' of note-issuers' accounts.

The divided roles of the chartered and private banks led to higher charges to the public; and they were attacked for over-investment in government stocks and under-investment in industry, as well as for neglect of private customers' needs. Several new banks established in 1825 were opposed to the older Scottish banks and directed a greater flow of finance to commerce and industry. The four main banks, however, met regularly to set interest rates and the lending policies of all the banks converged around this rate. A raft of new banks emerged in the 1830s and '40s to meet the needs of rapid industrial and commercial growth in the more dynamic west of Scotland. With many depositors and substantial investment from wealthy industrial and commercial families, they opposed the conservative policies of the Edinburgh banks.[56] When, in 1857, several firms that were heavily indebted to the new Western Bank went under, the Edinburgh banks did not provide significant help and the bank too collapsed.[57] The City of Glasgow Bank, with the most branches in Scotland, went the same way in 1878.[58]

Scottish banking was still considered more stable than England's, which suffered many more bank collapses in the early nineteenth century. Saville lists fifty new banks established in Scotland by mid-century, of which eight were 'exchange banks' prohibited from issuing their own notes.[59] Total deposits at Scottish banks increased from under £5m in 1825 to £35m by 1850, while advances doubled to £36m.[60] Despite rivalry between Edinburgh and west Scotland, the Scottish system financed rapid industrial and commercial growth. The banks also invested in a massive extension of the railway network which, with the electric telegraph, enhanced management of the branch system. The Bank of England, however, still wanted to reduce Scotland's note issue, even though it was profitable for the Scottish banks. Scots bankers and economists argued that convertible notes could not affect prices because 'if paper was in excess it would be immediately converted into gold'.[61] More gold had to be kept in Scotland to cover fluctuations in circulation that were formerly dealt with through bills drawn on London.[62]

The Scottish banks next decided that their branches should automatically follow changes in the Bank of England's minimum discount rate without reference

Table 8.1 The Scottish Banking System, 1802–1900

	1802	1825	1850	1900
Total bank assets	£12.3m	£24.4m	£51.9m	£137.7m
Total deposits	£ 5.8m	£14.6m	£35.0m	£107.3m
Total advances	£ 8.0m	£17.6m	£36.5m	£ 74.9m
Total branches and offices	92	173	407	959

Source: Checkland, 1975: 240, 423–7, 743.

to head office. Scottish banks opened facilities in London, against the vigorous opposition of the Bank of England and the City. The success of Empire trade and finance in the late nineteenth century reduced hostilities between London and the Scottish banks and diverted attention from the Scottish note issue. The share of the Scottish joint stock banks' branches in total turnover for Scotland, England and Wales fell from 40 per cent to 22 per cent between 1880 and 1900, while their share of assets and liabilities fell from 26 per cent to 17 per cent.[63]

The Scots also claim to have invented savings banks, the first being founded in 1810. These were important for small savers and attracted 'the better-off artisan and working class saver', the 'respectable' working class who supported the Liberal Party and the temperance movement. By 1900, the Scottish savings banks had deposits of over £16 million or some 18 per cent of the main bank's total, with half a million members and an average deposit of £33.[64]

Scotland's banking system quadrupled in size during the first half of the nineteenth century as a result of rapid industrialisation. Despite periodic booms and busts,

> by 1850, the Scottish banking system stood at the height of its prestige. Its public and joint-stock banks were large by British standards; it had suffered no public discredit by failure throughout the difficult 1820s, 30s and 40s. It was associated in the minds of informed men, both in Britain and abroad, with probity and reliability, as well as inventiveness and adaptability.[65]

As Checkland notes, the debate about Scottish banking autonomy continued, even though the Scottish banking system was now dependent on London.[66]

The Banking Acts of 1844–5 enforced the gold standard, a move unsuccessfully opposed by the Scottish banks. This imposed a costly requirement to hold reserves of gold, constrained the issue of Scottish notes and effectively stopped the formation of new banks, thus reinforcing the Scottish banking cartel. Moreover, it inhibited the expansion of Scottish banks into England, at least beyond London. The following half century or so was one of consolidation rather than growth. Moreover, limited liability became more general, despite the resistance of the three senior banks.

The number of banks trading in Scotland fell from about 17 in 1850 to 10 by the end of 1885 and stayed that way until the 1950s.[67] Checkland describes Scottish banking from 1850 to 1914 as 'respectable, stable and complacent'. So conservative was it that an imaginative proposal from the general managers of the British Linen and Union banks to establish a Scottish foreign exchange bank was rejected by all the other leading banks.

The banks had large holdings of government securities in 1918. Women and returning servicemen, lacking the old deferential attitudes, expected jobs in them. After a short post-war boom, depression set in until the late 1930s. The uncertainty and pessimism of this period strengthened the banking cartel. Growing competition from mutual and municipal savings banks was fended off by attracting small savers with interest-bearing accounts. Almost every branch of Scottish industry was in difficulty, so the banks committed again to government stocks (98 per cent of the Bank of Scotland's investments between 1931 and 1939). Total resources, advances and demand from commercial and industrial customers fell between the wars.[68]

The Scottish banks played an important role in funding government debt during the Second World War. They already had 57 per cent of their deposits invested in medium- or long-dated British Government securities or gilts by 1938, a ratio that stayed the same until 1945 – double the ratio of the English banks.[69] This preference for gilts was linked to reluctance between the wars to lend to heavy industry and engineering in west Scotland.

A cheap money policy was adopted during and immediately after the war, partly because this lowered the cost of servicing the large national debt, partly to depress rentier incomes. The State greatly increased its share of the economy by nationalisation of key industries and this reduced the banks' advances to firms.[70] In the early 1950s, the government returned to monetary controls, by changing the bank rate, for example, long held at 2 per cent. The Bank of England was no longer always 'open for purchases or sales of Treasury bills at market rates' and charged penal rates for 'last resort' loans to the banks. Further, government put pressure on the banks' liquidity ratio by converting part of their Treasury bills into securities that were no longer classified as 'liquid'.[71] The 1950s also saw banking amalgamations in Scotland, in response to the growth of giant corporations and to make them competitive with the larger English banks through 'economies of scale'.

Direct controls on bank lending imposed during the war were removed in 1958, but at the same time the banks were required to hold 'Special Deposits' (SDs) at the Bank of England. The ratio of SDs to gross deposits varied; but the rate for Scottish banks was half that for English banks, since they were required to hold Bank of England assets for the 'excess' portion of the Scottish note issue.[72] In 1959, the Radcliffe report relegated monetary policy to second behind fiscal policy as a means of government economic management. The report also warned against a narrow view of the money supply in the light of the explosion of monetary instruments including building society deposits, savings certificates, defence bonds, tax reserve certificates and many other short-term liabilities.

Banking controls were reintroduced in 1961, followed by a credit squeeze in 1964 and an embarrassing sterling devaluation in 1967. In 1969, the British banks abandoned their long-standing system of 'hidden reserves', which both disguised their true profitability and obscured their bad debts, moving to 'full disclosure'. In 1971, the Bank of England reduced the liquidity ratio requirement from 28 per cent to 12.5 per cent and extended this requirement to the Scottish banks, which were also given the same Special Reserve requirements as the English banks. This ended different rules for Scottish banks that had been earlier created in recognition of Scotland's special economic needs. The two countries' banks abandoned their cartels, setting the stage for greater competition between them.[73] These reforms generated new opportunities for banks and financial intermediaries, and money flowed into the real estate and financial services sectors, leading to a property bubble. A new financial instrument (sterling certificates of deposit) allowed investors to hedge against future interest rate rises, in which case lenders would be the losers. Secondary banks had advanced £4.5 billion to the property market and other financial schemes.[74] The subsequent crash was led by a secondary bank, the Scottish Co-operative Wholesale Society, for which the Scottish banks were the lead creditors,[75] but the ensuing melt-down cost the London secondary banking sector much more. In 1973, the Bank of England created a 'lifeboat' for the secondary banking sector, the costs of which fell on the clearing banks, and rushed in a number of ill-considered measures to forestall a collapse of asset values. 'The true extent of the loss, bad management, property speculation and financial greed, which in some cases involved fraud, was a salutary lesson'.[76] In 1974, the government introduced draconian controls on bank lending. The Scottish banks were dismayed, despite being less exposed to property speculation in the secondary banking sector. 'The needs of proprietors and of account holders were best protected by the Bank [of Scotland] having the self-confidence to think for itself and not be sucked into the current fashions of the City of London'.[77]

North Sea oil saved the British economy and the Scottish banks. The Bank of Scotland was a funder of BP's Forties Field under a risk-sharing arrangement.[78] Other active players were two Scottish banks and two dozen mutual assurance companies, investment trusts, holding companies and shipping lines.[79] But the oil boom also attracted larger English and foreign banks, bringing powerful competition, plus heavy deposits in UK banks from the Middle East oil-producing countries.

The election of Margaret Thatcher's Conservative government in 1979 brought dear money and a stronger pound, as well as declining support for nationalised industries and private 'lame ducks', which were over-represented in Scotland. Traditional manufacturing industry in Scotland, especially shipbuilding, steel, heavy engineering, vehicles and machine tools, collapsed at this time.[80] The Scottish banks were heavily committed to their own industries and bad debts increased, weakening the banks' ability to resist predatory attacks on their jealously guarded indigenous ownership and control. In 1979, Lloyds Bank attempted to take over the RBS. Subsequent bids by the Standard Chartered Bank and the Hong Kong and Shanghai Banking Corporation (HSBC) were turned down by the Monopolies and Mergers Commission.

The Bank of Scotland was happy to be 'the most boring bank in Britain'. An axiom of Scottish banking had long been that 'it was immoral to borrow beyond one's means and bank managers have a duty to refuse advances where there is doubt about the projected cash flow from which the loan will be repaid'.[81] This is why the Scottish banks survived.

Neither the Bank of Scotland nor the Royal Bank of Scotland remained 'boring' for long. The former made a hostile bid for the NatWest in the late

1990s, but lost out to its age-old rival. Still looking to become larger, in 2001 it merged with the Halifax Building Society, a mortgage company with over 20 per cent of the UK housing market, thereby creating the Halifax Bank of Scotland (HBOS). Like the RBS, HBOS peaked in 2007 with a market capitalisation of over £40 billion and a tangible book value of £18 billion. In 2009, HBOS was taken over by Lloyds TSB, which had the worst bad loan record of any bank. Today, what little shareholder value remains is because of the UK taxpayers' injection into HBOS and Lloyds TSB of £20.5 billion. The market value of the Treasury holding in Lloyds Banking Group is still £5 billion below the amount invested. HBOS makes fewer loans to retail customers and small- and medium-sized enterprises (SMEs); the banking market has shrunk and is less diverse. Sir James Crosby, Chief Executive of HBOS from its creation until 2006, told a Parliamentary Commission: '[My colleagues and I] always believed that we had a good understanding of the risks they were taking and we in aggregate as a bank had no evidence to the contrary.'[82]

This same Parliamentary Commission concluded that the collapse of HBOS was a 'classic banking failure' due to rapid and aggressive expansion of its real estate loan activities at twice the rate of growth of deposits, making the bank excessively exposed to risk of changes in both property values and the wholesale financing market which filled the growing gap between assets and deposits. Temporarily lucrative investment banking was not at fault nor was massive exposure to credit derivatives and other packaged securities, as in the case of RBS. Yet the lessons of the 1973 crisis had been totally forgotten.

So ended over three hundred years of Scottish banking, long known for its 'prudence'. No doubt the deregulation introduced by Mrs Thatcher's governments in the 1980s, subsequently deepened by the Blair-Brown reforms of the Bank of England, was partly to blame. The 1971 reforms also bear some responsibility by lowering minimum liquidity ratios to 12.5 per cent, which fell to 5 per cent in the 1980s. Leverage ratios also increased dramatically after 2000.

CURRENCY AND BANKING OPTIONS FOR SMALL OPEN ECONOMIES

We next examine the issues facing Scotland today in the light of Norway's experience since independence. The Norwegian banking system weathered crashes following boom years around 1850, in the 1920s and after banking deregulation in 1988–92. The last two were also periods of crisis in Scotland. Today, with a similar population to Scotland, Norway has its own currency – the kroner (NOK) – which since 1994 has been 'loosely' tied to other European currencies and since 1999 to the euro, but with rather wide margins and no commitment of its central bank to support the value of the NOK.[83] Indeed the regime is classified by the IMF, like Britain's, as 'free floating'. The present euro exchange rate has been close to the normal ECU/euro rate since the late 1980s. The Norges Bank has a government target of 2.5 per cent inflation that it largely succeeds in reaching.

According to the bank's guidelines, foreign exchange reserves should be invested so that at least SDR (Special Drawing Rights)[84] 10 billion can be used within a single trading day without appreciable losses. The money market portfolio is between SDR 3.5 billion and SDR 4.5 billion and invested in short-term fixed-income instruments.[85] The benchmark index for this is a composite of USD and EUR overnight money market and Treasury bill indices for the same currencies. The long-term portfolio is invested in equities and fixed-income securities. The benchmark index for the long-term portfolio is a composite of global equity and bond indices. The equity allocation for the strategic benchmark index is 40 per cent. The petroleum buffer portfolio ensures that the Government Pension Fund Global (GPFG) has an adequate supply of fresh capital. Funds accumulate in the portfolio through transfers of foreign currencies from the State's Direct Financial Interest (SDFI) in petroleum activities and through foreign exchange purchases. No benchmark index has been set for the petroleum buffer portfolio.

The bank's monetary policy instruments are intervening in foreign exchange markets and varying the interest rate. Interventions are made according to the bank's analysis of the 'operating parameters' of the Norwegian economy, including oil price trends. The danger is that speculators will believe the foreign exchange reserves of a small country are limited, however large Norway's may appear to be. This happened in November 1992 when the Norges Bank used over NOK 50 billion of its foreign exchange reserves in six trading hours over two days. Use of interest rates to manage foreign exchange also has limitations, and for similar reasons. Although raising interest rates may attract purchases of NOK and help to maintain a higher exchange rate against the euro, speculators may pull out when the policy becomes unsustainable because of deflationary effects on the domestic economy.

New Zealand is another small open economy with its own currency. A recent study examines New Zealand's choice of monetary, capital account and exchange rate policies in a context of comparing a number of countries.[86] It draws on the monetary policy 'trilemma' hypothesis,[87] which states that it is possible to have only two of the following at once:

- a fixed exchange rate;
- an independent monetary policy;
- free cross-border capital movement.

The authors argue that financial markets exert constant pressure to equalise returns across currencies. An open capital account allows funds to move across borders and between currencies to equalise returns on capital. Attempts by a country or central bank to control local interest rates will lead to arbitrage and thus move the exchange rate. If the authorities seek to stabilise the exchange rate, then capital flows will move interest rates. Any attempt to control both interest rates and exchange rates will conflict with cross-border arbitrage and confront the forces of foreign exchange and bond markets. The link between exchange rates and domestic interest rates can be broken by foreign exchange interventions and/ or partial or complete closure of the capital account. So both the exchange rate and domestic interest rates may be used as policy instruments. The cost, however, is possible loss of access to international capital markets and increased domestic borrowing costs. Alternatively, if foreign exchange market intervention is used, high reserves need to be maintained, which is itself expensive, while the policy is unlikely to be sustainable against very large currency market movements.

A number of small open economies with successful currency regimes, including Norway, opt for a mixed regime. The foundation is often floating exchange rates and inflation-targeted policy, allowing for exceptional intervention when the authorities consider that markets have moved out of line with 'fundamentals'. Norway's foreign exchange reserves in October 2013 were half its GDP and the Norges Bank is prepared to intervene with up to NOK 100 billion in a single day's trading. Nevertheless, the scale of the foreign exchange trade today means that intervention at this level could not be maintained for long, even with 'friendly' support from other Scandinavian countries.

The case of Denmark is also relevant for Scotland. The Danish krone is pegged to the euro, within a narrow band, and this has been maintained with foreign exchange reserves around 25 per cent of GDP, using intervention and interest rates as the main policy instruments. Real exchange rates have been stable there since 1990. This is because of the credibility of the Danish political and financial system and Denmark's close economic integration with the EU. Scotland could attempt something similar, especially if an oil fund were created like Norway's.

Both Denmark and Norway have some capital controls, for example over transactions in land, shipping and assets held by insurance companies, as well as Foreign Direct Investment (FDI) in the case of Norway. These are also important instruments giving some leverage over capital flows. The departure of the Baltic states from the USSR Rouble Zone in the early 1990s likewise offers varied monetary policy options.[88]

The question of the Scandinavian Currency Union's optimality is relevant to current debates over whether Scotland's membership of a UK currency area would be optimal. Members of an Optimal Currency Area (OCA) should in theory share a business cycle, so that interest rate changes, for instance, will not adversely affect one of them.[89] One condition is free movement of labour and capital within the OCA. While the economies of Scotland and England have lately moved quite closely together, this was not always the case and would be less likely after independence.[90]

Scotland's experience during the 'Lawson boom' of the 1980s is well documented: property prices in England increased by 52 per cent between 1986 and 1988, compared with 15 per cent in Scotland, which suffered very high interest rates designed to cool off house prices in England. More important, Scotland, as a small open economy, suffered asymmetrical shocks from fluctuations in oil and gas prices. Norway was likewise exposed when oil prices collapsed in 1986. Finally, Scotland's relative population and economic size – both one-tenth of the UK total – suggests that asymmetrical union is inevitable. Without control over monetary policy and with severe restrictions on fiscal policy, the case for independence would be significantly weakened.

Scotland would need its own currency, although this could be pegged to sterling, the euro or even the US dollar to avoid loss of confidence, at least in the early years. The experience of Norway after independence from Denmark is highly relevant to contemporary Scottish debates. The situation for money, banking and currencies is very different today from when silver and then gold standards were the norm. Now paper and electronic forms of money are standard and market confidence sets currency prices.

The turnover of foreign exchange markets averaged $5.3 trillion a day in April 2013, more than double the 1998 figure and up from $4.0 trillion in 2010 and $3.3 trillion in 2007. The annual volume of foreign exchange trading, at almost $2,000 trillion, is now twenty-seven times the Gross World Product (GWP). The foreign exchange reserves required to support any national exchange rate are so large as to be beyond all but the largest economies. Small countries have very little room for manoeuvre, but, as Norway has demonstrated, one with reasonable resources and money management skills can keep interest and exchange rates within fairly broad bands and so avoid the greater danger of being part of a sub-optimal currency union, such as the Eurozone.

Norway has maintained stability of exchange rates and inflation over long periods and with only minimal and occasional market intervention. This has supported domestic and international confidence in the kroner. Norway has also benefited from its Concession Laws, which require non-nationals to seek a permit to acquire property in Norway, thereby limiting speculative capital movements. Scotland might emulate Norway's example to maintain confidence in a Scots pound, while remaining convertible to sterling, the euro and the dollar. Scottish Concession Laws would help to restrain property prices and secure residence on rural land. While government and much other domestic business would be transacted in Scottish pounds, Scotland should follow the global trend to adopt a multi-currency regime, allowing other currencies also to be legal tender. The 'Latvian' solution to mint a 'parity coin' comprising combinations of currencies might be considered.[91]

BEYOND NATIONAL MONOPOLY CURRENCIES AND FIXED EXCHANGE RATE UNIONS

A single currency cannot address the needs of a large and diverse region like Europe that has not yet achieved the political coherence of the United States; and increasingly even small countries like Scotland must adapt to a plural monetary regime.

The European Union's ambition to become a federal power in the world economy was based on yoking member states to a system of fixed exchange rates whose logic harks back to Bretton Woods and before that to the gold standard. The contradictions of such a regime, conceived in the euphoria of the free market's 'victory' in the Cold War, were disguised by the long credit boom. The conversion of the whole world to free market capitalism ('neo-liberal globalisation') in the early 1990s coincided with a digital revolution in communications. Wall Street took the lead in exploiting these new possibilities. It was predictable that, of all the world's regions, the major and permanent loser in this economic crisis would be Europe.

The central problem today is not even mainly one of credit and debt, but rather a deep-seated shift in the world economy, with national and international political institutions now unable to influence a money circuit that has gone global. We have lived through an explosion of money, markets and telecommunications for three decades and are now experiencing the consequences. This hectic period of 'globalisation' represents a rapid expansion of society far beyond the twentieth-century norm when society was identified with the nation-state. In order to live in the world together, we have had to abandon the aspiration to achieve local self-sufficiency. So far this has been closely linked to the extension of society by means of markets and money. A universal communications network has two striking features: first, it is a highly unequal market of buyers and sellers fuelled by a money circuit that has become detached from production and politics; and second, it is driven by a digital revolution whose symbol is the internet.

Money has acquired its apparent preeminence because social regulation has been abandoned at all levels of the economy. Financiers used their new-found freedom from the social democracy of the 1940s to 1970s to loot the world in ways that must be repaired, if we can. But, in addition to drawing people *en masse* into unsustainable credit schemes, they also began to put in place some of the institutional mechanisms that could make the market work for all of us.

The removal of political controls over money in recent decades has led to a situation where politics is still mainly national but the money circuit is global and lawless. This process of social extension beyond national boundaries is fraught with danger. We need to extend systems of social rights to the global level before the contradictions of the market system collapse into world war – but local political organisation resists such a move. The current crisis should be seen as a moment in the history of money when the system that the world lived by in the twentieth century collapsed. This has been unravelling since the early 1970s, when a new regime of floating currencies emerged, and money derivatives were invented the year after the dollar was depegged from gold. As the need for international cooperation intensifies, the disconnection between the economy and political institutions is undermining effective solutions.

There is still a tendency to see the potential disaster we are living through in economic rather than political terms. In this respect, by attacking the free market rather than use of the State to siphon wealth to the top, neo-liberalism's detractors often reproduce the ideology they claim to oppose. We should ask not what is beginning, but what is ending. What is ending is 'national capitalism',[92] the synthesis of nation-states and industrial capitalism whose main symbol is national monopoly currency (legal tender policed by a central bank). It is the institutional attempt to manage money, markets and accumulation through a central bureaucracy within a cultural community of national citizens. It was never the only active principle in world political economy: cities, regional federations and empires are as old or older.

National capitalism's origins lay in a series of linked revolutions of the 1860s based on a new alliance between capitalists and traditional military enforcers. New governments launched a bureaucratic revolution in the late nineteenth century and sponsored large corporations in a drive towards mass production. The national system became generalised after the First World War, when states turned inwards to manage their economies in times of war and depression. Its apogee was the social democracy built in the thirty years after 1945.

People learn to understand each other as members of communities, and money is an important vehicle for this. They share meanings as a way of achieving their practical purposes together. Nation-states have been so successful in such a relatively short time that it is hard for us to imagine society in any other way. Five different types of community came together in the nation-state:

Political community: a link to the world and a source of law at home;
Community of place: territorial boundaries of land and sea;
Imagined or virtual community: the constructed cultural identity of citizens;
Community of interest: shared purposes in trade and war;
Monetary community: common use of a national monopoly currency.

The rise and fall of single currencies is therefore one way of approaching national capitalism's historical trajectory.

Mainstream economics says more about what money does than what it is. Its main function is held to be as a *medium of exchange*, a more efficient lubricant of markets than barter. Another school emphasises money's function as a *means of payment*, especially of taxes, and hence as 'purchasing power'. Some identify it as a *standard of value* or unit of account, emphasising the government's guarantee of the legal conditions for trade. Money as a *store of wealth*, according to John Locke, was a new form of property that allowed the accumulation of riches to escape from the limitations of natural economy.

Karl Polanyi[93] argued that only modern money in the form of national currency combines the four functions (payment, standard, store and exchange) in a few 'all-purpose' symbols. His approach offers profound insight into the causes of today's global economic crisis. Our challenge is to conceive of society once more as something plural rather than singular, as a federated network rather than a centralised hierarchy, the nation-state. The era of national monopoly currencies is very recent (beginning in the 1850s), and it took the United States, for example, half a century to secure an uncontested monopoly for its 'greenbacks'. 'All-purpose money', however, has been breaking up for four decades now.

The world economy has reverted to the plural pattern of competing currencies that existed before central banks learned how to control national economies in the late nineteenth century. The international rule system created by Bretton Woods was subverted by the creation of an offshore banking system which brought informal and illegal commerce to the heart of global finance. The separation of functions between different types of monetary instrument was also crucial to money's great escape from the rules of the Keynesian consensus. Central bank control was eroded by a shift to money being issued in multiple forms by a globally distributed network of corporations, not just governments and banks. The shadow banking system – hedge funds, money market funds, and structured investment vehicles that lie beyond State regulation – is now literally out of control. Money has come a long way in a short time. Consider Switzerland today, where euros are commonly accepted in shops alongside the national currency. If you pay with a card, you can often choose the unit of account (Swiss franc, euro, pound sterling, US dollar). But only francs are acceptable for the payment of local taxes.

Georg Simmel[94] considered money's twin anchors to be its physical substance (coins, paper, etc.) and the social institutions supporting the community of its users. He predicted that the first would wither away, making the second more visible. The digital revolution in communications has been transforming money's substance for two decades now. But globalisation has made national society seem a lot less self-sufficient than it did a century ago. Radical reductions in the cost of transferring information have introduced new conditions for engagement with the impersonal economy, and world society is increasingly driven by money, markets and telecommunications. The replacement of single currencies by numerous types of more specialised monetary instruments is one inevitable result of this.

Simmel's prophecy has been realised to a remarkable degree, as the digital revolution accelerates and cheapens electronic transfers. But if the essence of money is its use in a community with shared social institutions, national capitalism has lost its grip on reality. We must therefore move from singular (national) to plural (federal) conceptions of society. The infrastructure of money has already become decentralised and global, so a return to the national solutions of the 1930s or a Keynesian regime of managed exchange rates and capital flows is bound to fail.

The apparent triumph of the free market at the end of the Cold War induced two huge political blunders, both of them based on the premise that society should be shaped by the market economy rather than the other way round. First, the radical privatisation of Soviet bloc public economies ignored the common history of politics, law and social custom that shored up market economies in the West, thereby delivering economic control into the hands of gangsters and oligarchs. And second, the European single currency, which was supposed to provide the social glue for political union, was adopted without first developing effective fiscal institutions or economic convergence between northern and southern Europe.

The big mistake was to *replace* national currencies with the euro. An alternative proposal, the 'hard European Currency Unit' (ECU), would have floated nationally managed currencies alongside a low-inflation European central bank currency. Countries that didn't join the euro, like Britain and Sweden, have in practice enjoyed the privilege of this plural option, but Eurozone countries cannot devalue and so must reduce their debts through deflation or default. The euro was invented when money was already breaking up into multiple forms and functions. Whereas the Americans fought their Civil War before centralising their currency, the Europeans centralised theirs as a means of achieving political union. The EU is thus a neo-liberal experiment based on the dogma that markets logically precede politics.

The key problem for the Eurozone – and more generally – is the democratic deficit which has led governments to be accountable to finance rather than to their own people, as they largely were after 1945. Throughout the twentieth century, the Scandinavian countries showed that democratically accountable political elites could ensure among the highest rates of economic growth in the world. Scotland's economic history could support a similar observation in certain periods. Attempts to solve Europe's problems by fixing the euro alone will fail. The problem is political union itself. Equally, Scots must realise that independence would rest on political choices with economic consequences, especially concerning money.

CONCLUSIONS

Norway's example suggests that there are powerful Scandinavian precedents for Scotland if it becomes independent. We have also offered a detailed history of Scottish banking, before and after the Union, mainly as a reminder of the pitfalls of unequal partnership with London. Both exercises point to the need for firm regulation of finance in any future Scotland.

High leverage and low liquidity ratios suit commercial banks, especially if taxpayers carry much of the risk. Any new banking system in Scotland must be prepared to regulate. The requirements of Basel III by themselves are not strong enough. Large banks ('too big to fail') should be broken up into smaller units to avoid concentration. Banks should stick to the business of banking. A significant reserve fund should be created by all the banks to meet the needs of any that fails and to protect depositors without relying on taxpayers. Property bubbles should be avoided at all costs. None of these and many similar issues has yet entered the referendum debate, which seems odd given our recent economic history.

It is not surprising, however, that the future of the national currency is a focus of attention. The link between any future Scottish currency and the pound sterling, with its consequences for fiscal management, has inevitably dominated discussion. Our aim here has been to show that national monopoly currencies and fixed exchange rate currency unions are both endangered species. The world has entered another phase of multiple competing currencies since the early 1970s. Yet ideas about money have not kept up with this new reality. Scots must consider this disjunction between ideology and practice seriously. Ours is an age of new monetary possibility, as well as of the old order's decline. Money is still the main link between our local attempts to secure a community's rights and interests and the global conditions of its continuity. The terms of that link are changing fast, often in dangerous ways. We do not prescribe specific recipes, only the need to pay attention to our world's present and future, not just to its past.

Notes

1. The Scottish Fiscal Commission report and HM Government's Scotland Analysis report on currency and monetary policy (both published in April 2013).
2. '[In the seventeenth century] in a small country like Scotland, the currency was to a considerable extent made up of the coins of the states with which it traded' (Checkland, 1975: 11).
3. Bergman et al., 1993: 508.
4. Dollinger, 1964: 206–9).
5. For example, Welsh First Minister Carwyn Jones in a speech on 21 November 2013. http://www.bbc.co.uk/news/uk-scotland-scotland-politics-25034379 (accessed 26 Nov 2013).
6. Armstrong and Ebell, 2014.
7. Leverage is the ratio of bank assets to its capital. The 1850 ratio is derived from Checkland, 1975: 742.
8. Martin, 2013.
9. Broad liquidity is the ratio of sterling cash plus balances at the Bank of England, plus approved sterling bills and gilts, in effect, the required Bank of England balances held by Scottish banks to cover the issue of Scottish bank notes.
10. Day, 1957: 187.
11. Checkland, 1975: 188.
12. The Bretton Woods agreement of 1944 led to a global regime of fixed exchange rates pegged to the US dollar, which became the international reserve currency and was convertible into gold (Ferguson, 2008).
13. Arrighi, 2008: 197.
14. Eitrheim, 2012: 2.
15. Eitrheim, 2012: Figure 4.
16. Eitrheim, 2012: 7.
17. J. P. Morgan Global Emerging Market Bond Index (USD), 2012.
18. From www.tradingeconomics.com for Monday, 9 December 2013.
19. The national currencies were nevertheless used interchangeably because of their adherence to the gold standard.
20. Bergman et al. (1993) and Razgallah (2011).

21. Mo = Currency and Bank Reserves, known as the Monetary Base or 'narrow' money; M3 = Mo plus near substitutes for money plus large and long-term deposits; a wider definition.
22. Eitrheim, 2012: 7.
23. Martin Wolf, 'A Very Dangerous Game', *Financial Times*, 30 September 2003.
24. Writing in the *Financial Times*, 3 February 2009.
25. Basel III (2011) introduced stricter leverage and liquidity ratios as well as a counter-cyclical buffer that regulates equity ratios and increases capital requirements in good times and reduces them in bad.
26. Midthjell, 2010.
27. Beltratti and Stulz, 2009.
28. Norges Bank, 1985.
29. A bill of exchange is a promise to pay in a specified currency at a given date. A discount house purchases bills of exchange at a discount reflecting the risk and costs of recovery, as well as the time period involved.
30. Saville, 1996.
31. The official exchange rate was then £12 scots to £1 sterling.
32. Some wrongly claim that Paterson also founded the Bank of Scotland (for example, see Cooke and Donnachie, 1998: 141).
33. Saville, 1996: 33–8.
34. Neal, 2012.
35. Smith, 1776: 283.
36. Campbell, 1971: 71.
37. Cited but not named by Smout (1963: 252).
38. Campbell, 1971: 55.
39. Campbell, 1964: 55.
40. Saville, 1996: 84.
41. Campbell, 1964: 57.
42. Checkland, 1975: 59.
43. The Bank of England objected strongly to the charter for the 'Society of the Subscribed Equivalent Debt', with Paterson a major holder (Saville, 1996: 86).
44. Campbell, 1964: 69.
45. Devine, 1999: 105.
46. Saville, 1996: Chapter 6.
47. The British Linen Bank was amalgamated with the Bank of Scotland in 1971. The Labour government of the day strangely encouraged larger and fewer banks while also seeking greater competition in the banking sector (Saville, 1996: 680).
48. Saville, 1996: 87.
49. Smith, 1776: 269.
50. Smith, 1776: 275. Adam Smith's 'real bills' doctrine survived critique, for example by Thornton (1802), to be embodied in the US Federal Reserve Act of 1913, becoming one of the 'longest-lived economic fallacies of all time' (Blaug, 1968: 56).
51. Smith, 1776: 278–9.
52. Campbell, 1971: 135–6.
53. Saville, 1996: 172–5.

54. Ibid.: 178.
55. Saville, 1996: 228.
56. By 'conservative policies' we refer to the proportion of assets to be held in low-yielding government stocks, rather than in higher-yielding but riskier manufacturing and commercial investments.
57. Campbell, 1971: 143–4.
58. Wallace, 1905.
59. The prohibition was the result of the 1844 and 1845 Bank Charter Acts in England and Scotland, but it did not stop these banks from engaging in speculative or risky lending, and generally engaging in 'reckless competition and unsound practice' such that most of them had failed by 1850 (Saville 1996: 353).
60. Saville, 1996: 355.
61. Ibid.: 359.
62. Saville, 1996: 365.
63. Based on Table 15.2 in Saville (1996: 372).
64. Saville, 1996: 381.
65. Checkland, 1975: 398.
66. Ibid.: 447–8.
67. Ibid.: 497.
68. Saville, 1996: 556–77.
69. Ibid.: 606.
70. Day, 1957: 190–1.
71. Ibid.: 198.
72. Checkland, 1975: 627.
73. Ibid.: 632–4.
74. Reid, 1982: 61.
75. Saville, 1996: 698.
76. Saville, 1996: 700.
77. Saville, 1996: 702.
78. Saville, 1996: 705.
79. Saville, 1996: 707.
80. Payne, 1985.
81. Saville, 1996: 813.
82. House of Lords/House of Commons (2013).
83. Gjedrem, 1999.
84. SDR = Special Drawing Rights, a claim to special foreign exchange reserves in designated currencies managed by the International Monetary Fund. The value of SDR is defined by a weighted basket of four major currencies: the US dollar, the euro, the British pound and the Japanese yen.
85. NOK 1 million = 106,667.00 SDRs on 25 November 2013, so that SDR 10 billion is NOK 93.7 billion or some £9.5 billion at rates on that date.
86. Chetwin and Munro, 2013.
87. de Giovanni and Shambough, 2006.
88. Drēviņa et al., 2007.
89. Mundell, 1961.
90. Buxton, 1985.

91. The Latvian Bank minted one LAT 'Parity Coins' with the Latvian Lat and euro conversion rates on the reverse (1 LAT = 1.42 EURO) on 6 November 2013. The coin continued in circulation for one year after Latvia joined the EMU and adopted the euro on 1 January 2014.
92. Hart, 2009.
93. Polanyi, 1964.
94. Simmel, 1900.

CHAPTER 9

Religion in Scotland and Norway

Arne Bugge Amundsen and Michael Rosie

INTRODUCTION

Religion has loomed large in the development of both Norway and Scotland, contributing to their identities and popular history, and yet both countries are now largely secularised. In this chapter we hope to draw out the major contours of religion in both societies across the several last centuries, noting parallels and differences. Although there are some initial similarities – two small and, historically, Protestant countries of northern Europe, long governed within multi-national unions – there are also some very distinctive developments.

In this chapter we will outline some of the ways in which the Norwegian and Scottish experiences converge and differ. But we start with the present, since the broad contours of religious denomination in the early twenty-first century speak to how these two countries have found different (and largely 'regional') routes into a broadly secularised society. The different routes are summarised by Tables 9.1–9.3. These note, firstly, the broad religious affiliations in both the Nordic countries and the countries of the UK. Here we find that *disaffiliation*

Table 9.1 Religious Denominations in the United Kingdom, 2012

	England	Northern Ireland	Scotland	Wales
No religion	47	15	53	56
Protestant	38	43	32	37
Catholic	9	42	11	7
Base	2,799	1,168	1,229	164

Sources: England, Wales: British Social Attitudes, 2012; Scotland: Scottish Social Attitudes, 2012; Northern Ireland: Life and Times Survey, 2012.

Table 9.2 Religious Denominations in the Nordic countries, 2008

	Denmark	Finland	Norway	Sweden
No religion	14	18	16	30
Protestant	83	79	82	67
Catholic	1	–	1	1
Base	1,942	1,115	1,060	1,216

Source: International Social Survey Programme, 2008: Religion III (ISSP, 2008).

from religion is much more common in Scotland (where over half of respondents describe themselves as being of 'no religion') than in Norway (16 per cent). Norway is also more religiously homogenous, with the overwhelming majority of those belonging to a Protestant religion (and, here, specifically Lutheran). In Scotland, by contrast, the Protestant category is more varied, and also exists alongside a notable Catholic minority. In each of these respects both countries resemble their neighbours more than they resemble each other.

Yet although religious affiliation (at least in the loose sense of using it as a descriptor in a survey) is much more common in Norway, it does not follow that Norway is 'more religious' than Scotland. Table 9.3 notes claimed frequency of religious attendance in both countries. Here we find that rather more Scots than Norwegians claim to attend regularly *and* that more Scots say they rarely or never attend.

The differences reflect two aspects of history that we will explore in this chapter. Firstly, to some degree religious pluralism explains patterns in Scotland since much of the difference between the countries is explained by (i) the presence in Scotland of Catholics and (ii) a higher level of reported frequency of attendance among Catholics. But the patterns of attendance also speak to a sharper break from religion within Scotland. The evidence noted above suggests a greater propensity in Norway to be 'religious' in a rather nominal way: one need not go to church, nor perhaps believe in anything religious, and still be 'Lutheran'. This reflects a more formal and compulsory history of religious affiliation – specifically membership of the Lutheran State Church – in Nordic countries, which has meant a

Table 9.3 Claimed Religious Attendance

	Norway	Scotland
Regular (at least monthly)	7	18
Occasional (at least once a year)	28	10
Rare (less than once a year) or never	65	72
Base	1,060	1,229

Sources: Norway: International Social Survey Programme, 2008: Religion III (ISSP, 2008); Scotland: Scottish Social Attitudes, 2012.

disengagement between 'belief' and 'belonging' in a different way to how these concepts have disengaged in the United Kingdom.

In the UK it is common sense (indeed 'rational') for those who do not believe in religious things *not* to belong to religious organisations, nor to routinely attend their services. The process of secularisation in the UK has largely followed a break in practice/belonging, followed by a slower decline in belief.[1] In Nordic countries, by contrast, the break in practice has been more nuanced. Few Norwegians regularly attend church and a significant minority do not believe in 'any sort of spirit, God or life force': Eurobarometer[2] found that 29 per cent in Norway and 25 per cent in the UK took such a position. Yet 3.8 million Norwegians remain members of the Lutheran Church, and baptisms, confirmations and religious funerals remain the norm.[3] The second aspect to be explored in this chapter, therefore, is the relationship between Church and State, which has been markedly different in the two countries.

REFORMATION AND PROTESTANTISM IN NORWAY AND SCOTLAND

Norway and Scotland's paths to Protestantism were quite different and limit the extent to which we can identify any 'shared' sense of religious history. There were differences in terms of which segments of society supported Reform; differences in the particular theological influences at play; differences in how the 'new' church would be governed; and differences in how the lands held by monasteries and their like were to be redistributed after dissolution (see Chapter 1).

Since 1397, the three Scandinavian kingdoms of Norway, Denmark and Sweden had been united under one king. This union was dissolved in 1523, when after a rebellion Sweden demanded sovereignty with the prominent nobleman Gustav Vasa as its first king. Danish kings had no Norwegian competitors at the time. When a civil war in Denmark over hereditary and confessional issues ended in 1536 with nobility and cities supporting the Lutheran Prince Christian (III), the Norwegian Archbishop Olav Engelbrektsson tried to mobilise cultural and political resistance. In 1537, however, the archbishop had to flee Norway, and Danish Lutheran authorities imprisoned the Roman Catholic bishops, sieged the important military fortresses and declared Danish Lutheran rule valid in the Kingdom of Norway without any further negotiation or adaptation. Johannes Bugenhagen, Lutheran reformer from Wittenberg, finished the new church ordinance, ordained new Lutheran 'superintendents' to take the old bishops' positions, and crowned Christian III.[4]

From 1537, then, Lutheranism was superimposed on the Norwegian population, of which the dominant majority were peasants living in the countryside. This Reformation – a marked shift in confession, in liturgy and in religious practice – was in no way prepared, expected or wanted by the Norwegians themselves.

Rather, it was closely linked to strengthened Danish control and influence in the country. The old Norwegian elite groups (bishops and noblemen) were marginalised or simply removed, and the dissolution of the old church organisation represented a serious setback for social and cultural development.[5]

This meant that a more grounded implementation of Lutheran belief and practice in Norway needed several generations, and both a second and a third reformation had to take place. These new 'reformations' involved a strengthened Lutheran imprint on church interiors,[6] new prohibitions of old religious practices and an 'intensified' legislation aimed at controlling the religious conduct and feelings of the king's subjects. The most important parts of these new 'reformations' took place during the reign of King Christian IV (1588–1648).[7]

Little resistance to the new church regime is known from Norway except from the protests of the Roman Catholic bishops and the few monasteries still inhabited. There are indications, however, that common people resisted the changes by simply staying away from the new, reformed rituals, despised the new clergy and denied them their income, or simply made the former church rituals their own.[8]

The ordination of the new 'superintendents' was a clear separation from the old church organisation, and the new clergy never claimed any part in the apostolic succession as it was understood in the Roman Catholic Church. The king manifested his new power by being the one who appointed the new 'superintendents' – after a period of time normally called 'bishops'.

By sharp contrast, the Reformation in Scotland was at once a more 'indigenous' and (at least in the Lowlands) a more popular affair. Protestantism was, in many parts of Scotland, a movement from below as well as a mercantile/aristocratic endeavour. Reformation fed into, and was fed by, a shift in Scottish patriotism. That patriotism, historically anti-English, became increasingly anti-French in nature. A shared Protestantism and opposition to French intrigue built bridges between Scotland and England, in particular after the accession to the English throne of the staunchly Protestant Elizabeth. In 1560, the Scottish Church broke from Rome and established a Reformed Confession of Faith. The subsequent 'General Assembly' agreed a Book of Discipline which loosely established the Scots Church as Presbyterian, a form further ratified and entrenched by a Second Book of Discipline in 1581.

The Presbyterian governance of Scotland's Kirk and the Calvinist doctrine that underpinned it was to remain unstable and contested, however. Indeed, into the eighteenth century 'The Church of Scotland remained . . . contestable territory for all religious groups except the Catholics, with dissension being contained within it.'[9] While 'a fierce loyalty to the Presbyterian system' had developed across much of the Lowlands by c. 1750, in the north-east 'episcopacy and Catholicism retained considerable strength due to the protection afforded by landed and titled gentry'. Further, 'the religious complexion of the north was unusually confused, with religious traditions and practices intermingling'.[10] There was thus continued and sometimes deeply vexed conflict over the form of governance that the Scottish

Church should take, occasionally breaking out into violence/insurrection. King James VI of Scotland was Calvinist in doctrine, but Episcopalian in orientation, and his assumption of the English throne in 1603 strengthened the power of Scotland's bishops. This was deeply unpopular across many parts of Scotland, and the mid-seventeenth century saw Charles I impose a new Prayer Book on the Scottish Church. This prompted popular rioting and the signing of a 'National Covenant', with the Kirk's General Assembly of 1638 expelling the bishops and reestablishing Presbyterianism. In the Bishops' Wars that followed, the 'Covenanter' party proved victorious over the king and on the outbreak of Civil War in England, Scotland sided with the Parliamentary forces. With the restoration of the British monarchy in 1660, episcopacy was again imposed on the Kirk, with a resultant cycle of rebellion by, and the suppression of, the Covenanters. Only in 1690, after the ousting of the Stuart dynasty in the 'Glorious Revolution', was Presbyterianism finally established as the governing model for the Church of Scotland. Several pockets of Scottish Catholicism survived the Reformation in the north-east and in the Highlands, and these remained – along with some strands of Episcopalianism – a (potent) reservoir of Jacobite and pro-French mobilisation until their crushing military defeat at Culloden in 1746. Scotland's Presbyterianism was, therefore, popular and widespread and simultaneously under genuine political (and military) threat from c. 1560 to 1746.

By sharp contrast, there were few traces of open conflicts related to or protests against the new church regime in sixteenth- and seventeenth-century Norway; protests in most cases were represented by explicit wishes to reform religious tradition. The new authorities were cautious not to evoke radical protests. During the reign of Christian IV new regulations took place. Under the threat of the Roman Catholic counter-reformation, the king saw his rule challenged by both undercover missionaries faithful to Rome and by clergymen more or less silently sympathising with the old church. They were not many in number but their collegial and family networks made them quite influential. In 1613, Christian IV finally put an end to this crypto-Catholic culture of the Norwegian clergy. Interestingly, this culture had no parallel in Denmark, where the ideological and political whereabouts of the clergy was much more easily controlled. The next step was to strengthen the theological education at the University of Copenhagen and to expect future clergymen to have their testimonials from this strongly confessional institution (1629).[11]

The installation of Frederik III as the first Absolutist ruler of Denmark-Norway in 1660 made it permanently clear that the Lutheran king was the supreme ruler of the Church. The bishops became members of the new nobility – in their cases normally not hereditary – and in Norway the local *ius vocandi* disappeared totally and definitively. Until the introduction of Absolutism in 1660, local clergy in Norway to a certain extent were elected locally, their election later being confirmed by the king. Norwegian bishops, however, were exclusively appointed by the king both before and after 1660.[12]

In the 1680s, the next Absolutist ruler, Christian V, authorised a full revision of church rituals (*Kirkeritualet*, 1685) and church legislation (*Danske Lov*, 1683; *Norske Lov*, 1687) comprising all relevant acts and traditions in the Lutheran Church of his realm. These revised texts became the 'common ground' in the church life of Norway more or less until the last part of the nineteenth century. The theological and legal core of these revised regulations was that Denmark and Norway were exclusively linked to the Lutheran confession, that the king controlled and was the only earthly source of power in the Church, and that bishops and ministers were to execute the king's regulations and instructions. Religious opposition was prohibited in all respects of the word: adherents of non-Lutheran confessions were denied access to the realm (admittedly, this strict regulation had some marginal exceptions), the obligation to attend church services and Holy Communion was strictly controlled, and the Professors of Divinity at the University of Copenhagen were trusted with the task of State censorship of all printed material.[13]

During the eighteenth century, however, Pietism and Moravianism became important protest movements or agents of change within the State Church, advocating either extended freedom of conscience and devotion or at least the urgent need of strengthening the religious emotions and motivations among the king's subjects.

Already during the reign of King Frederik IV (1699–1730), Pietist influence resulted in sharpened regulations of church attendance, church discipline and – as a new strategy for strengthening of religious control and subordination – missionary strategies towards the Sami population in the northern parts of Norway and the Inuit population in Greenland. The Sami mission was headed by the Pietist clergyman Thomas von Westen, the Inuit mission by the orthodox minister Hans Egede. They were both of Norwegian origin, and brought with them experiences from Norwegian parishes to missionary actions towards these newly 'discovered' groups among the king's subjects.[14]

The Moravians started their activities in Denmark and Norway under the direct auspices of Count Nicholas von Zinzendorff. He was accredited at the Danish court during some important years in the 1730s. Since these new theological movements were favoured by the Absolutist king, a certain tolerance of religious groups not controlled by the representatives of the State Church dominated. In some Norwegian societies, groups of rather extreme Anabaptists created a sensation by their scandalous behaviour,[15] while others were more moderate in behaviour but accordingly also a bit more problematic for local church authorities. However, Christian VI started to nurture doubts about the development, and the growing number of quite extreme religious expressions in both Norway and Denmark in the 1730s finally necessitated the Conventicle Act of 1741 prescribing control of the Lutheran clergy over any religious groups outside the formal congregation and public services in the churches. Moravian communities still continued their activities in some of the larger Norwegian cities with the silent acceptance of the authorities despite the Act of 1741. They maintained their contacts with their ideological and organisational centre in Herrnhut, Saxony, through letters, printed material and visits. From 1772, an important link for these contacts was the Moravian colony of Christiansfeld in southern Jutland.[16]

The double ideological and political influence of Moravianism and Pietism, and hence of continental theological centres like Halle and Herrnhut, had lasting effects, among which reforms in religious life and education were the most important. In 1736, the rite of confirmation was established as the general duty of all the king's subjects. A new catechism authored by the leading Pietist court chaplain, Erik Pontoppidan, was authorised as the only handbook for confirmation instructions. This catechism (*The True Way to Piety/Sandhed til Gudfrygtighed*) was – with few alterations – the dominant handbook in Norway until the end of the nineteenth century. Pontoppidan's catechism did not advocate any radical change of religious observation and stayed within the frame of a Lutheran State Church, but at the same time it explained the duties of all individuals as basically Pietistic: anything that could threaten the individual way to a deeply felt conversion and religious sincerity should be avoided. This way of interpreting the Christian religion thus became dominant in Norway for the next 150 years. The individual approach to Christian piety was, however, interpreted through a collective lens – the obligatory rite of confirmation – through which all citizens were expected to renew their baptismal promise.[17]

In 1737, elementary schooling was introduced to all seven-year-old children in Norway. The most important handbook in the new school system was Pontoppidan's catechism, thus making a youth's education a preparation for the confirmation rite. Having finished this preparatory education at the age of 14–16, the new generations of the king's subjects were regarded as competent and full members of the society, ready to serve His Majesty as soldiers, servants, tenants, farmers, married couples and officials at different levels of local and national society. In Norway, the obligation to attend the confirmation rite lasted until 1912.[18]

With the Act of Confirmation 1736 and the Act of Elementary Schooling 1737, the last important parts of the religious framework of the Absolutist State in Norway were introduced. Church organisation in Norway was not regarded as 'Norwegian', but at the same time the cultural and social conditions in Norway were regarded as different from those in Denmark. Compared with Denmark, Norway had only a few, small cities and a small proportion of high officials and nobility, but at the same time the majority of Norway's population – the peasants – were regarded as freer and in many respects more capable than their Danish counterparts, secured as they were by the allodial rights, and strengthened by their willingness to defend king and nation during the many military conflicts with Sweden. Norwegians in general were also regarded as more conservative than the Danish, and many representatives of the clergy evaluated this in a positive way, seeing the Norwegians as defenders of the old religious traditions in the realm.[19]

Absolutism lasted in Norway until the breakdown of the twin monarchy of Denmark-Norway in 1814. From the dissolution of the Roman Catholic Church organisation in 1537, the Lutheran Church in Denmark-Norway was a State

Church in the sense that it was indisputably ruled by the king as 'the most prominent member of the church'. The confessional identity of this State Church was
also undisputed until 1814.[20]

Challenges *did* arise, though, based on theological conflicts and disagreement
on the religious ideals of the members of the State Church. In the late 1700s, open
critiques of ministers and of religious traditions were not uncommon in the higher
circles of Norwegian society, and the events of the radical French Revolution
made positive impressions even among some representatives of peasant elites.
In this situation, religious opposition in Norway suddenly came from within the
State Church structures. This is linked to one single lay individual, Hans Nielsen
Hauge (1771–1824). In 1796, he started to publicly distribute his message, which
was simple, conservative and radical at the same time: that belief in God should
result in good deeds, in an inner spiritual life, in loving community with other
believers, and in trust regarding one's worldly and heavenly fate. Hauge became
the leader of a popular movement unprecedented in Norwegian history. This
movement was proof of the successful implementation of Pietism as the State
religion in Norway since the 1730s. At the same time, its success challenged the
State Church that had nurtured Pietism with such enthusiasm. Hauge argued that
obedience to the State, the king and the law was necessary and unproblematic, but
such obedience did not necessarily have anything to do with true religion. The real
church was not embedded in the public rituals as described in the king's laws nor
represented by the clergy as the king's representatives.[21]

RELIGION, STATE AND UNION IN NORWAY

In 1814, the defeat of Napoleon ended the 400-year political union between
Denmark and Norway. The victorious states demanded that Norway be handed
over to the Kingdom of Sweden, which in 1809 had suffered the loss of Finland.
However, the Danish Viceroy in Norway, Prince Christian Frederik, led a revolt
resulting in a separate Norwegian constitution and his election as King of Norway.
After a short war, Christian Frederik abdicated from the Norwegian throne, but
the Swedish king accepted the Norwegian Constitution and its elected Parliament
(*Stortinget*). The union between Norway and Sweden was, therefore, dynastic in
nature. The kingdoms shared the same king, and their foreign policy and military strategy were united through the royal supremacy. In 1884, the Norwegian
Parliament unilaterally introduced Parliamentarism, forcing King Oscar II to
accept a non-violent political revolution within one of his kingdoms. A growing
nationalism and separatism led to the Norwegian Parliament dissolving the
two-state union in 1905 and establishing Norway as an independent kingdom.

There were no confessional differences between Norway and Sweden, but
the distinctively different church organisations of the two countries never
merged.[22] Norway's 1814 Constitution expected the king to adhere to the

Lutheran confession and to be the Defender of the Lutheran Church, its organisation and its rituals. The Norwegian Cabinet had its own Secretary of Ecclesiastical Affairs, a position that during most of the nineteenth century was held by a Minister.

The Norwegian Constitution of 1814 stated that the Evangelical Lutheran religion will 'remain the public religion of the State' (§2). The paragraph was an expression of continuity. The Absolutist monarchy was ended, but the new king was still expected to be 'the most prominent member of the church' and as such the defender of the confessional position and monopoly of the Lutheran Church in Norway. The Norwegian clergy continued to be State officials, they were appointed by the king, and, as explained in Chapter 5, they kept their central position in the administration and ideological control of the school system, they headed the poor relief organisation in the local communities, as well as assisting in fiscal, military and demographic registrations. The events of 1814 did not represent significant changes in the position and roles of the local clergy and there were no important changes in the ecclesiastical laws.[23]

In 1837, the Norwegian Parliament passed acts on local government administration. These acts formalised and strengthened the influence of members of the congregations on school and poor relief, and they reformulated the responsibilities of the local governments with regard to maintaining churches and chapels. No severe conflicts between the new local governmental bodies and the clergy were reported, but nonetheless the situation was radically changed. The local clergy after 1837 found itself with formal, politically elected counterparts in Church affairs.[24]

Considerably more aggressive and provocative were discussions in the Norwegian Parliament on ecclesiastical laws in the 1830s and 1840s. A radical Parliament in the 1840s forced the king and the Cabinet to abolish the Conventicle Act of 1741, thus making any religious organisation and practice within the Lutheran State Church legal. The same Parliament passed a Dissenter Act in 1845 allowing any adult to leave the State Church and legally establish or join any other kind of Christian society. After 1845, the most important among the new dissenter societies were the Methodists and the Mormons. Numerically none of these new religious societies became important, but their ideological influence was rather strong in many local communities.[25]

Both these reforms were fiercely attacked by the majority of the Lutheran clergy, and leading Norwegian theologians developed the concept of 'The Church of Norway'. This Church was seen as distinct from broader civil society and in need of institutions of its own – a Church Assembly at local and national level, Bishops' Conferences, and so on. The development of the 1840s and 1850s should thus be seen as the most radical change of position of national church organisation in Norway since the Reformation in the 1530s. Admittedly, the State religion continued to be Lutheran and the king was still the defender of the Lutheran Church, but from 1845 Norwegian citizens were not obliged to be members of the

State Church. This revolution in Norwegian church affairs started a long and still ongoing development of loosening the ties between civil society and the Lutheran State Church of 1537.[26]

Paragraph (§) 2 of the Constitution of 1814 also denied Jews and members of Roman Catholic monastic orders the right to enter the Kingdom of Norway. The paragraph was changed with regard to the Jews in 1851, and monastic orders in 1897, but members of the Jesuit order were not allowed to enter Norway until 1956, a change that was introduced as a result of the Norwegian ratification of the UN Declaration of Human Rights.[27]

Since 1845, the relationship between State and State Church in Norway has had to be renegotiated several times. The introduction of Parliamentarism in 1884 made the king as Head of Church dependent upon a secularising liberal majority within the Norwegian Parliament. This majority started to dissolve the strong historical and cultural links between the Lutheran Church and the school system, welfare and civil administration. In 1878, civil servants (judges from 1892) were no longer required to be members of the State Church and, in 1889, clerical control in public schools was diminished.[28]

The German occupation of Norway from 1940 to 1945 created severe conflicts between the bishops and the new Nazi Government. The new authorities expected the officials of the State Church to be loyal, but in 1942 all the bishops and an overwhelming majority of the clergy declared that their obligations as State officials were no longer valid. The theological arguments for their choice were formulated in the important document *Kirkens Grunn* (The Fundament of the Church).[29] After the war, some of the Norwegian bishops made an attempt at using this document as the ideological basis for reformulating the relationship between the Lutheran Church and the Norwegian State, but with no result. This episcopal project was soon overruled by the strategy for constructing a new Norway built on the ideology of the Social Democrats, now a major force in political life and with the majority in the Norwegian Parliament for decades. The ideological critique of religion and the social and cultural critique of the Lutheran State Church were quite dominant in the Social Democratic Party. The party to a certain extent came to accept the cultural and moral values of the State Church, but at the same time sought to control the Church as an institution and make it part of the Social Democratic project. This strategy meant that the Social Democrats explicitly worked to secure moral liberality and theological diversity within the Church, but it also led to widespread suspicion of the State Church developing a full organisation of its own.[30] Parish councils were introduced by law in 1920, diocesan councils and episcopal assemblies in 1934. The Church Act of 1953 did not develop church organisation further, but stated the legal primacy of the State Church based on a national, territorial principle. The 1964 revision of the Norwegian Constitution made an amendment to §2: 'All inhabitants of Norway have the right to practice their own religion'.

Parallel with this, State Church leaders worked strategically to develop a consistent, democratic and independent organisation for the Lutheran Church of Norway, and several national committees and parliamentary commissions worked on Church issues from the 1960s onwards. By an Act of 1984, the Church of Norway had its own National Synod, and from 2012 the Lutheran Church of Norway – its official name still being *The Church of Norway/Den Norske Kirke* – is no longer a State Church. The former §2 of the Norwegian Constitution was reformulated: 'Our values will remain our Christian and humanist heritage. This Constitution shall ensure democracy, a state based on the rule of law and human rights.' The Norwegian king is no longer the High Protector of the Lutheran Church, but the new §4 of the Constitution still reflects his historical role as 'the most prominent member of the Church: The King shall at all times profess the Evangelical-Lutheran religion'.[31]

UNION, STATE AND THE KIRK IN SCOTLAND

Two Unions are crucial to understanding modern Scotland: the dynastic 'Union of Crowns' in 1603, and the political 'Union of Parliaments' in 1707. While as noted above, the dynastic Union presaged almost a century of conflict over how the Scottish Church should govern itself, the 1707 Union guaranteed the continued Establishment of that Church. Indeed, Lindsay Paterson has described the continued independence of the Kirk as 'the cherished Scottish success of the union negotiations'.

> It was more than just a place of worship . . . it governed, it regulated, it policed behaviour, and it provided an occasion for popular participation of a sometimes semi-democratic sort. It also maintained, like the legal system, a pervasive link between the centre and the locality, and – far more than the rather arcane world of sheriffs and lawyers – was a way in which ordinary people, men and women, felt some involvement in the affairs of the nation.[32]

Political union thus entrenched the Kirk as a key social (and *national*) institution, and entrenched that church as Presbyterian. This aspect of the Union settlement helped contribute, by the mid-eighteenth century, to a widespread and popular 'buy in' to Britishness in lowland Scotland. This was particularly true after the suppression of the dynastic claims of the Stuarts in 1746 and once the economic and developmental benefits of union and Empire became evident. The continued fusion of Scottish patriotism and popular Protestantism became an important contributor to a very Scottish version of Britishness which dominated Scotland between c. 1750 and c. 1950 and has been aptly described as 'Unionist Nationalism'.[33]

The precise relationship between Church and State remained, however, a thorny issue. By the mid-eighteenth century the Church of Scotland could no longer contain dissent within itself. In particular, the authority of civil courts over church issues, not least the appointment of parish ministers, proved controversial. The issue of 'patronage' (who could appoint ministers) led to several secessions from 1733 and continued to provide the most potent threat to Presbyterian unity. The issue came to a dramatic head in the Disruption of 1843 when the Church of Scotland split, acrimoniously, in two. For several decades, two great national Churches wrangled over property, endowments and prestige. The resultant fierce enmity of these two Kirks, both of which claimed the mantle of the *de facto* (if not, in the case of the secessionists, *de jure*) 'Established' Church, deeply divided Scotland. These Churches were identical in Reformed doctrine/liturgy but increasingly opposite in political colouring, and their legal wrangling effectively compelled the Scottish/British State to be a neutral actor in its dealings towards them. The Established Kirk retained the formal status and most of the buildings, but the 'Free Kirk' had the popularity, the urban base and the political connections with the Liberal Party that dominated Scotland. As the Victorian doggerel had it:

The Free Kirk, the Wee Kirk,
The Kirk without the Steeple;
The Auld Kirk, the Cauld Kirk,
The Kirk without the People.

By the latter decades of the nineteenth century, Presbyterian fission had evolved into increasing fusion. As early as 1847, many of the earlier secessionist sects combined to form the United Presbyterian Church, which operated as the third sizeable major Presbyterian denomination until its merger with the Free Church in 1900. In turn, the resultant United Free Church merged with the Church of Scotland in 1929 after most of the latter's remaining State links had been severed. The Church of Scotland Act 1921 had guaranteed the independence of the Kirk in all spiritual matters, severing it from the State and transforming it from an Established Church into a 'National' one. The 1921 Act, in essence, codified the State neutrality that had, from expediency, followed the Disruption eighty years before.

PLURALISM AND SOCIAL DIVISION

It will be appreciated that the schismatic nature of Scotland's Church led to a religiously differentiated society. In 1851, a survey of religious worship was carried out for the first (and last) time in Britain alongside the decennial census. Although deeply flawed, the religious census does allow us to draw the broad contours of Scottish church life in the mid-nineteenth century. Table 9.4 reports the number of people recorded as attending the various services across religious denomination on the census Sunday in 1851. While the precise numbers need to be treated with extreme caution,[34] they do reveal the extent of pluralism: while Presbyterianism dominated the religious scene, it was a Presbyterianism fractured between three large churches: and there was a considerable variation in other kinds of Christianity.

Table 9.4 Religious Worship in Scotland, 1851

	Number at all sittings	Proportion of all sittings
(Established) Church of Scotland	368,668	26%
Free Church	485,693	35%
United Presbyterian Church	303,132	22%
Other Presbyterian Churches	26,563	2%
All Presbyterian sittings	**1,184,056**	**85%**
Episcopal Church	34,402	2%
Independents/Congregationalists	57,466	4%
Baptists	16,379	1%
Methodist Churches	18,019	1%
Evangelical Union	10,192	1%
Other Protestant Churches	3,345	0%
'Isolated Congregations'	7,545	1%
All Other Protestant sittings	**147,348**	**11%**
Roman Catholic	60,644	4%
Other Christian	3,825	0%
ALL CHRISTIAN SITTINGS	**1,395,873**	**100%**

Source: Adapted from HMSO, 1853.

Presbyterian division into three blocs, and the resultant informal compulsion on the State to remain neutral (rather than be seen to favour any one of the Presbyterian denominations over another), underpinned a *de facto* and broadening pluralism, and hastened secularisation. Over the nineteenth century, Scotland shifted from a largely agrarian society to a thriving urbanised and industrial powerhouse (see Chapter 6). The rise of Glasgow is emblematic: this 'squalid industrial megalopolis of textiles and engineering' witnessed 'a headlong rate of increase'. By 1841, 'at 275,000 it was twelve times as large as it had been in 1775, and between 1831 and 1841 it had grown by more than one-third'. By 1911, Glasgow's population stood at 784,000.[35] The towns and cities, factories and mills were fed by inward migration: from rural Scotland, and from Ireland and beyond. This brought increasing numbers of religious minorities – particularly Catholic and Episcopalian – into urban Scotland. These minorities were growing in numbers, 'respectability' and influence over the nineteenth century. The Episcopalian presence in Scotland rose from (an estimated) 12,000 in 1790 to 146,000 in 1914, while the Catholic population rose more dramatically over the same period from 25,000 to 546,000. While Episcopalians shrank over the latter twentieth century, Catholicism continued to grow, reaching 841,000 in the census of 2011, some 16 per cent of the population.

This religious and ethnic mixture brought with it the potential for very serious conflict, although that potential was rarely met. Bruce notes that the ingredients for sectarian conflict had developed unevenly in Scotland: while from the sixteenth century much of lowland Scotland embraced reformed theology, it was not until the latter eighteenth century that Presbyterianism made serious inroads into the Highlands. And by the time evangelical fervour was 'Calvinising' Highland districts, in much of the Lowlands 'the dominant form of Protestantism, for those who still had any, was moderate, rational, and ecumenical'. Lowland Scotland had lost the religious ideology essential for 'sustained ethnic tension' by the time religious minorities – most strikingly the Catholic Irish – began to arrive in substantial numbers.[36] Conservative Protestant evangelism gave nineteenth- and twentieth-century Highland Protestants the ideological basis for ethnic conflict, but the Highlands were characterised by emigration, not immigration. While there was, undoubtedly, intra-Christian friction over jobs, housing, political representation and symbolic status in many parts of urban Scotland, the impact of a 'sectarian' divide between Protestant and Catholic can be exaggerated. Martin Mitchell concludes that Catholic Irish immigrants in the early nineteenth century were participating in 'strikes, trade unions and political movements with native workers', and that socio-economic conflict between these groups should not be overstated.[37]

In the political realm, denominational and ethnic divisions did not straight-forwardly map on to partisan allegiances. Scottish politics across the nineteenth century was a two-party affair marked by class and geography: the landed gentry, and many rural districts, were strongly Conservative in hue, while urban districts and the Highlands were strongly Liberal. Free Kirkers gravitated towards the Liberals as part of their general class and social values: Irish Catholics because of the Liberal Party's position on Ireland. Thus (Free) Presbyterian – including Highland Calvinists – and (Irish) Catholic were in the same dominant political party (though not necessarily for the same reasons), while the social and class values of (Established) Presbyterian and Episcopalian gravitated towards the (less successful) Conservatives. It was thus difficult to sustain, for example, a common Presbyterian front against Catholics or Episcopalians, since such a front had the potential to undermine immediate political advantages. Likewise, Protestant alli-ances between Presbyterian and Episcopalian were largely limited because of the association of the latter with the Conservatives. Political cleavages, then, did not easily coincide with religious ones: indeed, they may well have served to limit actual religious conflict.

RELIGION, EDUCATION AND POLITICS IN NORWAY

In Norway, the dominant position of the Lutheran State Church made it an important target for politically or ideologically radical groups who either wanted a society built on values other than the Lutheran, the Christian, or one based on lay religious authority as opposed to that of the clergy. Still, the Lutheran clergy did not lose its *ex officio* position in local school councils until 1959, and only a School Act of 1969 ended the confessional status of religious education in public schools.[38] In 1946, the Social Democratic government made State control over teachers' education an important principle. Among the results of this new principle was State confiscation of the Oslo Teachers' College, established by the Norwegian Home Mission Society in 1932.[39] In 1956, the Norwegian Humanist Association – with 81,000 members by 2014 – was founded, with making public education and public symbols non-religious one of its major strategies.[40] The 1964 amendment to Clause §2 of the Norwegian Constitution laid down freedom of religion for all inhabitants of the country, thus giving priority to universal human rights over confessional State Church position in public schools.

Since religious education in the public schools was confessionally defined as the education of baptised members of the State Church, the Dissenter Act of 1845 made it possible for non-members to withdraw from these parts of the teaching schedules. After pressure from, among others, the Humanist Association, public schools from 1974 organised alternative teaching hours parallel with the teaching of religion. New debates on freedom of religion and – not least – the fact that non-Christian religions had become more important due to decades of non-Western immigration to Norway, led to a new definition and organisation of religious teaching in the public school system.

Increased immigration and growing numbers of asylum-seekers since the 1990s have put pressure on the public school system, so dominant in historically egalitarian and traditionally monocultural Norway, not least with regard to religious education. On the one hand, religious groups have argued their right to educate their own members in their faith and customs, while on the other, religious education in public schools has been criticised for being too much based on (Lutheran and) Christian perspectives. This situation has also been used by, for example, secularists to argue that (confessional) religion should not be part of the public educational system at all.[41]

In 1997, the curriculum in the public schools was changed into what was called 'Christianity, Religion and Human Values', obligatory for all to attend. This solution still created fury among some groups, finding the curriculum offensive and not sufficiently 'neutral' to their taste. They also found the obligatory attendance problematic. A few families took their case to court, with no positive result in Norway. The European Court of Human Rights, however, in 2007 judged the Norwegian curriculum not to be in accordance with the European Convention on Human Rights. As a result, the Norwegian Government in 2008 changed the curriculum and renamed it 'Religion, Human Values and Ethics'.[42]

RELIGION, THE STATE AND WELFARE IN SCOTLAND

The *de facto* neutrality of the State in Scotland's religion set the tone and the back-cloth for the expansion of the State's functions from the mid-nineteenth century onwards. There is a great historical irony that the ultimately *secularising* expansion of these functions was often driven by the desire among Presbyterian 'dissenters', in particular after 1843, to break the Established Kirk's remaining dominant position in Scotland's civic institutions. As Paterson notes:

> the various state takeovers of traditional church functions in the second part of the [nineteenth] century, although ostensibly secularising, were, in fact, victories for religious evangelicals, skilfully using the opportunities of state authority and finance to further their projects.[43]

Thus, clerical influence on local boards and committees continued well into the twentieth century – but that influence was, in effect if not intent, pluralistic. Three great Presbyterian Churches sought to involve themselves, as did, in particular places and contexts, representatives from the Episcopal, Catholic and smaller churches. In turn, the varied nature of representation opened up the opportunity for more secular platforms – not least 'ratepayer' caucuses standing for economy and, later, representatives from the labour movement. Throughout this process the reputation of the State – local and national – as the best-placed (and trusted) institution to provide and manage services grew, gradually undermining the role and relevance of the churches.

An exemplar of this process can be found in education. The theology of Scotland's Reformation, with its emphasis on *sola scriptura*,[44] had meant that the Kirk had long striven to provide both a church and a school in every parish. As Scotland urbanised and industrialised it became clear that the existing parish-focused system of schools (further undermined, post-Disruption, by the increased number of separate religious organisations providing their own schools) was failing to meet the needs of an increasingly complex society. Religion had proved a major stumbling block in the construction of a State education system in England. The English Education Act of 1870 restricted religious instruction in State schools to Bible-reading, forbidding the use of any catechism or formulary distinctive to any denomination. This was unacceptable to Catholics and – crucially – to the Church of England, and both these bodies remained outside the English State system. Thus, a majority of schools in England would receive no contribution from the locally levied education rate.[45] Scottish eyes were cast, anxiously, south-wards during these debates, not least since the Liberals were neither prepared to concede State-provided denominational schools nor able to impose a fully non-denominational solution.

The 1872 Education (Scotland) Act attempted to side-step these issues by going no further than allowing elected School Boards to provide religious instruction according to local opinion and practice. While in practice this 'compromise' allowed for Presbyterian instruction in Board Schools across most of Scotland, the refusal of its *statutory* status rankled the Churches. The segregated timetabling of religious instruction also meant that, as in England and Wales, Catholics and Episcopalians remained outside the new State system. While in England most schools had thus remained outside the State, in Scotland only a small minority remained in the 'voluntary' sphere. The key political result was that School Board elections were often fought on denominational lines as the various Churches sought to ensure that the feelings and interests of their communities were met. For the Presbyterian Churches this meant the protection of 'use and wont' in Board Schools. For the minority, Churches Board representation was essential: while their communities contributed to the education rate, their schools reaped little benefit, so there was an in-built interest in fiscal conservatism. 'Ratepayer' interests were increasingly active as educational provision and standards (and therefore expense) increased. By the 1890s, Scotland's larger School Boards were dominated by interests stressing 'economy'. The labour movement also entered into the education elections, though its record was dismal.[46]

The success of Board Schools over the next several decades left the voluntary religious schools – not least those provided by the Catholic Church – falling behind. The experience of Board politics, where denominational representatives worked together, also laid the grounds for a generous solution. In 1918, another Education (Scotland) Act brought Catholic and Episcopalian schools into the State system on a fully funded basis, with the religious character of the schools, and religious instruction within them, guaranteed by law. This was a far more progressive settlement than had brought English and Welsh denominational schools into the State system in 1902 and garnered far less opposition (despite the minority churches having won the statutory protection denied to Presbyterians in 1872). The architects of the 1918 Act had hoped to abolish local elected educational boards but were thwarted by the combined Churches – but by 1930 the success of the new system saw education fully taken over by local councils, with the Churches' role limited to guaranteed (but very modest) representation on the councils' education committees.

The Scottish story of religion and education is thus one of the success of the secular State in delivering high-quality education which, at least after 1918, met the religious needs of most families. Further, the longer-term impact of the 1918 reform was to reduce markedly the social inequalities between religious communities, not least between Protestant and Catholic. Paterson and Iannelli find that the State denominational sector has contributed markedly to the 'equalizing of educational attainment' between Scotland's major religious groups. In turn, 'These [educational] credentials are then rewarded in the labour market in broadly the same way for all religious groups, regardless of class of origin.'[47] In short, the intervention by the secular State to accommodate religious differences in education has markedly reduced the potential for religious differences to impact on educational attainment, subsequently reducing their impact on 'life chances'. That very success, ironically, has undermined the legitimacy (and, indeed, relevance) of religious bodies as key actors in educational provision beyond very specific circumstances (that is, 'Catholic' schools). By 1945, and the introduction of a comprehensive UK welfare system, it was the *State* – local and national – that was seen as the 'natural' provider and arbiter of welfare issues, leaving the Churches as voluntary – indeed 'private' – organisations relevant to individual conscience more than to public goods.

CHURCH, STATE AND WELFARE IN NORWAY

Given the fact that the Church – both the Roman Catholic, medieval church of Norway and the Lutheran State church since the 1530s – had a dominant position as the very organisation for social welfare, changes in this field came very slowly. It was recognised that the local clergy were the best informed about the social situation of the parishioners, and even after the introduction of municipal councils in 1837, the local vicar continued to be a member and chair of public assistance committees. This *ex officio* position was not removed until 1964. During the nineteenth century, a number of NGOs with public assistance and poor relief as their main clause developed. In the larger cities the Societies for Inner Mission included such clauses in their activities, and institutions for the education and practice of deaconesses (1868) and deacons (1890) were established. These are still prolific institutions, responsible for wide programmes for hospitals, religious care and education. The Roman Catholics, once being allowed entrance to Norway, also took up hospital and poor relief programmes in several cities.

These institutions have been problematic in the perspective of the Social Democrat welfare state ideology since 1945, and to be accepted as parts of the public welfare system they have had to adjust or reorganise the religious parts of their programmes.[48]

The Norwegian Church Aid (*Kirkens Nødhjelp*) was established in 1947, and this NGO – from a close connection with the Lutheran State Church now based in several Protestant denominations – has become a rather undisputed part of the emergency and foreign aid system in Norway.[49]

In Norway, religion from the 1970s has become part of the welfare system in that from 1971 the Norwegian State has supported economically all registered religious societies and denominations outside the Church of Norway. From 1981, this policy was extended to the Norwegian Humanist Association. In 1971, the new system covered religious societies with 110,000 members, of which 100,000 belonged to Protestant denominations and 10,000 to Roman Catholicism. In 2011, the same system for State economical support covered religious societies with

480,000 members. Among these, 80,000 belonged to the Humanist Association and 220,000 were members of non-Protestant and non-Christian religious associations and societies, half of which were Muslim.[50]

SECULARISATION IN SCOTLAND AND NORWAY

The key decade for religious decline in Scotland is the 1960s: 'Secularisation as a widespread breach of popular church connection . . . occurred only from about 1963–65. From then until the present, the slide in all indices has been very severe for most Protestant churches'.[51] Most markedly, membership of the Church of Scotland, which had numbered 1.3 million in 1960, entered steep decline in 1963. By 1980, it had fallen under 1 million, and by 2007 under 0.5 million. The latest figures, from 2013, put the Kirk's membership at under 0.4 million. The 'loss' of almost one million members in just half a century has been driven not by active abandonment of the Kirk by existing members but by its increasing failure to recruit young people. And it is that driver of decline – failure to recruit – that forms the key debate about the Scottish 1960s.

While Brown[52] points to the momentous social and cultural shifts of the 1960s themselves as presaging 'the death of Christian Britain', others argue that the roots of disengagement lie with the prior experiences of those who were *parents* in the 1960s. In other words, the dislocations of the Second World War and the boom that followed it may have as much to do with Scotland's (and Britain's) secularising moment than the more immediate cultural context.[53] Indeed, survey evidence from 2001 suggested that while most respondents born before 1965 had regularly attended religious services at some point in their lives (even if a large majority no longer did so), around 55 per cent of all respondents born after 1965 had *never* been regular attenders.[54]

Nor is this decline restricted to Scotland's Protestant churches. Catholic mass attendance in Scotland between 1950 and 2000 fell by 46 per cent, very similar to the decline in England of 49 per cent over the same period.[55] As Brown notes:

> Though the decline in the Scottish Catholic Church (as measured by a variety of indicators) only started in the mid-1970s, it has since the mid-1980s experienced an accelerating decline that has reached a gradient unmatched by any other Scottish church before. In short, Catholic Church decline started late, but it is proving to be incredibly sharp.[56]

Scotland, then, can be seen as a deeply secularised country along with other Northern European and historically 'protestant' societies (with the obvious exception of Northern Ireland). There is ample evidence of a broad and secular mindset in Scotland even among the religious.[57] Religion has a very limited voice in politics (it is at its loudest, and most unpopular, in the area of sexual morality), and religious identity is largely irrelevant in exploring both Scottish national identity and the pressing political issue over how Scotland should be governed.[58]

In Norway, secularisation as differentiation between different fields of society and culture can be traced as a process embedded in – and following not least as – political and ideological consequences of the Constitution of 1814 and the Dissenter Act of 1845. Still, the very close connections between the Lutheran king and the Lutheran Church, and between Lutheran Absolutism and Absolutist religious control, had an almost overwhelming psychological and cultural power in a monocultural nation. In the first phases of this development the 'opposition from within' seems to have been most important: the Pietists and the Dissenters claiming rights to practise their Christian conviction, and the radical Parliament claiming political power from the Old Regime, the civil servants and public religious authorities. In the last two decades of the nineteenth century these political debates were accompanied by a radical change in religious practice: declining Sunday service attendance and the extinction of the medieval tradition of going to Holy Communion once a year.[59]

However, not until the era of the Social Democratic 'One Party State' from 1945 was the position of the Lutheran State Church seriously politically challenged. The Social Democrats were not necessarily fighting the State Church as such but all attempts at narrowing what they conceived as intolerance, illiberal practices, restrictions of people's moral choices or undemocratically elected assemblies. Even the final dissolution of the Norwegian State Church in 2012 was a political compromise, accepting religious and moral freedom for all citizens, and at the same time identifying Christianity (not Lutheranism) as an important part of the national legacy and placing the monarch as constitutional member of The Church of Norway.

In 2013, a committee appointed by the government presented an overall programme for further change in the religious legislation of Norway, taking the full step into an 'open, neutral society'.[60] The committee was heavily influenced by radical Lutheran theologians and free church and secularist ideologies, and the future of its programme is still disputed.

In this connection, one should not disregard the fact that Norway has had a Christian Democratic Party (CDP) since 1933, counting several cabinet members since the 1960s and two prime ministers (1972–3, 1997–2000, 2001–5), and with considerable support in parliament elections (13.7 per cent in 1997, 5.5 per cent in 2009). The CDP has been in favour of what it considers to be Christian values in politics and society, but is not necessarily supportive of the Lutheran State Church system.

On the level below politics and committee programmes, the religious situation in Norway has indisputably changed during the last decades. In 1970, 94 per cent of all Norwegians were members of the State Church, in 2012, 77 per cent. Regular church attendance has diminished. In 1990, 81 per cent of all small children in Norway were baptised, in 2010, 67 per cent. In 1990, 81 per cent were subject to the ritual of confirmation, in 2010, 65 per cent. The most stable numbers relate to burial: in 1990, 96 per cent were buried according to the ritual of the State Church, in 2010, 91.5 per cent.[61]

It is more difficult to decide whether these numbers and percentages – combined with growing religious pluralism and religious conflicts – actually point to secularisation interpreted as diminishing or privatisation of religious belief and practice.[62] On the contrary, the many public discussions and conflicts on religious issues in recent years may indicate that Norway's long history as a monocultural and monoreligious country still has cultural importance and effects.

CONCLUSION

This chapter has demonstrated the very different histories of two small, neighbouring, historically Protestant, Northern European nations. The different trajectories of the Reformation, of church government, of the connection between Church and State, and differential experiences of pluralism all mark out distinctive experiences. In Scotland, the fissiparous nature of Presbyterianism – and in particular the fierce intra-Presbyterian conflicts around the Disruption – led to a *de facto* acceptance of religious pluralism, hastening a secularising process and leaving the State little practical option but to remain largely neutral in religious affairs. Where the State did intervene in religion tended towards the long-sighted and the progressive, as exemplified by the remarkable Education Act of 1918. Secularisation has bitten deep into religious membership in Scotland over the last half century, related probably to the social and cultural upheavals of the 1940s and 1960s. In Norway, by contrast, secularisation has taken a much longer historical trajectory, and has not greatly dulled the Norwegian appetite to 'belong' to the (former) State Church. Rather, formal pluralism from the 1840s and social democratic reforms in the twentieth century have chipped away at the political privileges of Lutheranism, leaving both a strong cultural attachment to religion and powerful secularist voices opposing it. Just as these neighbours found different routes into Protestantism, so they appear to be experiencing different routes out of and beyond it.

Notes

1. See, for example, Davie, 1994; Bruce, 1995; 2014.
2. Eurobarometer, 2010: 381.
3. Statistics Norway, 2013.
4. Oftestad, 1998: 40ff.
5. Rian, 2003: Part 3.
6. Amundsen, 2010a.
7. Amundsen (ed.), 2005: 221ff.

8. Amundsen (ed.), 2005: 171ff.
9. Brown, 1988: 145.
10. Brown, 1988: 145.
11. Amundsen and Laugerud, 2001: 62ff.
12. Oftestad, 1998: 53, 61.
13. Rian, 2010; Amundsen (ed.), 2005: 233ff.
14. Amundsen (ed.), 2005: 244ff.
15. Amundsen, 2008.
16. Amundsen and Laugerud, 2001: 164ff.
17. Amundsen, 1986.
18. Amundsen (ed.), 2005: 260ff.
19. Amundsen (ed.), 2005: 289.
20. Berge, 2001: 17ff.
21. Amundsen, 2007; 2010.
22. cf. Berge, 2001: 42ff.
23. Berge, 2001: 39ff.
24. Oftestad, 1998: 102ff.
25. Amundsen, 1987; Breistein, 2003: 60ff.
26. Berge, 2001: 135ff.
27. Breistein, 2003: 278ff.
28. Oftestad, 1998: Chapter 6.
29. Oftestad, 1998: 213ff.
30. Agøy, 2012.
31. Norwegian Constitution, 2012 Version.
32. Paterson, 1994: 38.
33. Morton, 1999.
34. Note that this figure sums the total sittings recorded at 'morning', 'afternoon' and 'evening' services held on Sunday, 30 March 1851. It thus cannot account for the (unknown) number of adherents who attended multiple sittings of their own denomination nor for the (unknown) number who may have attended services in more than one single denomination. For an overview of the deeply flawed nature of the 1851 religious census, see Pickering (1967).
35. Smout, 1986: 8, 41.
36. Bruce, 1988: 151.
37. Mitchell, 1998: 257. See also Rosie, 2004; Chapter 6 in this volume.
38. Breistein, 2003: 372ff.
39. Oftestad, 1998: 245.
40. Breistein, 2003: 294.
41. Det livssynsåpne samfunn, 2013: 47ff.
42. Det livssynsåpne samfunn, 2013: 55f.
43. Paterson, 1994: 58.
44. Literally 'by scripture alone'.
45. Rosie, 2004.
46. Rosie, 2004.
47. Paterson and Iannelli, 2006: 374–5.
48. Tønnessen, 2000: 281ff.

49. Tønnessen, 2007.
50. Det livssynsåpne samfunn, 2013: 47.
51. Brown, 1992: 54.
52. Brown, 2001.
53. See, for example, Bruce, 2002.
54. Rosie, 2002: 25.
55. Rosie, 2004: 35.
56. Brown, 2008: 33–4.
57. Rosie, 2002; 2004.
58. Rosie, 2004; 2013.
59. Sandvik, 1998.
60. Det livssynsåpne samfunn, 2013.
61. Det livssynsåpne samfunn, 2013: 45.
62. cf. Breistein, 2003: 415ff.

CHAPTER 10

The Nordic Welfare Model in Norway and Scotland

Mary Hilson and Andrew G. Newby

INTRODUCTION

More than a Millennium ago, Vikings first invaded and then controlled whole swaths of what is now Scotland. The Norsemen were in charge of the Orkneys, Shetland, the Hebrides, Caithness and Sutherland for several hundred years. Now Scotland could be looking to establish itself along the lines of a Nordic model once more. Parts of the Scottish National party, in their quest for independence, are keen to place Scotland alongside the likes of Norway, Sweden and Denmark by adopting similar social and economic policies.[1]

The idea of Scotland seeking to 'establish itself along the lines of a Nordic model', here reported by the *Financial Times* correspondent Richard Milne, has been a regular trope in Scottish political discourse, both before and after the reestablishment of the Scottish Parliament in 1999. Milne's article, written in the run-up to the 2014 independence referendum, demonstrates most of the classic elements of this discourse (as well as the slightly odd implication that 'Scotland' sought previously, a 'millennium ago', to establish a Nordic model via Norse invasion). He notes the 'superficial similarities' between Scotland and Scandinavia, such as geographical proximity in Northern Europe, borrowed linguistic elements in Scots, 'relatively small' populations, and a shared dourness underpinned by a particular religious outlook. None of this is new, although the apparently enduring Norwegian success story has led some supporters of Scottish independence to idealise Norway as a model. Conversely, opponents have highlighted the very distinct circumstances around Norway's Oil Fund, which have allowed high levels of public spending to create a social welfare blueprint that is the envy of many 'social democratic' onlookers.

The Nordic region has played a prominent role in the debates on Scottish independence for over four decades. Prior to the 1979 Scottish Referendum, and again in the 1990s, Nordic states provided examples of 'successful' countries which gave a rhetorical counterbalance to the 'great power' discourse of the British State. In addition to this constitutional comparison, it is clear that – particularly in the 1990s and the period of 'democratic deficit' during the Thatcher years – the idealised notion of a Nordic welfare model provided a fascinating example for many Scottish politicians. On the independence side, the SNP had its own 'social democratic' wing, which eventually gained internal party hegemony, aspiring to perceived Nordic ideals of social equality. For others, particularly in the Scottish Labour Party, the self-image or autostereotype of Scotland as a more democratic and egalitarian country than England also gave Scandinavia a particular allure, but generally it was believed that these social democratic ideals could be pursued either by using local powers or, particularly after 1999, using the existing powers of the Scottish Parliament. Nordic nirvana could be achieved without independence. Indeed, Richard Milne's article concludes by quoting Tom Johnstone, the Scottish-born CEO of Swedish multinational SFK. He suggested that pursuing a Nordic agenda in Scotland was a 'very good target', but wondered whether 'you need to be independent from Britain to do that'.[2]

The aim of this chapter, therefore, is to contextualise the Scottish portrayal of idealised Nordic – particularly Norwegian – society as a part of the independence debate. Firstly, we will summarise the main developments in the historical evolution of the Norwegian welfare state, within the broader context of the 'Nordic model' in both myth and reality, and considering also the similarities and differences between Norway and the other Nordic countries, especially Sweden. Secondly, we examine the rhetorical construction of the Nordic and Norwegian welfare states and the use of this rhetoric in the political discourse of the UK and, in particular, Scotland. We trace the growth of interest in Norway and the Norwegian welfare state in Scotland, starting with the referendum of 1979 but focusing in particular on the post-devolution debate.

We begin by introducing two apparent paradoxes. First, we note that recent Scottish interest in the 'Nordic model' – for the SNP at least – seems to be based on the autostereotype of Scottish egalitarianism. The Nordic countries have functioned in Scottish political discourse – as indeed in political discourses elsewhere – as both utopia and dystopia, helping to reaffirm Scottish self-images or autostereotypes.[3] The Nordic social democratic welfare model, it is argued, seems to be suited to a Scotland that is more egalitarian and less selfish than England or the UK as a whole. This autostereotype holds true even in the 'Better Together' rhetoric of unionist discourse. It was identified, for example, in the London *Guardian* in March 2014, which presented Scotland as 'already a country apart [a]nd a social democratic one', the point being that while the SNP and Labour might argue about the relationship between Scotland and London, they were both operating in a consensual, social democratic political context.[4] This deliberate and self-conscious reinforcement of an older Scottish autostereotype has been noted, for example, by Michael Keating, who posed the question of 'how Scotland might find its own synthesis of old and new elements and produce its own distinct form of social democracy', and whether that might follow 'continental or Scandinavian models'. Keating noted that although Scottish 'mass opinion is similar to that in England, political competition is skewed to the centre-left . . . Indeed, in the course of the 1980s and 1990s, Scottish political identity itself seems to have been reconstructed around progressive and left-of-centre themes.'[5] On the other hand, Norway and its Nordic neighbours remain tantalisingly out of reach for those who argue that Scotland is neither sufficiently egalitarian nor social democratic.[6]

Second, the idea of the 'Nordic model' seems to have enjoyed a resurgence recently – as seen for example in the special issue of *The Economist* devoted to the region in February 2013 – but there are also signs that it has lost its coherence.[7] Increasingly, the 'Nordic model' seems to exist either as a vague rhetorical construct, or as a set of detailed national policies which governments of the left and increasingly also of the right borrow from at will, to suit their particular political position. Commenting on British Prime Minister David Cameron's Nordic–Baltic summit in January 2011, *The Times* journalist Ian Birrell noted how,

> [t]here used to be an unwritten law in the Labour Party that if a policy came from Sweden, it had to be good. Today, in a weird reversal, a similar belief is spreading across the coalition . . . After all, as both parties know, if a policy is marked Made in Sweden it is much easier to sell, since everyone is a little bit dazzled by the Nordic Nirvana.'[8]

THE NORDIC WELFARE MODEL: HISTORICAL DEVELOPMENT

Although published nearly a quarter of a century ago, Gøsta Esping-Andersen's 'three worlds of welfare capitalism' remains an influential starting point for comparative analyses of the welfare state.[9] Drawing on a multi-case comparison, Esping-Andersen proposed a three-part typology. The first group of 'welfare regimes' consisted of the liberal welfare states of the Anglo-Saxon countries, where the State provided a basic safety net but where citizens also relied on the market and on private philanthropy for welfare. This model would include Scotland as a part of the United Kingdom. The second type was the conservative or corporatist welfare states of (mostly Catholic) Central Europe, where benefits were allocated according to recipients' status in the labour market, and which tended to reproduce traditional social structures and hierarchies based on the family. Finally, the Nordic countries formed a third, 'social democratic' group, distinguished by the extent to which social relations were 'decommodified' and the public sector had replaced the family and the market as the main provider of welfare.

It is important to remember that Esping-Andersen's three categories were intended as ideal types, rather than as empirical descriptions of different welfare states. Most welfare regimes include a mixture of different elements: in the words of two Nordic welfare scholars they are 'crossbreeds not purebreds'.[10] Thus, the supposedly 'liberal' welfare regime of the UK has a prime example of universal State-provided welfare in the National Health Service, still in 2014 – for the moment at least – free at the point of delivery for all citizens. Some scholars have extended Esping-Andersen's typology by adding further categories; others have questioned the concept of welfare models altogether.[11] As the field of welfare state studies has increasingly become a topic of interest for historians, the number of detailed empirical studies has grown. Indeed, comparative historical studies of welfare states have expanded enormously in the last decade or so, stimulated by international research networks such as the NordWel project coordinated by the University of Helsinki between 2007 and 2013.[12]

Nonetheless, there does still seem to be a consensus among scholars about the shared characteristics of the Nordic welfare states, as they have developed over the past century or more. In most accounts these would include some or all of the following:[13]

1   The welfare regimes of the Nordic countries are also welfare *states*, where until recently the State has been the dominant or indeed the only provider of welfare services. The division of responsibility between the national State and the local municipalities has varied, with a much greater role for the latter often noted as a particular characteristic of Norway, for example.[14]

2   The Nordic welfare states are tax-financed. Indeed, these states have shared notoriously high tax burdens, but at the same time they delivered welfare services that were largely characterised as comprehensive and universal: a 'luxury' model in contrast to the more residual welfare safety nets provided in the US, for example. The universalism of the Nordic welfare states has, however, been qualified in recent historical research.[15]

3   Welfare benefits were provided to citizens rather than according to individuals' status within the family or workplace. This favoured the development of a so-called 'dual breadwinner' model with very high rates of female labour force participation, which in turn has been linked to the relatively high levels of gender equality in the Nordic countries.[16]

As the designation 'social democratic' implies, the development of these features was partly shaped by the ideological influence of strong social democratic parties. In Norway and Sweden especially it is possible to speak of social democratic political hegemony at least for the three decades after 1935.[17] Leading social democrats – such as the Swedes Gunnar and Alva Myrdal, the Danes Th. Stauning and K. K. Steincke and the Norwegians Karl Evang and Einar Gerhardsen, to name a few – made significant contributions to shaping welfare policy. The social democratic vision of the welfare state was articulated most famously in Per Albin Hansson's concept of the *folkhem* or 'people's home' as a metaphor for the comprehensive cradle-to-grave Swedish welfare state.[18] The idea of the *folk* or people was also central to the ideologies of the other Scandinavian social democratic parties, expressed, for example, in the Norwegian Labour Party's 1936 election slogan, *Norge for folket* ('Norway for the people').[19] It is important to remember, however, that the *folk* was not an exclusively social democratic concept but had its roots also in the liberal and conservative political discourses of the late nineteenth century. Hansson's *folkhem* vision, first expressed in a speech in 1928, was borrowed from early twentieth-century conservative ideas.[20]

As this suggests, it should not be taken for granted that the Nordic welfare states were exclusively the products of strong social democratic parties. The development of welfare policy was pragmatic and incremental; the product of political compromise and consensus. Even within the social democratic parties there was never a comprehensive blueprint for welfare policy; instead its development should be seen as a pragmatic response to changing historical circumstances, and shaped by heterogeneous political influences from both home and abroad.[21]

Thus, whereas earlier research tended to emphasise the watershed of the 1930s and the coalition agreements negotiated across the region in that decade between the farmers' parties and social democratic parties, more recently the Nordic welfare states have come to be understood as rooted in distinctive Nordic 'paths to modernity'.[22] This includes the legacy of the strong State in partnership with the reformed Lutheran Church, and traditions of local democracy stretching back to the seventeenth century or even earlier. This reinforces the idea of the Nordic welfare state as something culturally and historically specific, and thus difficult to export. For example, those sceptical towards the idea of a Nordic model in Scotland and the UK have sometimes drawn attention to the apparent tolerance of the benign Nordic State and its influence in people's lives, in contrast to the traditional British aversion to the 'nanny state'.[23] The Nordic welfare state was not always benign, however. Its historic role in compromising individual freedom and promoting hegemonic social norms was questioned in the 1990s, in the context of debates over the use of eugenic sterilisation in all the Nordic welfare states during the 1930s and after.[24] Writing in *The Scotsman* shortly after the Norwegian Labour Party's severe electoral defeat in 2001, Bill Jamieson caricatured the Nordic welfare state – apparently rejected by Norwegian voters – as 'Big Nurse social welfarism':

> Norway has become this morning a most uncomfortable spectre at the Holyrood feast. It represents simultaneously everything that the political establishment here most wishes for – and the very voter rejection it dreads . . . Is this not the very model to which Scotland's left-wing progressives all aspire? True, alcohol and tobacco are taxed to the blue yonder and, yes, the suicide rate is strangely high for a system that trades so heavily on its reputation as a cradle-to-grave welfare provider. For here we have the state as all-wise nurse, the body politic as a psychiatric hospital, the nation as some 1930s Butlins with a whiff of eugenics: happy campers keeping Fit through Joy.[25]

Recent research has qualified the characterisation of the Nordic welfare state as something historically and culturally specific to the region by insisting on the

importance of the broader transnational context for understanding the evolution of the Nordic welfare regimes.[26] The Nordic welfare states were shaped by
contemporary social policy debates elsewhere in Europe, including, for example,
Bismarck's social conservatism of the late nineteenth century and Beveridge's
liberal welfare state ideas in the mid-twentieth century.[27] As Pauli Kettunen has
pointed out, international comparisons made possible by the statistical work of
institutions such as the International Labour Organisation (ILO) were extremely
important in shaping the development of welfare policy, perhaps especially so in
small states that considered themselves to be on the economic and cultural periphery of Europe.[28]

The idea of the Nordic welfare model was also shaped by international perceptions of the region as an ideological 'middle way' between the extremes of left and
right. This emerged during the 1930s and one of its most famous expressions was
in the American journalist Marquis Childs' *Sweden – The Middle Way*, which
became a bestseller after publication in 1936.[29] Like other reportage on the Nordic
region produced during the same decade, Childs' book did not deal specifically
with the welfare state – much of his book was about the consumer cooperative
movement – but it helped to establish an important and enduring image of the
region as a model of democracy and social harmony. This idea of the region was
strengthened by the geopolitical position of the Nordic countries during the Cold
War as neutral or semi-aligned states, though the region also had its detractors like
Eisenhower who saw the interventionist welfare state and the high taxes needed to
support it as dangerously socialist.[30]

The development of the Nordic welfare states was thus profoundly shaped
by transnational comparison and exchange. The most important source of ideas,
however, came from within the Nordic region. As Klaus Petersen has shown, the
construction of the 'Nordic' welfare state in its different national contexts was
influenced above all by Nordic inter-regional cooperation. Scandinavian social
policy experts began to meet regularly from the 1870s, as part of a general wave
of inter-Nordic cooperation among professionals and voluntary organisations
that flourished during the last decades of the nineteenth century.[31] From the late
1920s, regular Nordic social policy meetings became 'the backbone of a Nordic
social political epistemic community', in Petersen's words, strengthened also by
the regular meetings of Nordic social democratic politicians and trade unionists in
SAMAK (Nordic Social Democratic Cooperation Committee) from 1932.[32] Even
before the foundation of the Nordic Council in 1952, this cooperation had produced
some common initiatives, such as a 1929 convention on poverty guaranteeing some
degree of equal treatment for all Nordic citizens across the region.[33] In the 1950s,
these were followed by agreements on the common labour market in 1954 and the
social security convention of 1955, both under the auspices of the Nordic Council.

Nordic cooperation was always uneven, however, even if that lopsidedness
was never quite as marked as in the relations of the different nations within the
United Kingdom, for example, or indeed within the European Communities.

For Norwegian politicians in particular, the legacy of 1905 was difficult to over-come and during the inter-war period they remained suspicious of any initiatives towards Nordic cooperation that could be interpreted as potentially threatening Norway's recently gained independence.[34] Norwegian support for the Nordic Associations founded across the region in 1919 remained weak, especially in con-trast to the much greater enthusiasm found in the 'core' Nordic nations of Sweden and Denmark.[35] Norway's participation within international organisations such as the ILO and later SAMAK was also hindered by the bitter political divisions within the Norwegian labour movement during this period, during the Labour Party's brief membership of Comintern in the early 1920s.[36]

The inter-war period – the formative years of the Nordic welfare state – was thus to some extent a period of relative isolation for Norway, both within the Nordic region and beyond. Around the turn of the century it was Denmark – specifically Danish agriculture and agricultural cooperatives – that attracted most international attention, but from the 1930s the spotlight shifted towards Sweden.[37] For the next three decades at least, Sweden and the 'Swedish model' became more or less syn-onymous with the idea of *Norden* and the 'Nordic model'.[38] Even so, Norwegian examples were not entirely absent from the broader understanding of the Nordic model. Norway's democratic post-1814 'peasant state' had been an inspiration for British radicals from the early part of the nineteenth century.[39] As Glen O'Hara has noted, Norway was revered in the UK for its perceived heroism during the 1940–5 occupation and many British policymakers were as equally interested in Norwegian policies as they were in Swedish ones. In 1960, even Harold Macmillan described Norway as an admirable example of moderate socialism and his government looked to Norway in its attempt to reform housing policy.[40]

However, perhaps nowhere was the concept of the model stronger and more influential than within the Nordic region itself, at least during the two decades or so after the Second World War. Neutral Sweden, with its industrial sector undam-aged in the war, its innovative social policies and its reputation for modernity in architecture and design, was as important as a source of policy ideas and practice across the rest of the Nordic region as it was beyond.[41] It was especially important in Finland, where not only did Swedish reforms influence social policy debates, but several hundred thousand Finnish citizens also experienced the Swedish welfare state directly by migrating to take up work there during the 1960s.[42] But the example of Sweden was also influential and important in Norway, both as a source of policy ideas and also as a cultural 'other', shaped by recent memories of the nineteenth-century union.[43]

NORWAY AND THE NORDIC WELFARE STATE

In Norway, the development of the welfare state seems to fit the national 'rags to riches' narrative, helping to explain the transformation of a poor nation located on the periphery of Europe and until 1905 in a union with Sweden, into a wealthy, independent Nordic welfare state. No wonder the country has become so attractive for Scottish nationalists. However, as historians, we should approach this narrative with some scepticism, especially the suggestion that Norwegian society was unusually backward or peripheral in the context of nineteenth-century Europe. As part of the Danish kingdom until 1814, Norwegian merchants and entrepreneurs participated in the development of international maritime trade networks.[44] After 1814 and especially from the 1840s, Norway benefited from the liberalisation of British trade, which allowed not only commercial links but also the transfer of machinery, techniques and capital to flourish. This contributed to extremely high rates of economic growth during the late nineteenth century, especially in the fishing, forestry and shipping industries.[45] Despite high rates of emigration that in some estimates were second only to those of Ireland in the nineteenth century, the Norwegian population grew, as did real wages and standards of living.[46]

Although the majority of the population remained engaged in agriculture, the 'social question' of the late nineteenth century was also an industrial question, as it was in many other parts of Europe. Among the social reforms introduced to mitigate the effects of rapid industrialisation were labour protection laws introduced in the years 1892 to 1915, accident insurance for factory workers in 1895 and sickness insurance in 1909.[47] The model for all these benefits was Bismarck's social reforms, though they were also influenced by the self-help ideology of the politically dominant Liberal Party.[48] Despite the economic turbulence of the inter-war period, the Norwegian economy continued to grow very rapidly: according to one estimate, GDP per capita grew by 38 per cent during the period 1920–35.[49] Growth was partly generated by the rapid expansion of heavy industry based on the exploitation of hydro-electric power, supported and coordinated by the State.

Debates on welfare reform during the inter-war period were influenced by fears about declining population growth. Like the better-known example of Sweden, where Gunnar and Alva Myrdal's 1933 book *Kris i befolkningsfrågan* sparked a major debate, Norwegian social policy was shaped by faith in the ability of prophylactic social engineering to improve the health and efficiency of the population and thus contribute to national productivity.[50] This was to result in the passing of legislation permitting compulsory sterilisation on eugenic grounds in all four Nordic countries in 1934. Compulsory sterilisations carried out under this legislation peaked during the 1930s and 1940s – Nils Roll-Hansen cites the director of Norway's public health service Karl Evang's estimate that an average of eighty-seven 'feeble-minded' individuals was sterilised each year in the period 1945–54 – though Norway's 1934 law remained largely unaltered until 1977.[51] We should be cautious about assuming a link between the Nordic eugenics legislation and the racist theories that informed Nazi eugenics, though there were members of the scientific establishment that supported this more radical position, in Norway as elsewhere in Europe.[52]

More broadly, the 1930s marks the transition from the liberal order of the

nineteenth and early twentieth centuries to a 'social democratic' order that
was to dominate political debate in Norway – and, indeed, elsewhere in the
Nordic region – until the 1970s.[53] The Norwegian Labour Party (Det norske
Arbeiderpartiet, DnA) abandoned its earlier radical commitment to the class
struggle which had led it into Comintern in 1919, and in 1935 negotiated a crisis
agreement with the Agrarian Party (Bondepartiet; from 1959 Senterpartiet) which
gave it a stable parliamentary majority.[54] The agreement was modelled on similar
arrangements agreed in Denmark and Sweden in 1933. In the same year, representatives of the central trade union organisation AFL also signed an agreement
(*Hovedavtalet* or 'main agreement') with the Norwegian employers' federation
NAF. Both arrangements came to be seen as cornerstones of Norwegian politics
for at least three decades, marking the transition from a society that was bit-
terly divided along class lines to one united around a common commitment to
democracy, welfare and economic modernisation.

Where Norway differed from neutral Sweden was the extent to which this social
consensus was boosted by the experience of the Second World War. As is well
known, Norway was occupied by the Nazis from 9 April 1940. The king and the
government fled into exile in London, where they remained for the duration of
the war. Unlike Denmark, where the Social Democratic Party found themselves
compromised by the concessions they were forced to make to the occupying forces
as part of the wartime national coalition, the main Norwegian parties avoided
becoming tainted by allegations of collaboration. Leading members of the Labour
Party took part in the resistance, and in the elections of 1945 the party benefited
enormously from this, gaining an outright parliamentary majority for the first
time. The new leader of the Labour Party, Einar Gerhardsen, returned as a hero,
having been interned in a concentration camp.[55]

The spirit of national unity (*fellesskap*) and rebirth (*gjenreisning*) which characterised the post-war Norwegian Labour government is thus in many ways
comparable to the 1945 landslide election victory for the Labour Party in the
UK.[56] Indeed, as Donald Sassoon has pointed out, in 1945 Norway and the
UK – together with Sweden – were the only European countries where wartime
collectivism had translated into parliamentary majorities for social democratic
parties.[57] Moreover, in both cases the governing Labour parties could also draw
on a broad social and political consensus in support of their aims. Arbeiderpartiet's
1944 programme *Framtidens Norge* ('Norway of the Future') was influential on
the joint programme (*Fellesprogram*) agreed by the four main Norwegian political
parties in the autumn of that year, as the basis of the first post-war government.[58]
The strength of this consensus should not be over-estimated, however. Many of
Arbeiderpartiet's proposals for greater socialisation of the economy – including
economic planning, nationalisation and corporatist arrangements for labour
representation in industrial management – had to be scaled down or even abandoned, in the face of opposition from representatives of big business and the
bourgeois political parties.[59] Following the successful Communist coup d'état in

Czechoslovakia in 1948, the Labour government also aligned itself firmly with the emerging western block, accepting Marshall Aid and becoming a founder member of NATO in 1949.[60] The party's new programme adopted in 1949 marked the final break with its Marxist past, with its emphasis on cooperation and consensus and its optimism in the possibilities of capitalist economic growth to deliver prosperity and welfare for all.[61]

The 'golden age' of the social democratic welfare state in Norway during the post-war decades was thus connected to the ongoing process of economic indus- trialisation and modernisation. This did not happen in isolation. Even Lange has suggested that the immediate post-war period was one of greater liberalisation and internationalisation than ever before.[62] Norwegian exports – still dominated at this stage by shipping, forestry, fisheries and heavy industry based on the exploitation of hydro-electricity – benefited from the efforts to liberalise European trade but above all from connections with Britain. The challenge for Arbeiderpartiet was to ensure that the benefits of modernisation were spread evenly and that national prosperity could be achieved without abandoning the rural farming and fishing communities.[63] In some parts of rural Norway, modernisation was slow to make an impact: at the beginning of the 1950s many remote farms still lacked electricity or running water, for example.[64] Klas Åmark suggests that during the first post- war decade social progress was seen as following from industrialisation; only after 1955 was industrial policy matched by a similar focus on social policy.[65] Here, Arbeiderpartiet could draw on a well-established tradition of municipal socialism from the inter-war period and even earlier. The municipal reform of 1837 had created considerable autonomy for local councils, to a much greater extent than in the other Nordic countries, and during the 1920s and 1930s some municipali- ties had used this autonomy to provide extensive welfare services.[66] Yet even so, the Norwegian welfare state shared some of the centralising ambitions of other European welfare states, not least in the UK. Despite initiatives such as the Nord- Norge plan in 1951, the population of the urban and metropolitan areas around Oslofjorden in the south and east of the country grew at the expense of the rural districts in the west and north.[67] Some of the tensions that this produced were to emerge during the 1960s and 1970s, perhaps none so sharply as the Alta dam con- troversy of the late 1970s which brought the marginalised Sami minority mostly living in the north of the country into conflict with the Oslo-based government.[68]

THE NORWEGIAN WELFARE STATE IN THE ERA OF OIL

It is impossible to overlook the impact of petroleum on the recent history of the Norwegian economy and society, and indeed the welfare state. Oil was discovered in the North Sea in late 1969 and by the turn of the millennium it had become a very significant sector in the Norwegian economy. In recent years, the country has been widely cited as a model example for how to avoid the 'resource curse' in its responsible investment of oil revenues.[69] The extraordinary size of Norway's state petroleum fund tends to place Norway out of reach as a source of policy ideas, because it has become such an unusual economy. Yet at the same time, supported by the oil wealth, Norwegian activism in international affairs has increased, with some scholars seeing the Norwegian commitment to generous overseas aid programmes as an extension of the domestic welfare state.[70] What these contradictions mean for Scottish political discourse is explored further below.

Despite its wealth, the Norwegian welfare state has not been immune from the broader challenges to the welfare state that have emerged in the last thirty years or so. The beginning of the 1970s is often assumed to mark the high tide of the welfare state in Europe. In the case of Norway, the milestones were the completion of the national insurance system *Folketrygden* in 1967, and the national pension scheme of 1966 modelled on the Swedish system introduced in the late 1950s.[70] Many scholars have pointed out that the 1970s marked a convergence in the Nordic welfare states as a result of the rapid expansion of services across the region, especially in Finland, regarded traditionally as a latecomer.[72] Again, however, the provision of some of the trappings of modern welfare society was still patchy. For example, by 1980 all but the remotest Norwegian households were connected to mains electricity, but 100,000 were still without telephones.[73]

Moreover, this convergence of the Nordic welfare model occurred just at the same time as criticisms of the welfare state were emerging, from both the left and the right. On the left, the Scandinavian countries were all affected by the upsurge of radicalism in the late 1960s, but there was less direct confrontation than in other parts of Europe.[74] The challenge to social democracy was expressed in different ways: firstly, in criticisms that the welfare state was 'unfinished', in that it allowed the persistence of class inequalities and overlooked the problems of alienation and exploitation in the workplace; secondly, in the articulation of non-class inequalities, especially gender; and thirdly, in the environmental critique of the social democrats' enthusiasm for industrial modernity. As Francis Sejersted has pointed out, the energy sector became a major arena for conflict in both Sweden and Norway after 1970: in Sweden over the question of nuclear power and in Norway over hydro-electricity, especially the Alta dam conflict referred to above.[75]

One of the biggest changes in the Nordic welfare states after about 1970 was the decline of the so-called 'housewife contract'; in other words, the widespread acceptance of the nuclear family as the fundamental unit of society, based on a gendered division of labour and supported by the welfare system.[76] Comparative research has shown that historic support for the male breadwinner model was stronger in Norway than the other Nordic countries. Diane Sainsbury has described how Norwegian women gained civil, political and social rights earlier than their Swedish sisters, but that they were more likely to be allocated benefits on the basis of their status as mothers, leading to a deeper entrenchment of maternalist ideology in the Norwegian welfare state.[77] The strength of Norwegian family ideology also meant that Norway was slower than Sweden to move towards a dual-breadwinner model supported by the expansion of State day care during the 1970s, though female labour force participation did increase in Norway too.[78] It also explains why a centrist government in Norway was able in 1998 to introduce cash benefits (*kontantstøtte*) for parents whose young children were not in State-subsidised day care, in the name of freedom of choice.[79]

With hindsight, it is now clear that the challenges of the New Left were to have much less impact in the long term than the emerging neo-liberal criticisms of the welfare state. In Norway, this was seen first in the electoral success of a new anti-establishment populist party in the 1973 elections, which challenged the high tax regime.[80] Over the subsequent decades, and influenced strongly by international currents, this started to make an impact on the understanding of the relationship between the welfare state and economic growth, stimulated also by the first OPEC oil shock and subsequent recession of the early 1970s.[81] Arbeiderpartiet's initial response to this was to reassert its commitment to socialism, with a radical policy including the democratisation of the banking sector and increased nationalisation. Labour politicians interpreted the 1970s recession as a cyclical crisis and intervened in order to ease the situation of struggling industries and protect their employees.[82] Following electoral defeat in 1981, however, and under a new leader, Gro Harlem Brundtland, they abandoned this strategy for a 'third way' policy of deregulation and liberalisation that had absorbed parts of the neo-liberal critique. The earlier emphasis on solidarity and equality in the welfare state gave way to a new language of individual rights and individual choice, realised through efforts to open up welfare services to increased competition.[83]

Norway's oil wealth and the decision to create the State petroleum fund in 1990 meant that the Norwegian economy avoided the worst of the severe recession seen in Finland and Sweden during the early 1990s. Nor did Norway follow its Nordic neighbours into the EU in 1995, having rejected membership in a 1994 referendum. In Sweden in particular, the 'bourgeois' (centre-right) government of the early 1990s adopted some markedly neo-liberal rhetoric, even amounting to the explicit rejection of the idea of the Nordic model.[84] This rhetoric was not necessarily matched in policy, however. The consensus among scholars at the turn of the millennium was that despite some tinkering with the conditions attached to entitlements for benefits, many of the most distinctive characteristics of the Nordic welfare states remained intact. Globalisation 'do[es] not threaten Norway or its welfare system' was the upbeat assessment of two scholars writing at the peak of the economic boom in 2007.[85] Indeed, the examples of the Nordic countries were seen as a challenge to the idea that accelerating globalisation would render national governments increasingly powerless.[86]

Nonetheless, some of the domestic political critiques of the Nordic welfare model were also reflected in the changing xenostereotype of the region elsewhere, including in Scotland. Right-wing political commentator and journalist Andrew Neil had long highlighted what he saw as a dangerous 'social democratic' consensus in Scotland.[87] Soon after the 'Yes' devolution vote in 1997, which paved the way for a Scottish Parliament, Neil referred to Norway as a 'failing social democracy' and sought to highlight the dangers of Scotland attempting to emulate it:

> For nigh on 30 years, ever since the North Sea first promised untold riches, [the SNP] have blathered on about Norway being the template for an independent Scotland. The analogy was simple and (to some) alluring: Norway's four million people are even fewer than Scotland's five million but they enjoy independent status, general affluence, quality public services paid for by oil taxes and an egalitarian, social democratic ethos that Scotland is also supposed to share . . . Now Norway is in economic trouble, caught between the rock of overhigh public spending – a Scottish weakness too – and the hard place of commodity-based revenues being hit by falling oil prices . . . So much for wanting to be another state-aid addicted Norway.[88]

Prior to the 2007 Holyrood elections, the SNP revived the idea of an independent Scotland following Norwegian lines and replicating Norway's national success story. A broader device was constructed by Alex Salmond and his party to reinforce the message – the 'Arc of Prosperity'. Erasing national differences between some quite disparate economies, the 'Arc' comprised Ireland and the Nordic states, with Scotland imagined as a centre point.[89] In November 2006, Salmond took the opportunity to visit Norway as a means of underlining its potential as an economic and social comparator for Scotland. Conversely, opponents took the same opportunity to reiterate claims that a 'Norwegian model' implied taxes too high to be stomached by the Scottish electorate.[90]

Certainly, Norway is by no means immune to the profound structural challenges facing the Nordic and indeed other European welfare states in the twenty-first century. The main change is above all demographic, as the welfare states that were formed partly in response to fears of declining birth rates in the 1930s now face a new problem, namely the ageing population and the rising dependency ratios that this brings. One solution to this problem is of course immigration, but this brings its own political difficulties. Grete Brochmann has highlighted the reciprocal relationship between nation-building and the welfare state: the distinctiveness of the Norwegian welfare state is attributed to the strong sense of national cohesion, but the welfare state has also played a role in shaping national cohesion.[91] The portrayal of Norway as ethnically and socially homogeneous can be questioned, but the increases in immigration and ethnic diversity in the last three decades have often been portrayed as challenges to the future of the welfare state, rather than solutions to its problems. Immigration to Norway was relatively low in comparison to other parts of Europe until the mid-1970s, when the first restrictions were also introduced. Thereafter a high proportion of immigrants has been asylum-seekers and refugees admitted under Norway's international obligations, but the country has also been a member of Schengen since 1996 and labour migration from Eastern Europe rose following the 2004 EU enlargement.[92] Nor should the significance of inter-Nordic migration be overlooked: in 2012 the third-largest group of foreign immigrants, after Polish and Lithuanian nationals, consisted of Swedish citizens.[93]

The Norwegian response to increased immigration in the 1970s was influenced heavily by contemporary Swedish multi-cultural policy, which sought to support ethnic minorities in maintaining their own cultural traditions, while also assisting them to integrate into the labour market.[94] This differential treatment of specific groups was, as Grete Brochmann points out, a new departure for the welfare state: it was very different to the overwhelmingly assimilationist policies pursued for many decades with respect to the Sami minority, for example.[95] From the 1990s it was also criticised, with the Oslo Labour politician Rune Gerhardsen suggesting that *snillisme* or humanitarianism had to give way to a firmer emphasis on the rights and responsibilities of immigrants.[96] Across the Nordic countries there are indeed indications of relatively high levels of unemployment among ethnic minority groups in comparison to the majority white population, but at the same time there is also evidence that this may be attributed to labour market discrimination against these groups.[97]

A study conducted in 2008 and 2009 found that a similar proportion of the electorate in both Denmark and Norway supported 'welfare dualism', that is the restriction of entitlement to welfare benefits from individuals not holding full citizenship. This seemed to be based on the 'widespread belief' that immigrants were workshy and could not be trusted not to abuse the welfare state.[98] However, the authors of this study also noted how the politics of immigration was very different in the two countries. In Denmark, as is well known, the populist Danish People's Party (DFP) has campaigned forcefully on a platform of 'welfare chauvinism', and though it was not formally a member of the centre-right government in office from 2001 to 2011, in a supporting role it was able to have an important influence on Danish immigration and integration policy. In Norway, by contrast, the equivalent Progress Party (Fremskrittspartiet, FrP) has seemed less inclined to abandon its political roots as a low-tax, small-state party.[99] Yet after the election of September 2013, FrP became part of a two-party government led by the Conservatives (Høyre), and with one of its members (Solveig Horne) as Minister for Children, Equality and Social Inclusion might be expected to have some impact on Norwegian integration policy in the future.

INDEPENDENT SCOTLAND AND A 'NORWEGIAN' WELFARE STATE

Since gaining power in Holyrood in 2007, the SNP has not downplayed its previous interest in Norway as a potential role model. As Stephen Maxwell noted in 2009:

The movement in the SNP's understanding of social justice towards main-stream social democracy was also influenced by reference to Norway and other Scandinavian models. Norway was already popular with SNP activists because it provided an example of a small country successfully pursuing nationally oriented strategies on both oil and fisheries while, in the SNP's eyes, Scotland's oil and fisheries were being sacrificed to UK priorities. But the Scandinavian welfare model was also increasingly recommended as the solution, with the help of oil revenues, to Scotland's intractable social problems.[100]

Overall, the image of a specific 'Nordic model' has remained extremely strong in Scotland in general and Scottish political culture in particular. Certainly, the downturn in the Icelandic and Irish economies after 2008 allowed opponents to ridicule Alex Salmond's notion of an 'Arc of Prosperity', with the western side of the arc seemingly having collapsed.[101] Soon after Iceland's banking collapse, Scottish Secretary Jim Murphy (Labour) made a sarcastic jibe about the 'Arc of Insolvency'. This, in turn, infuriated Iceland's then Prime Minister, Geir H. Haarde, who accused the Westminster Labour Party of ridiculing his country in order to score political points over Scottish independence.[102] Andrew Neil continued his offensive against the Norwegians from a decade earlier, claiming triumphantly in 2008 that:

> Among the casualties of the banking crisis, we must now add Scotland's First Minister and SNP leader, Alex Salmond, whose dream to be part of an arc of pros-perity that included an independent Scotland, Ireland, Iceland and Norway now looks more like the stuff of nightmares.[103]

With a little distance, however, has come an acknowledgement that although Ireland and Iceland were badly hit by the financial crisis, there was not a general economic meltdown in other parts of Northern Europe. Styled as Scotland's 'most distinguished political commentator', Iain Macwhirter performed a u-turn in 2012 after claiming to have coined the 'arc of insolvency' soundbite. Seeking to rehabili-tate the idea of a Nordic Scotland, he argued that, '[w]hile some neoliberal small nations exploded because of their banks, the rest of the Nordic arc – Denmark, Sweden, Finland – passed through the eye of the storm largely unscathed.' Like many politicians, Macwhirter's perspective was changed by a short visit to Norway, where he perceived 'no sign of any financial hangover from the great crash'. Moving on to the Oil Fund, he continued:

> ...there are so many lessons for Scotland here, it's hard to know where to begin. Obviously, if Scotland had benefited from its oil wealth since 1970 it would be a very different country to the one it is today ... the 'feel' of Norwegian society is very much like Scotland, in terms of social expectations and outlook. Looking at Norway today, it is hard to argue that Scotland could fail to be an extremely

successful independent country . . . Scotland would probably find a place as one of the energy rich small nations of the true arc of Nordic prosperity.[104]

In the run-up to the 2014 independence referendum, unionists and nationalists alike were prepared to discuss the idea of Norway as a direct comparator to Scotland. The SNP committed itself to the establishment of a Scottish Energy Fund, to 'safeguard' the profits of oil and gas exploration, the merits of which have been debated in highly politicised terms. On the pro-independence side, the argument remained that – particularly in the event of Scotland being able to exploit its 'own' natural resources – this windfall would be used to instigate a long-term fund for promoting welfare and social equality.[105] Opponents were willing to engage with this, confident not only that the legal case for the oil reserves was far from clear, but also that any remaining reserves would not allow Scotland to build up anything like the surplus enjoyed by the Norwegians.[106] The Spring 2014 edition of *Yes!*, the newspaper of the pro-independence campaign, carried an article entitled 'Norway Shows The Way', its strapline proclaiming

With a population similar to our own, our neighbours across the North Sea only became independent in 1905. Like Scotland, Norway discovered oil in the 1970s. Today it provides Scotland with an example of what we too could do with the powers of independence.

The piece followed a familiar pattern, arguing that 'independence could bring Scotland the same kind of caring prosperity, allowing us to create a world-class welfare system ...'[107]

CONCLUDING REMARKS

After some years of scepticism and even outright rejection during the early 1990s, the idea of the 'Nordic model' recently seems to have enjoyed a resurgence in popularity. The search for new ideas in the wake of the global economic crisis that began in 2007–8 has stimulated a renewed interest in many aspects of the Nordic countries. Enthusiasm for the region has been strengthened by the proliferation of international league tables in which the Nordic countries perform well, not just on traditional social indicators such as life expectancy and GDP per capita, but also more nebulous measurements such as 'happiness'.[108] In the UK, interest has also been stimulated by the current popularity of Nordic cultural exports, especially the so-called 'Nordic Noir' phenomenon.

As we have discussed in this chapter, this interest in the region is not new but the construction and rhetorical use of the 'Nordic model' is a phenomenon with its own history. *The Economist*'s 2013 designation of the region as 'the next supermodel' has parallels with the rhetoric of the 'middle way' in the 1930s. As

Glen O'Hara has pointed out, we still need to know more about efforts to translate these broad visions into specific policies and the adaptations that policies have undergone during the process of transfer.[109] Moreover, constructions of the image of *Norden* or the Nordic xenostereotype are profoundly shaped by autostereotypes or self-images. For both sides in the Scottish independence debate, as for Westminster politicians of left and right, *Norden* is a pliable entity that can be used either to support or to undermine specific visions of the future of Scotland.

Notes

1. Milne, 2014.
2. Milne, 2014.
3. Andersson and Hilson, 2009. On auto- and xenostereotypes, see Musiał, 2002: 20–2.
4. Hetherington, 2014.
5. Keating and McCrone, 2007: 17–18, 30.
6. Newby, 2009: 319.
7. Wooldridge, 2013; Andersson and Hilson, 2009: 224.
8. Birrell, 2011.
9. Esping-Andersen, 1990.
10. Korpi and Palme, 1998: 669.
11. Kettunen and Petersen, 2011.
12. Nordic Centre of Excellence: The Nordic Welfare State – Historical Foundations and Future Challenges (NordWel), funded by NordForsk. See http://blogs. helsinki.fi/nord-wel/. Accessed 28 March 2014.
13. For summaries, see Christiansen and Markkola, 2006; Hilson, 2008: 90–1.
14. Halvorsen and Stjernø, 2008: 132ff; also Brandal and Bratberg in this volume.
15. Edling, 2006; Åmark, 2005.
16. On female labour force participation, see Åmark, 2006; for a discussion of the dual-breadwinner model, see Bergqvist, 1999.
17. Sejersted, 2011; Brandal and Bratberg in this volume.
18. Tilton, 1990: 126ff.
19. Elvander, 1980: 99; Lange, 2005: 23; also Brandal and Bratberg in this volume.
20. Dahlqvist, 2002.
21. Åmark, 2005.
22. Arnason and Wittrock, 2012; also Sørensen and Stråth, 1997.
23. For example, Bunting, 2008.
24. These debates are summarised in Broberg and Roll-Hansen, 2005: ix–xviii.
25. Jamieson, 2001.
26. Petersen, 2011.
27. See Brandal and Bratberg in this volume.
28. Kettunen, 2006; Kettunen, 2011: 22.
29. Childs, 1936; Marklund, 2009.
30. On Eisenhower, see Logue 1999: 164; cited in Andersson and Hilson, 2009: 220. On the Nordic states during the Cold War, see Hilson, 2008: 128–30.

31. Petersen, 2011: 48; also Petersen, 2006.
32. Petersen, 2006: 49; also Andersson, 1994: 51–2.
33. Petersen, 2011.
34. Hansen, 1994: 118; Andersson, 1994: 54.
35. Janfelt, 2005.
36. Halldor Heldal notes that of sixteen conventions on industrial policy adopted by the ILO between 1919 and 1926, only two were ratified in Norway. See Heldal, 1996: 269; Kettunen, 2009.
37. Musiał, 2002.
38. Andersson and Hilson, 2009.
39. For example, for Samuel Laing: see Porter, 1998.
40. O'Hara, 2008: 5–6.
41. Andersson and Hilson, 2009.
42. Engman, 1994. For examples of Swedish influences on the Finnish debate, see Bergholm, 2009.
43. On Swedish–Norwegian relations, see Sejersted, 2011.
44. Thue, 2008: 398.
45. Thue, 2008: 407–13.
46. Baines, 1985: 10.
47. Åmark, 2005: 52; Bjørnson, 2001: 201; Bjørnson and Haavet, 1994: 13.
48. Åmark, 2005: 46, 58.
49. Thue, 2008: 419–20.
50. Sejersted, 2011: 114–20; 257–60.
51. Roll-Hansen, 2005: 177–8.
52. Roll-Hansen, 2005: 180.
53. Thue, 2008.
54. Sejersted, 2011: 84–7. See also Brandal and Bratberg in this volume.
55. Elvander, 1980: 105.
56. For the 1945 Norwegian government, see Lange, 2005: 153, 158.
57. Sassoon, 1997: 118.
58. Lange, 2005: 160–1.
59. Hodne, 1983: 140.
60. Lange, 2005: 216; Hodne, 1983: 160; Sejersted, 2011: 297–8.
61. Elvander, 1980: 235.
62. Lange, 2005: 213.
63. Lange, 2005: 262.
64. Lange, 2005: 266.
65. Åmark, 2005: 132–3.
66. Bjørnson and Haavet, 1994. See also Brandal and Bratberg in this volume.
67. Lange, 2005: 259; Sejersted, 2011: 226.
68. Eidheim, 1997: 37.
69. Karl, 2007: 273.
70. Pharo, 2013: 83–4; Ingebritsen, 2002: 18–20.
71. Thue, 2008: 459; Sejersted, 2011: 398–9.
72. See Kosonen, 1993: 49.
73. Thue, 2008: 462.

74. On 1968 in Scandinavia, see Jørgensen, 2008.
75. Sejersted, 2011.
76. Sejersted, 2011: 247–9. On daycare, see also Cohen and Rønning in this volume.
77. Sainsbury, 2001; also Åmark, 2005: 260. However, Åmark also cautions against the idea that Sweden pursued a gender-equal welfare model from the 1930s: the radicalism of the Myrdals had relatively limited impact. Other factors cited by Sainsbury include greater class divisions among Norwegian feminists and the greater strength of religious influence in Norway.
78. Sejersted, 2011: 409–12.
79. Sejersted, 2011: 413–19.
80. The party was originally named 'Anders Lange's Party for a Drastic Reduction in Taxes, Rates and Public Intervention' but became Fremskrittspartiet (Progress Party) in 1977. Similar parties also emerged in Denmark and Finland during the early 1970s. See Arter, 1999: 103–7.
81. Andersson, 2003: 120–9.
82. Thue, 2008: 461–2.
83. Sejersted, 2011: 391–5.
84. Hilson, 2008: 180–1.
85. Halvorsen and Stjernø, 2008: 149.
86. Timonen, 2003.
87. Newby, 2009.
88. Neil, 1998.
89. Dinwoodie, 2005.
90. Dinwoodie, 2006; Fraser, 2007; Macdonell, 2006; all cited in Newby, 2009.
91. Brochmann, 2013: 193.
92. Halvorsen and Stjernø, 2008: 149–51.
93. Statistics Norway, 2012.
94. Brochmann, 2013: 209.
95. Brochmann, 2013: 206.
96. Brochmann, 2013; Sejersted, 2011: 407–8.
97. Vassenden, 1997: 117; Hilson, 2008: 171–2.
98. Bay et al., 2013.
99. Bay et al., 2013: 205.
100. Maxwell, 2009: 122.
101. Note that the Irish 'Celtic Tiger' as a model is given here as an example of a 'low-tax, low-regulation, business-friendly' approach, reflecting the neo-liberal 'Washington Consensus'. See Cuthbert and Cuthbert, 2009: 108.
102. Newby, 2009: 322.
103. Neil, 2008.
104. Macwhirter, 2012.
105. Mooney and Scott, 2012.
106. See, inter alia, Peterkin, 2014; Scottish National Party, 2014.
107. 'Norway Shows the Way', Yes!, Winter/Spring 2014, 10.
108. Stougaard-Nielsen and Napier, 2013.
109. O'Hara, 2008: 2–3.

CHAPTER II

Access, Nature, Culture and the Great Outdoors – Norway and Scotland

Lesley Riddoch

INTRODUCTION: A RIGHT TO ROAM?

Norway and Scotland are North Sea neighbours with a similar population, geology and landscape. However, their inhabitants have had very different experiences of nature and access to the outdoors through education, sport, leisure and the use of weekend huts and wooden cabins.

Both countries have 'right to roam' laws, mountain bothies, National Parks and a tradition of distinctive winter sports. Dig deeper, though, and differences quickly appear.

Norway has forty-three National Parks, the first established in 1962. Scotland has two National Parks, the first established in 2002, and neither Scottish park is a wilderness area owned by the government. This example sets a theme that crops up in almost every comparison of nature and outdoor access in Scotland and Norway. Formal rights of access to the outdoors in Scotland have typically occurred half a century later than in Norway, have been less far-reaching and have not changed or challenged the dominance of private sporting estates.

The Norwegians have always practised *allemannsretten* or 'freedom to roam'. In 1957, this was codified into an Outdoor Recreation Act giving the public rights of access to hike in the mountains, camp overnight, cycle on tracks and ski in forests during the winter – though not closer than 150 metres to any inhabited dwelling.

It took half a century longer for Scots to gain much the same package of legal access rights. Before that, Scots had the same long-standing belief in their traditional and informal 'right to roam', insisting trespass and 'Private – Keep Out' signs had no basis in Scots law. Some landowners – especially incomers with a different legal experience from south of the border – contested these customary rights, and during the foot and mouth outbreak of 2001 farmers were accused of closing the countryside for longer than necessary.[1] Nordic-style access laws were finally adopted in 2003 to resolve such disputes as part of the Land Reform (Scotland) Act. Yet despite this apparently similar customary and legal framework, the proportion of people actually using the outdoors today in Norway and Scotland is very different.

THE CULTURE OF EXERCISE

According to the most recent statistics, 82 per cent of Norwegian adults exercise regularly at least once a week (63 per cent in 1997), only 6 per cent never do any kind of sport (27 per cent in 1997) and the gender gap is small.[2] 81 per cent take regular walks in the forests and mountains, 45 per cent cycle on a regular basis, 42 per cent ski, 40 per cent jog, 39 per cent do strength-training, 26 per cent swim and 22 per cent do alpine sports.[3]

It is hard to compare Norway and Scotland because sporting activity is defined and measured differently. In Scotland, walking for 30 minutes is considered sporting activity. 59 per cent of Scots have done this in the previous four weeks (there's no measurement of regular year-round activity) but fewer than one-in-five has undertaken any other individual activity, with swimming the next most popular sport at 18 per cent.[4]

This compares poorly with Norway, where more people swim regularly than Scots, even though swimming is one of Norway's least popular sports. Equally, while 82 per cent of Norwegians hike regularly, only 42 per cent of Scottish adults visited the outdoors on a weekly basis in 2012. These visits did not necessarily constitute a 'hike' in Norwegian terms and the total was the lowest recorded since 2006.[5] Of those who did, most visited managed landscapes like parks (41 per cent),

Table 11.1 Participation in Outdoor Activities, Norway

Percentage participated in various activities during the last 12 months

	2007	2011
On a shorter trip for hikes in the forest or in the mountains		81
On a shorter trip skiing in the forest or in the mountains		42
On berry-picking or mushroom-picking	35	37
On fishing trip	43	45
	2007	**2013**
Jogging	38	40
Biking	40	45
Strength training	30	39
Exercise or train at least once a week	73	82

Source: Statistics Norway.

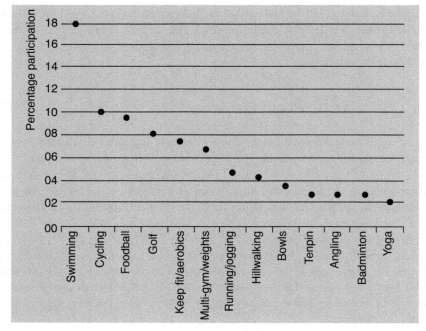

Figure 11.1 Participation in Sport in Scotland

with relatively few visiting mountains and moorland (10 per cent), and twice that number (21 per cent) recorded 'no particular reason' for not visiting the outdoors. A fifth of Scots made no visits outdoors in the previous year (up from 17 per cent in 2011.

In 2012, walking was the main way Scots reached outdoor destinations (64 per cent), with cars used by just 30 per cent of respondents.[6] This suggests the average Scot's experience of the Great Outdoors may be a walk round the block to the shops, bus stop or school. This differs significantly from the Norwegian understanding of the Outdoors as an immersion in nature.

OUTDOOR LIFE FOR CHILDREN: KINDERGARTEN AND SCHOOL

Outdoor experience begins almost at birth in Norway – informally in family weekend cabins (*hytter*) and formally in kindergarten.

Children in Norway not only have the right to affordable childcare between the ages of one and six, they also have the right to be outdoors at least one day per week. Many kindergartens achieve this by allowing children to spend virtually all of their time outdoors.

Anders Farstad, a kindergarten leader in southern Norway, has written about the learning benefits that come with open space:

> Nature gives us a lot of freedom. There are no walls or regulations to shut us in. So the children don't have to shout or fight to gain a bit of space or attention from grown-ups. The role of the kindergarten leader is also different outdoors. It is no longer a matter of keeping the children silent and engaged in quiet activities. Outdoors there are some simple rules like; 'Don't go any further than you can see a grown-up or we can see you.' In this way the children come to us for help or advice and watch how we do practical things.[7]

According to another comparative report, 'Being outdoors all the time, the [Norwegian] children stay healthy ... they are almost never ill compared to children in indoor kindergartens.'[8] The county of Nordland in the Arctic Circle has become a pioneer of outdoor, nature and farm kindergartens. Anita and Jostein Hunstad bought their farm near Fauske in 1983, 60 km inland from the coastal town of Bodø. They started with 150 sheep but predation by lynx became a problem. They built a new farmhouse in 1992 and Anita decided to diversify by starting a kindergarten in the old house. Locals were sceptical for the first year but now the kindergarten is full with a waiting list. Children spend the bulk of the day outdoors – often in snow and temperatures of minus 15 degrees – fully equipped by the school in thermal, waterproof gear. The children feed and play with the animals, collect eggs and wash them for sale, grow tomatoes, make hay and even watch slaughtered cows being dissected to learn more about animal biology. The Norwegian belief is that children divorced from the whole of nature – the cycles of life and death – become inactive, estranged from the outdoors and less independent, confident, cooperative and happy young adults.

At primary school, an outdoor activity centre in Bodø is also part of every Nordland pupil's week, especially children with autism, learning difficulties, hyperactivity and truanting tendencies. They drive on quad bikes, abseil on cliffs, climb trees, drive go-karts, and eat and learn outside around sheltered camp fires. As Nordland's educational pioneer Henny Aune puts it, 'Children simply have more physical energy than adults and children with attention issues have more energy still. They need to run it off. Then they can focus.'

So most Norwegian children start formal learning with five years' playing and learning outdoors under their belts – in every season and all weathers. This underpins sporting activity and attitudes to the outdoors in later life.

By contrast, Scottish children are still cooped up indoors for their early years and most of their school careers. Despite some special projects and a few Forest Schools organised by the Forestry Commission offering occasional visits of a day or two in length, there are fewer than ten outdoor kindergartens in Scotland. In 2012, one of these, the Secret Garden nursery in Fife, was threatened with closure by a Scottish Government safety quango for failing to use fresh water instead of wipes to clean the children's hands before eating as they played in the forest.[9] Fears over the application of health and safety legislation have also curtailed outdoor play and school trips, and security worries and the Dunblane School shootings in 1996 have created an atmosphere of lockdown in many schools. One Nordic-style outdoor kindergarten in Coatbridge was told to erect a wooden fence around the premises to prevent the children being watched. That made it more difficult for staff to pursue their original objective – encouraging the children to have confidence in and curiosity about the outdoors.

OUTDOOR ACTIVITY ORGANISATIONS

The organisations which support outdoor activity in Scotland and Norway also demonstrate differences of involvement and ease of access to nature.

The Norwegian Trekking Association (DNT) has 240,000 members in fifty-seven local member organisations across the country and a Children's Trekking Club with 16,000 members under the age of twelve.[10]

DNT owns 460 cabins and mountain huts throughout the country, some self-service, others staffed, and many serving dinner and breakfast. It means setting out for a few days' hiking doesn't have to mean carrying a heavy rucksack. The cabins range from large lodges with nearly 200 beds to small sheds with a few bunk beds. All hikers turning up for the night are guaranteed a place to stay – even if it's just a mattress on the floor at peak times in the busiest cabins. DNT was set up in 1868, owns all its own huts and cabins, and maintains one of Europe's largest marked hiking trail networks (20,000 km) and probably the world's most extensive cross-country skiing track network (7,000 km). DNT volunteers put in more than 175,000 hours every year.

By contrast, the Scottish Mountain Bothy Association was founded almost a century later in 1965 and arose from the practice of secretly staying overnight in half-ruined labourers' cottages in the years after the Second World War when the advent of jeeps, centralisation of farm production and eviction of tenant farmers left many farmsteads empty.[11] The MBA owns no bothies but maintains them subject to the agreement of landowners. According to the MBA website the huts are basic:

> You should only expect to find a wind and waterproof building with somewhere dry to sleep. Some bothies have a sleeping platform but at many you have to sleep on a wooden or concrete floor. Most have a fireplace or stove that can be used to provide warmth but you will usually need to carry fuel in. You will also need to take a stove for cooking and candles for light. Water comes from a stream or spring nearby. Do not expect the bothy to have toilet facilities.

No charge is made to use the bothies and they are not bookable. Like the DNT, the MBA is staffed by volunteers who maintain the huts. But the Scottish MBA has just 3,600 members compared to the DNT's quarter of a million – even though both countries have roughly the same population size.

Of course, youth hostels provide another way for Scots to access the Great Outdoors: in 2013, there were seventy hostels with 18,747 members. But Norway's Hostel Association (Norske Vandrerhjem) exceeds that with seventy-seven hostels.

HUNTING AND FISHING

The range of activities practised by locals on the land, rivers and lochs of Scotland is also restricted compared to Norway.

Allemannsrett gives Norwegians the right to swim and canoe in lakes and rivers, and fishing is relatively cheap for locals on most rivers. By contrast, rivers in Scotland are usually managed by riparian owners, and many of the best rivers have been timeshared, effectively halting local and casual use indefinitely.

Deer, fish (and until 2003 even trees on crofts) technically belong to the land-owner in Scotland, while in Norway – and indeed all the Nordics – hunting is a classless activity. Permits are relatively easy to acquire and many municipalities organise an annual cull of deer and elk on communally owned land involving the whole community. Children often take the day off school to act as 'beaters', women are involved in shooting and after the set number of deer are culled, the meat is hung and divided among those taking part. The day often ends with a party.

By contrast, in Scotland the restriction on local access to lochs, rivers and land for hunting, shooting and fishing has turned poaching into a counter-cultural activity, vividly described by Neil Gunn in *Highland River*:

> The salmon flailed the dry stones with desperate violence but Kenn was now in his own element . . . thrusting at the gills until his hands were lacerated and bleeding. He dragged that fish over fifty yards into the grass park before he laid it down. And when it heaved a last convulsive shudder he at once fell upon it as if the river of escape still lapped its tail.

All these restrictions have combined, over time, to make the non-landowning majority of Scots feel uncertain about their rights and even their place in a countryside that appears to be the preserve of a landed elite. In Norway, land is more usually owned by the *kommune* (council) or the average citizen than the titled feudal superior. So the outdoor sporting and leisure activities that take place in Norway are generally affordable, easy to access and uncontested. The biggest difference between Scots and Norwegians is their experience of the outdoors surrounds the ownership and use of huts and cabins, which allow families to stay comfortably in the countryside and access even the most remote areas on a weekly basis.

HUTS AND CABINS

Norway has one of the highest rates of second home ownership in the world, with a cabin for roughly every ten Norwegians. There were 429,093 holiday homes in 2010, of which 398,884 were basic wooden cabins (*hytter*), most without running water or electricity. Half the Norwegian population (4.9 million people) has access to a *hytte* for relaxation, connection with nature, exercise, escape from city pressures and strengthening family ties. They are not alone. In 1991, there was one cabin per 12 Swedes, one per 18 Finns and one per 33 Danes, along with widespread cabin ownership in Russia, the Czech Republic, Germany, Spain and other parts of Central and Southern Europe, as well as the northern states of America and Canada.[12] Scots alone at our latitude have virtually no hut or cabin culture and the lowest rate of second home ownership in Northern Europe, with one holiday home per 173 Scots and just 600 wooden weekend cabins.[13]

The Big Difference: Friluftslif

In Norway, nature is used and actively experienced every weekend. In Scotland, it seems to be admired from a distance. The father of the Norwegian nation, explorer and humanitarian Fridhof Nansen, articulated his country's preoccupation with the great outdoors:

> The first great thing is to find yourself, and for that you need solitude and contemplation: at least sometimes. I tell you, deliverance will not come from the rushing, noisy centres of civilization. It will come from the lonely places.[14]

King Haakon rallied public spirits in the post-war rationing years by taking the public tram to the ski slopes above Oslo; Gerhardson, Norway's first Prime Minister, was regularly pictured in hiking gear; and the great composer Grieg worked best in a humble wooden cabin:

> It boasted just one tiny room, and was poised on the edge of the fjord, in the midst of the exquisite beauty of Ullensvang, with the dark, deep fjord below, and the glittering ridge of the Folgefonna glacier on the other side of the water. In the heart of this matchless amphitheatre of nature, surrounded by the most sublime and majestic scenery in Norway, Grieg placed his grand piano and his writing desk. Here he sat, like an Orpheus reborn, and played in his mountain fastness, among the wild animals and the rocks.[15]

The Norwegians have a word for this kind of existence – *friluftsliv* or leading a simple life outdoors.[16] Much of the pleasure associated with that simple life derives from fond memories of the traditional *sætre* or high pasture shieling. Until relatively recently, life on most farms involved spending the summer in a *hytte* or *sætre* – high summer farms used mainly by women who tended cattle feeding on high pastures and produced supplies of cheese and butter. Farmers often had two houses on one farm and would switch to the smaller house in the summer because it was easier to maintain and keep clean and the bigger house was closed for the season. *Sætre* were multi-purpose production areas during the summer season, with wild berry-picking, trout-fishing and providing accommodation to hikers – and given their remoteness from the constraints of normal daily life, they also offered young people opportunities for intimacy and privacy.[17] Thus, *sætre* and *hytter* were associated with freedom, fun, summer weather and the natural diversions of *friluftsliv*. This attractive part of the rural idyll was lost through urbanisation but positive memories remained – even if the reality of life in sub-Arctic fjords had been tough.

An old woman remembers the late 1890s when she was newly married to a cottar. She describes how hungry she sometimes was. But she didn't dare to touch the food because she had barely enough for the children. Then her husband started work in a wood pulp factory, his weekly wage was doubled, and they could afford sufficient food for all family members, even for the mother.[18]

And yet, Norwegians retain positive folk memories of those days, partly because *friluftsliv*, the *bonde* (peasant) life became associated with the political project of building the Norwegian nation.

The widespread landownership enjoyed by ordinary Norwegians and discussed in Chapter 1 prompted the Constitution-writers of 1814 to enfranchise male peasants (*bonder*) long before other European nations – and that same Constitution paved the way for peaceful independence from Sweden in 1905. This might not have been achieved without the active support of Norwegian people mobilising with public celebrations on 17 May every year – and sport was a pivotal part of the day. Constitution Day encouraged sporting competition to evolve into something more attuned to distinctive Norwegian skills and sensibilities – away from the British 'pastime model' of sport towards a more practical and purposeful sense of activity.

Constitution Day brought sport and nationalism together. An important part of the festivities were sporting contests. Climbing, wrestling, running, gymnastics and sailing were all ingredients of the celebrations. Rowing – a traditional activity – was the dominant athletic event. Sport was used as a deliberate means to extend the popularity of Constitution Day celebrations.[19]

Most of the rowers in the city of Bergen, for example, came from the pre-industrial working class complemented by local rural crofters and fishermen. A new national ideology of sport was explicitly promoted by the Central Association for the Spread of Physical Exercise and the Practice of Arms[20] to confront British thinking. It tried to make sport serve higher purposes than pastime and competition for its own sake – the creation of better soldiers and improved public health.

Above all, Norwegian sport was more concerned with the concept of *idræt* than 'sport.' *Idrett* (in modern usage, *bokmål*) is hard to translate but means activity, not rule-bound games.

Thus, according to rowers in Bergen:

> The British way of rowing, less rational [and] involving crafts only suited to shallow waters and competition, was doomed . . . our fraternities are too much adapted to the people's and nature's practical requirements.[21]

Perhaps the man who personally embodied and most powerfully articulated this new idea of sport as *idrett* was Fridtjof Nansen, scientist, sportsman, explorer and humanist, whose book on his expedition across Greenland on skis in 1889 was published simultaneously in English and German. The impact on public opinion and nationalist fervour of his triumphant 1896 return from presumed death in the Arctic after trying to ski to the North Pole and prove a theory about ocean currents, can hardly be exaggerated. Nansen so disliked the British concept of sport that he urged all Norwegians to 'practise *idræt* and detest sport and record-breaking'. In *The First Crossing of Greenland*, Nansen wrote;

> Skiing is the most national of all Norwegian sports and a thrilling sport it is. Nothing . . . teaches the quality of dexterity and resourcefulness, calls for decision and resolution, like skiing. Can there be anything more beautiful and noble than the northern winter landscape when the snow lies foot-deep, like a soft white mantle over wood and hill?[22]

The explorer was also a central figure in the Lysaker Group (*Lysakerkrets*) – a nationalist cultural and political circle which included artists like Erik Werenskjold, academics like Moltke Moe and the historian Ernest Sars.

The group's ideology of national cohesion attempted to reconcile the gap between rural and urban culture and to combine the traditional with the modern, making Norwegians more aware of their national character.[23]

After independence in 1905, sport was again used in Norway to define and reinforce political goals. The powerful workers' movement (*Arbeidersbevegelsen*) maintained a strict and explicit policy of separate class-based cultural development from 1918 until 1935, believing members of Norway's National Association for Sport were strike-breaking and training for military service.[24] The Workers' Sports Federation (AIF) was founded in 1924 and had 100,000 members by 1940. Its members trained quite separately from 'national' teams and competed in the Socialist Workers Sports International (SASI) Workers' Olympics in 1925, 1931, 1937 and the revolutionary Red Sports International (RSI), 'Spartacus Olympiads', in Oslo and Moscow in 1928. The two organisations merged to fight fascism in the 1930s and the Workers' Federation finally merged with the Norwegian National Association on the eve of the Second World War.

Before then – in the wake of the Russian Revolution – Norway had passed an important law to limit the working day and legislate for leisure. 'Eight hours work, eight hours recreation, eight hours rest', the Labour Movement's slogan since 1889, was finally realised in 1918–19.[25] But with the *åtte timer arbeid* (eight-hour working day legislation) was placed more than just a limit on work. Uniquely in Europe perhaps, Norway's legislation divided each day into three equal portions – work, leisure and rest. The inclusion of leisure as a State-sanctioned activity – perhaps even a statutory obligation – had a profound impact on public attitudes. Workers got twelve statutory days of paid annual holiday in 1937 but holiday agreements were already being won by well-organised trade unions from 1919. It was no coincidence that the first large hutting settlements on islands in Oslo fjord began a few years later, partly prompted by an anxious backlash among professionals. In 1919, the journal *Sociale Meddelelser* published an article with the title, 'What are working people going to use their freetime for?', which argued a 10–11 hour working day had been the norm for such a long time that it was impossible for workers to know how to use free time properly. The journal concluded that workers should be taught about leisure and the State started research projects and competitions to find the most constructive free-time ideas.

Prohibition meant alcohol was not an easy option. Hutting ticked all the boxes – it was cheap, self-starting, popular, healthy and constructive family-oriented leisure.

So the campaigns to defend Norway's Constitution, create a 'genuine' national identity and avert post-independence class division all deployed *friluftsliv* (a simple life in nature) and made *idrett* (purposeful outdoor 'sporting' activity) an integral part of national identity.

The story in Scotland was quite different. In 1775, James Boswell said Voltaire was amazed when he announced an intention to visit the Scottish Highlands; 'he looked at me as if I had talked of going to the North Pole'. The fearsome nature of Scottish weather and landscape had kept visitors away from Scotland's Great Outdoors until Queen Victoria braved the elements to set up a second home at Balmoral. Deer stalker-clad southerners and wealthy lowland Scots followed her north to shoot deer and grouse in deer 'forests' on 'sporting' estates freshly emptied of local people. Scotland was transformed from a place with nothing to see before 1760 into the most fashionable holiday location for the wealthy in Europe.

A. V. Seaton observes: 'Overnight a forbidding wilderness was turned into a genteel pleasure ground, an alien and hostile race into an object of sentimental myth, and a climate regarded as brutish into an environment of challenge and grandeur.'[26]

By the 1820s, newspapers such as the *Inverness Courier* were commenting on the influx of visitors: 30,000 arrived after the publication of Scott's *Lady of the Lake* in 1810, which established the vogue for cruising along Loch Katrine. By the 1850s, a railway through the Highlands was being proposed with an estimated 50,000 passengers a year. Highland Scotland had become an adventure park for those with the money or connections to experience its pleasures.

But the Scottish outdoors was a destination for literate middle- and upper-class English, German and French visitors – not for Scots. The home market only developed when working time legislation produced time off in the second half of the nineteenth century with cheap rail and steamer day trips to seaside resorts. After the Holidays with Pay Act of 1938, there could be longer stays in rented accommodation. This resulted in holiday apartheid as different parts of Scotland catered for different classes of tourist, and seems to have had a lasting impact on attitudes towards access, nature and the Great Outdoors in Scotland.

In his *Theory of Practice*, Pierre Bourdieu, the French sociologist, argued that taste and cultural preferences are determined by class and social position. Cultural preferences feel 'natural' and 'familiar' so individual group members are reluctant to 'let the side down' by adopting the habits, preferences and pastimes of other social classes. Since hunting, shooting and fishing were all the preserve of the laird and county set, working-class Scots may have decided the countryside itself was part of an alien habitus.

In Norway, things have long been different. Across the Nordic countries – but particularly in Norway – a long tradition of easy access to land, an absence of large aristocratic estates, a development-oriented local planning system and relatively low property taxes have all combined to create widespread participation in sport and weekly connection with nature in *hytter*.

Five weeks of paid holiday, extending to six for those over sixty years old, and the opportunity of exchanging overtime work for extended weekends, meant there was plenty of time available to spend in the second home.

Thor Flognfeld Jr articulates the classic explanation offered by most writers on the exponential growth of second homes in Norway.[27] The combination of holidays, flexible working patterns and more disposable income inevitably resulted in high demand.

But Scotland shows these factors alone don't create a 'cabin culture'. Income levels in Scotland are lower today than in modern Norway. But Britain is still within the top ten economies of the world by GDP. When the first post-war expansion of cabins and *hytter* began across Norway (and the rest of Scandinavia), Scots had much the same level of disposable income. Yet the number of second homes was then and is still now very different.

In Norway, it is assumed any right-minded person would own a *hytte* if they possibly could – maybe two. Many Norwegians own a *hytte* in the *fjell* (mountain) for winter skiing and another in the fjord for summer bathing. In Scotland it is assumed no right-minded person would want a second home – but if they did it would be a timeshare in Spain or Florida, not a 'shabby' wooden hut.

Is that because Scots don't value nature? Is it because we have more mobile pastimes like cycling, mountain-climbing, camping and caravanning? Or is the truth the other way around? Have Scots opted for peripatetic pleasures like

Munro-bagging[28] because staying put in one place has been so difficult and expensive?

According to Eric Simpson in *Going on Holiday*, the first climbing clubs were middle class and exclusive. The Scottish Mountaineering Club was formed in 1889 and the Ladies' Scottish Climbing Club in 1906. Workers' hiking and cycling clubs were quite separate (like Norway):

> Some Glasgow shop workers toiling of necessity till late on Saturdays could count themselves fortunate if they caught the last train or bus out of the city. Many lived rough, finding primitive forms of shelter such as caves or overhanging boulders. Rough and ready howffs were made using old tarpaulin for roofing material. For these proletarian pioneers the campfire was at one and the same time a comradely expression of freedom and a practical necessity. 'We carried no tents', said Jock Nimlin, one of the working class trailblazers, 'and some of us carried no blankets or sleeping bags. It hardly seemed worthwhile as we had so little time for sleep.'[29]

Nimlin and his fellow 'Mountain Men' were hardy in the extreme. They caught the last bus or walked from Glasgow to Balloch, rowed up Loch Lomond to Tarbert, slept in a cave, rose the next day to climb the Arrochar Alps, did the same on Sunday, rowed back down the loch and walked into Glasgow having generally missed the last bus. This herculean physical effort was then repeated the next weekend. Nimlin and other working-class men used caves, bothies, self-built rooms beneath road bridges and even hollowed-out trees for overnight shelter and were reportedly contemptuous of those using youth hostels or indoor accommodation. Was that making a virtue of necessity? Or did they assume that asking for permission might only result in humiliating rejection? Perhaps the terrible living conditions endured in Glasgow bred a self-reliance which depended on never asking for help – especially from perceived 'class enemies'?

This comfort-averse outlook made Scottish hill-walking a physically demanding, hardy and very male endeavour. By contrast, Norway's emphasis on having a place to stay in the Great Outdoors encouraged whole families to experience nature together. Perhaps this explains why second homes are viewed as unproblematic by Norwegians who nonetheless inhabit one of the world's most equal societies. In Scotland, second home owners are often viewed as greedy incomers pricing young people out of the local housing market. And yet Scotland contains enough land to accommodate tens of thousands of people in huts, cabins, mountain cottages and seaside shacks. So why won't Scottish landowners sell small patches of land for huts? Why won't Scots demand them?

Traditionally it was thought the earlier industrialisation and urbanisation experienced by Scots severed all practical, emotional and family links with the land, so that by the 1920s – when the Norwegian Government started the ball rolling by giving hut sites to the poorest Oslo citizens – urban Scots were five or six generations away from the countryside and blocked from easy access to land by feudal ownership. So Scots were emotionally and physically 'locked out' of the countryside in the 1920s and hutting communities never really got off the ground.

That at least has been the explanation. But recent research suggests it isn't true.

In 1999, a Scottish Government researcher, Hugh Gentleman, identified hutting communities in sixty-two locations across Scotland at the request of the Scottish Executive.[30] The new Parliament had been petitioned for help by hutters from Carbeth, 12 miles north of Glasgow, who were facing eviction after rent rises and a rent strike. The Government wanted to see how many other hutters might be in the same situation – without rights because of their temporary, not permanent, occupation of huts. Gentleman's report found most of the hut sites had indeed begun between the wars – exactly the same moment of birth as hutting communities across the rest of Europe and Norway – fuelled by a collapse in land values, fear of revolution, concern for the health of soldiers returning from war and the growth of outdoor activities encouraged by socialist movements.

The research showed Scottish hutting communities didn't fail to start, but that unlike their Nordic counterparts, they failed to survive. Why?

Scotland's first and longest-surviving hut site made a faltering, unplanned start 12 miles north of Glasgow in 1920. Carbeth was effectively started by Sgt William Ferris of the Highland Cyclist Battalion while he was stationed in Ballinrobe in Ireland. In 1918, Ferris wrote to an officer in the HCB asking him to intervene on the Battalion's behalf with the owner of Carbeth, Allan Barns Graham. Ferris mentioned that he and two fellow soldiers had camped at Craigallian Loch near Carbeth before the war and viewed it 'as a favourite camping site'. The men had formed a small club saving money throughout the war (collecting £30 by 1918) with a view to the joint purchase of a small hut at Carbeth afterwards.

According to the current landowner, Allan Barns Graham Jr, his grandfather refused but offered them the chance to camp instead. It is not clear why the well-crafted request was so swiftly and emphatically rejected, but the period was a fractious one in the west of Scotland with successful rent strikes in 1915 and a General Strike of 70,000 workers in 1919 supporting the engineers' call for a maximum 40–hour week. This provoked riots in George Square in Glasgow. According to historian Richard Finlay:

> *The Glasgow Herald* estimated that the potential revolutionaries could call on the support of over 100,000 people. To the middle class the threat seemed real. After all there were militant workers going on strike and a mass movement had forced the government to intervene in the payment of rent, something the middle classes regarded as sacrosanct to the market. And the workers appeared to be led by committed socialists. The middle class took the leaders of the workers at their word and believed that they were about to abolish the market and take over private property.[31]

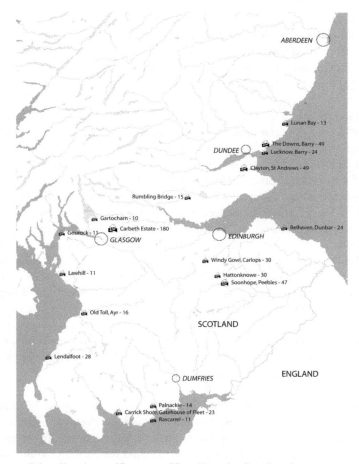

Figure 11.2 Distribution of Largest Hut Sites in Scotland, 1999

The largest site (hut nos)
Carbeth Estate, Stirling **180**
Large sites (c. 50)
The Downs, Barry **49**; Clayton, St Andrews **49**; Soonhope, Peebles **47**
Medium sites (c. 20–30)
Windy Gowl, Carlops **30**; Hattonknowe, Eddleston **30**; Lendalfoot, Girvan **28**; Belhaven,
Dunbar **24**; Lucknow, Barry **24**; Carrick Shore, Gatehouse of Fleet **23**
Smaller sites (c. 10–20)
Old Toll, Ayr **16**; Rumbling Bridge **15**; Palnackie, Castle Douglas **15**; Carronbridge **14**;
Corbie Knowe, Lunan Bay **13**; Craigendownie, Glen Lethnot, **11**; Cloch Road, Gourock **11**;
Rascarrel, Auchencairn **11**; Lawhill, West Kilbride **11**; Aber Mill, Gartocharn **10**

Ferris was requesting access to land at a time viewed by many as the high point of revolutionary fervour in Scotland, but whereas in Norway concessions were made to discontented workers, the strategy in Scotland was very different.

Ferris wrote again to Barns Graham from Glasgow in 1919 after being demobbed and perhaps pinpointed the source of the landowner's anxiety:

It was kind of you to let me see that postcard you received from the anonymous 'Soldier' who is so certain that you entertained each weekend a few 'bolshies'. I thought it might interest you to know the war history of the 'Bolshies' mentioned on your Postcard. There are five of us. Robertson was in the RNOR at the outbreak of war and has Antwerp, Jutland and a broken leg as his war honours. Fraser joined when the Post Office allowed him (1915) and managed to have a few years' holiday in France where he collected a few wounded stripes until demobbed a few months ago. Smith visited Gallipoli, Egypt and France perhaps on 'bolshie' propaganda, but his three gold bars indicate that he did not have it all his own way. McCallum and myself both joined voluntary on September 1914 and came with the others to enjoy the lovely district of Carbeth just a few weeks after being demobbed. I wish sincerely that such gentlemen as 'A Soldier' would not hastily rush to conclusions.

Barns Graham relented the following year after getting to know William Ferris. More hutters followed, and it seems some hatched the idea of regular visits to Carbeth at a socialist summer camp on Arran. Ailsa McNicol recalls:

My grandfather was a member of the Social Credit movement in Glasgow at that time. His name was Tommy Wood and he was an electrical engineer at John Brown's Shipyard. He used to come to Arran a lot. So in the 1920s he and his brother Jimmy got on their bikes and scouted round the island for a suitable campsite to bring workers and their families for a holiday. They found a site at Catacol and from then it was known as the Clarion Camp. It was close to the Lochranza ferry and the tenant farmer was a bit of a socialist.

Many of the Arran holiday-makers ended up at Carbeth. In 1927, there were just five huts. In 1929, the Carbeth Swimming Pool or Lido was opened (finally closing in 1972) – and the ever-helpful William Ferris was Secretary of the Club. The big growth in huts occurred during the 1930s. At one 1936 event there were fifty hutters present (though most wanted to be called hut-owners or walkers, not hutters). Soon a village of self-built but similar-looking huts, with bitumen roofs and green timber walls, sprouted throughout the forest landscape, built by the hutters themselves. They paid a nominal rent and facilities were primitive.

Most of the hutters came from the west side of Glasgow; from Scotstoun, Yoker and Clydebank. Many walked to Carbeth and by the 1930s the camp had become a hub for climbers, cyclists and

... the unemployed from the shipyards of Scotstoun and Clydebank. Climbers, many of them in the legendary Creag Dhu, met at Craigallion Loch, a little south of the huts, where a fire was reputedly never allowed to go out, such was the coming and going of walkers, mountaineers, and tramps.[32]

In 1941, Clydebank Council asked permission to build forty-seven huts to house families made homeless in the Blitz, and by 1947 there was a grand total of 191 huts. But the administrative burden fell largely on one man – William Ferris. His son Murray recalls that his father didn't actually have a hut himself but made hutting possible for everyone else by holding meetings at his stamp and book shop in Glasgow between 1920 and 1943. During this time Ferris also co-founded the Citizens Theatre after being active in the Clarion Players, an offshoot of the Clarion Socialist movement set up by Robert Blatchford. Ferris was also a keen cyclist, like many Glaswegians of the time, often cycling to Carbeth – even when he finally had a car. His son recalls that a special design of bike was produced in Glasgow to help cyclists cope with hills and to carry panniers with tents. A Greenock firm produced a tent with collapsible poles – again the kit was designed to fit onto these first 'mountain bikes'. The Socialist Sunday School movement was also heavily connected with the Great Outdoors. And yet little archive material of this period seems to exist.

William Ferris went on to become vice-president of the Camping Club of Great Britain and Ireland, vice-chairman of the Scottish Council of Physical Recreation, Chairman of the Scottish Rights of Way Society, Scottish Ramblers Federation and member of the Scottish Tourist Board – and founded Britain's first youth hostel at Rowardennan. Ferris was an outdoors evangelist. And yet none of the organisations he set up seems to have kept any record of his efforts.

By all accounts Carbeth was run with military precision by an elected executive committee with strict rules about membership and behaviour in the camp which could only be occupied between 1 July and 30 September each year.[33] The landowner behaved a bit like 'a benevolent dictator'. Hutters were only allowed at weekends, and Barns Graham himself went round the site after the last bus each Sunday to check every chimney was cold, and each hut empty. Yet the site continued to expand.

This is uncannily similar to the origins of *hytte* islands in Inner Oslo fjord, which were divided into hut sites in 1922 by their landowner – the Norwegian Government – offering holiday homes to *barnerike* (literally 'child-rich') families from the poorer East End of Oslo. The first Norwegian hutters were also campers, transporting kit in small rowing boats kept at the mouth of the Aker River. They too faced tough conditions – the first leases gave no duration and required hutters to move after a month's notice should the island be needed for anything else. But the 600 summer hutters on Lindoya, Nakkholmen and Bleikoya had some advantages over the Carbeth hutters. They had a constant State owner – not a succession of private landlords. And although they had no security of tenure until the 1980s and faced constant opposition from *friluftsliv* activists objecting to their 'privatisation' of the fjord and development attempts by Oslo *kommune*, the Norwegian hutters had something valuable on their side – a middle-class hutting movement with individual huts dotted discreetly all over the mountains, lochs and fjords of Norway. The long-term problem for Scottish hutters was that Scotland's middle classes opted not to spend their time and money the same way, and that left working-class hutters exposed. As time passed, the original landowners of Scotland's hutting communities died, and with each passing generation goodwill diminished and personal ties weakened.

By the time he died in 1957, Allan Barns Graham had undergone a total change of heart towards the hutters he once shunned – and perhaps had a premonition about the changing priorities of his sons. He wrote in his will: 'My estate of Carbeth shall not be feued or leased in such a manner as to interfere with the tenancies or rights of the original hutters', and he instructed his heir to 'look after the hutters without remuneration'.

Within a year the spirit of the will was bent, if not broken, by his son. According to hutter May Macgregor, Barns Graham's son Patrick doubled rents soon after inheriting Carbeth estate in 1959 to invest in mains water. May's husband Bill started a tenants' association when no water appeared. Patrick Barns Graham took Bill and May to court and won: they were evicted in May 1961 but the judge ordered that no new huts could be built on their site.

According to another hutter, Netta Wallace, a neighbour was evicted around the same time for merely cutting down a tree. In 1962, Patrick did bring mains water to the estate, with seventeen standpipes for hutters. During the 1970s and '80s the community struggled. In 1972, the swimming pool closed, many huts were derelict or vandalised, and in 1999 the remaining 150 hutters went on strike in protest at raised rents. Legal advice suggested the hutters had no tenants' rights under Scottish law because they were only temporary occupants of their huts. Stirling Council intervened to designate the huts a Conservation Zone – deterring rival bidders for the land. It took a community buyout in 2013 to resolve the stand-off and secure the land for the hutters. Other inter-war hut sites were not so lucky.

A study for Carnoustie District Council in Angus in the late 1970s recorded thirty-seven huts at a site on Barry Downs in 1937/8, increasing to a peak of 159 in the early 1960s before dropping to around 110 in 1978. The sixty-five remaining hutters were evicted in 2012.

It was a similar story at Rascarrel in Galloway. Some hutting sites like Seton Sands in East Lothian became caravan sites: it is not clear whether this was at the instigation of landowners, hutters or the council.

DIG FOR VICTORY: ALLOTMENTS IN SCOTLAND AND NORWAY

The history of allotments has a similar theme.

In Britain, the appetite for growing food was stimulated by the Defence of the Realm Act 1917, which urged patriotic Britons to get outdoors and plant food to ease the pressure for imports. Straight after the First World War, resumption of the use of ground for building and other purposes was scheduled for over 100 acres of allotments. The same pattern emerged before and after the Second World War. 'Dig for Victory' urged the use of urban land for planting, but plotholders were expected to hand the land back on the cessation of hostilities. Although some allotments survived, their status is generally still precarious, demand outstrips supply and the rules strictly forbid any overnight stays in sheds.

Meanwhile, in Norway 'colony gardens' (*kolonihager*) have been longer-lasting and more successful. The *kolonihager* are fenced-off collections of plots on *kommune*-owned land designed to give city residents without gardens the chance to grow their own fruit, trees and vegetables. They began in the early 1900s, but today there are nine allotment gardens with around 1,600 plots in Oslo and 3,000 across Norway. The Kolonihager Association has other member gardens in Stavanger, Trondheim and Drammen, and there are unaffiliated *kolonihager* in Kristiansand and Tønsberg. The colonists have long-term leases on the land and, unlike in Scotland, every Norwegian plot has a hut to which many owners move for the entire summer.

So effectively Norwegians use allotments to provide yet another opportunity for hut-living: Scots do not and cannot use their allotments in the same way.

The same triggers used to explain the decline of huts in 1960s Scotland – more leisure time, statutory holidays, better transport and higher incomes – are used to explain their massive growth in 1960s Norway.

So other factors must have been at work. By the 1960s and '70s, hut sites needed substantial capital investment in sanitation, water, electricity and services. By then, however, landowners had become distanced from the post-war relationships which prompted their grandfathers to lease land in the first place. Some wanted better returns from picturesque, high-quality cottages. Meanwhile, without any security of tenure or chance to gain security by land purchase, hutters may have been reluctant and unable to make major improvements to water and sanitation themselves. When wooden cabins needed major renovation – by the 1960s – hutters had to decide if the effort was worth it. By then, cheap holidays abroad had become popular.

Nonetheless, the allure of two weeks in the sun didn't replace the year-round appeal of weekend huts in Norway. For whatever reason, middle-class Scots – unlike their Nordic or working-class Scottish counterparts – didn't hanker after the weekend hutting habit. Perhaps makeshift huts in Scotland were seen as shabby reminders of a poverty many Scots had only just left behind.

Landowners still have great indirect power to shape the leisure lives of Scots. If they are cooperative, long-distance paths can be developed like the West Highland, Speyside and Southern Upland ways. If they are not (as in the 'Far North' of Scotland), a local population will miss out. If landowners are willing to rent out small plots of land, then weekend cabins or caravans allow working people to create an affordable weekend escape. If they won't rent out small, affordable pockets of land, caravans can only be berthed in large managed coastal parks where owners have no protection against arbitrary eviction or sudden price hikes.

Scottish councils still discourage hutters with planning policies that seem modelled upon the aesthetic of the 'empty glen'. A vital factor was the UK 1947 Town and Country Planning Act whose post-war determination to restore food production as the primary function of the countryside tended to exclude competing land-use developments like huts. According to Colin Ward, the Act was responsible for clearing thousands of inter-war huts built around London by the 'plotlanders'.[34]

In summary, the average Scot has traditionally had less access to and ownership of land than the average Norwegian. Scots have therefore had less chance to invest in land, river, loch, forest or home (until 1993 a majority of Scots rented their homes), so there has been one big way to spend rising incomes since the war: Scots have tended to consume them, spending on food, drink and cars. The Norwegians, by contrast, have invested their cash in weekend huts, skis, ski-mobiles, and systems to support their dual life in towns and in nature. Without radical change to patterns of landownership and attitudes to nature, Scots will take a very long time to catch up with their outdoor-oriented, sporting Norwegian cousins.

Notes

1. http://www.heraldscotland.com/sport/spl/aberdeen/lines-drawn-in-the-battle-of- dunnet-1.718263
2. http://www.ssb.no/en/kultur-og-fritid/statistikker/fritid
3. Football is relatively less popular in Norway and played during the summer only, but for decades the most popular Oslo team, Vålerenga, also hosted speed-skating and track-and-field events at their ground.
4. http://scotland.gov.uk/Publications/2007/03/07105145/5
5. http://www.snh.gov.uk/docs/A1020956.pdf : Table 6, p. 16.
6. Ibid.: Table 19, p. 35.
7. Cohen and Milne, 2007.
8. Bergstrom and Ikonen, 2005.
9. http://www.scotsman.com/news/lesley-riddoch-this-demand-simply-won-t-wash-1-807612
10. http://www.visitnorway.com/uk/media--press/ideas-and-features/hiking-in-norway/

11. http://www.mountainbothies.org.uk/mba-history.asp
12. Statistics Norway, Sweden, Finland and Denmark.
13. The Scottish holiday home total is taken from 2006/7 Council Tax returns and the hut total comes from H. Gentleman, *Huts and Hutters*, Scottish Office Central Research Unit, 1999: http://www.chrissmithonline.co.uk/files/huts-and-hutters-in-scotland---1999-draft-research-materials.pdf
14. Nansen, 1897.
15. Grönvold, 1883.
16. Literally translated as 'free air life'.
17. Flogenfeldt, 2004.
18. Bull, 1956.
19. Goksøyr, 1996.
20. Centralforeningen for Udbredelse af Legemsøvelser og Vaabenbrug.
21. *Njørd Journal* (1901),
22. Nansen, 1891.
23. Libaek and Stenersen, 1991.
24. Larsen, 1979.
25. Kjeldstadli, 1993.
26. Seaton, 1998.
27. Flognfeldt, 2004.
28. A 'Munro' is a Scottish mountain over 3,000 ft above sea level. 'Munro-bagging' refers to the practice of climbing as many of these as possible.
29. Simpson, 1997.
30. Gentleman, 1999.
31. Finlay, 2004.
32. Mitchell, 2007.
33. Jamieson, 2000.
34. Ward and Hardy, 1984.

CHAPTER 12

Education in Norway and Scotland: Developing and Re-forming the Systems

Bronwen Cohen and Wenche Rønning

OVERVIEW

We examine here the development of public education systems in Norway and Scotland and the ways in which both systems have responded to new challenges. Our focus is on the policies adopted for democratising access to schools and democracy within the schools, the means and mechanisms used in developing Early Childhood Education and Care (ECEC) services and school-age childcare services, and the relationship between schools and communities. We find that national autonomy has made a difference, and that local identity and democracy have also been significant in the three areas examined here. In ECEC, there is a yawning gap in levels of provision between Scotland and Norway, where, from 1975, a strong partnership between local authorities and national government developed a fully integrated system. Post- devolution, growing divergence in educational principles and models between Scotland and England suggests that Scotland should look more to its northern than its southern neighbour in developing some aspects of policy.

EARLY HISTORY

Norway and Scotland both have a long history of school education, dating from the Protestant Reformation and predating the formal establishment of their national education systems. Various versions of religious education existed in Norway from the sixteenth century. This became compulsory through an Education Act passed by Denmark in 1739, requiring Norwegian children from the age of seven in rural areas to learn religion and reading for five years in schools, using the official language of Danish.[1]

A long campaign led to Norway obtaining its first university, in Oslo, in 1811, joined in 1859 by the Agricultural University (now known as the University of Life Sciences or NMBU) in Ås, Akershus. Independence from Denmark in 1814 gave Norway greater control over its institutions, and subsequently the language used for teaching. The nature of the relationship between the Church and schools changed as education became the subject of public debate and the aspirations of newly enfranchised property owners, including small farmers and fishermen (see Chapters 1 and 9). In 1864, inspired by the Danish educationalist Nikolaj Grundtvig, Norway established its first *folkehøgskole* or folk high school, mentioned later in this chapter. Schools had developed separately in rural and urban areas, with those in rural areas generally taking the form of *omgangsskole*, a peripatetic school where the teacher travelled around. Urban schools had their own school buildings. A Commission set up in 1885 on the future of education led to legislation in 1889 with separate Acts for rural and urban schools. Schools would no longer be Church schools but became *folkeskole* (people's school) managed through local school boards.[2] Following Norwegian independence in 1905, people's schools would develop based on the *enhetsskole* or unity school concept, described as running 'like a red thread through a democratically inspired schools policy from the mid-nineteenth century until now'.[3]

In Scotland, the basic shape of the education system up until the late nineteenth century was developed prior to the Acts of Union with England in 1707. Unlike Norway this included universities. The first three of these were established in the fifteenth century[4] and by the end of the following century it had five, 'at the heart' of the eighteenth century humanist and rational Scottish Enlightenment.[5]

In common with Norway, Scotland from the seventeenth century had an extensive system of burgh and parish schools dating back to the Reformation, and marked by the Education Act 1633 of Scotland's then still independent Parliament, which required a locally funded, Church-supervised school to be established in every parish in Scotland, later joined by a variety of other providers.[6] From the 1840s, these received State subsidies and other forms of State support, and were subject to inspection. By the late 1860s, the proportion of Scottish children on the school roll was close to Prussian levels, where education was already compulsory.[7]

Scottish State education legislation followed over three decades of debate and was passed two years after equivalent legislation in England. The 1872 Education (Scotland) Act established non-sectarian 'board' schools, managed by elected school boards. Education was made compulsory in Scotland (and from 1892, free) for all children aged 5–13 years, and teachers in charge of the schools had to hold a certificate of competency.[8] For a period of time the new system was supervised from London, prompting George Davie[9] to describe 1872 as the year when 'the effective control of Scottish education was transferred to London and put under English authority...' Davie pointed to the delay in Scotland achieving a State education system, despite the lengthy campaigning for this in Scotland from the 1840s, citing a 1919 booklet on the surrender of Scotland's longer-established 'ideals and practice' to England.[10] Paterson, in his 1994 analysis of the extent to

which Scotland effectively retained control of some areas, offers a different explanation, pointing to internal divisions within Scotland as a reason for the delay.[11]

Written just over a decade later, the Napier Commission (1884) provides some
insight into the impact of the 1872 legislation in the Highlands and Islands. The
Commission's report is notable for the issues it raises around the relationship
between schools and communities, which remain in a number of respects as pertinent today as they were then. The Commission had harsh words, and (largely
unimplemented) recommendations about the discouragement it found for using
Gaelic in the schools, and asked questions about the neglect of traditional singing
and music, and flexibility in the school calendar for the household economic
activities.[12] Commission evidence highlighted the extent to which families relied
on children themselves for the care of other siblings as well as household income,
with one Shetland teacher complaining about absenteeism: 'Any frivolous excuse
is considered good enough, such as keeping the house, or minding the child, or
going "gipping" [gutting] herring ...'[13]

DEMOCRATISING ACCESS TO SCHOOLS

In the 1930s, both Norway and Scotland were exploring educational reform which
would lead to the development of the concept of the *enhetsskole* or unity school
in Norway and comprehensive education in Scotland. In Norway, where its first
Labour government took office in 1935, the unity school was seen as a vehicle for
reducing economic and social inequalities in Norwegian society. While drawing
on the powerful ideas around *folkeskole* from the previous century, it also drew on
international educational reformers, making Norway's public education system
a laboratory for some of these ideas, supported by a Pedagogical Research Unit
established at the University of Oslo in 1938. In 1945, after five years of war, the
main focus became that of securing education for all and on extending the length
of compulsory education from seven to nine years, eventually secured through
1969 legislation.

The unity school concept has been described as having four dimensions.[14]
Adequate **resources** ensure an equitable educational provision irrespective of
local economic, geographical and demographic circumstances, secured until
1986 by ring- fenced funding, now replaced by block grant. A **social** dimension
requires that children in a designated geographical area receive their education in
a common public school, limiting the development of private schools, a dimension
which is challenged by right-wing parties, including the current government.
A third dimension is **culture**, focusing on the responsibility for ensuring that
the children in Norwegian schools gain access to and learn about their cultural
heritage through a common national curriculum. For many years this included
giving pupils a 'Christian and moral upbringing', but following a 2007 European
Court of Human Rights decision, education legislation recognises Norway as an

increasingly culturally diverse nation.[15] The fourth dimension is **diversity**, which is interwoven with the concept of *tilpasset opplæring* or 'adapted education'. This is a principle intended to accept and adapt individual and group differences, so that diversity and not equality of provision is the guiding principle.

The concept of the unity school has proved long lasting and its administration has been undertaken within the context of increasing local authority powers, from the right in 1968 to decide their own property tax rate to the introduction of block grants in 1986. This process was associated with reforms of the Norwegian national curriculum from 1974 and subsequently in 1984 and 1997, reinforcing the local dimension in the Norwegian education system. As we see later, this has required all schools to develop their own local version of the national curriculum.

In Scotland, the concept of comprehensive schools first emerged in the 'omnibus' schools in Scotland (and 'multilateral' schools in London) in the 1920s. Secondary omnibus schools shared to some degree the basic democratic principle of Norway's 'unity' school of being for all children from a designated neighbourhood, although in Scotland at this time it was only those who passed the qualifying exam. By the late 1920s, these made up around one-third of all secondary schools in Scotland.[16]

Comprehensive education as a formal policy came not as a direct result of the omnibus schools or from the proposals of the 1947 Advisory Council on Education for Scotland for a comprehensive system of secondary schools, although both may have influenced UK discussions around the principle.[17] Comprehensive education was brought in across Britain in 1965, and while Scotland, as a result of its omnibus schools, started in a different place from England and Wales, it was 'a British policy applied to Scotland'.[18] In Scotland, it was brought in through Circular 600, which was intended to end selection and establish one 'unified' school that in all areas (except those sparsely populated) would provide a full range of courses for all pupils in a designated district for all ages from 12 to 18. Circular 600 confirmed the intention to raise the school leaving age to 16 and abolished any remaining fee-charging in education authority schools. By 1982, all selection in the public sector had ended.[19]

In Norway, the unity school concept has been closely linked with social democracy and, combined with the welfare state model developed from 1945, has been a powerful tool in supporting the development of a more equal society. Different governments have introduced some modifications, including allowing local authorities to introduce an element of parental choice of school, although few have chosen to do so. Essentially, the concept of children receiving their education in a school common to their community or geographical area remains for all but a few children.

In Scotland, as elsewhere in the UK, the principle of parental choice was introduced in 1981 by the then Conservative government. Enacted through the 1981 Education (Scotland) Act, the presumption in Scotland remained that of parents being allowed to ask for a place other than the one allocated, rather than indicating their own preferences from the outset. Placement requests were initially very low but now account for 24 per cent of the P1 primary school roll and 14 per cent of the S1 secondary school roll.[20] Devolution in 1999 has undoubtedly built a more effective wall between Scottish education and some more recent 'marketisation' developments in England, including the development of self-governing City Academy schools. These will soon constitute more than half of secondary schools in England, prompting its Department for Education to commission research on whether 'parental choice works well in an increasingly autonomous school system'.[21] The principle of parental choice is still supported in Scotland by both the Scottish Government and the Scottish Parent Teacher Council but is seen by some others as having undermined one of the key goals of comprehensive education in Scotland: achieving a social mix of pupils.[22]

We look now at the way both countries have addressed the understanding and practice of democracy within their schools.

DEVELOPING DEMOCRATIC RIGHTS FOR PARENTS, CHILDREN AND YOUNG PEOPLE WITHIN THE EDUCATION SYSTEMS

In Norway, the development of the education system, the *folkeskole*, was supported by increasingly strong local municipal and government institutions. From 1814, Norwegian local authorities were elected by a wider suffrage than in most other countries of the time (see Chapters 1, 3 and 5). A long tradition of local representative government, and an extended period of devolving many aspects of decision-making, including education, to local authorities, may be seen as contributing to the emphasis on democratic rights for initially parents, and, subsequently, children and young people.

In Norway, these rights are seen primarily in terms of governance. The 1998 Norwegian Education Act (Section 1-1) stipulates that 'Education and training in schools and training establishments shall **in collaboration and agreement with the home** [authors' emphasis] open doors to the world'. In primary and lower secondary schools all parents are members of the parents' council which, among other tasks, '…shall work to promote an atmosphere of solidarity between home and school, lay a basis for well-being and positive development for the pupils and foster contact between the school and the local community' (Section 11-4). The parent council elects an executive committee, which in turn elects representatives to sit on the school's coordinating committee, typically consulted on the school's aims and priorities, and budget. Parents are also represented on the school's environmental committee in 'creating a satisfactory school environment' (Section 11-1a). Nine out of ten parents are satisfied, although issues remain over the involvement of the most disadvantaged families.[23]

Similarly, children's participation in schools and kindergartens in Norway is seen as a democratic right and includes a governance role as well as being seen as a means of 'developing their democratic ideals and understanding the importance of active and committed participation in a multicultural society'.[24] This is seen as starting in the kindergarten, where young children have a legislative right 'to express their views on the day-to-day activities of the kindergarten' and must regularly be given the opportunity to take an active role in planning and assessing the activities.[25] It is followed by a legislative entitlement for children in schools to actively participate in how education services are developed and operate. From Year 5, when children are ten years old, schools are required to have a pupil council with representatives from all classes.[26] Pupil council members are represented on the school environmental and coordinating committees. The curriculum highlights the importance of a learning environment which encourages not only cooperation and dialogue, but also 'difference of opinion'.[27] However, while pupil involvement is extensive, Furre et al. found that pupils only to a limited degree reported being involved in planning and assessing learning work and progress.[28]

In Scotland, following the introduction in 1981 of the principle of parental rights to choice in schooling, the Scottish Schools (Parental Involvement) Act 2006 was enacted by Scotland's own Parliament and was intended to 'make further provision for the involvement of parents in their children's education and in school education generally' and set up parent councils. Curricular guidance also emphasises the role played by parents in supporting their children's learning and encourages parental participation through the parent councils. Research examining early experiences of parental involvement in primary school activities found that fewer than a quarter had attended a parent council.[29] The most common activity (involving 86 per cent of parents) was visiting their child's classroom, followed by attending a school event (81 per cent).

As in Norway, the rights of children and young people are now embedded in various Scottish legislative acts, dating from the Children (Scotland) Act 1995 to most recently the Children and Young People Act 2014. Within education, the Standards in Scotland's Schools Act 2000 (Section 2.2) required education authorities to have 'due regard, so far as is reasonably practicable, to the views ... of the child or young person in decisions that significantly affect that child or young person', leading subsequently to the setting up of pupil councils in most schools. This has been lent additional support by the Curriculum for Excellence, in which the development of responsible citizens is one of the four key capacities for schools to develop.[30] Research indicates that while examples of meaningful involvement of children and young people and citizenship education can be found in Scottish schools, teaching staff and pupils have somewhat different views on what it should involve.[31] Staff are most likely to see it in terms of consultation, and external to the core of classroom-based teaching and learning, while pupils see it relating to precisely these areas, that is, being taught democratically.[32]

At a pre-school level there is encouragement but no requirement equivalent to the Norwegian Kindergarten Act, which gives children the right to express their views on the day-to-day activities of the kindergarten. Scottish guidance emphasises the rights of the child and refers to children being 'consulted naturally in decision-making, for example about resources and snacks' and, for older pre-school children, helping them to become responsible citizens 'through encountering different ways of seeing the world, learning to share and give and take, learning to respect themselves and others, and taking part in decisions'.[33]

Unlike the results in international tests such as the Programme for International Student Assessment (PISA), where Norwegian pupils score on or below average, Norwegian pupils achieved very good results in the 2009 International Civic and Citizenship Education Study, which researches pupil attitudes to, and understanding of, democracy.[34] Involvement in day-to-day discussion of activities in kindergartens and schools, and learning environments in which difference of opinion is valued, represents the kind of approach advocated by a recent Scottish study of pupil participation in schools. Hulme et al., in their 2011 study of pupil participation in Scottish schools, conclude that 'advancing the participation agenda in Scotland's schools requires serious engagement with the notion of deliberative democracy'.[35]

Although beyond the scope of this chapter, it is worth noting that since upper secondary education reform in 1994, young people in Norway have a legislative right of up to four years of free upper secondary education to use until they are twenty-five years old.[36] Outside the university system, some make use of a one-year boarding course at a government-supported *folkehøgskole* (Norwegian Folk High School) of which there are currently seventy-eight across Norway. These offer an exam-free space for young people at an important time in their lives and have a particular focus on social interaction and democratic participation.[37]

DEVELOPING EARLY CHILDHOOD EDUCATION AND CARE AND SCHOOL-AGE CHILDCARE

In common with much of the Minority World, following industrialisation one of the major challenges for education systems in Norway and Scotland over the last half century has been their relationship to those services meeting the varied needs of young children and their families prior to the age of compulsory schooling, and outside school hours.

Scotland, which industrialised earlier, could draw on a more extensive history in this area and a very early example of Early Childhood Education and Care (ECEC). Visitors today to the World Heritage site of New Lanark in South Lanarkshire can see what may be described as the world's first integrated school, nursery and out-of-school service, opened in 1816 by the millowner and education reformer Robert Owen for his employees and their children.[38]

As Scotland continued to industrialise, some other employers opened nurseries. By 1905 there were four in and around Dundee.[39] Both the 1914–18 and

1939–45 wars brought nursery programmes throughout the UK to enable women to work.[40] These programmes, which provided 'childcare', subsequently lost their funding. Instead, both wars were followed by legislation across Britain to enable local authorities to provide nursery education for children from the age of two.[41]

Norway had far fewer pre-school services than Scotland in 1945. Industrialising later, the first services had developed towards the end of the nineteenth century in the larger cities as 'children's asylums', offering free full-time care, supervision and education for orphans and children living in extreme conditions of poverty.[42] The first public kindergarten (*barnehage*) was opened in Oslo in 1918.[43] Most services, including kindergartens, were for disadvantaged families. Unlike Denmark and Sweden, there was no major expansion in the first half of the twentieth century in the provision of kindergartens.

In both Norway and the UK, the immediate post-war periods saw the development of their welfare states but neither country anticipated the need for either leave provision or services to support maternal employment. In Norway, where, as in the UK, there was a widespread view that women with young children should not work, the level of provision continued to be very low. The early postwar period saw some funding for day care services (*daghjem*), which were few in number. It was not until 1963, when only just over 8,500 children attended kindergartens, that any form of general funding for kindergartens was put in place.[44]

In both countries, from the late 1960s, the women's movement focused attention on gender inequality and discrimination, and services required to support women's education and employment. Maternal employment rates, while still low, were beginning to rise. In the UK, the 1970s brought equality legislation and in 1975 a package of employment provisions, including maternity leave. In Norway, where maternity leave was introduced at the beginning of the twentieth century, it was extended to eighteen weeks.

As Table 12.1 shows, in 1975 levels of provision were higher in Scotland than in Norway but involved a variety of services, mostly part time. These included part-time nursery education for three- and four-year-olds; only a small number of two-year-olds were included. While Scottish statistics did not separate out nursery from primary school places at this time, a decade later it would cover 28 per cent of three- and four-year-olds. This, with places in day nurseries (nine out of ten in local authority provision) and childminders (covering 3 per cent of under-fives) and a new informal service called playgroups (attended on average 6–9 hours a week), amounted to ECEC for 24 per cent of Scotland's under-fives at the time.[45]

Norway had provision at this time for only 10 per cent of children aged one to six (see Table 12.1). However, 1975 was a watershed. A commission set up in the late 1960s to examine services to support women's employment and for young children themselves, led to the 1975 Kindergartens Act. A common name was adopted for the two elements of care and education that it brought together. *Barnehage*, or kindergarten, was seen as a term that belonged to neither schools

Table 12.1　Paid Parental Leave, Maternal Employment Rate and ECEC
Provision in Norway and Scotland in mid-1970s and 2010/12

		Norway[a]	Scotland[b]
	Paid parental leave[c]	12 weeks[d]	6 weeks[e]
1975-77	Maternal employment	43%[f]	[g]27%/60%
	ECEC provision	10%[h]	24%[i]
	Paid parental leave[j]	49/50 weeks[k]	39 weeks[l]
2010-12	Maternal employment	83/86%[m]	66 %[n]
	ECEC provision	90%[o]	57 %[p]

Sources: Norway: BFD, 1996; Jensen, 2000; Havnes and Mogstad, 2014; Moafi and Bjorkli, 2011.
Scotland and UK : Scottish Government; Cohen, 1988; Moss and Fonda, 1980; National Records of Scotland, 2014; Scottish Government Statistical Unit, 2014a and b; Care Inspectorate, 2014.

Notes:
[a]　1976 and 2010.
[b]　1975, 1985 and 2012.
[c]　Maternity leave only.
[d]　12 weeks' full pay.
[e]　UK 6 weeks at 90% (+ maternity allowance).
[f]　Mothers with children aged 0-7, i.e. below school starting age.
[g]　(GB) Mothers with children 0-4/5-10.
[h]　Kindergarten provision. No figures available for other (limited) provision.
[i]　Children aged 0-4 in day nurseries, nursery education (1985), family daycare and playgroups. Predominantly part-time.
[j]　UK maternity leave only; Norway leave for both parents.
[k]　Current (2014) regulations: 49 weeks at 100% pay or 59 weeks at 80% pay.
[l]　6 weeks at 90% and 33 weeks at flat rate.
[m]　Mothers with children aged 0-2: 83 %; children aged 3-5: 86 %; 52 % work full-time - 35 hours or more per week.
[n]　Mothers with children aged 1-10; 57 % part-time.
[o]　Children aged 1-5 in kindergartens, predominantly full-time.
[p]　Children aged 1-4; nurseries, crèches, childminders and playgroups, predominantly part-time.

nor day care, conveying instead an emphasis on free and creative play, in keeping with the Froebelian influence on Norway's early services.[46] The kindergarten was defined as a pedagogical institution for the child and not just a safe place while parents were at work or in providing preparation for school. The kindergarten manager and group leaders had to be trained as *førskolelærere* or pre-school teachers (a term which in Norway refers to a qualification in a holistic early years' pedagogy in which learning, care and 'upbringing' are seen as inseparable). The Act also gave children with disabilities a right to a kindergarten place, based upon

the principle of inclusion.[47] Following the legislation, a number of training institutions began to be set up for the *førskolelærere* required for the kindergartens.
Kindergartens – as also argued in Chapter 11 – generally have a major focus on the
use of the outdoors and the arts.[48]

As kindergartens developed, the age of compulsory schooling came under the
spotlight, together with the short length of the Norwegian school day. Public
debate also focused on the schools' curriculum content, which was seen as too
formal and rigid for children used to the Froebelian approach of the kindergartens. In 1997, the age of compulsory schooling was reduced to six years, and the
National Curriculum was reformed to include play as an approach to learning. In
addition, pre-school teachers were allowed to work in school, provided they took a
post-graduate course on teaching reading, writing and basic mathematics, a development which may have been helped by both pre-school teachers and teachers
being represented in the same main teacher union.

To compensate for the short school day, which at the time was only three to four
hours a day, *SkoleFritidsOrdning* or SFO (school-age childcare) was introduced as a
statutory requirement from 1997. All local authorities are required to provide SFO
for children in the first four years of primary education, including the school holiday
period. In 2010, more than 60 per cent of all six- to nine-year-olds (including 75
per cent of all six-year-olds) attended SFO in Norway.[49] The great majority of the
services are provided within schools.[50] Despite the increase, challenges remain,
particularly the need to improve the qualifications of staff and the cost that is now
higher than a kindergarten place.[51]

In 2006, the new Red-Green (Labour, Socialist and Centre parties) coalition
government fulfilled an election promise that every child from the age of one,
irrespective of their parents' employment status, should be entitled to a full-time
place in kindergarten. Associated with this, the kindergartens became the responsibility at national level of the Ministry of Education and Research, receiving an
increased budget. A 2010 survey found that 90 per cent of children between the
ages of one and five attended kindergarten full time, compared with 62 per cent a
decade earlier. Of the 10 per cent that did not attend kindergarten, 9 per cent spent
their day with their parents and 1 per cent used other forms of day care such as
relatives and family day care, or au pairs.[52]

In Scotland, as concerns over the fragmented structure and levels of provision
grew, some local authorities sought to develop a more integrated approach to
the plethora of services and, in particular, to bring together services providing
childcare for parents with nursery education, but with only limited success.[53]
The election of a Labour government in 1997 brought a (renewed) commitment
to provide part-time nursery education for all three- and four-year-olds (but
not two-year-olds) and strategic commitments, within broadly similar UK and
Scottish strategies, to provide good-quality childcare for children aged from
birth to fourteen 'in every neighbourhood' on the basis of 'better integration of
early education and childcare'.[54] They brought together responsibility at national

level for education and childcare services, and initiated major investment in a range of services.

In 1999, the Scottish Parliament brought the expectation that Scotland would build on its own system in what was seen as a devolved area of policy. For example, one possibility to which the introduction to the Scottish Childcare Strategy refers, is that of using a New Community Schools programme, introduced in 1998, to pilot the integration of early education extended day care.[55] However, the choices open to the new Scottish administration were limited by the strategy itself and by prior and subsequent decisions taken at a UK level.[56] These UK decisions included the use of demand funding through tax credits and other measures, and the decision to fund a range of providers as well as schools to deliver the new pre-school entitlement, with new bodies called Childcare Partnerships, bringing together the various providers to plan and develop services. The structure reflected the growing market economy in services in England. Local authorities were given a stronger role within Childcare Partnerships in Scotland than in England but their leadership role was undermined by losing their regulatory function and associated expertise at a critical time.

In 2007, the Scottish National Party (SNP) took office, initially as a minority government, with a manifesto commitment to increase the hours of nursery education and to work 'towards an entitlement for every child from the age of one to 12 or 14 to a place in a pre-school service, school age childcare or whole day school'.[57] It has led to an extension in the hours of free 'early learning and child-care', increased under 2014 legislation from 475 hours a year to approximately 15 hours a week for 40 weeks for three- and four-year-olds, and some two-year-olds. The Scottish Government's Independence White Paper envisaged that by the end of the second Parliament, in an independent Scotland, all children from the age of one would be entitled to 1,140 hours a year. Independence, it argued, by giving it full powers over tax and benefit systems, would enable investment in services rather than in subsidising demand.[58]

School-age childcare is also an area in which Scotland has a longer history than Norway. In recent times, the first formal out-of-school childcare service started in Scotland in 1981.[59] By the end of the decade, Scotland provided twice as many places for primary school children as in the UK as a whole, although still only available for less than 0.5 per cent of children in this age group.[60] Lottery funding led to a growth in centres, reaching its highest level in 2007, when the total number of services numbered 1,118.[61] Since then, the number of centre–based services has decreased, numbering in total 970 in 2012. Holiday care is also currently decreasing.[62] As in Norway, but to a lesser extent, out-of-school care centres make use of school premises. In 2010, 61 per cent of out-of-school clubs and 54 per cent of holiday play schemes used school premises.[63] However, less local authority support is now available. The Scottish Out of School Care Network (SOSCN) 2012 membership survey found fewer free premises and less than a quarter with subsidised premises. Other forms of support, including training and development officer support posts, have also decreased.[64]

As Table 12.1 shows, there is now a yawning gap in ECEC services between Norway and Scotland. Despite Scotland's historical lead, Norway has outstripped Scotland, with its kindergartens attended mostly full time by approximately 90 per cent of all children aged one to five years, prior to starting compulsory school at the age of six. The overwhelming majority of kindergartens are open for up to ten hours a day, although attended on average 30–35 hours per week.[65] They are staffed by a workforce that, under 2012 proposals, will involve 50 per cent of staff having a graduate teacher/pedagogue qualification.[66]

Kindergartens are not free but they are heavily subsidised, and parents' fees have been capped since 2003 at NOK 2330 (£230) per month. There is very little demand for any other services and a controversial cash-for-care benefit introduced in the 1990s has been virtually discontinued, following a massive decline in take-up.[67] From having very low levels of school-age childcare and part-time schooling until 1997, SFO has also developed as a major area of provision.

Scotland's ECEC is now not only less than two-thirds that of Norway but is also predominantly part time and provided through a variety of services and informal care, with grandparents continuing to play a major role and a 'sizeable minority' using multiple arrangements.[68] Even following the extension in the 'early learning and childcare entitlement' hours to 600 hours a year, Scotland's children will be attending for approximately half the time Norwegian children on average attend. And while in Scotland these hours are free, the additional hours of care required by parents in paid employment are high, with net childcare costs (after benefits) estimated by the OECD as making up 27 per cent of family income, compared with 11 per cent in Norway.[69]

Unlike the consideration given to school staffing in Norway when the school starting age was lowered, workforce reviews of schools and pre-schools in Scotland have remained separate. This may partly be a result of a UK-wide framework for developing competency-based qualifications set up just prior to the Scottish Parliament, which reinforced the separation of vocational from professional qualifications.[70] But it also marks a continuing divide between schools and the childcare components of ECEC.

While school-age childcare centres developed earlier in Scotland, they now offer places for far fewer children than in Norway and less than they did over five years ago, and an increase in child-minding has not filled the gap left by the loss of centres.[71] Maternal employment in Scotland has increased significantly and is now higher than in England. However, it remains lower than in Norway, where most women also work full time (see Table 12.1).

Why has Norway achieved so much more over such a short period? Funding itself does not seem to be the issue but rather the way it has been used. In 2007, the UK had the third-highest expenditure (after Denmark and Norway) on childcare and pre-primary education in the OECD, representing 1.1 per cent of GDP.[72] Local authorities have played a key role in Norway, in partnership with government, which set targets and provided ring-fenced funding to support the expansion until 2011, when block grants, based on potential demand, have replaced ring-fenced funding.[73] It may well have been easier for a fully independent country, with 'all the levers', to take the necessary decisions, and, in particular, invest in the supply of rather than demand for services, as the Scottish Government has indicated it would like to do.[74] The mixture of funding has made it more expensive and more difficult to shape the system, and weakened local authority leadership.

The development of the system was also hindered by a lack of clarity over responsibilities in the newly devolved context, and failure at a UK level to take account of the different histories and institutional frameworks in what were known as the devolved 'territories'. Within Scotland, one impediment may have come from Scotland's 'inheritance'. Multiple stakeholders and separate trade unions made more difficult the creation of an integrated system, achieved by Norway in 1975. It may also not have been helped by the nature of Scotland's education policy community for at least some of this period, described for much of the twentieth century as tending to be 'male, from small-town rural backgrounds, and to have teaching careers that took them to schools that, through longevity, had acquired the status of national icons'.[75] Also significant was a discourse shared across the UK and indeed to a large extent the Anglophone world, which encourages a vocabulary of 'targeting' 'vulnerable two-year-olds' and 'early intervention' as a cure for a wide range of social and economic ills. This may be said to run through UK early years policy as strongly as the 'red thread' through Norway's democratically inspired school system.

BEYOND THE SCHOOL GATES: HOW DO SCHOOLS RELATE TO THEIR COMMUNITIES?

We have considered the challenges posed to the education systems by socio-demographic changes and the rights of women and children. We look now at how both systems conceptualise the relationship of schools to communities within the curriculum.

In 1939, on the eve of war, the Norwegian Government issued a curriculum (N39) for its *folkeskole*. Its emphasis, reflecting the influence of educational reformers such as Dewey and Piaget, was on active learning and a cross-curricular approach intended to connect school work with real life, using authentic teaching resources, including nature, as a teaching area, and engagement with pupils as a means of ensuring the learning content of activities is adapted to the individual pupil.[76]

The N39 curriculum was never fully implemented in Norway, partly because of the war, but its thinking contributed to later curriculum frameworks and an approach which was to lay the basis for high levels of school engagement with community.

After 1945, the education system had become increasingly centralised, and in 1969, when compulsory schooling was extended from seven to nine years, the system was reviewed. A 1972 survey of ninth-grade pupils found that many felt schools were preparing them for academic study in upper secondary school or life in urban areas rather than in areas such as fishing and farming.[77] This led to reform of the Norwegian national curriculum in 1974 and, subsequently, 1984 and 1997, and required all schools to develop their own local version of the national curriculum: a local curriculum in which schools should develop and describe their use of the local environment as a learning arena and define their role in relationship to the local community. The 1997 curriculum, which formed part of wider changes in the whole education system, went further in a number of ways, requiring all schools for children up to the age of sixteen to implement thematic cross-curricular approaches and project work, making use of local issues and local learning resources. For years one to four at primary school level, a minimum of 60 per cent of work had to be done through cross-curricular themes, reducing to 40 per cent at upper-primary level and 20 per cent at lower-secondary level.[78] Reform 97 included a Sami curriculum (L97S) in the North Sami language and including as subject areas Sami traditions and culture as well as Sami as a mother tongue and second language.[79]

Decentralisation in education paralleled political devolution, devolving decision-making down to the lowest efficient organisational level and financial responsibility to the local authorities. Norwegian local authorities are small and have clearly defined local identities. They have been given considerable freedom to develop services in ways which have supported implementation of educational reforms, enabling, for example, extensive use of the arts and promoting environmental awareness. Links with the community are very evident from the kindergartens to lower and upper secondary schools; from farms, which form part of the ECEC system, or are used by schools for various subjects, to local employers who take responsibility for helping to deliver the curriculum to older children as they gain work experience. Nearly all children (97.5 per cent) attend their local school and, in rural areas, their local kindergarten. Many children also take part in activities organised and run by the local Culture School, a municipal service providing education in music, drama and the arts for children and adults.

The 1997 curriculum was replaced in 2006 and cross-curricular requirements were removed. This reflected in some measure concerns raised by Norway's positioning in the Programme for International Student Assessment (PISA) league tables and an increasing focus on measurable outcomes.[80] Over recent years, the growth of quality assurance has led to more national control, including some national testing and a web portal showing school results.[81] But the concept of 'giving responsibility to the one who knows where the shoe pinches' still remains, underpinning the system and making possible a variety of flexible arrangements between schools and communities.

In Norway, the growth of kindergartens has accompanied the greater emphasis on a local curriculum over the last few decades, and partnership with communities in delivering active, place-based learning is probably most evident now in what has become the first stage of the education system.[82]

Since the reestablishment of the Scottish Parliament in 1999, Scotland has had more parliamentary time and freedom to develop its own education system, and this is now visible in a number of aspects of educational policy. It has taken a different approach to the curriculum. Initiated in 2004, Curriculum for Excellence, covering ages three to eighteen, is less reliant on exams. It is intended to 'declutter' the curriculum, particularly in primary, with more emphasis on active learning and space for a wider range of activities, including sport and the arts, sustainable development and enterprise, and, as in the Norwegian 1997 curriculum, more cross-subject activity. Guidance documents which have subsequently been produced cover outdoor learning, interdisciplinary and community learning, and development and school community partnerships, encouraging schools to work with people in the community. The Scottish Parliament, and the referendum on independence, have focused more attention on issues around local and national identity in Scotland. Cultural strategies have led to recognition, particularly in the Scottish islands, of the contribution of cultural activities to 'creating and sustaining socially and economically healthy communities'.[83] Local authorities were given greater freedom to strengthen relationships between schools and communities through the 2007 Concordat between the new SNP government and local government. Access issues for pre-school children and subsequently parental choice of schools can mean that this is less straightforward than in most parts of Norway. In the Highlands and Islands, schools are taking part in a programme, Crofting Connections, intended to develop awareness of their crofting heritage, and this is just one example of how the community can contribute to cross-curricular activity. A growing number of community-owned estates and woodlands are forging links with their local schools and more use is being made of local crofts and crafts, arts and businesses in contributing to the experiences young people can gain during the latter years of their schooling. In these respects, Scotland's curriculum framework is making possible developments that are familiar in Norway, although both countries share the same pressures from global expectations of educational standards. Greater use of the outdoors and the arts – sometimes combined – has opened up many opportunities for links between kindergarten, schools and their local communities, rooting children in their local environments, and communities. In Norway, these have been systematic approaches for some time. Currently they are being developed by the local culture schools and nationally through the Cultural Rucksack, which brings arts and artists to schools and local kindergartens, and most recently through the national project, the Natural Rucksack, which focuses on the use of the outdoors to promote health and support the teaching of science and sports.

FINAL THOUGHTS

Our comparison of the development of these two educational systems suggests that national autonomy can make a difference. Norway, as part of Denmark, only achieved its first university four centuries after Scotland, as an independent country, had founded its own universities. During this period, Norwegian school education initially developed as in Scotland, through their respective churches, involving in Norway a shared Lutheran Church with Denmark and the use of Danish within the schools. The nature of the union of Scotland and England, subsequently becoming the UK, has been different and latterly has restored to Scotland its own Parliament. However, it does raise the question over the extent to which such partnerships can benefit or constrain developments, or both of these.

While not explored in any detail in this chapter, Norwegian educational reformers drew on the ideas of Danish and Swedish reformers, as well as those elsewhere.[84] Norwegian folk high schools originated in Denmark, and while Norway's development of its education system has been distinctive, it has also drawn on the discourse within those countries and, in many respects, a shared social welfare 'Nordic' model (see also Chapter 10). It has developed and retained 'like a red thread', since the mid-nineteenth century, an educational system which now embodies principles of universalism and equity, from services for very young children through to higher education. It has adapted the system to new understandings of democracy and to respond to socio-economic developments and to changes in family roles and life. These adjustments have taken time in a country in which democratic discussion is extensive and the principle of devolving decision-making through local authorities and community institutions to individuals is now well embedded. Norway's sense of itself does not only rest in its national heritage but also in the strong sense of identity which exists within each local authority. Defining this in ways which are welcoming of new Norwegians is one of the challenges Norway currently confronts.

Union with England brought relatively few initial changes in Scotland's education system, but since the nineteenth century the impact of union can be seen. The depiction of Scotland's education system as meritocratic and democratic is now seen by some as to some extent mythologised, but, nevertheless, a potent force in enabling Scotland to retain and develop its own separate system, unimpeded by the UK Government. Paterson quotes a senior civil servant in the Scottish Education Department in the late 1960s as saying: 'I cannot think offhand of any important matter on which Scotland has been prevented . . . from taking a decision that ministers wanted to take'.[85] But any serious examination of the development of the system reveals that the major legislative decisions for much of this period from 1872 onwards, until at least 1999, were all taken at a UK level. They might, or might not, have been different or differently timed if taken within Scotland but would almost certainly not have included, for example, the 1981 legislation introducing parental choice in schools, a principle which stands in contrast to the continuing emphasis within the Norwegian *enhetsskole* concept that children in a designated geographical area should receive their education in a common public school. Scottish education at this time was less separate than we like to think.

Devolution and the Scottish Parliament now enable more decisions to be taken in Scotland. And there are many examples of the difference that this has made, including the right given to all children within the first new education legislation enacted by the new Parliament, the Standards in Scotland's Schools Act 2000, to school education 'directed towards the development of their personalities, talents, and mental and physical abilities', a provision which has underpinned improvements in particular for children with additional learning requirements.

However, the current division of responsibilities remains problematic in a number of areas of educational policy. We explored this in some detail in the development of ECEC services, and touched on the difficulties posed to workforce reform through vocational qualifications forming part of a UK framework while professional qualifications are devolved. In the other areas examined, national status may be less significant than the historical development and experiences of Norwegian local government democracy, visible in the development of the *enhetsskole* concept and writ large in the democratic provisions within school governance and in the local curriculum within schools.

The concept of active place-based learning has been particularly important in protecting Norway's rural areas, and is an aspect of educational policy equally relevant to Scotland.[86] Indeed, our review has shown that there are a number of such areas that might usefully form the basis for collaborative learning and practice programmes, from place-based learning to democracy within schools. Like Norway with its former partners, Scotland has been able to share ideas across the UK and beyond, into the wider Anglophone world. But it may be that the growing divergence in educational principles and policy between Scotland and England means that Scotland should look more often to its northern than southern neighbour in developing these aspects of its system over the coming century.

Notes

1. Ness, 1989: 17–18.
2. Myhre, 1992: 50.
3. Myhre, 1992: 41.
4. St Andrews in 1412, Glasgow in 1451 and King's College Aberdeen in 1495. Dickinson, 1961: 6.
5. Devine, 1999: 389, 68.
6. University of St Andrews, 2007–14.

7. Devine, 1999: 397, 394.
8. Paterson, 2003.
9. Davie, 1961: 76
10. Ibid.: 76.
11. Paterson, 1994: 68.
12. Napier, 1884 (digitalised 2007): 80–1.
13. Napier 1884 (digitalised 2007): para.19664.
14. Telhaug, 1994.
15. 1998 Education Act, amended 2008.
16. Stocks, 2002: 27–8.
17. Paterson, 2003: 137.
18. McPherson and Raab, 1988: 394.
19. Paterson, 2003: 137–8.
20. Scottish Government, March 2010.
21. Allen et al., 2014: 5.
22. *The Herald*, 2014.
23. Westergård, 2012: 163.
24. Utdanningsdirektoratet, 2006: 3.
25. 2005 Kindergarten Act, Section 3.
26. 1998 Education Act, Section 11–2.
27. Utdanningsdirektoratet, 2006.
28. Furre et al., 2006: 41.
29. Bradshaw et al., 2012.
30. Scottish Government, 2004.
31. Maitles and Deuchar, 2006.
32. Hulme et al., 2006: 141.
33. HMIE, 2007: 6; Learning Teaching Scotland, 2010: 20, 23.
34. Fjeldstad et al., 2010.
35. Hulme et al., 2011: 141.
36. Education Act, Section 3–1.
37. Knutas, 2013.
38. Cohen et al., 2004: 95.
39. Gordon, 1991: 166.
40. Braybon and Summerfield, 1987: 19–20.
41. Cohen, 2004: 94–5.
42. Balke, 1995: 59.
43. Ibid., 243.
44. Wilhjelm, 2013.
45. Cohen, 1988: 31.
46. Bø, 1993: 399.
47. Balke, 1979: 138.
48. Cohen and Rønning, 2014.
49. Moafi and Bjørkli, 2011: 56.
50. Ibid., 56.
51. Scheistrøen, 2013.
52. Moafi and Bjørkli, 2010: 10.

53. Cohen, 2004: 96.
54. Scottish Office, 1998: 3.
55. Cohen, 2013: 8.
56. Ibid., 8.
57. Cohen, 2013: 11.
58. Scottish Government, 2014b: 78,186.
59. Audain, 2014.
60. Cohen, 1990: 28.
61. Scottish Government, 2007.
62. Care Inspectorate, 2013.
63. Scottish Government, 2002: Tables 6 and 7.
64. SOSCN, 2013: 40.
65. Ellingsæter, 2014: 56–7.
66. Ibid., 67.
67. Ellingsæter, 2014: 54–61.
68. Scottish Government, 2009.
69. Naumann, 2013: 18, 83.
70. Cohen, 2013: 9.
71. SOSCN, 2013.
72. Naumann, 2013: 18.
73. Ellingsæter, 2014: 62.
74. Scottish Government, 2014b: 194.
75. Paterson, 1994: 125.
76. Rønning, 2010: 49–51.
77. Cohen and Milne, 2007: 27.
78. Ibid., 27.
79. Hirvonen and Keskitalo, 2004: 202–3.
80. Karseth and Engelsen, 2013: 44–5.
81. Rønning, 2010: 81.
82. Cohen and Rønning, 2014.
83. Cohen and Rønning, 2014: 117.
84. Rønning, 2010.
85. Patterson, 1994: 124–5.
86. Cohen et al. (forthcoming, 2016).

CHAPTER 13

Norway and the United Kingdom/Scotland after the Second World War

Tore T. Petersen

NORWAY–BRITAIN RELATIONS AFTER THE SECOND WORLD WAR

In the autumn of 1956, the Norwegian Prime Minister, Einar Gerhardsen, and his wife Werna were invited to the United Kingdom for an official visit. The invitation was a direct consequence of the Gerhardsens having paid a State visit to the Soviet Union the year before. British sources reported that the Norwegian premier had been much taken in by the Soviet system, hence the invitation to London to counteract these impressions and influences and to strengthen Norway's adherence to the Atlantic alliance. The Norwegian premier had strongly indicated that he saw himself as a kind of bridge-builder between the East and the West. Gerhardsen belonged to the Norwegian Labour Party, Arbeiderpartiet, which had excellent relations with its British counterpart Labour. But Labour had been out of power since 1951. The Conservative government in Britain wanted to strengthen and maintain good relations with Norway, also to show that the Tories had no intention of dismantling the British welfare state, but rather to maintain and strengthen it. The planners in London took great care to showcase for Gerhardsen different aspects of the successful British welfare state. Interestingly, apart from these more general considerations, the absence of genuine Anglo–Norwegian relations is striking. The interlocutors simply did not have much in common or much to talk about.[1] But this is not only the case for 1956, for the whole period under consideration here there was little in terms of real-life alliance politics and relations, despite much official rhetoric to the contrary.

It was standard operating procedure in Whitehall that prior to State visits, the Foreign Office mandarins provided background material and briefing papers for the ministers. This material routinely consisted of a summary of the most important bilateral relations between the United Kingdom and the country of origin for the visiting head of state, a discussion and analysis of the state of affairs, and suggestions for the politicians on how to handle the issues. Going through the material in the National Archives in Kew, it is quite astonishing that there are hardly any Anglo–Norwegian issues that should warrant high-level political discussions. Having said that, there might be some obscure files that have avoided my attention, but comparing the way the material is organised on Norway in the National Archives, which is quite similar to how material from other countries is organised, there are no indications that the Norway material is filed any differently. And after many research trips to the National Archives, with my first in 1987, I feel reasonably confident that my conclusions are correct. Furthermore, the National Archives is very well organised and catalogued, making anything pertaining to Norway easily available. Unfortunately, the cache for Anglo–Norwegian relations is exceedingly limited.[2]

Research in the archive of the Norwegian foreign ministry also had very limited success, and when I inquired of the custodian, Jacob Sverdrup, about the files of Norwegian Foreign Minister Halvard Lange he confirmed the impression that there were no particular issues of any substance between Norway and the United Kingdom in 1956. There was therefore little of importance that Gerhardsen and the British Prime Minister, Anthony Eden, could discuss. The visit was, then, largely symbolic. Even the looming Suez crisis caused no concern among the Norwegians. According to Sverdrup, there is no reference to the Suez crisis in Lange's papers. This is also indirectly confirmed by Einar Gerhardsen in his memoirs: 'Before noon on October 29, I had talks with prime minister Anthony Eden and foreign minister Selwyn Lloyd. Although the conversation was specifically directed towards Anglo–Norwegian relations, we were mainly concerned about the international situation.' While Gerhardsen is a far better source for his political attitudes, and much less reliable on actual events, the Norwegian Prime Minister here confirms the absence of important Anglo–Norwegian relations. It is a reasonable assumption if the talks had covered topics of importance that Gerhardsen would at the very least have alluded to them, but here the Norwegian premier's account confirms the impression from the archives.[3] When given access to the Norwegian files, the foreign ministry warned me that the material on Gerhardsen's London visit was sparse with almost no political content, the reason being that the visit was broken off because of the Suez crisis. There are no memorandum of conversations from the visit or minutes from political conversations.[4]

Still, there was one episode that loomed large in Anglo-Norwegians relation in the autumn of 1956. We let Prime Minister Einar Gerhardsen give his version first:

A traditional audience with the Queen would be of limited interest if not for a special reason. Some Norwegian newspapers made a fuss over the fact that Werna – in response to a question – explained that she refused to courtesy for the Queen. But of the many heads of state she had met, she had always behaved properly, and I do not believe anyone had reason to complain at her behavior. She kneeled but did not courtesy. She had no difficulty behaving respectfully towards people in a position to require it. But it was not natural for her to kneel and therefore she abstained from doing it. We had a pleasant conversation with the Queen, who I did not think registered the 'crime' against her Majesty.[5]

But what was the fuss all about? On 11 October 1956, the newspaper *Verdens Gang* interviewed Werna, who explained it was against her nature to courtesy. The only exception she made was for the Norwegian King Håkon, whom Werna held in high regard. But Queen Elisabeth was evidently not for Werna in the same category. The queen according to Werna was a sweet and natural young lady and well liked by the Norwegian premier's wife.[6] But the British ambassador, J. Scarlett, was also paying attention and reported to the Foreign Office:

You will no doubt bring this piece of tactlessness to the notice of Buckingham Palace. I do not for one moment suppose it to be ill-meant, but it will surely get publicity at home. I expect to see Andersen tomorrow to discuss the programme and unless you stop me I shall tell him as a friend, that this advance publicity is most embarrassing.

The gap between the upper-class monarchical Great Britain and the Arbeiderpartiet (Labour)-dominated Norway was evidently quite wide. The Arbeiderpartiet had a majority in the Norwegian Parliament in the period 1945–61, and with the exception of three weeks in 1963 was in government until 1965. These were the days of rationing and a tightly controlled economy in order to rebuild Norway after the ravages of war. Luxury was, if not banned, frowned upon in this period. Vacationing in Italy, which most Norwegians could not afford to do, even then Gerhardsen demonstrated his common touch, camping in an old-fashioned pyramid- shaped canvas tent, much to the amusement of the mandarins in the Foreign Office. Scarlett had earlier reported home on Gerhardsen: 'He is a man of extreme austerity and I have never yet met him on other than the most formal occasions. Anything more than the minimum wining and dining would I feel sure be an embarrassment to both of them.' Pencilled on the telegram was the following missive from someone in the Foreign Office: 'Mrs Gerhardsen is a strong, not to say bigoted, Social Democrat, and no doubt thinks she is asserting her principles this way.'[7] Eden, too, liked the Mediterranean, but he planned to be going in a style slightly different from the Gerhardsens. On this, the prime minister noted, just prior to Egyptian dictator Gamal Abdul Nasser nationalising the Suez Canal Company:

When the July days came our thoughts turned to our holiday plans. The year before they had not worked out, but this time my wife and I had firm hopes of three weeks' rest in August. We both longed above all things for hot sunshine and seas in which to bathe. The Governor of Malta, Sir Robert Laycock, had most kindly found for us one of the loveliest villas in the island, by the sea.[8]

Small by today's standards, but enough to shake Werna, a veritable press storm broke loose, mostly from the conservative press, while the Norwegian Labour Party's papers simply ignored the issue. Sarcastic comments followed that Werna refused to courtesy because she considered herself Norway's sovereign, being married to Einar – what she wanted, he did.[9] An editorial in the Christian daily *Vårt Land* was strongly critical, urging Werna to gain sufficient flexibility of her back to show the proper respect for the British Queen. Werna should understand that when Queen Elizabeth granted an audience, it was not because she was a sweet and natural young lady. If unwilling to courtesy, Werna better stay home.[10] The op-ed pieces in the conservative press were filled with critical comments both from journalists and the general public, augmented by several drawings making fun of Werna. The negative press reactions worried the Gerhardsens sufficiently to ask for a meeting with Scarlett, apologising for the situation. Scarlett reported: 'Mrs G. had been caught off guard. Mrs. G. added that of course she would conform to British court etiquette and she hoped that I would reassure her future hosts on that score.' She also felt the need to apologise publicly to the readers of *Verdens Gang*, and assured the readership that she would behave properly.[11] Scarlett summed up the affair this way: 'Local Press comments have been pretty cruel and the average Norwegian is frankly infuriated.' Scarlett noted with satisfaction that nobody came to Werna's defence:

> If then by any outside chance, which I personally discount from the start, her indiscretion was a piece of kite-flying, then those concerned have shown quite clearly how strongly respect for royalty is felt in this country. [...] *ARBEIDERBLADET*, the government newspaper has avoided all mention of the subject, which suggests that the party are no whit less embarrassed than the general public. Werna was asking for trouble. She has had it to no mean tune. And how clear it is from all this rough stuff that Norwegians despise women with political ambitions.[12]

It says something of the unimportance of Anglo–Norwegian relations when the British ambassador pays so much attention to a relatively minor matter. Scarlett is milking the episode for all it is worth, and finally he has the attention of his superiors in the Foreign Office. Otherwise, the British ambassador to Norway must have been seriously under-employed to pay so much attention to a rather trivial matter. Werna would be visiting as the spouse of the Norwegian Prime Minister, she herself did not have a sufficiently prominent position in Norway to have justified an invitation for a State visit to Britain. After having expressed her regrets to the Norwegian public and British Government, Werna grew tired of the entire business and wanted to avoid going on the State visit to the United Kingdom. She was persuaded to go after having consulted the Norwegian ambassador to London, the ambassador, Prebensen, advising her to come as long as she courtesied properly at the court.[13]

Two more different characters than Anthony Eden and Einar Gerhardsen would be difficult to find or imagine. About the only thing they had in common was that they were born in the same year, 1897, and married much younger wives, albeit this was for Eden the second time around, underscoring the difference, and that there was a slight difference in social background between Clarissa Eden, Winston Churchill's niece, and Werna. But in a strange way they both epitomised the British and Norwegian experience. Eden fought in the First World War, Einar did not, rather in the inter-war years serving time for resisting the draft. Eden's commanding officer wrote of the future prime minister: 'A young but capable and energetic Brigade Major. Cool and resourceful in battle and possessed of a staying power his appearance doesn't suggest.' Eden is furthermore described as 'delicate'.[14] But while Einar ended up a draft-resister, not having seen actual fighting, and experiencing the Second World War from the inside of Sachenhausen concentration camp, Anthony Eden was Foreign Secretary during the war. Both men were accomplished politicians in their own right, and, as we have seen, Eden was no pushover, but Einar was by far the toughest. Having clawed himself up to the top in the fiercely rough politics of the Norwegian Labour Party, it was said about Gerhardsen that he could shoot when somebody had to be killed. Close associate and later rival, Håkon Lie, described Gerhardsen thus: 'Einar Gerhardsen was not only one of us. He had also an outstanding ability to unite the party.' This he combined with a strong will to have power.[15] Few, if any, politicians have dominated Norwegian politics as Einar Gerhardsen did in the period 1945 to 1965. He was one of the chief architects of modern Norway, what historians have labelled the corporatist state, where the different elites cooperated and negotiated national policies. Gerhardsen and his associates succeeded in including Norwegian unions in this corporative framework, making major strikes phenomena that were few and far between in Norway. Eden and his successors did not succeed in including the unions in the British political scene to the same extent as in Norway, or at the very least not in a corporate framework. It would be very hard to imagine a Norwegian Arthur Scargill or a Norwegian equivalent of the British winter of discontent in 1979.

Even when resigning the premiership in 1951, Gerhardsen held a dominant position on the Norwegian political scene, and even more so when he resumed as premier in 1955. In semi-retirement after 1965 (he would not hold any government office), Einar Gerhardsen had considerable influence on his beloved Labour Party in particular and on the Norwegian political scene in general. Eden's position, even as Prime Minister, was considerably more precarious. When leaving office in favour of Anthony Eden in April 1955, Winston Churchill remarked: 'No two men have ever changed guard more smoothly.' But this was far from the truth; Churchill had hung on to the premiership as long as he possibly could. Eden had been designated Churchill's heir apparent as early as 1942. As Eden resignedly remarks in his memoirs: 'The long era as crown prince was established, a position not necessarily enviable in politics. Perhaps this experience helped to dampen my exhilaration when the time came to succeed.'[16] In contrast to Gerhardsen, Eden had to contest with fiercely ambitious rivals, most notably R. A. Butler and Harold Macmillan. Einar was down to earth, looking back to his roots and his former workmates, and his time as a common labourer. Eden was anything but, being of a highly strung and nervous temperament. This side of the Prime Minister was viciously summed up by one of his foremost rivals in the Conservative Party, R. A. Butler: 'Anthony's father was a mad baronet and his mother a very beautiful woman. That's Anthony – half mad baronet, half beautiful woman.'[17] Speaking about the leader of the Conservative Party in this way signifies a total lack of respect, and Butler's malicious tongue, of which Eden was not the only victim, was partly to blame for him not succeeding Eden as Prime Minister. But the other challenger, Harold Macmillan, did. Eden was forced to fall on the sword of his own creation – the failed Suez crisis. His closest associates, in tandem with the Americans, were stunningly disloyal.[18] On this, David Carlton explains:

> For though [US President Dwight D.] Eisenhower had probably delivered the coup de grace, the conduct of some of Eden's principal colleagues had been so disloyal as to leave him with little self-confidence to resist the President. It is difficult to be sure whether he resented most the conduct of Eisenhower, Butler, [Lord] Salisbury or Macmillan.[19]

The contrast with Einar Gerhardsen is quite astonishing, as after 1945 he probably never lived in fear of being backstabbed by any of his colleagues. On the contrary, Gerhardsen was quite ruthless against potential rivals in his own party, forcing Prime Minister Oscar Torp to retire in 1955 and conducting a devastating personal attack in public against the general secretary of the Labour Party, Håkon Lie, at the annual conference of the Norwegian Labour Party in 1967. There are no indications that Torp, Lie or others paid Gerhardsen back with the same coin.[20]

But while there was nothing much to be concerned about in Anglo–Norwegian relations, great power politics intruded during the Gerhardsens' visit. On the same evening, Anthony Eden and the British Cabinet gave a State dinner for their Norwegian guest of honour, British planes bombed Egyptian airfields (this was in the middle of the Suez crisis). Gerhardsen strongly implies in his memoirs that he did not believe Eden's assurances ('I swear you') that Britain was not in cohoots with Israel when the Jewish nation attacked Egypt.[21] Werna was furious, and the day after the State dinner she joined in the demonstrations against Eden. Luckily for Werna, neither British nor Norwegian officials were cognisant of this break in diplomatic protocol; State visitors do not usually join demonstrations against their hosts. In this case, Werna's judgement was not the best, but Gerhardsen does not criticise his wife in the aftermath.[22]

The whole courtesy episode is of little historical interest except, perhaps, for its comical aspects. More important, when this minor episode becomes the most serious aspect of Anglo–Norwegian relations in 1956 it attests to how little the two powers seriously interacted. In addition, the episode clearly demonstrates the connection between stagecraft and statecraft in international diplomacy. At the time of the Suez crisis, Norway had one of the largest merchant marines in the world. The future management and potential closure of the Suez Canal was thus a major Norwegian national interest. After Britain, Norwegian shipowners were the largest users of the canal. Despite the future of the Suez Canal being a major Norwegian concern, there is no hint in the declassified record or the literature that these concerns played any role whatsoever in the British decision-making process.[23] Gerhardsen's visit to the UK is not mentioned in Eden's memoirs, nor is it a concern of Eden's 'official' biographer.[24] Apart from the much-repeated mantra about Great Britain being Norway's closest ally – if Norway had to choose sides in both World Wars it would be with Britain – it is largely an empty slogan. In reality, it is the absence of genuine Anglo-Norwegian relations for the entire period from 1918 to the mid-1960s that is striking. Nowhere in the literature have I found any genuine Anglo–Norwegian relations beyond the official phrase-making. This is an image that is strikingly confirmed in the official histories of Norwegian foreign policy.[25] Britain ignoring Norway's key interests rings more than a little hollow when Eden indignantly describes in his memoirs the United States, in his view, disloyally and publicly undermining the British position in terms of its willingness to use force against Egypt's seizure of the Suez Canal:

> Yet here was the spokesman of the United States saying that each nation must decide for itself and expressing himself as unable to recall what the spokesman of a principal ally had said. Such cynicism towards allies destroys true partnership. It leaves only the choice of parting, or a master and vassal relationship in foreign policy.[26]

While Eden indignantly describes the United States as disregarding important British interests, the British themselves were, perhaps, just as ruthless towards lesser powers, not to mention the clients of the British Empire. Leaving the Aden federation (Southwest Arabia), Britain callously abandoned its allies and clients of long standing. As Clive Jones has observed:

> the Labour government of Harold Wilson, despite assurances given to the Federal potentates that Britain would honour its commitments to safeguard the transition to independence and beyond: for those rulers and their followers who had thrown in their lot with the British, their sense of betrayal was profound. As the old Arab adage had it, 'It is better to be the enemy of the British than their friend: if you are their friend they will sell you, whereas if at least you are their enemy they'll attempt to buy you.'[27]

This may seem crude and ruthless, but well under the dictum of British foreign policy of then foreign minister Henry Temple Palmerstone, who in a speech to Parliament on 1 March 1848 said: 'We have no eternal allies, and we have no perpetual enemies. Our interests are eternal and perpetual, and those interests it is our duty to follow.'[28]

Official rhetoric apart, how could it be otherwise? In the inter-war years, Great Britain was the only power with a global reach. In fact, it would maintain its global reach until its withdrawal from the base complexes east of Suez in 1971, which supplemented and complemented the American ability for force projection during the Cold War. Norway, of course, was anything but a great power, its only global reach being its ability of late to write cheques. While other countries willingly take Norwegian money, it is far from certain that it buys Norway much influence. Whatever the case presently, it is, however, outside the scope of this study. Eden's quote above is probably also an apt description of the state of Anglo–Norwegian affairs for the period under consideration, but now with Britain as the disrespectful ally. Both Norway and Great Britain seem to have little regard for each other; behind a veneer of rhetorical alliance politics, there is a blatant lack of respect.

Still, Paul Kennedy uses the British example to argue in *The Rise and Fall of the Great Powers* that all great powers will come to an end, much like the trajectory of Great Britain.[29] Peter Hennessy is solidly in the Kennedy school, while listing the impressive British military might at the end of the Second World War: a Royal Navy with 929 capital ships, 137 submarines, 6,485 patrol boats, landing crafts and auxiliary vessels, the Royal Air Force with 55,469 aircraft, and over a million personnel. Demobilisation saw draconian cuts in British military might, but the demands of Empire kept large numbers of British service personnel abroad. Hennessy argues that even in decline, 'Britain was a superpower in 1945, as it had been in the nineteenth century, for a single reason: its possession of a global empire.'[30] The British elite certainly had no wish or intention to dismantle the Empire, epitomised in Churchill's famous war-time quip that he had not 'become the King's First Minister to preside over the liquidation of the British Empire'.[31]

Evelyn Shuckburgh, Anthony Eden's private secretary, notes in his diaries: 'The British position in the Middle East in the early 1950s is unrecognizable in terms of today. We were the dominant power throughout the area.' Britain had more than 80,000 soldiers stationed along the Suez Canal in a massive base complex. The Mediterranean as well as the Persian Gulf were for practical purposes British lakes, as Britain controlled Gibraltar and had bases on Malta and Cyprus, as well as a huge naval base in Aden. Britain paid and commanded the Arab Legion in Jordan, and controlled the foreign and defence policies of the Persian Gulf sheikdoms from Kuwait to Aden. Compounding this, the Iranian oil concession was an exclusive British interest. While overstretched, there was no clamour among British elites for withdrawal. Britain was the dominant power in the Middle East and determined to remain so.[32] With 75 per cent of British imported oil going through the Suez Canal, Egyptian dictator Gamal Abdul

Nasser's nationalisation of the Suez Canal Company was seen as a direct challenge to the British position in the Middle East. Winston Churchill, in retirement, confided with his physician Lord Moran:

> Moran: Nasser is not the kind of man to keep his job for long?
> Winston: Whoever he is, he's finished after this. We can't have that malicious swine sitting across our communications. [...]
> Moran: What will the Americans do?
> Winston: We don't need the Americans for this.[33]

The contrast to Norway was, of course, enormous. Having gained its independence from Sweden in 1905, the main goal of the young state was to secure the continued existence of an independent Norway. That meant a cautious foreign policy, or almost no foreign policy at all, to avoid provoking the greater powers. Underlying it all was the assumption in the early years, 1905–20, that beyond the veneer of neutrality and belief in international law, Norway's independence was guaranteed by Britain and secured by its fleet. Also because Britain in its own interest did not want a competing power to control Norway.[34] Typically, when Norway came into conflict with Great Britain over fishery boundaries in 1924–5, Norway was unable and unwilling to stand up for its rights. As Odd-Bjørn Fure laconically notes, there was no equality between a great naval power and a small coastal state. In the inter-war years, Norway had no empire of colonies and no wish to gain either apart from a hare-brained scheme to occupy eastern Greenland by Norwegian trappers, a claim to Norse polar imperialism that was shot down by the international court in The Hague.[35] Not only shot down, but Norway suffered a humiliating defeat – the international court found for Denmark on all issues.[36]

In 1897, when Einar and Anthony were born, Queen Victoria celebrated her diamond jubilee, the British Empire being at the peak of its powers. Since then, according to the Kennedy school, there has been nothing but a slow decline.[37] But Britain actually increased its influence by being late in choosing its alliance partners before the First World War. Europe had, since the Franco-Russian alliance of 1894, essentially been divided into two camps, Britain, by choosing the Russo-French alliance, became the determining factor in the Triple Entente winning the war. Britain before the First World War faced many real and potential challengers; the British economy was only the third-largest in the world after the United States and Germany. Furthermore, Britain had until its alliance with Russia in 1907 been engaged in a more than century-old competition with Russia for influence from Constantinople to the Far East. While officially ending the competition, I strongly suspect the powers were still covertly jockeying for position. Britain came out of the war strengthened, most of its competitors and rivals being either devastated by the war or having taken themselves out of the competition. The Soviet Union was internationally ostracised and embroiled in a civil war, Germany was defeated, the United States refused any binding political commitments towards Europe, while France hunkered down behind the Maginot Line. Great Britain was thus the only power with a global reach in the inter-war years, its power resting on the tripod of Empire, world-class navy and the world's largest overseas investment. One historian has aptly titled his book *The British Empire as a Superpower, 1919–1939*.[38] A further indication of strength was the ten-year rule. The War Cabinet instructed its different military services on 15 August 1919 to operate on the assumption 'that the British Empire will not be engaged in any great war during the next ten years, and that no Expeditionary Force is required for this purpose'. The ten-year rule was placed on a permanent basis in 1928 and was cancelled first in March 1932 after the Japanese attack on China.[39] Gordon Martel comments on the importance of the ten-year rule thus:

> For more than a decade after the armistice [1919], Great Britain did not need to stretch her resources to the utmost simply to survive as an independent state or a great power; the reality and the reputation of her power were sufficient to meet her strategic needs.[40]

How did Norway compare, let alone interact, with this colossus? The answer, of course, is that it did not compare, having neither the reality nor the reputation of power like Great Britain. Norway had just gained its independence from Sweden in 1905, and the first priority of any Norwegian government would be to secure its new-found freedom. Internationally, this made for a cautious foreign policy, and when interacting with Britain (interacting is probably too strong a word) the Norwegians usually did what the English told them to do.

THE NORWEGIAN AND SCOTTISH EXPERIENCE COMPARED

Comparing the Norwegian and Scottish experience after both world wars has been a little like comparing apples and oranges; the only meaningful way in my view has been to see the two entities through the eyes of the British Empire, if we at all can talk about meaningful Anglo–Norse relations for the period under consideration beyond the customary phrases like 'close allies', 'Norway's westwards orientation', and so on. But it is important not to confuse rhetoric with reality, for during the period under consideration here, Norway has been nothing but a client of the powerful British Empire. Scotland has largely followed Norway's (and Britain's) trajectory after the Second World War. Also, in Scotland one talks about the lost generation after the First World War, but the inter-war years were a period of economic crisis and stagnation in both Norway and Scotland.[41] Interestingly, while Scotland was largely in the economic doldrums, or more precisely suffered low or uneven economic growth, after the First World War, Norway experienced rapid and extensive economic growth (see also Chapters 1, 6 and 7). Norway presently has a GDP per capita more than twice the size of Scotland's, which is quite startling when they were about equal after the Second World War.[42] A reasonable inference may be that the Empire actually hampered economic growth at this point, while Norway's position as an independent country actually facilitated growth. Entering the realm of a more speculative analysis, Norway has largely been a land of political consensus, while Great Britain, particularly under Margaret Thatcher's premiership, was a land with a more confrontational political culture, changing the political landscape most notably in northern England and Scotland, where the Tories have been more or less wiped off the political map. Labour dominates in northern England and in Scotland, sharing the spoils and parliamentary seats with the Scottish National Party. I am well aware that the Liberal Democrat Party also plays an important role in Scottish politics, but in recent times the party had little chance of power before joining the Tories nationally to form a UK coalition government. In the period from 1980 to the advent of Tony Blair as Prime Minister, Labour was the dominant party in Scotland. The Tories therefore had little incentive to pay particular heed to Scotland because any chance of winning elections there seemed remote. Paradoxically, this has also been the case for Labour until recently, where there has been no need to pay special attention to Scotland's concerns, particularly at the expense of voters south of the border, since Labour had by and large received the Scottish vote anyway. The contrast to Norway is interesting, since all serious Norwegian parties at one time or another have formed a government, giving Norwegian politicians a great incentive to court voters in the entire country, not to write off parts of the electorate as in Great Britain.

Notes

1. The most important documents pertaining to Norway in The National Archives (TNA) in Kew; England for 1956 is in the Political Correspondence of the Foreign Office, in the following folders: 'Foreign Policy of Norway', FO 371/128755; 'Political Relations Norway–UK', FO 371/128788; and 'Visit of PM of Norway to UK', FO 3711222573-74 (hereafter cited as FO 371 with appropriate filing designations).
2. Ibid.
3. In the archive of the Norwegian Ministry of Foreign Affairs, I have gone through the following material: *om Statsministerens reise til England* [The Prime Minister's trip to the United Kingdom], *norsk-britiske politisk relasjoner* [Norwegian–British political relations], *Suez-krisen* [the Suez crisis], *fiskerigrensekommisjonen* [fisheries border commission], *skandinavisk-britisk økonomisk samarbeid* [Scandinavian–British economic cooperation]. The Gerhardsen quote: '*Om formiddagen 29. oktober var det samtaler med statsminister Anthony Eden og utenriksminister Selwyn Lloyd. Selv om disse samtalene kom innpå de særlige britisk-norske forhold, dreide de seg først og fremst om den internasjonale situasjonen,*' is in Gerhardsen, 1972: 244.
4. Letter from Norwegian Department of Foreign Affairs to author, 26 October 1990: '*Imidlertid må vi gjøre dem oppmerksom på at det overnevnte materialet er*

forholdsvis sparsomt og inneholder praktisk talt intet av politisk interesse. [...] Noen rapporter eller referater fra politiske samtaler foreligger derfor ikke.'

5. Gerhardsen, 1972: 251. *'Et tradisjonelt besøk hos dronningen hadde vært liten grunn til å omtale hvis det ikke hadde vært en spesiell årsak. Noen norske aviser hadde før vår avreise gjort et visst oppstyr av at Werna på et spørsmål hadde svart at hun ikke kom til å neie til gulvet for Dronningen. Nå falt det i hennes lodd å hilse på mange statsoverhoder. Hun gjorde det etter min mening både tekkelig og pent, og jeg tror ikke noen hadde grunn til å beklage hennes oppførsel. Hun neiet, men hun knelte ikke. Hun hadde ingen vanskelighet med å vise respekt for mennesker som blant annet i kraft av sin stilling hadde krav på det. Men det ville være unaturlig for henne å knele, derfor gjorde hun det heller ikke. Men vi hadde en hyggelig liten samtale med Dronningen, og jeg er ikke en gang sikker på at hun registrerte "majestetsforbrytelsen".'*

6. VG, 11 October 1956.

7. Scarlett to John Ward, 11 October 1956, with notes by Martin Charteris, FO 371/122574/N 1631/32.

8. Eden, 1960: 419.

9. *Dagbladet*, 12 October 1956.

10. *Vårt Land*, 12 October 1956.

11. For Norwegian press reactions, see VG, 12 October, *Aftenposten*, 13 October, *Nationen*, 15 October, *Adresseavisen*, 15 and 17 October; all 1956; Scarlett to Ward, 13 October 1956, FO 371/122574/N 1631/32; Werna to VG, 13 October 1956.

12. Scarlett to Ward, 17 October 1956, FO 371/122574/N 1631/32. Emphasis in the original.

13. Notat Jacobsen on conversation with ambassador Prebensen, 19 October 1956, DU/Oslo. 11.7./8, *'Statsministerns reise til UK'* (Prime Minister's visit to the UK). Prebenson on advice to Werna: *'Det viktigste for Ambassadøren var selve den realitet at fru Gerhardsen nå tydeligvis var villig til å neie, og han var beroliget ved å høre dette.'*

14. Rhodes James, 1987: 56.

15. Lie, 1975: 15. *'Einar Gerhardsen var ikke bare en av oss. Han hadde også en fenomenal evne til å forene oss.'*

16. Eden, 1960: 265, 266.

17. Cosgrave, 1981: 12.

18. On this, see Petersen, 2000.

19. Carlton, 1981: 453–4.

20. On this, see Lahlum, 2009.

21. Gerhardsen, 1972: 250.

22. Gerhardsen, 1972: 252.

23. Waage, 1998: 3, 2011–241 analyses Norwegian policy but does not mention Gerhardsen's London visit during the crisis. For a summary of the current state of research on Suez, see Smith, 2008.

24. Eden, 1960; Rhodes James, 1987.

25. Fure, 1996; Svedrup, 1996; Eriksen and Pharo, 1997.

26. Eden, 1960: 484.

27. Jones, 2004: 11.

28. Palmerston, speech to Parliament, 1 March 1848, Hansard, HC debates 01 March 1848, CC66–123.
29. Kennedy, 1987. For a trenchant critique of Kennedy, see Martel, 1991: 662–94. 'The dominant interpretation of British decline may be regarded as having reached its climax in the work of Kennedy because he turned the tale of Great Britain as a great power into a paradigm: what was true of the British and their power has been true of all states at all times.'
30. Hennessy, 1993: 91.
31. Charmley, 1995: 60.
32. Shuckburgh, 1986: 207–10.
33. Gilbert, 1988: 1201. It is interesting to note that while Winston Churchill was the most important spokesman for a union of the English-speaking peoples, that is, Anglo–American unity, a concept he even argued for before the Second World War. But as the Americans saw it, it was nothing but a ploy for the US to under-write and pay for the British Empire, and as we have seen during the Suez crisis, this the Americans were not willing to do. When the Americans were not willing to play their part, the most eager supporter of an Anglo–American condominium, Churchill, as seen from the quote above, was willing to go it alone.
34. Berg, 1995: 311.
35. Fure, 1996: 87; 'Greenland', 131.
36. Furre, 1991: 141.
37. In addition to Kennedy, see for instance Friedberg, 1988.
38. Clayton, 1986; McKercher, 1991: 751–83.
39. Reynolds, 1991: 121–2. Incidentally, in a book with this title and the scope of the narrative, Norway is barely mentioned, and when mentioned it is only in passing, confirming the main thesis of this essay; the absence of genuine Anglo–Norwegian relations.
40. Martel, 1991: 662–94.
41. See Harvie, 1992: 47; Lynch, 1992: 423.
42. See Chapter 1, Table 1.1.

CHAPTER 14

Conclusions

John Bryden, Lesley Riddoch and Ottar Brox

What do we finally draw from this comparison of Norway and Scotland over the past two hundred and more years? The evolution of public institutions and values, including what Adam Smith calls the 'just rule of law', seems to be a critical and fairly obvious factor: governments in democracies must ultimately be tested by the way that they manage a rather wide range of public and semi-public goods that they, *and only they*, can manage in the interests of the people that they are elected to represent. We are referring here in particular to the management of Polanyi's triad of natural resources, human beings and money, but also to education, health and the security of the individual. The goal of this management is deeply connected to the social contract that underpins the relations of people to the State and the notions of justice and equity that are linked to that. Only the State can guarantee such things, and the desired outcomes of freedom, equity and justice for all. The 'market' cannot do so, and nor can individuals acting alone.

Scotland's place within Britain and its globally dominant Empire during the first 150 years after 1800, and the hundred or so years before that, gave it a completely subordinate position in British politics within which, for most of the period, people were disenfranchised and the governments in Westminster neither secured people's interests in Scottish public goods, nor delivered freedom, equity and justice for all. The Scottish elite broadly went along with this because, being better motivated by greater poverty and better equipped by education, they were able to take considerable personal advantage from the British Empire, as capitalists, traders, military men, educators and administrators. But, as we see in Chapters 6, 7 and 8, the great wealth that was accumulated by the elite in this period did not filter down to the majority of workers who were less well paid, living in poor and unhealthy housing, and with lesser access to education when compared to their counterparts in Norway or indeed England. There was no government in Britain, and far less in Scotland, with the kind of representation given to Norwegians after

1814, while the *Ancien Régime* retained considerable direct and indirect political clout. Before the Attlee post-Second World War Labour government, little was done to alleviate the pressing problems of urban poverty, poor housing and poor health of the people who worked in Scotland's noteworthy industries, such as coal-mining, for the previous century and more.

As Chapter 3 makes clear, Norway's independence in 1814 was a defining moment in Norwegian political and social development. Such as it was, Norway's *Ancien Régime* had, for reasons advanced in Chapter 1, effectively died long before this point, and the moment to create a relatively liberal franchise for its time was seized by the peasants who gained political power, and, as Chapter 5 makes clear, who already had political experience in the various forms of local governance before that. As we see in Chapters 6 and 7, these same peasants became the industrial workers, there being no clearances, no enclosures and no creation of a large property-less working class. Norway's industrial history was very different from that of Scotland's, both for this reason and because industrial development was rooted in hydro-electricity, which was naturally distributed across the country, including the north and the west. Norway's industrialisation was decentralised and diffused, rather than concentrated in a few urban centres, as it was in Scotland. Norway developed the political and institutional conditions to ensure that the public goods of land, fish, hydro power and forests were used for the benefit of the majority of the people, rather than being captured by a small elite. That was reflected in the Concession Laws in the early 1900s, the Fresh Fish Acts of the 1930s, in the laws around the sale and transfer of farms, and in the stimulation of cooperatives for processing and marketing. So, when resources – initially minerals, fish, forests, hydro power and later oil – were exploited, the State both regulated them and was often financially and managerially involved.

Chapters 1 and 3 show clearly that the basic conditions of widespread ownership of land and property, a wide franchise and popular political participation, assured that the Norwegian (central and local) State was focused on the stewardship of resources, including, importantly, the natural resources and the people. As articulated in Chapters 11 and 12, this in due course also led to free primary, secondary and university education for all – a very democratic education system and one that also deals with the practice of political participation and the outdoor life from a very early age. Related egalitarianism led to a generous and fairly universal system of social protection, as we find in Chapters 3 and 10.

The strong states in Scandinavia have been criticised both internally and externally as being 'nanny states', especially by neo-liberals and right-wing parties that have been in the ascendency everywhere since the 1970s. This is further explored in Chapter 10. While there is some substance in this critique, especially in matters pertaining to minority groups and eugenics, it is in our view a serious diversion. In particular, the critique entirely misses Polanyi's point that *only* the State can – and has the moral duty to – protect the natural and human resources from over-exploitation and ultimately their degradation and despoliation. If history teaches us anything in the past two hundred years, it is that Polanyi was absolutely right on this point: the efforts of liberal economists in cahoots with the finance industry to financialise common property resources and to liberalise labour markets have led to environmental disasters and growing (and by now very serious) inequality. If it is not the primary duty of the State to do these things, then what, one might ask, is the State for at all?

The study of the economic, social and political development of Norway and Scotland since the 1700s, and in some cases earlier than that, highlights the importance of both historical institutional analysis and path dependency, both of which were used specifically in Chapter 3. If we claim that Scotland and Norway looked 'fairly similar' in the early Middle Ages, and we think there is sufficient evidence to support such a claim, the significant differences that we observe today can only be explained by the very different evolution of land and property ownership, the different agrarian and industrial revolutions of the period after about 1750, and the impact of these on political institutions. Independence from Denmark in 1814 was a defining moment in Norwegian history, and it made a large difference to Norway's development thereafter. Equally, Scotland's Union with England in 1707 was a defining moment for Scotland which gave it the opportunities presented by large resources and markets of the Empire, but which created a class of property-less urban industrial workers, and lost it the power to act at home in terms of the stewardship of natural resources and people, essential public goods and the distribution of wealth and income. In the words of Brandal and Bratburg (Chapter 3), Scotland became a country subject to 'top-down containment'.

Of course, all of Scotland's ills cannot be blamed on the Union. Religious conflicts, even if sometimes exaggerated, were a significant hindrance to working-class solidarity in the nineteenth century, as we see from Chapters 6 and 9. This did not happen in Norway. Equally significantly, the Scottish elite were as complicit in accepting the 'clearances' and 'enclosures' as necessary (if a necessary evil) in the eighteenth and nineteenth centuries (see Chapter 4), as, later, in accepting that the death of shipbuilding and heavy engineering had no future (Chapter 6). Scottish banks and bankers were also at the centre of the banking collapse in 2007 (see Chapter 8). And Scots were at the heart of the exploitation and governance of the British Empire that Sir Anthony Eden was so focused on preserving in the 1950s (see Chapter 13).

Equally, if we have shown that Norway's peaceful independence from Denmark in 1814 was a 'defining moment' which allowed it to develop its own political, social and economic institutions, and its own identity within the Scandinavian family of nations, the weight of the path dependencies and institutions established in Scotland since 1707 will make it a challenging task to do the same in Scotland, now or at some future point. It is not a simple matter of transferring existing policies. As is clear from many chapters in this book, the political conditions and institutions have to be 'right' and 'fit for purpose'. Among the many reforms of the political and institutional framework suggested by this comparison, we can include land reform,

reform of local government, abolition of NDPBs, reform of money and banking, tax reforms, and reform of the education system. No doubt there are others. Suffice to say that although a vote for independence in September 2014 would lead to many challenges of this kind, it would also open up many new and interesting opportunities, among which a restoration of the former alliance with its nearest continental country Norway, and through that with the Nordics, has obvious attractions.

Whatever the result of the independence referendum, it could be argued that Scotland is effectively entering a constitutional stage embarked upon by Norwegians two centuries back. It can also be argued that the level and intensity of political discussion in Scotland has reached a new high because of the referendum. As part of that process, the impact of Nordic thinking on the Scottish democratic process has been profound. 'Nordic Horizons' speaker Professor Jon Kvist from the University of South Denmark was a member of Nicola Sturgeon's Welfare Commission, Alex Salmond mentioned the Icelandic Constitutional Commission as a possible template for drawing up a written Constitution (but then opted for a draft to be written behind closed doors), and the Norwegian system of childcare was explicitly referenced by SNP leaders when they made transformational improvements in early years care their key post-independence pledge. Currently a new group is being formed to argue for an increase in participatory democracy, irrespective of the referendum outcome. According to Robin McAlpine of the Jimmy Reid Foundation, 'Practices of decision-making which include much wider and more representative groups of citizens are well-established and have been shown to be effective elsewhere. Whatever the outcome of the referendum, the participative process it has instigated has created fertile ground for a major transformation of how society collectively can make decisions on its own behalf.'

The cooperative, consensual decision-making envisaged in this and other groups arises from recent experience of the Norwegian model . . . or perhaps even from similar external conditions that allowed a consensual society to develop across the North Sea in the first place.

But there is also criticism of the SNP and suggestions that the party would prefer to collect 'low-hanging fruit' rather than reorder Scottish society. Michael Keating, Director of the Scottish Centre on Constitutional Change, said: 'Taxes would have to be higher, there's no doubt about it. This is a costly model. The people in Nordic countries are generally willing to pay those taxes, because they appreciate what they get back from it.' He told *The Times* newspaper: 'You have to make a choice and my criticism of the white paper is that we see a hybrid of those two models there, and they don't fit together very comfortably.'

At the time of writing, we do not know what the outcome of the referendum will be. However, we can be sure that Norway, and indeed the Nordics, will remain both an inspiration to those who cherish greater independence for Scotland, and that its example will remain a source of ideas. However, what is unrealistic is to expect an immediate transfer of Nordic policies to a reborn Scotland. Not only do the prior political conditions and institutions need to be first fostered, but what was possible for Norway in the past is not necessarily going to be possible, or even always desirable, in today's very different global, national and regional conditions. The issue is perhaps most clearly exemplified in Chapter 8, dealing with money and banking.

If Scottish people have recognised that Norway's history and institutions have some relevance for their future options, it has to be said that the reverse is not the case. Norwegian people do not look to Scotland as a role model today. Indeed, it is often said that Norway has a special relationship with England because of the fact that the king and his government functioned from London during the Second World War, and because so many Norwegians fought alongside the allies when their country was occupied by the Germans. Although this view must – at least – be modified by Petersen's account of post-war relations between Norway and Britain, it has recently been reinforced by the two gas pipelines constructed to bring Norwegian gas to England. Yet Norway is currently embarked on some risky policy changes, promoted by the present Populist and Conservative coalition, and showing the continuing influence of Margaret Thatcher. Although many of these ideas will no doubt fail to gain a majority in the *Storting*, the fact that they are there at all perhaps indicates that the political and bureaucratic elites in Norway need to take heed of what such policies have done to Scotland since the 1970s.

The Contributors

Arne Bugge Amundsen is Professor of Cultural History in the Faculty of Humanities at the University of Oslo and Head of Department of Cultural Studies and Oriental Languages. He specialises in the cultural history of Northern Europe 1500–1800, with a particular interest in church history. His other publications include Arne Bugge Amundsen and Henning Laugerud (eds): *Religiøs tro og praksis i den dansk-norske helstat fra reformasjonen til opplysnings-tid ca. 1500–1814* (2010); Arne Bugge Amundsen and Andreas Nyblom (eds): *National museums in a global world* (2008); (ed.): *Revival and Communication. Studies in the History of Scandinavian Revivals 1700–2000* (2007); (ed.): *Norges religionshistorie* (2005).

Eberhard 'Paddy' Bort is Academic Coordinator of the Institute of Governance and Director of the Parliamentary Programme at the Academy of Government, University of Edinburgh. Publications include (ed., with Neil Evans), *Networking Europe: Essays on Regionalism and Social Democracy* (2000); with Malcolm Anderson, *The Frontiers of the European Union* (2001); (ed.) *Commemorating Ireland: History, Politics, Culture,* (2004); (ed.): *View from Zollernlick: Regional Perspectives in Europe* (2013).

Nik. Brandal is a Historian at the University of Oslo whose research interests range from extremist political movements of post-war West Germany and the United States to the history and ideology of the Scandinavian labour movement. He is a co-author of *The Nordic Model of Social Democracy* (2013).

Øivind Bratberg is a Political Scientist at the University of Oslo who completed his PhD in 2011 on the topic of British party politics following devolution. He has edited one academic volume on comparative political systems in Norway and the UK and is a co-author of *The Nordic Model of Social Democracy* (2013).

Ottar Brox is a former Professor of Sociology at the University of Tromso and Senior Research Associate at NIBR (Norwegian Institute for Regional Research) in Oslo. He is a former Member of the Norwegian Parliament representing North Norway. He has published widely on Norwegian development issues over the long term, and a selection of his works was recently published as *The Political Economy of Rural Development: Development without Centralisation* (2006) (edited and introduced by John Bryden and Robert Storey).

John Bryden is a political economist, currently Research Professor at the Norwegian Institute for Bioeconomy Research in Oslo and Emeritus Professor of Human Geography at the University of Aberdeen in Scotland. He held the Chair of Human Geography at Aberdeen University between 1995 and 2004, when he was also co-Director of the Arkleton Institute for Rural Development Research. His other publications include *Tourism and Development* (1973); *Agrarian Change in the Scottish Highlands* (1976: with G. Houston); *Towards Sustainable Rural Communities* (1994); *A New Approach to Rural Development in Europe* (2004: ed. with Keith Hart); *Towards Sustainable Rural Regions in Europe* (2011: ed. with S. Efstratoglou, T. Ferenczi, T. Johnson, K. Knickel, K. Refsgaard and K. J. Thomson) . He has also written many book chapters and journal articles on economic development, Scottish dependency, agrarian change, land reform, regional and rural policies, academic freedom, and on innovation in rural regions. He is a Scot who has lived and worked in Norway since 2008. He is the lead and corresponding editor. See also http://www.johnbryden.com.

Bronwen Cohen is Honorary Professor in the School of Social and Political Science at the University of Edinburgh, with over thirty years' experience in social and educational policy and research at NGO, government and university levels, including twenty years as Chief Executive of Children in Scotland. Her current area of research is place-based learning in Scotland, Norway and the US, and her recent publications include 'Developing ECEC Services in Regionalised Administrations: Scotland's Post-devolution Experience', *International Journal of Early Childhood*, 2013, vol. 45, and (with Wenche Rønning), 'Place-based Learning in Early Years Services: Approaches and Examples from Norway and Scotland', in Miller and Cameron (eds), *International Perspectives in the Early Years* (2014).

Keith Hart is Centennial Professor of Economic Anthropology at the London School of Economics, Co-director of the Human Economy Programme, University of Pretoria and former Director of the African Studies Centre, University of Cambridge. He was Senior Research Fellow at the Arkleton Institute for Rural Development Research in Aberdeen University, and has taught at the universities of Manchester, Yale, Michigan, Chicago and West Indies, among others. He is author of *The Memory Bank: Money in an Unequal World* (2000) and editor of *The Human Economy* (2010: with Jean-Louis Laville and David Cattani).

Agnar Hegrenes is a retired Senior Agricultural Economist and Researcher, formerly with the Norwegian Agricultural Economics Research Institute in Oslo. He has written a number of book chapters and papers on Norwegian agricultural development and policy.

Mary Hilson is Professor of History at the School of Culture and Society, Aarhus University. Work for this book was completed while she was employed at the Department of Scandinavian Studies, University College London. She has previously been a visiting researcher at the universities of Jyväskylä, Helsinki and Uppsala. She is the author of *The Nordic Model: Scandinavia since 1945* (2008) and co-editor (with Silke Neunsinger and Iben Vyff) of *Under the North Star: Labour, Unions and Politics in the Nordic Countries c.1600 to 2000* (forthcoming 2017). Her current research is concerned with the history of the co-operative movement in the Nordic countries and beyond.

Andrew G. Newby is Senior Research Fellow of the Finnish Academy, and Associate Professor in European Area and Cultural Studies at the University of Helsinki. He is specialist in the history and society of northern Europe in the nineteenth and twentieth centuries, and principal investigator of the research project '"The Terrible Visitation", Famine in Finland and Ireland, c. 1845–1868: Transnational, Comparative and Long-Term Perspectives.' He is the author of *The Life and Times of Edward McHugh* (2004) and *Ireland, Radicalism and the Scottish Highlands* (2007); and co-editor of *Michael Davitt: New Perspectives* (2009), *Language, Space and Power: Urban Entanglements* (2012), *Famines in European Economic History* (forthcoming, 2014) and *Ireland and Finland 1800–1923: Comparisons and Transnational Perspectives* (forthcoming, 2015).

Erik Opsahl is Associate Professor in the Department of Historical Studies at Norwegian University of Science and Technology (NTNU), Trondheim. Opsahl is a medievalist with a particular interest in Late Medieval Scandinavian History. He is one of the authors in *Norske Historie 750–1537 I & II* (1999/2007, 2003) and *Norsk innvandringshistorie I, I kongenes tid* (2003), and has written several articles on subjects including aristocracy, State formation, political culture, military history and national identity.

Tore T. Petersen is Professor in the Department of History, NTNU, Trondheim. His dissertation was on '"The Special Relationship that Never Was": The United States, Britain and France, 1953–1959'. Publications include *Richard Nixon, Great Britain and the Anglo-American Alignment in the Persian Gulf and Arabian Peninsula: Making Allies out of Clients* (2009/2011); *The Decline of the Anglo-American Middle East, 1961–1969: A Willing Retreat* (2006); *The Middle East between the Great Powers: Anglo-American Conflict and Cooperation, 1952–7* (2000); *Challenging Retrenchment: The United States, Great Britain and the Middle East, 1950–1980* (2010); (with Clive Jones) *Israel's Clandestine Diplomacies* (2013).

Forthcoming publications include *Power, Restraint and Influence: Anglo-American Relations in the Persian Gulf and Arabian Peninsula, 1978–1985* (2014); and *The Military Conquest of the Prairie: Native American Resistance, Evasion and Survival, 1865–1890* (2014).

Karen Refsgaard is an Ecological Economist who studied at the University of Copenhagen and the University of Life Sciences at Ås, Norway. She is Deputy Director (Research) in NORDREGIO, Stockholm. Karen was co-author (with Ingrid Guldvik) of a chapter on Norwegian local governance for a recent book edited by B. S. Baviskar and A. Roy on local governance on five continents, published by ISR Delhi and the Government of India.

Lesley Riddoch is a journalist, author and broadcaster currently completing a PhD at Strathclyde University on the history of 'hutting' in Norway and Scotland. Lesley studied PPE at Oxford and was President of the Oxford Union. She is a popular journalist and broadcaster, her latest book being *Blossom* (2013), about what Scotland needs to do to make life better for all, and referring to Nordic examples. In 2010, Lesley set up Nordic Horizons, an informal group of Scottish professionals who want to raise the standard of knowledge and debate about life and policy in the Nordic nations. The group holds public meetings in Edinburgh to allow Nordic specialists to discuss how they do things with decision-makers, practitioners, MSPs, academics and the interested public in Scotland. See also: http://www.lesleyriddoch.co.uk.

Wenche Rønning is Vice Dean for research and Associate Professor in pedagogy at the University of Nordland and Senior Researcher at Nordland Research Institute, both located in Bodø, Norway. In her research, Rønning has focused on issues concerning school in society, teacher-thinking and classroom research, and initiatives such as outdoor education and entrepreneurship in education. In her PhD she focused on active learning in the Norwegian context, historically, but also how teachers today interpret and view active learning in the current educational context.

Michael Rosie is Senior Lecturer in Sociology in the School of Social and Political Science at the University of Edinburgh, Director of the Institute of Governance, and Associate Editor of *Scottish Affairs*. His key research has centred around national identities, nationalism and (ir)religion, with a particular focus on Scotland and its UK neighbours. He is author of *The Sectarian Myth in Scotland: Of Bitter Memory and Bigotry* (2004) and co-author of *Sectarianism in Scotland* (Edinburgh University Press, 2004), and serves on the Scottish Government's independent Advisory Group on Tackling Sectarianism. Recent publications have focused on the ethnic boundaries of Scottish identity, on immigration and politics in Scotland, and on liaison models of protest policing.

Bibliography

Agøy, N. I. (2012). 'Kontrollere eller bekjempe? Det norske Arbeiderparti og stat-skirkespørsmålet 1887–1940', in Birger Løvlie et al. (eds), *Kirke, kultur, politikk: Festskrift til professor dr. theol. Bernt T. Oftestad på 70-årsdagen*, Trondheim: Tapir, pp. 213–24.

Aidta, T. S., Duttab, J. and Loukoianovac, E. (2006). 'Democracy comes to Europe: Franchise extension and fiscal outcomes 1830–1938', *European Economic Review*, 50.

Allen, R., Burgess, S. and McKenna, L. (2014). *School performance and parental choice of school: secondary data analysis*, London: Department for Education/Centre for Understanding Behaviour Change.

Almås, R. (ed.) (2004a). *Norwegian Agricultural History*, Trondheim: Tapir Academic Press.

Almås, R. (2004b). 'From State-driven modernization to green liberalism 1920–2000', in Almås 2004a, pp. 294–357.

Åmark, K. (2005). *Hundra år av välfärdspolitik. Välfärdsstatens framväxt i Norge och Sverige*, Umeå: Boréa.

Åmark, K. (2006). 'Women's labour force participation in the Nordic countries during the twentieth century', in N. F. Christensen et al. (eds), *The Nordic Model of Welfare: A Historical Reappraisal*, Copenhagen: Museum Tusculanum Press, pp. 299–333.

Amundsen, A. B. (1986). 'Fromme Borgeres Vindskibelighed og Dyd'. Perspektiver på konfirmasjonens sosialhistorie frem mot siste århundreskifte', in Brynjar Haraldsø (ed.), *Konfirmasjonen i går og i dag. Festskrift til 250 års jubileet 13. januar 1986*, Oslo: Verbum Forlag, pp. 242–64.

Amundsen, A. B. (1987). 'Vekkelser og religiøse bevegelser i Smaalenene (Østfold) på 1800-tallet', in *Kattegat-Skagerrak projektet. Meddelelser nr. 15-1987*, Kristiansand: Kattegat-Skagerrak projektet, pp. 95–135.

Amundsen, A. B. (2007). 'Books, Letters and Communication. Hans Nielsen Hauge and the Haugean Movement in Norway, 1796–1840', in Arne Bugge Amundsen (ed.), *Revival and Communication. Studies in the History of Scandinavian Revivals 1700–2000* (Bibliotheca historico-ecclesiastica lundensis 49), Lund: Lunds Universitets Kyrkohistoriska Arkiv, pp. 45–64.

Amundsen, A. B. (2008). 'The Drammen Pietists: Messengers of a New Order in Norway in the 1740s?', in Fred van Lieburg and Daniel Lindmark (eds), *Pietism, Revivalism and Modernity, 1650–1850*, Newcastle upon Tyne: Cambridge Scholars Publishing, pp. 63–88.

Amundsen, A. B. (2010a). 'Churches and the Culture of Memory. A Study of Lutheran Church Interiors in Østfold, 1537–1700', *Arv. Nordic Yearbook of Folklore*, 66, pp. 117–42.

Amundsen, A. B. (2010b). 'Haugeanism between Liberalism and Traditionalism in Norway 1796–1840', in Jonathan Strom (ed.), *Pietism and Community in Europe and North America, 1650–1850*, Leiden and Boston: Brill, pp. 291–306.

Amundsen, A. B. (ed.) (2005). *Norges religionshistorie*, Oslo: Universitetsforlaget.

Amundsen, A. B. and Laugerud, H. (2001). *Norsk fritenkerhistorie 1500–1850*, Oslo: Humanist forlag.

Andersson, J. A. (1994). *Nordiskt samarbete: Aktörer, idéer och organisering 1919–1953*, Lund: Lunds Grafiska.

Andersson, J. (2003). *Mellan tillväxt och trygghet: Idéer om produktiv socialpolitik i social-demokratisk socialpolitisk ideologi under efterkrigstiden*, Uppsala: Uppsala University.

Andersson, J. and Hilson, M. (2009). 'Images of Sweden and the Nordic Countries', *Scandinavian Journal of History*, 34: 3, pp. 219–28.

Anon. 'Norway Shows the Way', *Yes!*, Winter/Spring 2014, p. 10.

Aresvik, O. (1954). 'Kornproduksjonens utvikling i Norge', in *Statens Kornforretning 1929–1954*. Oslo.

Armstrong, A. and Ebell, M. (2014). 'Monetary Unions and Fiscal Constraints', *National Institute Economic Review*, 228, May.

Arnason, J. P. and Wittrock, B. (eds) (2012). *Nordic Paths to Modernity*, New York: Berghahn.

Arrighi, G. (2009). *Adam Smith in Beijing: Lineages of the Twenty-First Century*. London and New York: Verso.

Arter, D. (2008). *Scandinavian politics today*. Manchester: Manchester University Press.

Audain, I. (2014). Scottish Out of School Care Network, personal communication to authors, 3 February.

Austvik, O. G. (2012). 'Landlord and Entrepreneur: The Shifting Roles of the State in Norwegian Oil and Gas Policy', *Governance*, 25: 2, April, pp. 315–34.

Baines, D. (1985). *Migration in a Mature Economy: Emigration and Internal Migration in England and Wales, 1861–1900*, Cambridge: Cambridge University Press.

Bay, A.-H., Finseraas, H. and Pedersen, A. W. (2013). 'Welfare Dualism in Two Scandinavian Welfare States: Public opinion and party politics', *West European Politics*, 36: 1, pp. 199–220.

Balke, E. (1979). 'Utviklingen av barnehagen i Norge', in Simmons-Christenson, G., *Førskolepedagogikkens historie*, Oslo: J. W. Cappelens Forlag.

Balke, E. (1995). *Småbarnspedagogikkens historie. Forbilder for vår tids barnehager*, Oslo: Universitetsforlaget.

Barne-, likestillings- og inkluderingsdepartementet, Tidslinje (2011). <http://www. regjeringen.no/nb/dep/bld/kampanjer/allmenn-stemmerett/tidslinje.html?id =661778> (last accessed 15 April 2014).

Barrow, G. W. S. (1983). 'Scandinavia, Contact With', in Derick S. Thomson (ed.) *The Companion to Gaelic Scotland*, Oxford: Blackwell.

Bartlett, R. (1993). *The Making of Europe: Conquest, Colonization and Cultural Change, 950–1350*, London: Penguin.

BFD (1996). *NOU 1996: 16. Offentlige overføringer til barnefamilier*, Oslo: Barne- og familiedepartementet.

Belassa, B. (1969). 'Industrial Development in an Open Economy: The Case of Norway', *Oxford Economic Papers*, New Series, 21: 3, November, pp. 344–59.

Beltratti, A. and Stulz, R. M. (2009). *Why Did Some Banks Perform Better during the Credit Crisis? A Cross-Country Study of the Impact of Governance and Regulation*, ECGI Working Paper Series in Finance.

Berg, R. (1995). *Norge på Egen Hånd 1905–1920*. Oslo: Universitetsforlaget.

Berge, L. J. (2001). 'Løs Baandene, lad Kræfterne udvikles…'. En beskrivelse og analyse av kirkeforfatningsdebatten i Norge fra 1840 til 1859 med tanke på dens historiske og kirkelige forutsetninger, KIFO Perspektiv 10, Trondheim: Tapir.

Bergholm, T. (2009). 'The Making of the Finnish Model', *Scandinavian Journal of History*, 34: 1, pp. 29–48.

Bergman, M., Gerlach, S. and Jonung, L. (1993). 'The Rise and Fall of the Scandinavian Currency Union 1873–1920', *European Economic Review*, 37: 2–3, pp. 507–17.

Bergqvist, C. (1999). 'Childcare and Parental Leave Models', in Bergqvist et al. (eds), *Equal Democracies? Gender and Politics in the Nordic Countries*, Oslo: Scandinavian University Press, pp. 121–36.

Binswanger, H. (1986). 'Agricultural Mechanisation: A Comparative Historical Perspective', *The World Bank Research Observer*, 1, pp. 27–56 at www.jstor.org/ stable/3986307 (last accessed 10 March 2014).

Binswanger, H. P., Deininger, K. and Feder, G. (1995). 'Power, distortions, revolt and reform in agricultural land relations', in Hollis Chenery and T. N. Srinivasan (eds), *Handbook of Development Economics*, 1st edn, vol. 3, chapter 42, pp. 2659–772. Elsevier.

Birrell, I. (2011). 'Why Cameron is inviting a Viking invasion', *The Times*, 19 January.

Bjørklund, T. (2005). *Hundre År med Folkeavstemninger*, Oslo: Universitetsforlaget.

Bjørnson, Ø. and Haavet, I. E. (1994). *Langsomt ble landet et velferdssamfunn. Trygdens historie 1894–1994*, Oslo: Ad Notam Gyldendal.

Bjørnson, Ø. (2001). 'The Social Democrats and the Norwegian Welfare State: Some perspectives', *Scandinavian Journal of History*, 26: 3, 197–223.

Blaug, M. (1962). *Economic Theory in Retrospect*, London: Heinemann.

Bloch, M. [1961] (1967). *Feudal Society*, I and II, paperback edn, London: Routledge.

Bort, E., McAlpine, R. and Morgan, G. (2012). *The Silent Crisis: Failure and Revival in Local Democracy in Scotland*, Biggar: The Jimmy Reid Foundation, http:// reidfoundation.org/portfolio/the-silent-crisis-failure-and-revival-in-local-democ-racy-in-scotland/ (last accessed 15 April 2014).

Bradshaw, P., Hall, J., Hill, T., Mabelis, J. and Philo, D. (2012). *Growing Up in*

Scotland: Early Experiences of Primary School – parental involvement in school activities, Research Findings No. 3, Edinburgh: Scottish Government.

Brandal, N., Bratberg, Ø. and Thorsen, D. E. (2013). *The Nordic Model of Social Democracy*, Basingstoke: Palgrave Macmillan.

Bratberg, Ø. and Nordby, T. (2012). 'Britisk og norsk parlamentarisme: Grunnleggende prinsipper, likhetstrekk og aktuelle utfordringer' (British and Norwegian parliamentarianism: Basic principles, similarities and current challenges), in Øivind Bratberg and Kristin M. Haugevik (eds), op. cit.

Braybon, G. and Summerfield, P. (1987). *Women's Experiences in Two World Wars*, London: Pandora.

Breistein, I. F. (2003). 'Har staten bedre borgere?' *Dissenternes kamp for religiøs frihet 1891–1969*, KIFO Perspektiv 14, Trondheim: Tapir.

Broberg, G. and Roll-Hansen, N. (eds) (2005). *Eugenics and the Welfare State: Sterilization Policy in Denmark, Sweden, Norway and Finland*, 2nd edn, first published 1996, East Lansing: Michigan State University Press.

Brochmann, G. (2013). 'Citizenship and welfare in the Norwegian welfare state: the immigration challenge', in Andrzej Marcin Suszycki (ed.), *Welfare citizenship and welfare nationalism*, Helsinki: NCoE NordWel, pp. 193–226.

Brown, C. G. (1988). 'Religion and Social Change', in Tom Devine and Rosalind Mitchison (eds), *People and Society in Scotland, Volume I, 1760–1830*, Edinburgh: John Donald.

Brown, C. G. (1992). 'Religion and Secularisation', in A. Dickson and J. H. Treble (eds), *People and Society in Scotland, Volume III, 1914–1990*, Edinburgh: John Donald.

Brown, C. G. (2001). *The Death of Christian Britain: Understanding Secularisation 1800–2000*, London: Routledge.

Brown, C. G. (2008). 'The secularisation decade: what the 1960s have done to the study of religious history', in Hugh McLeod and Werner Ustorf (eds), *The Decline of Christendom in Western Europe, 1750–2000*, Cambridge: Cambridge University Press.

Brown, C. (2013). 'Report on Glasgow autonomy', *The Scotsman*, 7 September.

Brox, O. (1984). *Nord-Norge: Fra allmenning til koloni*. Oslo University Press.

Brox, O. (1993). 'Let us now praise dragging feet', in N Åkerman (ed.), *The Necessity of Friction*, Heidelberg: Physica-Verlag.

Brox, O. (2006). *The Political Economy of Rural Development – Modernisation without Centralisation?*, Delft: Eburon.

Brox, O. (2012). *Økonomisk og politisk demokrati I Norge etter 1814: Et forsøk på historisk komparasjon*. Forelesning, Hegra. 27 September.

Bruce, S. (1988). 'Sectarianism in Scotland: A Contemporary Assessment and Explanation', in David McCrone and Alice Brown (eds), *The Scottish Government Yearbook 1988*, Edinburgh: USGS.

Bruce, S. (1995). *Religion in Modern Britain*, Oxford: Oxford University Press.

Bruce, S. (2002). *God is Dead: Secularization in the West*, Oxford: Blackwells.

Bruce, S. (2014). *Scottish Gods: Religion in Modern Scotland, 1900–2012*, Edinburgh: Edinburgh University Press.

Bryden, J. M. and Houston, G. (1976). *Agrarian Change in the Scottish Highlands*, Glasgow Series in Social and Economic Research Studies 4, London: Martin Robertson.

Bryden, J. M. (1979). 'Scotland', in Seers et al. (eds).

Bryden, J. M. (1980). 'Core–Periphery Problems – The Scottish Case: A post-script'. ESRC Seminar, Edinburgh University, 21 March, unpublished.

Bryden, J. (1985). 'Scottish Agriculture 1950–1980', in Saville, R., *The Economic Development of Modern Scotland 1950–1980*, Edinburgh: John Donald.

Bryden, J. M. (1995). 'Scottish Agriculture 1950–1990', *Scottish Tradition*, Canadian Association for Scottish Studies, vol. 20.

Bryden, J. M. (1996). *Land Tenure and Rural Development in Scotland*. The 1996 McEwen Lecture on Land Tenure in Scotland. Rural Forum and A. K. Bell Library: Perth.

Bryden, J., Courtney, P., Atterton, J., Timm, A. and Hart, K. (2004). 'Scotland', in J. Bryden and K. Hart (eds), *A New Approach to Rural Development in Europe: Germany, Greece, Scotland and Sweden*, Lewiston, NY: The Edwin Mellen Press.

Bryden, J., Refsgaard, K., Westholm, E., Vihinen, H., Voutilainen, O. and Tanvig, H. (in press). *Equity, Equality, and Territorial Equivalence and their Significance for Rural Development and Inclusion: the Nordic Case*. Sociological Trends.

Bryden, J. M. (2006). 'From an Agricultural to a Rural Policy in Europe: Changing Agriculture, Farm Households, Policies and Ideas', in P. J. Stewart, and A. Strathern (2006), *Landscape, Heritage and Conservation*, Durham, North Carolina: Carolina Academic Press.

Bryden, J. M. and Geisler, C. (2007). 'Community-based Land Reform: Lessons from Scotland', *Land Use Policy*, 24, pp. 24–34.

Bryden, J. M. and Hart, K. (2000). 'Land Reform, Planning and People: An Issue of Stewardship?', in G. Holmes and R. Crofts, *Scotland's Environment: The Future*, Edinburgh: Tuckwell Press.

Bryden, J. M., Efstratoglou, S., Ferenczi, T., Johnson, T., Knickel, K., Refsgaard, K. and Thomson, K. J. (2012). *Towards Sustainable Rural Regions in Europe*. New York: Routledge.

Bull, E. (1956). 'Autobiographies of Industrial Workers', *International Review of Social History*.

Bull, E. and Tvedt, K. A. (2013). 'Den Industrielle Revolusjon', in *Store norske leksikon*. Retrieved 5 March 2014 from http://snl.no/den_industrielle_revolusjon.

Bukve, O. (2002). 'Demokrati, effektivitet og debatten om kommunestrukturen' (Democracy, effectiveness and the debate about the municipal structure), *Norsk Statsvitenskaplig Tidsskrift*, 18: 263–83.

Bunting, M. (2008). 'We may admire the Nordic way, but don't try to import it', *The Guardian*, 15 August.

Burns, R. (2001). *The Canongate Burns: The Complete Poems and Songs of Robert Burns*, ed. A. Noble and P. S. Hogg, Edinburgh: Canongate.

Burton, J. H. (1897). *The History of Scotland*, Edinburgh and London: William Blackwood & Sons.

Buxton, N. (1985). 'The Scottish Economy, 1945–79: Performance, Structure and Problems', in R. Saville (ed.), *The Economic Development of Modern Scotland 1950–1980*, Edinburgh: John Donald.

Bø, I. (1993). 'Norway', in Cochran, M. (ed.), *International Handbook of Child Care Policies*, Westport/London: Greenwood Press.

Callander, R. F. (1987). *A Pattern of Landownership in Scotland*, Finzean: Haughend Publications.

Cameron, E. A. (2010). *Impaled Upon a Thistle: Scotland since 1880*, Edinburgh: Edinburgh University Press.

Campbell, R. H. (1965). *Scotland since 1707*, Oxford: Basil Blackwell.

Campbell, R. H. and Dow, J. B. A. (1968). *Source Book of Scottish Economic and Social History*, Oxford: Basil Blackwell.

Campbell, R. H. (1971). *Scotland Since 1707: The Rise of an Industrial Society*, Oxford: Basil Blackwell.

Campbell, R. H. (1980). *The Rise and Fall of Scottish Industry, 1707–1939*, Edinburgh: Edinburgh University Press.

Campbell, R. H. and Skinner, A. S. (1982). *The Origins and Nature of the Scottish Enlightenment*, Edinburgh: John Donald.

Cappelen Dam (2014). Mennesker i tid 2. Verden og Norge etter 1750. Historie VG3, <http://menneskeritid2.cappelendamm.no> (last accessed 3 April 2014).

Care Inspectorate (2013). *Childcare Statistics 2012, The provision and use of registered daycare of children and childminding services in Scotland as at December 2012*, Dundee: Care Inspectorate.

Care Inspectorate (2014). Ad hoc 2246, 2013 Childcare Statistics, Table 8b.

Carlton, D. (1981). *Anthony Eden: a Biography*, London: Allen Lane.

Carter, I. (1979). *Farmlife in Northeast Scotland 1840–1914: The Poor Man's Country*, Edinburgh: John Donald.

Charmley, J. (1995). *Churchill's Grand Alliance: The Anglo-American Special Relationship 1940–1957*, London: Hodder & Stoughton.

Checkland, S. G. (1975). *Scottish Banking, a History: 1695–1973*, Glasgow and London: Collins.

Chetwin, W. and Munro, A. (2013). *Contemporary exchange rate regimes: floating, fixed and hybrid. Reserve Bank of New Zealand*. Paper for a joint Reserve Bank-Treasury Forum on the Exchange Rate, Wellington, 26 March. http://www.rbnz.govt.nz/research_and_publications/seminars_and_workshops/Mar2013/5200818.pdf (accessed 27 November 2013).

Childs, M. (1936). *Sweden – the Middle Way*, New Haven: Yale University Press.

Christiansen, N. F. and Markkola, P. (2006). 'Introduction', in Niels Finn Christensen et al. (eds), *The Nordic Model of Welfare: A Historical Reappraisal*, Copenhagen: Museum Tusculanum Press, pp. 9–29.

Clarke, J. and Glendinning, C. (2002). 'Partnerships and the Remaking of Welfare Governance', in C. Glendinning, M. Powell and K. Rummery (2002), *Partnerships, New Labour, and the Governance of Welfare*, Bristol: The Policy Press.

Clayton, A. (1986). *The British Empire as a Superpower, 1919–1939*, London: Macmillan.

Cohen, B. J. (1988). *Caring for Children. Services and Policies for Childcare and Equal Opportunities in the UK*, Report for the European Commission's Childcare Network, London: European Commission.

Cohen, B. J. (1990). *Caring for Children. The 1990 Report*, London: FPSC.

Cohen, B. J., Moss, P., Petrie, P. and Wallace, J. (2004). *A New Deal for Children? Re-forming education and care in England, Scotland and Sweden*, Bristol: Policy Press.

Cohen, B. J. and Milne, R. (2007). *Northern Lights: Building better childhoods in Norway*, Edinburgh: Children in Scotland.

Cohen, B. J. (2013). 'Developing ECEC services in regionalised administrations: Scotland's Post-devolution Experience', *International Journal of Early Childhood*, vol. 45, no. 1, Springer.

Cohen, B .J. and Rønning, W. (2014). 'Place-based learning in early years services: approaches and examples from Norway and Scotland', in L. Miller and C. Cameron (eds), *International Perspectives in the Early Years*, London: SAGE, Chapter 8, pp. 112–27.

Cohen, B., Rønning, W., Adams, J. and Shelton, J. (2016, forthcoming). *Place Matters: Linking Learning to the Lives of Children and Young People*. London: IOE Press.

Collier, A. (1953). *The Crofting Problem*, Cambridge: Cambridge University Press.

Cooke, A., Donnachie, I., MacSween, A. and Whatley, C. A. (1998). *Modern Scottish History 1707 to the Present. Volume 1: The Transformation of Scotland, 1707–1850*, Edinburgh: Tuckwell Press.

Coppock, J. T. (1976). *An Agricultural Atlas of Scotland*. Edinburgh: John Donald.

Cosgrave, P. (1981). *R. A. Butler: An English Life*, London: Quartet Books.

CoSLA (2013). Local Matters, <www.cosla.gov.uk/sites/default/files/documents/local_matters.pdf>.

CoSLA (2014). Interim Report, Commission on Strengthening Local Democracy, 24 April, <www.localdemocracy.info/wp-content/uploads/2014/04/Local-Commission-April-2014.pdf>.

Crouzet, F. (1985). *The First Industrialists: The Problem of Origins*, Cambridge: Cambridge University Press.

Curtice, J., McCrone, D., McEwen, N., Marsh, M. and Ormston, R. (2009). *Revolution or Evolution? The 2007 Scottish Elections*, Edinburgh: Edinburgh University Press.

Cuthbert, J. and Cuthbert, M. (2009). 'SNP Economic Strategy: Neo-Liberalism with a Heart', in Gerry Hassan (ed.), *The Modern SNP: From Protest to Power*, Edinburgh: Edinburgh University Press, pp. 105–19.

Dahlqvist, H. (2002). 'Folkhemsbegreppet: Rudolf Kjellén vs Per Albin Hansson', *Historisk Tidskrift*, 122: 3, pp. 445–65.

Dalton, G. (1995). *The contribution of alternative farm enterprises to farm business development in the Highlands of Scotland*, SAC.

Danielsen, R. (1987). 'Frihet og likhet. Det lokale selvstyrets dilemma', in H. E. Næss et al., *Folkestyre i by og bygd*, Oslo: Universitetsforlaget AS, pp. 31–315.

Darling, F. F. (1955). *West Highland Survey: An Essay in Human Ecology*, Oxford: Oxford University Press.

Davie, G. (1961). *The Democratic Intellect*, Edinburgh: Edinburgh University Press.

Davie, G. (1994). *Religion in Britain Since 1945: Believing Without Belonging*, London: Wiley-Blackwell.

Davies, T. (2012). '"Power to the people" must have meaning', *The Scotsman*, 10 May.

Day, A. C. L. (1957). *Outline of Monetary Economics*, Oxford: Oxford University Press.

Derry, T. K. (1979). *A History of Scandinavia*, 10th printing 2000, Minneapolis and London: University of Minnesota Press.

Devine, T. (1994). *Clanship to Crofters' War. The Social Transformation of the Scottish Highlands*, Manchester: Manchester University Press.

Devine, T. (1996). *Farm Servants and Labour in Lowland Scotland, 1770 to 1914*, Edinburgh: John Donald.

Devine, T. (1999). *The Scottish Nation 1700–2000*. London: Penguin.

Devine, T. M. and Wormald, J. (eds) (2012). *The Oxford Handbook of Modern Scottish History*, Oxford: Oxford University Press.

De Vreis, J. (1984). *European Urbanisation 1500–1800*, Cambridge, MA: Harvard University Press.

Di Giovanni, J. and Shambaugh J. (2006). 'The impact of foreign interest rates on the economy: the role of the exchange rate regime', IMF Working Papers WP/06/37.

Dickinson, W. C. (1961). *Scotland from the earliest times to 1603. A New History of Scotland Vol. I*, Nelson.

Dinwoodie, R. (2005). 'Oil will fuel an economic rebirth, says SNP', *The Herald*, 4 February.

Dinwoodie, R. (2006). 'Salmond points north for a new future for Scotland', *The Herald*, 12 August.

Donaldson, G. (1992). *The Northern Commonwealth: Scotland and Norway*, Saltire Press.

Drēviņa, K., Laurinavičius, K. and Tupits, A. (2007). 'Legal and Institutional Aspects of the Currency Changeover following the Restoration of the Independence of the Baltic States'. ECB Legal Working Papers no. 7, July 2007.

Dunbabin, J. P. D. (1974). *Rural Discontent in Nineteenth-Century Britain*, London: Faber & Faber.

Dyrvik, S. (2005). *Året 1814*, Oslo: Det Norske Samlaget.

Dørum, K. and Sandvik, H. (eds) (2012). *Opptøyer i Norge 1750–1850*, Oslo: Scandinavian Academic Press.

Eden, A. (1960). *Full Circle: The Memoirs of Anthony Eden*, London: Cassell.

Edling, N. (2006). 'Limited Universalism: Unemployment Insurance in Northern Europe 1900–2000', in Niels Finn Christensen et al. (eds), *The Nordic Model of Welfare: A Historical Reappraisal*, Copenhagen: Museum Tusculanum Press, pp. 99–143.

Eidheim, H. (1997). 'Ethno-political development among the Sami after World War II', in Harald Gaski (ed.), *Sami Culture in a New Era: The Norwegian Sami Experience*, Kárášjohka: Davvi Girji OS, pp. 29–61.

Eitrheim, Ø. (2012). *Money and banking in Norway 1816–2016*. Background paper for Economic History Workshop, Rutgers University, 1 October 2010.

Ellingsæter, A. L. (2014). 'Towards universal quality early childhood education and care: The Norwegian model', in L. Gambaro, K. Stewart and J. Waldfogel (eds), *An Equal Start? Providing quality early childhood education and care for disadvantaged children*, Bristol: Policy Press, pp. 53–77.

Elvander, N. (1980). *Skandinavisk arbetarrörelse*, Stockholm: Liber Förlag.

Engman, M. (1994). 'Är Finland ett nordiskt land?', *Det Jyske Historiker*, pp. 69–70, 62–78.

Eriksen, K. E. and Pharo, H. Ø. (1997). *Kald Krig og Internasjonalisering 1949–1965*, Oslo: Universitetsforlaget.

Esping-Andersen, G. (1990). *The Three Worlds of Welfare Capitalism*, Cambridge: Polity.

Eurobarometer (2010). Eurobarometer 73.1: Biotechnology, Brussels: TNS Opinion & Social.

European Commission (1991). *The Development and Future of the Common Agricultural Policy: Proposals of the Commission, 2/91*, Brussels: Commission of the European Communities.

Falkinger, J. and Grossman, V. (2012). *Oligarchic Land Ownership, Entrepreneurship, and Economic Development*. This refereed paper is available at: http://www.unifr.ch/makro/assets/files/workingpapers/Oligarchic%20Land%20Ownership%20Entrepreneurship%20and%20Economic%20Development.pdf

Fenton, A. (1987). *Country Life in Scotland*, Edinburgh: John Donald.

Ferguson, N. (2009). *The Ascent of Money: A Financial History of the World*, London: Penguin.

Finlay, R. (2004). *Modern Scotland 1949 to 2000*, Profile Books.

Firn, J. (1975). 'External Control and Regional Policy', in J. G. Brown (ed.), *The Red Paper on Scotland*, Edinburgh: EUSPB.

Fjeldstad, D., Lauglo, J. and Mikkelsen, R. (2010). Demokratisk beredskap. Kortrapport om norske ungdomsskoleelevers prestasjoner og svar på spørsmål i den internasjonale demokratiundersøkelsen, International Civic and Citizenship Education Study (ICCS 2009), Oslo: Universitetet i Oslo.

Flognfeldt, T. (2004). 'Second homes as a part of a new rural lifestyle in Norway', in C. M. Hall and D. K. Miller (eds), *Tourism, Mobility and Second Homes: Between Elite Landscapes and Common Ground*, Cleveden: Channel View, pp. 233–43.

Formannskapslovene hos Stortinget (1837). <https://www.stortinget.no/no/Stortinget-og-demokratiet/Historikk/Historisk-dokumentasjon/Formannskapslovene-av-1837/> (last accessed 15 April 2014).

Formannskapslovene (2014). <http://lokalhistoriewiki.no/index.php/Formannskapslovene> (last accessed 3 April 2014).

Fougstad, C. A. (1834). *The Norwegian Storting, 1833*.

Fraser, D. (2007). 'Salmond: Set England Free', *New Statesman*, 26 March.

Frater, A. (1993). 'Aig an Fhaing'/'At the Fank', in Christopher Whyte, *An Aghaidh na Siorraidheachd/In the Face of Eternity*, Edinburgh: Polygon, pp. 27, 77.

Friedberg, A. L. (1988). *The Weary Titan: Britain and the Experience of Relative Decline*, Princeton: Princeton University Press.

Frydenlund, B. (2013). 'Før unionspartiet: omstridte forbindelser og norske møter om helstatens fremtid 1809–1814', in B. Frydenlund and O. A. Storsveen (eds), *Veivalg for Norden: 1809–1813*, Oslo: Akademika.

Frydenlund, B. (2014). *Spillet om Norge: Det Politiske Året 1814*, Oslo: Gyldendal.

Frydenlund, B. and Storsveen, O. A. (eds) (2013). *Veivalg for Norden: 1809–1813*, Oslo: Akademika, pp. 23–42.

Fure, O. B. (1996). *Mellomkrigstid 1920–1940*, Oslo: Universitetsforlaget.

Furre, B. (1991). *Vårt Hundreår: Norsk Historie 1905–1990*, Oslo: Det Norske Samlaget.

Furre, H., Danielsen, I. J., Stiberg-Jamt, R. and Skaalvik, E. M. (2006). *Analyse av den nasjonale undersøkelsen 'Elevundersøkelsen'*, Kristiansand: Oxford Research AS. ·

Gentleman, H. (1999). *Huts and Hutters*, Scottish Office Central Research Unit.
Gerhardsen, E. (1972). *I Medgang og Motgang: Erindringer, 1955–1965*, Oslo: Tiden.
Gerschenkron, A. (1962). *Economic Backwardness in Historical Perspective. Essays*, Cambridge, MA: The Beknap Press of Harvard University Press.
Gilbert, M. (1988). *Never despair: Winston S. Churchill 1945–1965*, London: Heinemann.
Gjedrem, S. (2009). 'Financial Crisis: lessons from the Nordic experience', *Financial Times*, 3 February.
Gjerdåker, B. (2004). 'Continuity and modernity 1815–1920', in: Almås (2004a), pp. 234–93.
Glenthøj, R. and Nordhagen Ottosen, M. (2014). *Experiences of War and Nationality in Denmark and Norway, 1807–1815*, Basingstoke: Palgrave Macmillan.
Goksøyr, M. (1996). 'Norway's Utilisation of International Sport', in J. A. Mangan (ed.), *Tribal Identities*, London: Portland.
Gordon, E. (1991). *Women and the Labour Movement in Scotland 1850–1914*, Oxford: Clarendon.
Graham-Campbell, J. (1998). *Vikings in Scotland: An Archaeological Survey*, Edinburgh: Edinburgh University Press.
Grant, E. (1994). *Abernethy Forest: Its people and its past*, Oxford and Nethy Bridge: The Arkleton Trust.
Grepstad, O. and Nerbøvik, J. (eds) (1984). *Venstres Hundre År*, Oslo: Gyldendal.
Grimley, O. B. (1937). *The New Norway: A people with the Spirit of Cooperation*, Oslo: Bye & Co. Griff Forlaget.
Grosjean, A. and Murdoch, S. (2005). *Scottish Communities Abroad in the Early Modern Period*, Leiden: Brill.
Grönvold, A. (1883). *Norske Musikere*.
Gunn, N. M. (1937). *Highland River*, Edinburgh: Canongate.
Hagen, R. (2003). 'At the Edge of Civilisation: John Cunningham, Lensmann of Finnark 1619–1651', in A. MacKillop and S. Murdoch (eds), *Military Governors and Imperial Frontiers c. 1600–1800. A Study of Scotland and Empires*, Leiden: Brill, pp. 35–7.
Hagen, R. (2009–11). Biography of Petter Dass (with Hanne Lauvstad). Store Norske Leksikon.
Hagen, T. P. and Sørensen, R. (2001). *Kommunal organisering*, Oslo: Universitetsforlaget.
Hall, C. M. and Müller, D. K. (eds) (2004). *Tourism, Mobility and Second Homes: Between Elite Landscape and Common Ground*, Clevedon: Channelview Publications.
Halvorsen, K. and Stjernø, S. (2008). *Work, Oil and Welfare: The Welfare State in Norway*, Oslo: Universitetsforlaget.
Handley, J. E. (1953). *Scottish Farming in the Eighteenth Century*. London: Faber & Faber.
Hansen, S. O. (1994). 'Foreningerne Norden 1919–1994 – ambisjoner og virkelighet', *Det jyske Historiker*, pp. 69–70, 114–31.
Hart, K. (2009). 'Money in the making of world society', in C. Hann and K. Hart (eds), *Market and Society: The Great Transformation Today*, Cambridge: Cambridge University Press, pp. 91–105.

Hart, K., Laville, J. L. and Cattani, A. D. (eds) (2010). *The Human Economy*, Cambridge: Polity.

Harvie, C. J. (1994). *Fool's Gold: The Story of North Sea Oil, How a £200 Billion windfall divided a kingdom*, London: Penguin Books.

Harvie, C. (1998). *No Gods and Precious Few Heroes: Twentieth-Century Scotland*, 3rd edn, Edinburgh: Edinburgh University Press.

Havnes, T. and Mogstad, M. (2014). *Is universal child care levelling the playing field?* Discussion Paper no. 774, Oslo: Statistics Norway.

Haydecker, R. (2010). 'Public policy in Scotland after devolution: convergence or divergence', *POLIS Journal*, vol. 3, Winter 2010, University of Leeds.

Hegrenes, A., Hval, J. N., Asheim, L. J. and Svennerud, M. (2012). *Fleire dyr på sommerferie? Evaluering av beiteordningene*, NILF, Notat 2012–7.

Heidar, K. (2001). *Norway: Elites on Trial*, Oxford and Boulder, CO: Westview Press.

Heldal, H. (1996). 'Norway in the International Labour Organisation 1919–1939', *Scandinavian Journal of History*, 21: 4, pp. 255–83.

Hennessy, P. (1993). *Never Again, Britain 1945–1951*, New York: Pantheon Books.

Her Majesty's Stationery Office (1853). *Census of Great Britain 1851: Religious Worship and Education, Scotland*, London: HMSO.

Herald, The (leader) (2013). 'A fair wind for island councils', 26 July.

Herald, The (2014). 'Education expert hits out at right to choose school', 13 January.

Hetherington, P. (2014). 'Scotland is Already a Country Apart: And a Democratic One', *The Guardian*, 11 March.

Hetland, T. (2010). <http://www.humiliationstudies.org/documents/Hetland-KnowNorwayBook.pdf> (last accessed 9 June 2011).

Higgs, J. (1965). *The Land*, London: Readers' Union Studio Vista.

Hilson, M. (2008). *The Nordic Model: Scandinavia Since 1945*, London: Reaktion Books.

Hirvonen, V. and Keskitalo, J. H. (2004). 'Samisk skole – en ufullendt symfoni?', in K. J. Solstad and T. O. Engen (eds), *En likeverdig skole for alle? Om enhet og mangfold i grunnskolen*, Oslo: Universitetsforlaget.

HMIE/Scottish Qualifications Authority/Learning Teaching Scotland (2007). *A Curriculum for Excellence. Building the Curriculum 2. Active learning in the early years*, Edinburgh: Scottish Executive.

Hodne, F. (1983). *The Norwegian Economy 1920–1980*, London: Croom Helm.

Hodne, F. and Grytten, O. H. (1992). *Norske Økonomi 1900–1990*. Oslo: Tano.

Hommerstad, M. (2012). 'Politiske bønder: bondepolitikk og Stortinget 1815–1837'. PhD Dissertation, Faculty of Humanities, University of Oslo.

Hommerstad, M. and Nordhagen Ottosen, M. (eds) (2014). *Ideal og Realitet: 1814 i Politisk Praksis for Folk og Elite*, Oslo: Akademika.

House of Lords/House of Commons (2013). Parliamentary Commission on Banking Standards: 'An accident waiting to happen': The failure of HBOS. Fourth Report of Session 2012–2013 HL Paper 144 HC 705 Published on 4 April 2013 by authority of the House of Commons, London: The Stationery Office Limited.

Hovland, E., Nordvik, H. W. and Tveite, S. (1982). 'Proto-Industrialisation in Norway, 1750–1850: Fact or Fiction?', *Scandinavian Economic History Review*, 30: 1.

Hovland, E. (1987). 'Grotid og glanstid. 1837–1920', in H. E. Næss et al., *Folkestyre i by og bygd*, Oslo: Universitetsforlaget AS, pp. 31–155.

Hovland, E. (1990). 'Den forhaandenværende nødstilstand. Bønder, organisasjoner og tollbeskyttelse 1893–1905', in E. Hovland, E. Lange and S. Rysstad (eds), *Det som svarte seg best. Studier i økonomisk historie og politikk*, Oslo: Ad Notam Forlag AS.

Hulme, M., McKinney, S., Hall, S. and Cross, B. (2011). 'Pupil Participation in Scottish Schools: How far have we come?', *Improving Schools*, 14: 2, July, pp. 130–44, SAGE.

Hume Brown, P. (1893). *Scotland Before 1700 from Contemporary Documents*, Edinburgh: David Douglas.

Hume Brown, P. (1907). *A History of Scotland*, Edinburgh and London: Oliver & Boyd.

Hunter, J. (1976). *The Making of the Crofting Community*, Edinburgh: John Donald.

Hutchison, I. G. C. (1996). 'Government', in T. M. Devine and R. J. Finlay (eds), *Scotland in the Twentieth Century*, Edinburgh: Edinburgh University Press, pp. 46–63.

Hutchison, R. (2012). *In the Doorway to Development: An Enquiry into Market oriented Structural Changes in Norway ca. 1750–1830*, Leiden: Brill.

Imsen, S. and Winge, H. (1999). *Norsk historisk leksikon*, 2nd edn, Oslo.

Imsen, S. (2010). *The Norwegian Domination and the Norse World c.1100–c.1400*, Rostra Books.

Ingebritsen, C. (2002). 'Norm entrepreneurs: Scandinavia's role in world politics', *Cooperation and Conflict*, 37: 1, pp. 11–23.

Innes, C. (1860). *Scotland in the Middle Ages*, Edinburgh: Edmonston & Douglas.

Innes, C. (1872). *Lectures on Scotch Legal Antiquities*, Edinburgh: Edmonston & Douglas.

Jamieson, B. (2001). 'Warning for Scotland in Nordic Rebellion', *The Scotsman*, 11 September.

Jamieson, F. (2000). *Carbeth Estate*, Area Character Appraisal for Stirling Council.

Janfelt, M. (2005). *Att leva i det bästa av världar. Föreningarna Nordens syn på Norden 1919–1933*, Stockholm: Carlssons bokförlag.

Jareg, K. (2011). *Øyene i vest Hebridene, Orknøyene og Shetland*, Oslo: Cappelin Damm.

Jensen, R. S. (2000). *Kvinner og jobb etter småbarnsfasen. Rapport 2000:10*, Oslo: Institutt for samfunnsforskning.

Johnson, T. (1909). *Our Scots Noble Families*, Glasgow: Forward Publishing.

Jones, C. (2004). *Britain and the Yemen Civil War, 1962–1965: Ministries, Mercenaries and Mandarins. Foreign Policy and the Limits of Covert Action*, Brighton and Portland: Sussex Academic Press, 2004.

Jørgensen, T. E. (2008). 'The Scandinavian 1968 in a European Perspective', *Scandinavian Journal of History*, 33: 4, pp. 326–38.

Kane, A. and Mann, M. (1992). 'A Theory of Early Twentieth-Century Agrarian Politics', *Social Science History*, 16: 3 (Fall 1992), pp. 421–54.

Karl, T. L. (2007). 'Ensuring Fairness: The Case for a Transparent Fiscal Social Contract', in Marcartan Humphreys, Jeffrey D. Sachs and Jospeh E. Stiglitz (eds), *Escaping the Resource Curse*, New York: Columbia University Press, pp. 256–86.

Karseth, B. and Engelsen, B. U. (2013). 'Læreplan for Kunnskapsløftet. Velkjente tråkk og nye spor', in B. Karseth, J. Møller, and P. Aasen (eds), *Reformtakter. Om fornyelse og stabilitet i grunnopplæringen*, Oslo: Universitetsforlaget.

Keating, M., Stevenson, L., Cairney, P. and Taylor, K. (2003). 'Does Devolution make a Difference? Legislative Output and Policy Divergence in Scotland', *The Journal of Legislative Studies*, 9: 3, pp. 110–39.

Keating, M. (2005a). *The Government of Scotland: Public Policy Making after Devolution*, Edinburgh: Edinburgh University Press.

Keating, M. and McCrone, D. (2007). 'Social Democracy and Scotland', in M. Keating (ed.), *Scottish Social Democracy: Progressive Ideas for Public Policy*, Brussels: Peter Lang, pp. 17–38.

Keilhau, W. (1938). *Det norske folks liv og historie*, vol. 11: Vår egen tid. Oslo.

Kemp, A. (2012). *The Official History of North Sea Oil and Gas, Vol II: Moderating the State's Role*, London: Routledge.

Kendle, J. (1997). *Federal Britain. A History*, London: Routledge.

Kennedy, P. (1987). *The Rise and Fall of the Great Powers: Economic and Military Conflict from 1500 to 2000*, New York: Random House.

Kenny, M. and Mackay, F. (2013). *Still Counting? Women and the 2012 Local Government Elections, Gender Politics at Edinburgh* (blog, 11 February), http://genderpoliticsatedinburgh.wordpress.com/page/3/

Kettunen, P. (2006). 'The Power of International Comparison – A Perspective on the Making and Challenging of the Nordic Welfare States', in Niels Finn Christensen et al. (eds), *The Nordic Model of Welfare: A Historical Reappraisal*, Copenhagen: Museum Tusculanum Press, pp. 31–65.

Kettunen, P. (2009). 'The Nordic model and the International Labour Organisation', in Norbert Götz and Heidi Haggrén (eds), *Regional Co-operation and International Organizations: The Nordic model in transnational alignment*, London: Routledge, pp. 67–87.

Kettunen, P. (2011). 'The International Construction of National Challenges: The Ambiguous Nordic Model of Welfare and Competitiveness', in Pauli Kettunen and Klaus Petersen (eds), *Beyond Welfare State Models: Transnational Historical Perspectives on Social Policy*, Cheltenham: Edward Elgar Press, pp. 16–40.

Kettunen, P. and Petersen, K. (2011). 'Introduction: Rethinking Welfare State Models', in Pauli Kettunen and Klaus Petersen (eds), *Beyond Welfare State Models: Transnational Historical Perspectives on Social Policy*, Cheltenham: Edward Elgar Press, pp. 1–15.

Keynes, J. M. (1936). *The General Theory of Employment, Interest and Money*, London.

Kile, E. (1997). *Landbruksskulen 1825–1990. Mål, innhald og arbeidsmåtar*, Oslo: Landbruksforlaget.

Kjeldstadli, K. (1993). 'Åtte timer arbeid', in I. G. Klepp and R. Svarverud (eds), *Idrett og fritid*, Oslo.

Kjellberg, F. (1990). 'Kommunalt selvstyre og nasjonal styring – Mot nye roller for kommunene' [Municipal local governance and national governance – Towards new roles for the municipalities], *Norsk Statsvitenskaplig Tidsskrift*, 1, pp. 45–63.

Knutas, A. (2013). 'People's high schools in Scandinavia: a contribution to democracy?', *International Journal of Lifelong Education*, 32: 6, pp. 780–95.

Knox, W. W. (1999). *Industrial Nation: Work, Culture and Society in Scotland, 1800–Present*, Edinburgh: Edinburgh University Press.

Knox, W. W. (SCRAN n.d.). 'Poverty, Income and Wealth in Scotland 1840–1940', Chapter 5 in *SCRAN, A History of the Scottish People*, www.scran.ac.uk (accessed 9 March 2014).

Knox, J. (2010). 'Analysis: mayors the way to combat cuts?', *Caledonian Mercury*, 22 February, http://politics.caledonianmercury.com/2010/02/22/mayors-the-way-to-combat-cuts/

Korpi, W. and Palme, J. (1998). 'The Paradox of Redistribution and Strategies of Equality: Welfare state institutions, inequality and poverty in the western countries', *American Sociological Review*, 63: 5, pp. 661–87.

Kosonen, P. (1993). 'The Finnish Model and the Welfare State in Crisis', in Pekka Kosonen (ed.), *The Nordic Welfare State as a Myth and as Reality*, Helsinki: Renvall Institute, pp. 45–66.

Krasner, S. (1984). 'Approaches to the state: alternative conceptions and historical dynamics', *Comparative Politics*, 16: 2, pp. 223–46.

Kresl, P. K. (1976). *The Concession Process and Foreign Capital in Norway*, Norges Bank Skriftserie No. 4, Oslo.

Kvist, J., Fritzel, J., Hvinden, B. and Kangas, O. (eds) (2012). *Changing Social Equality: The Nordic welfare model in the 21st century*, Bristol: The Policy Press.

Labrousse, C. E. (1932). *Esquisse du movement des prix et des revenus en France au XVIIIe siècle*.

Lahlum, H. O. (2009). *Håkon Lie: Historien, Mytene og Menneskene*, Oslo: Cappelen Damm.

Lie, H. (1975). *Slik jeg ser det*, Oslo: Tiden norsk forlag.

Landbruks- og matdepartementet (2011). *Landbruks- og matpolitikken – Velkommen til bords*. Meld. St. 9 (2011–12).

Lang, T. and Heasman, M. (2004). *Food Wars: The Global Battle for Mouths, Minds and Markets*, London: Earthscan.

Lange, E. (1977). 'The Concession Laws of 1906–1909 and Norwegian Industrial Development', *Scandinavian Journal of History*, 2, pp. 311–30.

Lange, E. (2005). 'Samling om felles mål', vol. 2 of Knut Helle (ed.), *Aschehougs Norges historie*, Oslo: Aschehoug (first published 1996).

Langeland, N. R. and Michalsen, D. (eds) (2014). *Politisk Kompetanse: Grunnlovas Borgar 1814–2014*, Oslo: Pax.

Larsen, H. O. (2007). *Local government in Norway: Between autonomy and integration*. Paper presented at the India–Norway Seminar on Local Government the 29th of October 2007 in New Delhi.

Larsen, P. (1979). *Med AIF-stjerna på brystet*, Oslo: Tiden Norsk Forlag.

Lavergne, L. de (1855). *The Rural Economy of England, Scotland and Ireland*, Edinburgh and London: William Blackwood & Sons.

Learning Teaching Scotland (2010). *Pre-Birth to Three Positive Outcomes for Scotland's Children and Families, National Guidance*, Glasgow: Learning Teaching Scotland.

Lee, C. H. (1979). *British Regional Employment Statistics 1841–1971*, Cambridge: Cambridge University Press.

Leneman, L. (1989). *Land Fit for Heroes? Land Settlement in Scotland after World War I*, Aberdeen.

Lewis, W. A. (1954). *Economic Development with Unlimited Supplies of Labour*, The Manchester School, May.

Libaek, I. and Stenersen, O. (1991). *A History of Norway: from the ice age to the oil age*, Oslo: Grøndahl & Søn.

Lidtveit, A. (1979). *Jordbruket i Noreg 1914–1974. Tiltak under Landbruksdepartementet*, Oslo.

Lillehammer, A. (1986). 'The Scottish Norwegian Timber Trade in the Stavanger Area in the Sixteenth and the Seventeenth Centuries', in T. C. Smout (ed.), *Scotland and Europe 1200–1850*, Edinburgh: John Donald.

List, F. [1841] (1885, English translation). *The National System of Political Economy*, London: Longman.

Local Government Act (1992). Act of 25 September 1992 concerning municipalities and county municipalities, No. 107.

Logue, J. (1999). 'The Swedish Model: Visions of Sweden in American Politics and Political Science', *Swedish–American Historical Quarterly*, 50: 3, pp. 162–72.

Loughlin, J. and Martin, S. with assistance from S. Lux (2005). *Options for Reforming Local Government Funding to Increase Local Streams of Funding: International Comparisons*, Cardiff: Cardiff University, < http://ourcampaign.org.uk/user_files/axethetax/International_comparisons.pdf>.

Lunden, K. (2004). 'Recession and new expansion 1350–1814', in Almås (2004a), pp. 142–232.

Lynch, M. (1992). *Scotland: A New History*, London: Pimlico.

Lynch, P. (2001). *Scottish Government and Politics: An Introduction*, Edinburgh: Edinburgh University Press.

Løyland, M. and Dørum, K. (2012). 'Oppvakning og overvakning 1848–1851', in K. Dørum and H. Sandvik (eds), *Opptøyer i Norge 1750–1850*, Oslo: Scandinavian Academic Press (SAP).

MacAskill, J. (2006). '"The most arbitrary, scandalous act of tyranny": The Crown, Private Proprietors and the Ownership of the Scottish Foreshore in the Nineteenth Century', *The Scottish Historical Review*, Vol. 85, No. 2: No. 220, October, pp. 277–304.

Macdonell, H. (2006). 'Critics jump on SNP hint of taxes rises', *The Scotsman*, 21 November.

MacEwen, J. (1977). *Who Owns Scotland?*, Edinburgh: EUSPB.

MacSharry, R. (1991). Foreword to *The Development and Future of the Common Agricultural Policy: Proposals of the Commission*, Green Europe 2/91.

Macwhirter, I. (2013). *Road to Referendum*, London: Cargo.

Macwhirter, I. (2012). 'Norway, Scotland and Why I was Wrong about the Arc of Insolvency', *The Herald*, 24 November. Published online at: http://iain-macwhirter2.blogspot.fi/2012/11/norway-scotland-and-why-i-was-wrong.html (accessed 24 March 2014).

Mahoney, J. (2000). 'Path dependence in historical sociology', *Theory and Society*, 29: 4, pp. 507–48.

Maitles, H. and Deuchar, R. (2006). 'We don't learn democracy, we live it! Consulting the pupil voice in Scottish schools', *Education, Citizenship and Social Justice*, SAGE 1, pp. 249–66.

Marklund, C. (2009). 'The Social Laboratory, the Middle Way and the Swedish model: Three frames for the image of Sweden', *Scandinavian Journal of History*, 34: 3, pp. 264–285.

Martel, G. (1991). 'The Meaning of Power: Rethinking the decline and Fall of Great Britain', *The International History Review*, 13: 4 (November).

Martin, I. (2013). *Making It Happen: Fred Goodwin, RBS and the Men Who Blew up the British Economy*, London: Simon & Schuster.

Mather, A. S. (1978). *State-Aided Land Settlement in Scotland*, Aberdeen: University of Aberdeen Press.

Maxwell, S. (2009). 'Social Justice and the SNP', in Gerry Hassan (ed.), *The Modern SNP: From Protest to Power*, Edinburgh: Edinburgh University Press, pp. 120–34.

McConnell, A. (2004). *Scottish Local Government*, Edinburgh: Edinburgh University Press.

McDowall, S. (1985). 'Coal, Gas and Oil: The Changing Energy Scene in Scotland. 1950–1980', in R. Saville (ed.), *The Economic Development of Modern Scotland 1950–1980*, Edinburgh: John Donald.

McGarvey, N. and Cairney, P. (2008). *Scottish Politics: An Introduction*, Basingstoke: Palgrave Macmillan.

McGarvey, N. (2009). 'Centre and Locality in Scottish Politics: From Bi- to Tri-partite Relations', in C. Jeffery and J. Mitchell (eds), *The Scottish Parliament 1999–2009: The First Decade*, Edinburgh: Luath Press (in association with Hansard Society), pp. 125–31.

McPherson, A. and Raab, C. D. (1988). *Governing Education*, Edinburgh: Edinburgh University Press.

McCalla, A. (1994). *The CGIAR in the 21st Century. Options for Change*, CGIAR.

McKercher, B. J. C. (1991). '"Our Most Dangerous Enemy": Great Britain Pre-Eminent in the 1930s', *The International History Review*, 13: 4 (November).

Mendels, F. (1972). 'Proto-Industrialisation: the First Phase of the Industrialisation Process', *Journal of Economic History*, XXXII, pp. 241–61.

Mendelsohn, O. (1969). *Jødenes Historie i Norge gjennom 300 År*, Oslo: Universitetsforlaget.

Michalsen, D. (2013). 'Grunnlovens menn', *Levende historie*, 11, pp. 42–5.

Midthjell, N. L. (2010). *Finanspolitikk og finanskrise – hvilken effekt har egentlig finanspolitikken?* Norges Bank, Penger og Kreditt 2/2010 (årg. 38), pp. 32–46.

Midwinter, A. (1995). *Local Government in Scotland: Reform or Decline?*, Basingstoke: Macmillan.

Milne, R. (2014). 'Scottish Nationalists Look To Nordic Model for Independence', *Financial Times*, 2 February.

Mitchell, I. R. (2007). *Walking through Scotland's History*, National Museums of Scotland.

Mitchell, J. (1996). 'Scotland in the union, 1945–1995: the changing nature of the union state', in T. M. Devine and R. J. Finlay (eds), *Scotland in the Twentieth Century*, Edinburgh: Edinburgh University Press, pp. 85–101.

Mitchell, M. (1988). *The Irish in the West of Scotland, 1797–1848*, Edinburgh: John Donald.

Mitchison, R. (2000). *The Old Poor Law in Scotland: The Experience of Poverty, 1574–1845*, Edinburgh: Edinburgh University Press.

Moafi, H. and Bjørkli, E. S. (2011). *Barnefamiliers tilsynsordninger høsten 2010, Rapport 34/2011*, Oslo: Statistisk Sentralbyrå.

Mooney, G. and Scott, G. (2012). 'Devolution, Social Justice and Social Policy: The Scottish Context', in Gerry Mooney and Gill Scott (eds), *Social Justice and Social Policy in Scotland*, Bristol: Policy Press, pp. 1–24.

Morton, G. (1999). *Unionist Nationalism: Governing Urban Scotland, 1830–1860*, East Linton: Tuckwell Press.

Morton, G. (2008). 'Scotland', in G. H. Herb and D. H. Kaplan (eds), *Nations and Nationalism: A Global Historical Overview, Volume 1: 1770 to 1880*, Santa Barbara, CL: ABC-CLIO, pp. 232–43.

Morgan, G. (2009). 'What is the Shetland Charitable Trust?', *The Shetland Times*, 3 April.

Moseng, O. G., Opsahl, E., Pettersen, G. and Sandmo, E. (2007). *Norsk historie I, 750–1537*, 2nd edn, Oslo.

Moss, P. and Fonda, N. (1980). *Work and the Family*, London: Temple Smith.

Mundell, R. A. (1961). 'A Theory of Optimum Currency Areas', *American Economic Review*, 51: 4, pp. 657–65.

Murdoch, S. (2003). *Britain, Denmark–Norway and the House of Stuart, 1603–1660*, East Linton: Tuckwell Press.

Murdoch, S. (2003). 'Scotsmen on the Danish–Norwegian Frontier, 1589–1680', in S. Murdoch and A. Mackillop (eds), *Military Governors and Imperial Frontiers c.1600–1800*, Leiden: Brill.

Murdoch, S. (2006). *Network North: Scottish kin, commercial and covert association in Northern Europe 1603–1746*, Leiden: Brill.

Murray, D. (1883). *The York Buildings Company. A Chapter in Scotch History*, Edinburgh: Bratton.

Musial, K. (2002). *Roots of the Scandinavian Model: Images of Progress in the Era of Modernisation*, Baden-Baden: Nomos Verlagsgesellschaft.

Myhre, J. E. (2012). *Norsk historie 1814–1905: Å byggje ein stat og skape ein nasjon*, Oslo: Det Norske Samlaget.

Myhre, R. (1992). *Den norske skoles utvikling. Idé og virkelighet*, Oslo: ad Notam Gyldendal.

Nansen, F. (1891). *The First Crossing of Greenland*.

Napier, Lord Francis (1884). *The Report of Her Majesty's Commissioners of Inquiry into the Condition of the Crofters and Cottars in the Highlands and Islands of Scotland. Vol. 2*, digitalised and accessed, University of the Highlands and Islands. http://www.whc.uhi.ac.uk/research/napier-commission

Naumann, I., McLean, C., Koslowski, A., Tisdall, K. and Lloyd, E. (2013). *Early Childhood Education and Care Provision: International review of Policy, Delivery and*

Funding, Edinburgh: Scottish Government Social Research Unit. http://www.scotland.gov.uk/Topics/Research/About/Social-Research (accessed 10 February 2014).

Neil, A. (1998). 'SNP's Nordic star begins to fade', *The Scotsman*, 4 September 1998.

Neil, A. (2008). 'Is There a Plan B?', Andrew Neil's BBC Blog, 16 October. Available at http://www.bbc.co.uk/blogs/dailypolitics/andrewneil/2008/10/is_there_a_plan_b.html. (accessed 24 March 2014).

Ness, E. (1989). *Det var en gang... Norsk skole gjennom tidene*, Oslo: Universitetsforlaget.

Nerbøvik, J. (2000). *Nasjonsbygging og Modernisering: Tema med Variasjonar. Artiklar og Talar 1990–2000*, Volda: Høgskulen i Volda.

Nerbøvik, J. (1999). *Norsk Historie 1860–1914: Eit Bondesamfunn i Oppbrot*, Oslo: Det Norske Samlaget.

Newby, A. (2003). 'Edward McHugh, the National Land League of Great Britain, and the Crofters' war, 1879–1882', *The Scottish Historical Review*, LXXII: 213, April.

Newby, A. G. (2009). '"In Building a Nation Few Better Examples can be Found": Norden and the Scottish Parliament', *Scandinavian Journal of History*, 34: 3, pp. 307–29.

Norges Bank (1985). *The Norwegian Monetary and Credit System*, Norges Banks Skriftserie No, 15, Oslo.

Norwegian Constitution, 2012 Version, available at https://www.stortinget.no/en/In-English/About-the-Storting/The-Constitution/The-Constitution/ (accessed 3 May 2014).

NOS (1921). *Utvandringsstatistikk*, NOS VII 25, Kristiania.

NOU (1988). *Nye mål og retningslinjer for reformer i lokalforvaltningen* [New goals and directions for reforms in the local management], NOU, 38.

NOU (1990). *Forslag til ny lov om kommuner og fylkeskommuner* [Proposal for a new Act about municipalities and counties], NOU, 13.

NOU (2005). *Samspill og tillit – Om staten og lokaldemokratiet. Utredning fra Lokaldemokratikommisjonen* [Norway's official reports, Interaction and trust – About the state and national democracy. Study from the Local Democracy Commission], NOU, 06.

NOU (2013). *Det livssynsåpne samfunn. En helhetlig tros- og livssynspolitikk*, Norges offentlige utredninger, 1.

NRK Østlandssendingen (2003). 'Et frekt statskupp 17. Mai 1814', 16 May, <http://www.nrk.no/nyheter/distrikt/nrk_ostlandssendingen/sendinger_nrk_ostlandssendingen/lang_lunsj/2765204.html> (accessed 15 April 2014).

Næss, H. E. (1987). 'Det lokale selvstyrets røtter. Tiden fram til 1837', in H. E. Næss, E. Hovland, T. Grønlie, H. Baldersheim and R. Danielsen, *Folkestyre I by og bygd*, Oslo: Universitetsforlaget AS, pp. 11–30.

O'Donnell, G., Schmitter, P. and Whitehead, L. (eds) (1986). *Transition from Authoritarian Rule*, London: Johns Hopkins University Press.

OECD (2007). Governance Issues. OECD Territorial Reviews: Norway, <http://www.oecd-ilibrary.org/urban-rural-and-regional-development/oecd-territorial-reviews-norway-2007/governance-issues_9789264038080-5-en> (accessed 9 June 2011).

Offerdal, A. (2007). *Political and administrative structures and processes in Norwegian municipalities.* Paper presented at the India–Norway Seminar on Local Government 29 October 2007 in New Delhi.

Oftestad, B. T. (1998). *Den norske statsreligionen: Fra øvrighetskirke til demokratisk statskirke,* Kristiansand: Høyskoleforlaget.

O'Hara, G. (2008). 'Applied Socialism of a Fairly Moderate Kind', *Scandinavian Journal of History,* 33: 1, pp. 1–25.

Olmstead, A. L. and Rhode, P. W. (2001). 'Reshaping the Landscape: The Impact and Diffusion of the Tractor in American Agriculture, 1910–1960', *The Journal of Economic History,* 61: 3 (September), pp. 663–98.

Orwin, C. S. and Whetham, E. H. (1964). *History of British Agriculture, 1846–1914,* London: Longmans.

Ottosen, M. N. (2013). 'Stormaktspolitisk perspektiv på 1814', *Norges forsvar: organ for Norges forsvarsforening,* 6, pp. 20–5.

Øye, I. (2004). 'Farming systems and rural societies ca. 800–1350', in Almås (2004a) pp. 79–140.

Paterson, L. (1994). *The Autonomy of Modern Scotland,* Edinburgh: Edinburgh University Press.

Paterson, L. (2003), *Scottish Education in the Twentieth Century,* Edinburgh: Edinburgh University Press.

Paterson, L. and Iannelli, C. (2006). 'Religion, social mobility and education in Scotland', *British Journal of Sociology,* 57: 3, pp. 353–77.

Payne, P. (1985). 'The Decline of the Scottish Heavy Industries, 1945–1983', in R. Saville (ed.), *The Economic Development of Modern Scotland 1950–1980,* Edinburgh: John Donald.

Peden, G. C. (2012). 'DeIndustrialization', in T. M. Devine and J. Wormald (eds), *The Oxford Handbook of Modern Scottish History,* Oxford: Oxford University Press.

Pedersen, N. Ø. (2005). 'Scottish Immigration to Bergen', in A. Grosjean and S. Murdoch, *Scottish Communities Abroad in the Early Modern Period,* Leiden: Brill.

Pentland, G. (2006). 'The Debate on Scottish Parliamentary Reform, 1830–1832', *The Scottish Historical Review,* vol. LXXXV, 1: No. 219, pp. 102–32.

Pentland, G. (2013). 'By-elections and the Peculiarities of Scottish Politics, 1832–1900', in T. G. Otte and P. Readman (eds), *By-elections in British Politics, 1832–1914,* Woodbridge: The Boydell Press.

Peterkin, T. (2014). 'Scottish Independence: SNP Oil Fund Questioned', *Scotsman Online,* 9 April (accessed 10 April 2014).

Peters, B. G., Pierre, J. and King, D. S. (2005). 'The politics of path dependency: political conflict in historical institutionalism', *Journal of Politics,* 67: 4, pp. 1275–300.

Petersen, K. (2006). 'Constructing Nordic Welfare? Nordic social political co-operation 1919–1955', in N. F. Christensen et al. (eds), *The Nordic Model of Welfare: A Historical Reappraisal,* Copenhagen: Museum Tusculanum Press, pp. 67–98.

Petersen, K. (2011). 'National, Nordic and trans-Nordic: Transnational perspectives on the history of the Nordic welfare states', in P. Kettunen and K. Petersen (eds),

Beyond Welfare State Models: Transnational Historical Perspectives on Social Policy, Cheltenham: Edward Elgar Press, pp. 41–64.

Petersen, T. T. (2000). *The Middle East between the Great Powers: Anglo-American Conflict and Cooperation, 1952–7*, London: Macmillan.

Pharo, H. Ø. (2013). 'Side Show to Centre Stage: The Transformation of Norwegian Development Aid', in Thorsten Borring Olesen et al. (eds), *Saints and Sinners: Official Development Aid and its Dynamics in a Historical and Comparative Perspective*, Oslo: Akademika forlag, pp. 51–88.

Pickering, W. S. F. (1967). 'The 1851 Religious Census: A Useless Experiment?', *British Journal of Sociology*, 18, pp. 382–407.

Pierson, P. (2000). 'Increasing returns, path dependence, and the study of politics', *The American Political Science Review*, 94: 2, pp. 251–67.

Ploeg, J. D. van der (2003). *The Virtual Farmer: Past, present and future of the Dutch peasantry*, Assen: Royal Van Gorcum.

Polanyi, K. (1977) [1964]. 'Money objects and money uses', in *The Livelihood of Man*, New York: Academic Press, pp. 97–121.

Polanyi, K. (1944, 2001 edition). *The Great Transformation: The Political and Economic Origins of our Time*, Boston: Beacon Press.

Porter, B. (1998). 'Vice and Virtue in the North: The Scandinavian Writings of Samuel Laing', *Scandinavian Journal of History*, 23: 3–4, pp. 153–72.

Pryser, T. (1999). *Norsk Historie 1814–1860: Frå Standssamfunn mot Klassesamfunn*, Oslo: Det Norske Samlaget.

Raaum, N. C. (1999). 'Women in parliamentary politics: Historical lines of development', in C. Bergqvist et al. (1999), *Equal Democracies? Gender and Politics in the Nordic Countries*, Oslo: Scandinavian University Press, pp. 27–47

Randall, J. N. (1985). 'New Towns and New Industries', in R. Saville (ed.), *The Economic Development of Modern Scotland 1950–1980*, Edinburgh: John Donald.

Reform Scotland (2012). *Renewing Local Government*, Edinburgh, http://reformscotland.com/public/publications/Renewing_Local_Government.pdf (last accessed 15 April 2014).

Reinert, E. S. (2007). *How Rich Countries Got Rich . . . and Why Poor Countries Stay Poor*, London: Constable & Robinson Ltd.

Reinton, R. (1961). *Sæterbruket i Noreg III Institutt for sammenlignende kulturforskning*, Serie B: Skrifter XLVIII. Oslo.

Reynolds, D. (1991). *Britannia Overruled: British Policy and World Power in the 20th Century*, London: Longman.

Rhodes, J. R. and Eden, R. A. (1987): *Anthony Eden: A Biography*, London: Weidenfeld & Nicolson.

Rian, Ø. (2003). *Maktens historie i dansketiden* (Makt- og demokratiutredningens rapportserie, 68), Oslo: Makt- og demokratiutredningen.

Rian, Ø. (2010). 'Sensuren i Danmark-Norge, 1536–1814', in Hilde Sandvik (ed.), *Demokratisk teori og historisk praksis*, Oslo: Scandinavian Academic Press, pp. 123–60.

Richards, E. (1973). *Leviathan of Wealth: The Sutherland Fortune in the Industrial Revolution*, London: Routledge & Kegan Paul.

Richards, E. (1982). *A History of the Highland Clearances*, London.

Riddoch, L. (2007). *Riddoch on the Outer Hebrides*, Luath Press Ltd.

Riddoch, L. (2010). 'Mini-councils will energise Scotland's communities', *The Scotsman*, 28 June.

Riddoch, L. (2013). *Blossom*, Edinburgh: Luath Press.

Riis, T. (1988). *Should auld acquaintance be forgot: Scottish–Danish relations c. 1450– 1707* (Odense University studies in history and social sciences), Odense University Press.

Rodger, R. (ed.) (1988). *Scottish Housing in the 20th Century*, Leicester.

Rognstad, O, and Steinset, T. A. (2012). *Landbruket i Norge 2011*, Oslo: Statistics Norway.

Rokkan, S. (1975). 'Scotland vs. Norway: Points for a possible analysis of similarities and differences'. Note for the Bergen–Strathclyde Conference June–July 1975, unpublished.

Rokkan, S. and Urwin, D. W. (1982). *The Politics of Territorial Identity: Studies in European Regionalism*, London: Sage.

Roll-Hansen, N. (2005). 'Norwegian eugenics: Sterilization as social reform', in G. Broberg and N. Roll-Hansen (eds), *Eugenics and the Welfare State: Sterilization Policy in Denmark, Sweden, Norway and Finland* (2nd edn, first published 1996), East Lansing: Michigan State University Press, pp. 151–94.

Rønning, W. (2010). *Norwegian Teachers' Conceptions of and Stances towards Active Learning*. PhD thesis, Leeds: University of Leeds, School of Education.

Rosie, M. (2002). 'Death by Committee', *Theology in Scotland*, IX: 2.

Rosie, M. (2004). *The Sectarian Myth in Scotland: Of Bitter memory and Bigotry*, Basingstoke: Palgrave.

Rosie, M. (2013). 'Tall Tales: Religion and Scottish Independence', *What Scotland Thinks*, 15 August, http://blog.whatscotlandthinks.org/2013/08/tall-tales-religion-and-scottish-independence/

Rålm, P. C. (ed.) (2013). *Mat og industry 2013*, Norsk institutt for landbruksøkonomisk forskning.

Sainsbury, D. (2001). 'Gender and the making of welfare states: Norway and Sweden', *Social Politics*, 8: 1, pp. 113–43.

Sandvik, B. (1998). *Det store nattverdfallet. En undersøkelse av avsperring og tilhørighet i norsk kirkeliv* (KIFO Perspektiv 2), Trondheim: Tapir.

Sassoon, D. (1997). *One Hundred Years of Socialism: The West European Left in the Twentieth Century*, London: I. B. Tauris.

Saville, R. (ed.) (1985). *The Economic Development of Modern Scotland 1950–1980*, Edinburgh: John Donald. References are to Saville's Introductory Chapter, 'The Industrial Background to the Post-War Scottish Economy'.

Saville, R. (1996). *Bank of Scotland: A History 1695–1995*, Edinburgh: Edinburgh University Press.

Scheistrøen, J. (2013). 'Lavere barnehagesatser, høyere SFO-satser', http://www.ssb.no/utdanning/artikler-og-publikasjoner/lavere-barnehagesatser-hoyere-sfo-satser

Scott, P. H. (1992). *Andrew Fletcher and The Treaty of Union*, Edinburgh: John Donald. (Page references are to the 1994 Saltire Society paperback edition.)

Scottish Government (2002). *Summary Results of the 2002 Pre-school and Daycare Census Tables 6 and 7*, Edinburgh: Scottish Executive. http://www.scotland.gov.uk/Publications/2002/09/15401/10854 (accessed 3 March 2014).

312   NORTHERN NEIGHBOURS

Scottish Government (2004). *A Curriculum for Excellence*, Edinburgh: Scottish Government. https://www.scotxed.net/ScotXed%20Web%20Parts/Data%20Exchanges.aspx (last accessed 7 February 2014).

Scottish Government (2007). *Pre-school and Childcare Statistics 2007 Tables 1 and 4*, http://www.scotland.gov.uk/Publications/2007/09/26094517/0 (last accessed 7 February 2014).

Scottish Government (2009). *Growing up in Scotland: Multiple Childcare Provision and its Effect on Child Outcomes.* http://www.scotland.gov.uk/Publications/2009/03/13143410/6 (last accessed 17 March 2014).

Scottish Government (2010). *Placing requests in Schools 2008/9, Table 7.* http://www.scotland.gov.uk/Publications/2010/03/19130022/11 (last accessed 31 March 2014).

Scottish Government (2013). *Scotland's Future: Your Guide to an Independent Scotland*, www.scotland.gov.uk/Publications/2013/11/9348/14 (last accessed 15 April 2014).

Scottish Government (2014a). *Additional Data Set Employment rates of mothers by age of youngest child 1993–2012*, unpublished.

Scottish Government (2014b). *Scotland's Future. Your Guide to an Independent Scotland*, Edinburgh: APS Group Scotland.

Scottish Government Statistical Unit (March 2014). *Ad hoc Parents Hours of Work.*

Scottish National Party (2014). 'Norway Oil Fund Soars Past £500bn mark', published online 28 February 2014. Available at https://www.snp.org/mediacentre/news/2014/feb/norway-oil-fund-soars-past-£500bn-mark (accessed 10 April 2014).

Scottish Office (1998). *Meeting the childcare challenge: A childcare strategy for Scotland*, Edinburgh: The Stationery Office.

Scottish Out Of School Care Network (2013). *Symposium Report*, Glasgow: SOSCN.

Seaton, A. V. (1998). *The History of Tourism in Scotland*, Oxford: International Thomson Business Press.

Sejersted, F. (2011). *The Age of Social Democracy: Norway and Sweden in the Twentieth Century* (trans. R. Daly, ed. M. B. Adams), Princeton: Princeton University Press. Also printed in Norwegian as *Sosialdemokratiets tidsaler. Norge og Sverige I det 20. Årehundre*, Oslo (2005).

Seers, D. et al. (eds) (1979). *Under-Developed Europe: Studies in Core–Periphery relations*, Hassocks: The Harvester Press.

Senghass, D. (1977). *Weltwirtschaftsordnung und Entwicklungspolitik. Plädoyer für Dissoziation* [World Economic Order and Development Policy: A Plea for Dissociation], Frankfurt: Suhrkamp Verlag (5th edn 1987).

Senghaas, D. (1985). *The European Experience: A Historical Critique of Development Theory*, Leamington Spa/Dover, NH: Berg.

Sharpe, L. J. (1970). *Theories and Values of Local Government.* Political Studies 2.

Sheenan, H. (1892). *Boundaries of Counties and Parishes in Scotland. Asselled by the Boundary Commissioners under the Local Government (Scotland) Act, 1889*, Edinburgh: William Green & Sons.

Shuckburgh, E. (1986). *Descent to Suez: Diaries 1951–1956*, London: Weidenfeld & Nicolson.

Shucksmith, M., Thomson, K. J. and Roberts, D. (eds) (2005). *The CAP and the Regions: The Territorial Impact of the Common Agricultural Policy*, Wallingford: CABI.

Shuldham-Shaw, P. and Lyle, E. B. (eds) (1983). *The Greig-Duncan Folk Song Collection*, Aberdeen: Aberdeen University Press in association with the School of Scottish Studies, University of Edinburgh. Vol. 2 of eight volumes.

Simmel, G. (1978 [1900]). *The Philosophy of Money*, London: Routledge.

Simon, E. (1985). *And the Sun Rises with the Farmer* (Og solen står med bonden op). The Philosophical History of the Nordic Folkhighschool. Lectures given by Simon at the Nordic Folk Academy (Kungälv, Sweden). Translation by Kathryn Parke. See http://www.peopleseducation.org/resource-center/and-the-sun-rises-with-the-farmer/ (last accessed 3 February 2014).

Simpson, E. (1997). *The Cairngorm Mountaineering Club*, National Museums of Scotland.

Sinclair, D. (1997). 'Local Government and a Scottish Parliament', *Scottish Affairs*, 9, pp. 14–21.

Smellie, K. B. (1946). *The History of Local Government*, London: Allen & Unwin.

Smith, A. (1961 [1776]). *An Inquiry into the Nature and Causes of the Wealth of Nations*, London: Methuen. References are to the 1910 Everyman's edition, London: J. M. Dent & Co.

Smith, N. J. (2011). *The Sea of Lost Opportunity: North Sea Oil and Gas, British Industry and the Offshore Supplies Office*, Oxford and Amsterdam: Elsevier.

Smith, S. C. (ed.) (2008). *Reassessing Suez 1956: New Perspectives on the Crisis and its Aftermath*, Aldershot, Hampshire: Ashgate Publishing.

Smout, T. C. (1963). *Scottish Trade on the Eve of the Union*, Edinburgh and London: Oliver & Boyd.

Smout, T. C. (1969). *History of the Scottish People, 1560–1830*, London: Collins.

Smout, T. C. (1986). *A Century of the Scottish People, 1830–1950*, London: Fontana.

Smout, T. C. (1994). 'Scottish emigration in the seventeenth and eighteenth centuries', in N. Canny (ed.), *Europeans on the Move*, Oxford.

Smout, T. C. (2012). 'A New Look at the Scottish Improvers', *The Scottish Historical Review*, vol. XCI, 1: no. 231 (April).

Sogner, S. (1996). *Krig og fred 1660–1780*. Vol. 6 of *Aschehougs Norges historie*.

Statistics Norway (1955). *Økonomisk utsyn* [Economic Survey] 1900–1950 (Samfunnsøkonomiske studier no. 3), Oslo, p. 60. At https://www.ssb.no/a/histstat/sos/sos_003.pdf (accessed 12 March 2014).

Statistics Norway (2011a). 'Members and reelected members of the local councils, by county 2011', <https://www.ssb.no/a/english/kortnavn/kommvalgform_en/tab-2011-12-19-06-en.html> (last accessed 15 April 2014).

Statistics Norway (2011b). 'Municipal and county election, 2011', <https://www.ssb.no/en/valg/statistikker/kommvalg> (last accessed 3 April 2014).

Statistics Norway (2012). *Immigration and emigration*. Available at http://www.ssb.no/en/befolkning/statistikker/innvutv/aar (accessed 25 March 2014).

Statistics Norway (2013). *The Church of Norway 2012*, available at http://www.ssb.no/en/kultur-og-fritid/statistikker/kirke_kostra/aar/2013-06-19#content (accessed 4 April 2013).

Statistics Norway (2014a). *Hjemmehørende folkemengde – historisk statistikk*, <http://www.ssb.no/a/histstat/tabeller/3-1.html> (last accessed 3 April 2014).

Steen, S. (1989). *1814*, Oslo: Cappelen.

Steuart, J. (1767) [1966 edn ed. Skinner]. *An Inquiry into the Principles of Political Œconomy*, 2 vols, Edinburgh and London: Oliver & Boyd.

Stocks, J. (2002). 'Social class and the secondary school in 1930s Scotland', *Scottish Educational Review*, 34, pp. 26–39.

Stortinget (2014a). 'Grunnloven av 4. november', reprinted in *Skjebneåret 1814: Fire Dokumenter som Formet Norge*, Oslo: Stortinget.

Stortinget (2014b). 'Kieltraktaten av 14. januar', reprinted in *Skjebneåret 1814: Fire Dokumenter som Formet Norge*, Oslo: Stortinget.

Stortinget (2014c). 'Kongeriget Norges grundlov af 17.de mai 1814', reprinted in *Skjebneåret 1814: Fire Dokumenter som Formet Norge*, Oslo: Stortinget.

Stortinget (2014d). 'Mossekonvensjonen av 14. August', reprinted in *Skjebneåret 1814: Fire Dokumenter som Formet Norge*, Oslo: Stortinget.

Stougaard-Nielsen, J. and Napier, D. (2013). *Should we trust the Danes? The World Happiness Report 2013*, UCL European Institute. Available at http://www.ucl.ac.uk/european-institute/highlights/2013-14/happiness (accessed 25 April 2014).

Streeck, W. and Thelen, K. (2005). 'Introduction: institutional change in advanced political economies', in W. Streeck and K. Thelen (eds), *Beyond Continuity: Institutional Change in Advanced Political Economies*, Oxford: Oxford University Press, pp. 1–39.

Sumner Maine, H. (1890). *The Early History of Institutions*, London: John Murray.

Sumner Maine, H. (1901). *Ancient Law, its connection with the early history of society*, London: Routledge.

Sundt, E. (1855). *Om Giftermaal I Norge* [On Marriage in Norway. Trans. M. Drake.] English edn published by Cambridge University Press, 1980, http://www.rhd.uit.no/sundt/bind2/eilert_sundt_bd2e.html (accessed 11 March 2014).

Sverdrup, J. (1996). *Inn I Storpolitikken 1940–1949*, Oslo: Universitetsforlaget.

Sørensen, Ø. (1988). *Anton Martin Schweigaards Politiske Tenkning*, Oslo: Universitetsforlaget.

Sørensen, Ø. (ed.) (1994). *Nordic Paths to National Identity in the Nineteenth Century*, Oslo: The Research Council of Norway.

Sørensen, Ø. (ed.) (1996). *Nationalism in Small European Nations*, Oslo: Research Council of Norway.

Sørensen, Ø. (ed.) (1998). *Jakten på det Norske: Perspektiver på Utviklingen av en Norsk Nasjonal Identitet på 1800-tallet*, Oslo: Ad notam Gyldendal.

Sørensen, Ø. (2004). 'Det nye Norge i det nye Norden 1814–1850', in M. Engman and Å. Sandström (eds), *Det Nya Norden efter Napoleon: 25:e Nordiska historikermötet, Stockholm, den 4–8 augusti 2004*, Stockholm: Almqvist & Wiksell International, pp. 55–78.

Sørensen, Ø. and Nilsson, T. (eds) (2005). *1905: Nye Perspektiver*, Oslo: Aschehoug.

Sørensen, Ø. and Stråth, B. (eds) (1997). *The Cultural Construction of Norden*, Oslo: Scandinavian University Press.

Tansey, J. and Rajotte, T. (2008). *The Future Control of Food: A Guide to International*

Negotiations and Rules on Intellectual Property, Biodiversity and Food Security, London: Earthscan.

Taugbøl, T. (2013). 'Den Andre Industrielle Revolusjon', in *Store norske leksikon*, retrieved 5 March 2014 from http://snl.no/den_andre_industrielle_revolusjon.

Telhaug, A. O. (1994). *Utdanningspolitikken og enhetsskolen*, Oslo: Didakta.

Thelen, K. (2003). 'How institutions evolve', in J. Mahoney and D. Rueschemeyer (eds), *Comparative Historical Analysis in the Social Sciences*, Cambridge: Cambridge University Press.

Thomson, W. P. L. (2008). *The New History of Orkney*, Edinburgh: Birlinn.

Thue, L. (2008). 'Norway: A resource-based and democratic capitalism', in S. Feldman et al. (eds), *Creating Nordic Capitalism: The Business History of a Competitive Periphery*, Basingstoke: Palgrave Macmillan, pp. 394–493.

Tilton, T. (1990). *The Political Theory of Swedish Social Democracy: Through the Welfare State to Socialism*, Oxford: Clarendon Press.

Timonen, V. (2003). *Restructuring the Welfare State: Globalization and Social Policy Reform in Finland and Sweden*, Cheltenham: Edward Elgar.

Tracy, M. (1982). *Agriculture in Western Europe: Challenge and Response, 1880–1980*, 2nd edn, London: Granada.

Transactions of the Highland and Agricultural Society of Scotland (1886), Fourth Series. Vol. XVIII.

Transactions of the Highland and Agricultural Society of Scotland (1885–1933). Annual publication.

Tveite, S. (1990). 'Den nye jordbruksteknologien – slåmaskina' in E. Hovland, E. Lange, and S. Rysstad (eds), *Det som svarte seg best. Studier i økonomisk historie og politikk*, Oslo: Ad Notam Forlag AS.

Tønnessen, A. V. (2000). *'Et trygt og godt hjem for alle'? Kirkelederes kritikk av velferdsstaten etter 1945* (KIFO Perspektiv 7), Trondheim: Tapir.

Tønnessen, A. V. (2007). *Kirkens Nødhjelp: Bistand, tro og politikk*, Oslo: Gyldendal.

Ugulen, J. R. (2005). 'On the distribution of Norwegian landed property', in T. Iversen and J. R. Myking (eds), *Land, Lord and Peasants*, Trondheim.

UNEP (2011). *Ecosystems for Food Security*.

University of St Andrews (2007–14), Records of the Parliaments of Scotland to 1707 database, http://www.rps.ac.uk.

Utdanningsdirektoratet (2006). The Quality Framework, http://www.udir.no/Upload/larerplaner/Fastsatte_lareplaner_for_Kunnskapsloeftet/5/prinsipper_lko6_Eng.pdf?epslanguage=no

Vabo, S. (2002). *Tid for hamskifte? En diskusjon av nye utfordringer for de folkevalgtes rolle i kommunen* [Time for political transformation? A discussion of new challengess for the role of the elected representatives in the municipality]. Nordisk Administrativt Tidsskrift (4).

Van Bath, S. B. H. (1963). *The Agrarian History of Western Europe AD 500–1850*, London: Edward Arnold.

Vassenden, K. (1997). *Innvandrere i Norge: Hvem er de, hva gjør de og hvordan lever de?*, Oslo: Statistisk Sentralbyrå.

Waage, H. H. (1998). 'Norway and a Major International Crisis: Suez – the Very Difficult Case', *Diplomacy & Statecraft*, 9: 3.

Wallace, W. (1905). *Trial of the City of Glasgow Bank Directors*, Glasgow and Edinburgh: William Hodge & Company.

Ward, C. and Hardy, D. (1984). *Arcadia for All: the Legacy of a Makeshift Landscape*, London: Mansell.

Westergård, E. (2012). 'Læreren i skole-hjem samarbeidet', in M. B. Postholm, E. Munthe and R. Krumsvik (eds), *Lærere i skolen som organisasjon*, Kristiansand: Cappelen Damm Høyskoleforlaget.

Whatley, C. A. (1989). 'Economic Causes and Consequences of the Union of 1707: A Survey', *The Scottish Historical Review*, 68.

Whatley, C. A. (1997). *The Industrial Revolution in Scotland*, Cambridge: Cambridge University Press.

Wheatley Report (1969). *The Report of the Royal Commission on Local Government in Scotland. Report and Appendices.* Cmnd. 4150. Edinburgh, HMSO.

Wightman, A. (1996). *Who Owns Scotland?*, Edinburgh: Canongate.

Wilhjelm, H. (2013). *Barnehage – hus og hage fra 1630 til 2010*, Oslo: Gyldendal Akademisk.

Williams, E. (1970). *From Columbus to Castro: The History of the Caribbean 1492–1969*, London: André Deutsch.

Willumsen, L. (2008). *Seventeenth-Century Witchcraft Trials in Scotland and Northern Norway*. PhD thesis, University of Edinburgh.

Winson, A. (1993). *The Intimate Commodity: Food and the development of the Agro-Industrial Complex in Canada*, Toronto: Garamond Press.

Wooldridge, A. (2013). '"Northern Lights": Special report on the Nordic Countries', *The Economist*, 2 February.

Woolf, A. (2007). *From Pictland to Alba: Scotland 789–1070* (Edinburgh New History of Scotland), Edinburgh: Edinburgh University Press.

Young, C. (1995). 'Financing the Micro-Scale Enterprise: Rural Craft Producers in Scotland, 1840–1914', *Business History Review*, 69, pp. 398–421.

Youngson, A. J. (1973). *After the Forty-Five: The Economic Impact on the Scottish Highlands*, Edinburgh: Edinburgh University Press.

Zickermann, K. (2005). '"Briteannia ist mein patria": Scotsmen and the "British" Community in Hamburg', in A. Grosjean and S. Murdoch (eds), *Scottish Communities Abroad in the Early Modern Period*, Leiden: Brill, pp. 249–77.

Index

M	2	
WT	2	
CC	2	

Ship To:
MYRA CHRISTIE
19 SILVER STREET
KINCARDINE
ALLOA, CLACKMANNANSHIRE,
FK10 4NS
UNITED KINGDOM

C9 10002

3 Dec 2018 07:56

BetterWorldBooks   62686178